Science Fiction as Legal Imaginary

This book examines how science fiction informs the legal imagination of technological futures.

Science fiction, the contributors to this book argue, is a storehouse of images, tropes, concepts and memes that inform the legal imagination of the future, and in doing so generate impetus for change. Specifically, the contributors examine how science fictions imagine human life in space, in the digital and as formed and negotiated by corporations. They then connect this imaginary to how law should be understood in the present and changed for the future. Across the chapters, there is an urgent sense of the need for law – as it is has been, and as it might become – to order and safeguard the future for a multiplicity of vulnerable entities.

This book will appeal to scholars and students with interests in law and technology, legal theory, cultural legal studies and law and the humanities.

Alex Green is Senior Lecturer in Law at the University of York, UK.

Mitchell Travis is Director of the Centre for Law and Social Justice at the University of Leeds, UK.

Kieran Tranter is Chair of Law, Technology and Future at the School of Law, Queensland University of Technology, Australia.

Part of the TechNomos: Law, Technology and Culture series

series editors

Kieran Tranter, *School of Law, University of Queensland, Australia*

Edwin Bikundo, *Griffith University, Australia*

for information about the series and details of previous and forthcoming titles, see https://www.routledge.com/TechNomos/book-series/LTC

A GlassHouse book

Science Fiction as Legal Imaginary

Edited by Alex Green, Mitchell Travis and Kieran Tranter

Routledge
Taylor & Francis Group
a GlassHouse Book

First published 2025
by Routledge
4 Park Square, Milton Park, Abingdon, Oxon OX14 4RN

and by Routledge
605 Third Avenue, New York, NY 10158

Routledge is an imprint of the Taylor & Francis Group, an informa business

A GlassHouse book

British Library Cataloguing-in-Publication Data
A catalogue record for this book is available from the British Library

Library of Congress Cataloging-in-Publication Data
Names: Green, Alex, 1988- editor. | Travis, Mitchell, editor. | Tranter, Kieran, editor.
Title: Science fiction as legal imaginary / edited by Alex Green, Mitchell Travis, and Kieran Tranter.
Description: Abingdon, Oxon [UK]; New York, NY: Routledge, 2025. | Series: Technomos | Includes bibliographical references and index.
Identifiers: LCCN 2024032423 (print) | LCCN 2024032424 (ebook) | ISBN 9781032534374 (hardback) | ISBN 9781032534831 (paperback) | ISBN 9781003412274 (ebook)
Subjects: LCSH: Science fiction. | Science and law. | Technology and law.
Classification: LCC K487.S3 S337 2025 (print) | LCC K487.S3 (ebook) | DDC 809.3/936–dc23/eng/20240714
LC record available at https://lccn.loc.gov/2024032423
LC ebook record available at https://lccn.loc.gov/2024032424

ISBN: 9781032534374 (hbk)
ISBN: 9781032534831 (pbk)
ISBN: 9781003412274 (ebk)

DOI: 10.4324/9781003412274

Typeset in Sabon
by Deanta Global Publishing Services, Chennai, India

Contents

Preface

This volume is another illicit, monstrous offspring of the 'Jurisprudence of the Future' project. The horror first began, as many other horrors did, during the extraordinary times of 2020 and 2021. The pandemic and its various public health responses (or *non*-responses) generated a moment of creative reflection. There was anxiety and change experienced quietly and alone. Science fiction became lived experience during those years: a reality that seemed stranger by far than the wildest of inventions. Within the genre, the pandemic narrative is a common vector through which the normal present transmogrifies into a dystopic future. There was this sense of future, not only in the macro of pandemics and the possible end of the world as we knew it but also in the micro, where the cultural imaginary of 'working from home' became the everyday new normal: of video conferences, of 'you're on mute' and of the endless accumulation of digital 'bells' – tribute for a capitalistic raccoon within Nintendo's *Animal Crossing: New Horizons* (2020).

For law and humanities scholars, the science fictionality of pandemic times was hyperfuel. There was already a small body of scholarship that engaged with science fiction as a window into questions of law and justice. The pandemic and its social, legal and everyday manifestations emboldened scholars who had already thought that science fiction and law needed more exploration.

Into this confluence of opportune circumstances, in 2021 Alex Green and Mitchell Travis innocuously organised a call for papers for a panel for the 2022 Socio-Legal Studies Association Annual Conference on 'Jurisprudence of the Future', inviting papers that creatively and critically engaged with science fiction in the context of law and justice. The response was overwhelming. From that initial call, two things happened. First, a follow-up conference panel, 'Jurisprudence of the Future II', was called and held for those located in the southern hemisphere of the planet at the 2021 Law, Literature and Humanities Association of Australasia Conference. Second, papers presented at both panels went on to be published in the Jurisprudence of the Future symposium in volume 4(2) of *Law, Technology and Humans* in November

2022. It is from the community of scholars who presented and engaged with both conference panels, and with the subsequent symposium, that the chapters for this volume and its sibling, *Cultural Legal Studies of Science Fiction* (Routledge, 2024), emerged.

Edited volumes are collective endeavours. First and foremost, we would like to thank the contributors who have trusted us with their work. There is a generosity and courage to be found in sharing work and collaborating with others to do something new and different. We would also like to thank Susan Jarvis, who assisted us and the authors in copyediting the manuscript, and the Humans Technology Law Centre at the Queensland University of Technology for providing a small grant to cover the editorial process. Also, special thanks to Bruce Arnold, Honni Rijswijk, Jordan Belor, Paul Burgess, Antonia Waltermann, Craig Finnegan, Penny Crofts, Katie Szilagyi and Yeliz Döker, who read and commented on chapters. Finally, many thanks to Edwin Bikundo as series editor for the TechNomos series for sharing the vision of the volume, and Colin Perrin and Naomi Round Cahalin at Routledge for their support.

Alex Green, Mitchell Travis and Kieran Tranter, April 2024

Notes on contributors

Renae Barker is Senior Lecturer in Law at the University of Western Australia, where she researches in the area of law and religion. Her particular areas of interest are state–religion relationships and the impact of law on minority faiths. ORCID ID: 0000-0003-3034-320X.

Jordan Belor is a PhD student in the School of Law and Society, University of the Sunshine Coast. He has published on the cultural legalities of Netflix's *The Punisher*. His current research focuses on the cultural legalities of corporate technology, encompassing critical readings of the representation of corporations, artificial intelligence and technology in science fiction film and television. ORCID ID: 0000-0002-9537-0148.

Meredith Blake is Associate Professor of Law at the University of Western Australia. Her research interests include criminal responsibility, health law and ethics. She has a particular interest in the balancing of individual and collective interests in health law and policy. ORCID ID: 0009-0006-8893-5709.

Paul Burgess is Senior Lecturer at Monash University. He is interested in all things related to the rule of law. Most of his time is spent trying to figure out exactly what the rule of law is, and trying to think about the way that the concept can most clearly be expressed, discussed and used. In doing this, he works within and is interested in legal theory, legal history, political theory, public law, economics and constitutional theory. The rest of his time is spent wondering how the law (and rule of law) will need to evolve to cater for and understand AI in all its guises. ORCID ID: 0000-0002-5674-1735.

Yeliz Figen Döker is a PhD researcher at the European University Institute (Florence, Italy). Her doctoral studies focus on the legal conditions of experiential learning of machine ethics by artificial intelligence. She is also co-founder and head of the Science Fiction section of the Digital

Constitutionalist Blog (DigiCon) and co-builder of the Metaverse Exhibitions of DigiCon. ORCID ID: 0000-0002-2661-0013.

Christina Fawcett is Contract Faculty in the Department of English, University of Winnipeg. Her research examines cultural intersections and participatory narratives in science fiction, horror and fantasy texts, both literary and new media. ORCID ID: 0000-0003-2123-7958.

Thomas Giddens is Chair of Jurisprudence at Dundee Law School. Taking its cues from the humanities heritage of the legal discipline, his research focuses on critical and cultural legal studies, with a particular interest in visuality and form. He is the author of *Judgment* (2022) and *On Comics and Legal Aesthetics* (2016). ORCID ID: 0000-0002-1525-4615.

Alex Green is Senior Lecturer at the York Law School. His research lies in the intersections of political philosophy and international law, with a particular interest in statehood and the nature of political communities. His recent book, *Statehood as Political Community: International Law and the Emergence of New States*, was published in 2024. ORCID ID: 0000-0001-7889-2852.

Stacey Henderson is Senior Research Fellow in Law at the College of Business, Government and Law at Flinders University. Her research focuses on the protective capacity of international law, the responsibility to protect (R2P), governance of outer space and space technology, commercial space activities and sustained human presence in space. ORCID ID: 0000-0003-1369-5510.

Evie Kendal is a bioethicist and public health researcher in the Department of Health Sciences and Biostatistics at Swinburne University of Technology. Her research interests include ethical dilemmas in emerging biotechnologies, space ethics and utopian science fiction. ORCID ID: 0000-0002-8414-0427.

Daniel Chia Matallana is a lawyer from the School of Law of the Pontificia Universidad Javeriana in Bogota, Colombia. He obtained an LLM in international law and politics from the University of Canterbury in New Zealand. As a current PhD candidate, he is working on an interdisciplinary project that uses science fiction as its principal approach to provide marks and hints for a jurisprudential speculation of artificial intelligence. He is also interested in the relationship between science and law, and in how to build bridges between them. ORCID ID: 0009-0008-4533-8482.

Emily Wati Muir is a PhD student at Queensland University of Technology. Her research is focused on Japanese popular culture and the legal imagining of children. She is currently a solicitor in private practice based in Canberra. ORCID ID: 0000-0002-4903-1583.

Dhiraj Nainani is Postdoctoral Fellow at the Asia Research Institute, National University of Singapore. A legal geographer, his research focuses primarily on law and urban space in Asia. He is especially interested in how the legal materialities of surveillance and regulation can be generated, resisted, aestheticised and even reproduced. ORCID ID: 0000-0003-4216-3951.

Georgios Pavlidis is the holder of a UNESCO Chair and a Jean Monnet Chair funded by the European Union. He is an Associate Professor of International and EU Law at Neapolis University Pafos, Cyprus. His research interests include international and EU financial law, regulation of financial markets and anti-money laundering (AML), including uses of artificial intelligence (AI) in AML. ORCID ID: 0000-0001-6311-3086

Timothy D Peters is Associate Professor of Law at the School of Law and Society, University of the Sunshine Coast, Australia, Adjunct Research Fellow at the Law Futures Centre, Griffith University and the president of the Law, Literature and Humanities Association of Australasia. He is also the recipient of an Australian Research Council Discovery Early Career Researcher Award (project number DE200100881), funded by the Australian Government, examining 'New Approaches to Corporate Legality: Beyond Neoliberal Governance'. ORCID ID: 0000-0001-5644-5402.

Deniz Seval is a PhD researcher at the University of Ottawa in Canada. Her doctoral studies focus on the interplay between law and technology from a feminist perspective. Currently, she is conducting her doctoral research and advising technology start-ups on a freelance basis. In addition, Deniz is also an editor at the Digital Constitutionalist (DigiCon) for the Science Fiction section. ORCID ID: 0000-0002-0401-6056.

Kritika Sharma is a doctoral researcher at the Luxembourg Centre for European Law, University of Luxembourg, and a PhD candidate at Leiden University, the Netherlands. ORCID ID: 0000-0002-2409-1432.

Katie Szilagyi is Assistant Professor at the Faculty of Law, University of Manitoba. Her research focuses on artificial intelligence and the law, including privacy, property, autonomy and transdisciplinary approaches to engineering ethics. ORCID ID: 0000-0003-4821-1504.

Erika Techera is Professor of Law at the University of Western Australia. She teaches and researches in international and comparative environmental law, space and satellite law and heritage governance. She has a particular interest in the intersection of science and law. ORCID ID: 0000-0001-8283-2967.

Kieran Tranter is Chair of Law, Technology and Future at the School of Law, Queensland University of Technology. His current projects focus on the foundational features of digital legality and the techno-legal utopianism of Australia. ORCID ID: 0000-0003-1683-2939.

Mitchell Travis is Associate Professor of Law and Social Justice at the University of Leeds. He is increasingly occupied by the links between jurisprudence, temporality and futurity. Every time he gets out, they pull him back in. ORCID ID: 0000-0001-6245-7354.

Antonia (AM) Waltermann is Assistant Professor of Legal Theory and Philosophy, Foundations and Methods of Law in the Faculty of Law, Maastricht University. Antonia's research focuses on non-human agents within the law and in the social construction of law, combining socio-ontological theories of law with law and the cognitive sciences. ORCID ID: 0000-0003-1643-5028.

Melissa de Zwart is Professor at the Andy Thomas Centre for Space Resources, University of Adelaide. Melissa is a thought leader in the area of law and technology and has a strong international profile in the fields of internet law and the regulation of access to and uses of outer space. ORCID ID: 0000-0002-9372-1530.

Chapter 1

The legal imaginary and science fiction

Alex Green, Mitchell Travis and Kieran Tranter

The legal imaginary

Law is haunted by ghosts, fictions and the speculative.[1] This is more than just the spectres of law's victims haunting those left behind[2] and dwelling at sites of incarceration and execution.[3] There is an ectoplasm surrounding the formal activities of law – an oozy, illuminous goo that is the very opposite of the alleged sharpness and hardness of law. This spectral supplement cannot be 'busted' by characters conjured by Ivan Reitman, Dan Aykroyd and Harold Ramis.[4] Indeed, its presence should not be expelled, for without this haunting, law would be nothing.[5] It would have no content, no substantive meaning; it would just be a machine remaking matter and time without sense or direction.[6]

This ghostly haze that surrounds law, that gives it substance and meaning, is culture.[7] The separation of law from the very culture that calls law forth and sustains it is the enduring crime of positivism. The search for a legal science according to formalist nineteenth-century paradigms led, in positivist hands, to the exorcising of culture from law. Law became identifiable by abstract formulas of habitual obedience, *grundnorms* or rules of recognition, and consideration of legal practice devolved to the arid mechanics of textual manipulation.[8] The inevitable failure of the *sacramental exorcizamus* of positivism to expel culture from the understanding and practice of law was felt as a recurring trauma throughout the twentieth century – a trauma in the real

1 Eslava (2018); Nash (2006); Dick (1972); Dayan (2011).
2 Horton (2022).
3 Carlton (2023).
4 Greene (2022).
5 Tranter (2018), pp 32–33.
6 This image of modern law as a machine remaking matter and time without any preconceived content belongs to Carl Schmitt (1985), p 48. See further Dyzenhaus (1994); Goding and Tranter (2021).
7 Cover (1983).
8 Nonet (1990).

DOI: 10.4324/9781003412274-1

with the need to deal with the horrors of authoritarianism's legalities,[9] and witnessed in legal theory through a seemingly endless succession of 'law and' movements.[10] Indeed, the energy within legal studies over recent decades has been how to think of and understand law as culturally infused and embedded, and not as an alien empire beyond and above the lived experience of humans.

This reckoning has taken many forms. Sociological studies of lawyers, their clients and the practice communities they form have emphasised how the everyday of law is not the mechanical application of positive rules but sociocultural interactions of shared and conflicting meaning-making.[11] Others have tracked how cultural artefacts – the music of Bob Dylan or quotes and characters from science fiction franchises – have infiltrated the texts of legal judgments.[12] There has been a renewed appreciation for the relationships between law and the visual:[13] the spaces and architecture of courts and their buildings,[14] the cultural aesthetics that prefigure and frame the law[15] and the circulation of images within legal writing and sites.[16] One celebrated legal scholar has even explored the parallels between *Star Wars* and US constitutionalism.[17]

The zenith of the reunification of law and culture has been the emergence of a distinct field of cultural legal studies that sees law, justice and legal concepts within and through popular culture.[18] Cultural legal studies moves beyond the rules to take the cultural penumbra that surrounds law seriously.[19] Through reading cultural practices and artefacts as law, cultural legal studies uncovers a *lex populi*, the laws, justice and legalities that reside beyond the official institutions and practices of law.[20] The contributions to the companion volume to this book, *Cultural Legal Studies of Science Fiction*,[21] are located firmly within this tradition. In that volume, there is a presentation of science fictional texts, experiences and artefacts as revelatory of legal concepts, such as personhood and sovereignty, within the technocultural milieu of the anthropogenic present.[22] In contrast, the contributions in this volume

9 Hart (1958); Fuller (1958).
10 Minda (1995).
11 Sarat and Felstiner (1995); Mather et al (1995). See generally Robertson and Tranter (2007).
12 Long (2011); Browning (2014).
13 Douzinas and Nead (1999).
14 Mulcahy (2011).
15 Goodrich (2013).
16 Sherwin (2011); Crawley and Tranter (2019).
17 Sunstein (2016).
18 Sherwin (2000); Crawley and Peters (2018).
19 Peters (2022), p 16.
20 MacNeil (2007).
21 Green et al (2024a).
22 Green et al (2024b).

reconnect culture back to law in a way that is both narrower and broader than the contributions in *Cultural Legal Studies of Science Fiction*.

The narrower way unifies all the contributions herein: a particular connection of law to the cultural elements of science fiction. All the contributors engage with science fiction texts, tropes and memes as part of a *legal imaginary*. Contemporary ideas of the imaginary have their origins in the post-Marxist work of Cornelius Castoriadis, who presented the ideal of the 'social imaginary' that mediates between institutions and the experiences of social life:[23]

> This element – which gives a specific orientation to every institutional system, which overdetermines the choice and the connections of symbolic networks, which is the creation of each historical period, its singular manner of living, of seeing and of conducting its own existence, its world, and its relations with this world, this originary structuring component, this central signifying-signified, the source of that which presents itself in every instance as an indisputable and undisputed meaning, the basis for articulating what does matter and what does not, the origin of the surplus of being of the objects of practical, affective and intellectual investment, whether individual or collective – is nothing other than the imaginary of the society or of the period considered.[24]

Castoriadis used his development of the imaginary to explain the lived material diversity between societies. Marxism focused on the abstract institutional arrangements that emerged due to political economic forces: Castoriadis's social imaginary went to explain the symbolism and myths 'that articulate meaning … and what should and should not be done'.[25] Like the postwar project of overcoming positivism's separation of law and culture, Castoriadis's account of the social imaginary allowed critical theory to moderate the abstract forces of Marxism and think about located praxis within sociocultural communities.[26]

Subsequently, the *imaginary* has become a flexible and much-deployed concept within critical thought.[27] As Moira Gatens and Genevieve Lloyd observe, 'the imaginary endures through time and so becomes increasingly embedded in all our institutions, our judicial systems, our national narratives, our founding fictions, our cultural traditions'.[28] The idea of the imaginary

23 Castoriadis (1994).
24 Castoriadis (1987), p 145.
25 Castoriadis (1987), p 146; Thompson (1982), pp 164–67; Ross (2018).
26 Rundell (2001).
27 Frank (2017), pp 16–17; Kølvraa and Forchtner (2019), p 229.
28 Gatens and Lloyd (1999), p 143.

– how collective memes and myths are 'given a concrete form in the sphere of cultural production and communication'[29] – has been used to think about nation,[30] the collective construction and accounting for ageing and dementia[31] and colonial framings and practices.[32] Ideas about colonial imaginaries have been significant for critics within settler-colonial states such as Australia and Canada, in thinking about relations between law and enduring colonial projects.[33] There has been identification of how settler cultural texts, tropes and narratives frame, explain and justify occupier sovereignty and carceral projects of criminalising and removing First Nations peoples.[34]

Indeed, it is possible to identify a sense of the *legal imaginary* focusing on how legal discourses – judgments, legislation and scholarly legal literature – are informed, constructed and reify the imaginary.[35] One location where this has occurred is in relation to law and technology.[36] It is almost trite to observe that writing about law and technology tends towards the speculative.[37] The 'what if' of technological change is a foundation for speculation about how law can and should respond. Often this speculation is informed by science fiction itself. For example, contemporary discussions of lethal autonomous weapon systems tend to be framed around popular filmic representations of killer robots.[38]

The contributions in this volume engage more explicitly with science fiction as the legal imaginary. Science fiction falls ready-to-hand for legal scholars because of the importance of time within and upstream from legal analysis.[39] As a general definition of a genre, science fiction – distinct from other speculative genres such as fantasy or horror – has a sense of futurity, a sense of temporal connection with the present.[40] For legal scholars, this dynamic of a present connected to the future is deeply familiar. The positive enterprise of making law explicitly involves actions in the present to affect the future.[41] The synergy between science fiction and legal scholarship focused on what law *should be* is strongly evident within law and technology, but it does not stop there. Legal discourses that think, desire and anticipate a future through

29 Yar (2014), pp 3–4.
30 Moraru (2011); Yip (2004).
31 Kontos et al (2020); Kothari (2020).
32 Brosch (2021); Lynch (2014)
33 Coombe (1993); Van Rijswijk (2018); Unger (2023).
34 Anthony et al (2023), pp 63–78.
35 Grear (2020).
36 Robb and Tranter (2023).
37 Tranter (2011).
38 See, for example, Crootof (2015), p 1840; Douglas (2023), p 525. More broadly on robot law and the science fiction robot canon, see Goding and Tranter (2023).
39 Travis (2022).
40 Menadue et al (2020).
41 Tranter (2018), p 35.

law are inherently science-fictional. The futurity embedded within the imaginary of the technoscience culture of the present is articulated through science fiction.

This is what makes the contributions broader than was evident in *Cultural Legal Studies of Science Fiction*. In that volume, the chapters interrogated concepts such as sovereignty, personhood and relations with 'others'; in this volume, science fiction as the legal imaginary informs reflection on more substantive legal areas: international law, space law, contemporary concerns about the digital and the corporation.

The chapters

The remaining chapters in this book, unified by an explicit recognition of and engagement with science fiction as legal imaginary, manifest three discrete themes. The first of these is explored in Part I: 'Law of Space(s)'. The chapters within this theme focus on supra-law, public international law and imagining of shared lawful space beyond the sovereign nation.

In Chapter 2, Alex Green continues a critical legal tradition of engaging with the novels of China Miéville, a Marxist international lawyer and science fiction scholar, who crafts fiction that problematises both law and legality.[42] Green focuses on Miéville's *The City and the City* (2009)[43] and the international law of state continuity. Focusing on Small Island Developing States (SIDS), he utilises Miéville's story about two cities overlapping each other critically and inspirationally. Within the critical register, he observes the discipline and structures whereby the inhabitants of Miéville's cities 'unsee' each other and parallels the remarkable unseeing in which the international community and its law of statehood are engaged regarding the alleged legal consequences of sea-level rise for SIDS. Insightfully, Green draws upon Miéville's imagining of geographically convergent states as an intuition pump for the possibility that international law can and should go beyond the idea of territory as land.

Like Green, Kritika Sharma engages with a science-fictional imaginary and international law in Chapter 3. However, whereas Green turns towards the weird fiction of Miéville, Sharma turns towards the extreme pop of the mainstream American superhero comic publishing houses. For Sharma, the ways in which these cultural juggernauts play with time are instructive. She identifies a repeated tendency within the multiverses presented by Marvel and DC Comics to portray time as intimate and non-linear. Sharma exemplifies this through the recent Marvel Cinematic Universe (MCU) television series *Loki* (2021–). She turns to two international law decisions, emphasising how the

42 Doherty (2016); Hourigan (2013, 2018).
43 Miéville (2009).

judges, like the titular Norse god of mischief in *Loki*, are blending time, travelling back to points in the past and reaching out to the future from an experiential location of the present. Within the texts of their judgments, there is a fluidity across, and a looping of, time that mirrors the temporal fluidity celebrated and screened within *Loki* itself.

Chapter 4 by Emily Muir shifts the visual focus from Sharma's emphasis on texts from the West to the East yet remains concerned with international order. Muir's point of reference is the celebrated Japanese anime series *Neon Genesis Evangelion* (1995–96)[44] and its presentation and critique of the *jus in bello* principles within international law. The principles of *jus in bello* present a foundational perspective on right conduct in warfare. Muir examines how the show's child-soldier protagonists, vulnerable yet violent, victims and aggressors, undermine the abstract rationality within the principles. She demonstrates how the representations of child soldiers, even genetically engineered child soldiers who battle aliens while merged with giant, biomechanical robots, turn from agency to collective responsibility.

Whereas Green, Sharma and Muir focus on international law and ordering firmly located on Earth, in Chapter 5, Erika Techera, Renae Barker and Meredith Blake blast off to other spaces. Their focus is on the adequacy of international space law for space-faring futures. Noting a coalescence between science fiction imaginaries of space futures and the contemporary renaissance of the space industry and technologies, they identify a site for rethinking space governance. They focus particularly on the imaginary of rights-based orders, particularly *human* rights-based orders, in space. Working through a range of screened science fictions, from the Hollywood *Solaris* film[45] to the celebrated space opera franchises of *Babylon 5* and *Star Trek*, they identify imagined conflicts and coordination problems that are possible in space futures, not just in the engagement with truly alien others but those manifested by diversity, difference and resource inequality within extraterrestrial human communities. They conclude by emphasising the need for a space governance that takes responsibility for harm, rather than merely the assertion of rights, seriously finding inspiration with the Prime Directive from *Star Trek*.

Chapter 6 by Stacey Henderson and Melissa de Zwart zooms into one of the problems of imagined space futures that Techera, Barker and Blake noted. This chapter is located at the disjunction between the imaginary that underpinned the mid-twentieth-century emergence of international space law (that of sovereign nations competing for space resources) and the emerging twenty-first-century space activity, which largely features private corporations. They note that the corporatisation of space has often been imagined

44 Seager (2023).
45 Soderbergh (2002) *Solaris*.

within science fiction, and they focus particularly on celebrated 'neo-hard' science fictions of a near-future, near-Earth solar system exploration, colonisation and exploitation, such as Kim Stanley Robinson's *Mars* trilogy.[46] They identify an imaginary where corporate space actors are corrosive to the potential benefits of humanity's space-faring future. In doing so, Henderson and de Zwart identify a lacuna within our existing international ordering of space: that the state-centric focus of contemporary international law obscures where the driver for funding and technology for space exploration (and exploitation) is really developing. A next generation of space legality is required, which can engage and regulate corporate space actors.

A theme that is present in the space law imaginaries discussed by Techera, Barker and Blake, and also within the Henderson and de Zwart chapter, is that of space and human vulnerability. Humans are vulnerable to violence and deprivation on Earth, the planet on which our species evolved. Space holds another level of vulnerability. For human life to endure in space, there must be absolute dependence on artificial environments to maintain the basic parameters of heat and oxygen. The imagining of such environmental vulnerability among space humans, and how the law might respond, is the focus of Chapter 7 by Evie Kendal. Drawing upon a substantial cross-section of science fiction narratives unified by a focus on what can go wrong with artificial space environments, Kendal examines issues of workplace health and safety, mining and incarceration. She identifies how earthbound vulnerabilities are imagined as intensified when translocated to space. The artificial environments of space habitation are seen as allowing for sites of total exploitation and total information control: opaque black spaces of dehumanisation. In doing so, she highlights the need for law and order to mitigate the dystopian potential of space habitation.

Part II: 'Dealing with the Digital' focuses on the relationships between the decades of science fiction narratives, tropes and texts that imagine robots, artificial intelligence (AI) and networked societies, and the legalities called forth by the digital present. Chapter 8 by Paul Burgess and Daniel Chia Matallana utilises Ted Chiang's *The Lifecycle of Software Objects* (2010).[47] Chiang's novella presents a world of digital personalities ('digients') and foregrounds three ways in which such entities could be deployed: from employees to corporate directors to sexual partners. Burgess and Chia Matallana take these tropes and examine them through existing rule of law theories. They find that such theories struggle to accommodate the powers and vulnerabilities of digital entities. Digital entities – especially the digients in the novella that grow and develop over time – problematise orthodox accounts of legal

46 Robinson (1992, 1993, 1996).
47 Chiang (2010).

personality that inform rule-of-law theories, leading to the collapse of concepts such as ownership and consent.

Whereas Burgess and Matallana explore the legal *protection* of digital entities, in Chapter 9, Georgios Pavlidis focuses on protecting human economies and societies from digital entities – or, more precisely, by AI systems used by organised crime. Pavlidis reviews the long imaginary of malevolent AI in science fiction and the repeated representations of attempts to police and bring to justice rogue robots. He notes, however, a parallel imaginary where the robot or AI is utilised by a human criminal to facilitate crimes. Pavlidis sees this secondary imaginary reflected in contemporary forms of AI-enabled crime. Focusing on AI use in money laundering, he identifies an escalating intensification of AI-based tools being deployed by organised crime to launder money; in turn, these are counteracted with AI-based tools by financial institutions and state-based law enforcement agencies. Pavlidis concludes that this battle of the machines, also imagined within various science fiction works, creates substantial problems for established legal principles centred around transparency and accountability.

Some ways to start thinking about how to entrench desirable values into AI systems are examined in Chapter 10 by Yeliz Figen Döker and Habibe Deniz Seval. They engage deeply with two of the paradigmatic representations of AI in science fiction: Asimov's robot stories and Philip K Dick's *Do Androids Dream of Electric Sheep?* (1968).[48] They highlight two very different legalities manifested within each of these texts. The first is that Asimov's famous 'Three Laws of Robotics' show the limit of AI compliance by design. Internal safeguards, although a good everyday framework, require refinement through learning from experience. In contrast, Dick's world reveals a legality of violence and a failure to provide any sort of framework for AI. By constructing a detailed dialogue between the worlds of Asimov and Dick, Döker and Seval generate an ethical imperative, not in the contemporary AI engineering sense of a placeholder for social responsibility, but rather in a sense of an empathy-driven framework for living with the artificial other.

AM Waltermann, in Chapter 11, focuses further on the values that should inform AI law. For her, the science-fictional imaginary of robots as possessing something akin to human personality is misleading. Looking at two screened legal reckonings with AI, the celebrated *Star Trek: Next Generation* episode 'Measure of Man' (1989)[49] and the more recent *Westworld* series (2016–22), she identifies that the focus on representing AI as embodied and human-like is a poor imagining of agency in both humans and other entities. Drawing upon more recent neuroscience critiques of moral agency theories, Waltermann identifies that the clarity of the traditional accounts of a will to

48 Dick (1972); see Goding and Tranter (2023).
49 Scheerer (1989) 'The Measure of a Man'.

choose action within a context of awareness of the likely consequences of action is compromised within human reasoning by a multitude of cognitive biases. For her, rather than engaging in talk about personality for digital entities from the perspective of a legal regime that seeks to identify pre-existing moral agents worthy of legal protection, progress should be made by a law of personhood that constructs rights and obligations *for* entities. From this perspective, the imaginary of this new law should be guided by broader social concerns regarding the benefits and disadvantages of legislating rights and obligations onto entities – digital, human or other.

This brings us to Chapter 12, by Katie Szilagyi and Christina Fawcett. Whereas the contributions thus far have focused on living with and making laws for digital entities, Szilagyi and Fawcett connect the digital back to its corporate location and the speculative imagining of a digitalised society and economy. Their focus is on the entities behind platform capitalism: the giant tech companies (Google, Apple, Meta, Amazon) and their extraction, collection and profiting from data. They observe that Neal Stephenson's fabulous cyberpunk novel *Snow Crash* (1992)[50] has a complicated legacy. What should perhaps be read as a more light-hearted satire of the tropes within 1980s cyberpunk has seemingly been interpreted by many in Silicon Valley as an imaginary for desirable digital environments, particularly virtual worlds. (The transformation of Facebook to 'Meta' is a direct reference to the cultural impact of Stephenson's work.) However, Szilagyi and Fawcett also read the novel as a critique of the neoliberal corporate agenda of our contemporary tech giants. *Snow Crash*, they argue, reveals a world of corporate excess, where the state has been dismantled and privatised, and information transcends money. Social harmony has disintegrated, financial systems are depleted and human wellbeing is in decline. In short, *Snow Crash* reveals large corporations acting as villains. Szilagyi and Fawcett suggest that dealing with the digital should not be preoccupied with digital, artificial beings that might resemble the science-fictional imaginary of robots or general AI, but with the very real and very powerful artificial beings of the present that are crafting digital futures: the corporate tech giants.

This leads directly to Part III: 'We are Borg – Imagining the Corporate Form'. In Chapters 5 and 6, we saw in the confluence of the science fiction imaginaries of corporatised space exploration and contemporary corporate space activities a concern that profit and privatisation could undermine beneficial space futures. Moreover, in Chapter 12, through *Snow Crash*, Szilagyi and Fawcett saw tech companies as undermining the digital present. This part contains three chapters that each explicitly connects science fictional accounts and representations of the corporation and collective commercial forms to theories of the corporation and corporate law.

50 Stephenson (1992).

Chapter 13, by Timothy D Peters and Thomas Giddens, sets the approach and establishes the concerns that unify all three. Peters and Giddens undertake a cultural legal studies reading of the Netflix series *Snowpiercer* (2020–). *Snowpiercer*, specifically the 1001-carriage titular train that traverses a frozen Earth, manifests corporate sovereignty in a more material and grounded way than the cartoonish representations of corporate sovereignty that Stephenson presents in *Snow Crash*. Peters and Giddens draw particularly on Peter Goodrich's work on legal symbolism and imagery to observe how the collective (in the form of 'Wilford Industries', the corporate entity behind both the physical train and the train as a techno-social entity) and individuals (the absent, then present, Mr Wilford and the diverse passengers) are bound together. In particular, they identify how the symbolism within images and myths of absence intertwine with 'somatic' power – that is, power over the biological life in the form of corporal punishment – to stabilise and disrupt the collectives. Significantly, Peters and Giddens emphasise that engaging with symbolic forms of power, through which corporate sovereignty rules the world, is not a speculative task. Understanding and thinking critically about the relations between various corporate forms and the somatic power that corporations wield is an urgent need of the present.

Chapter 14 by Dhiraj Nainani takes this urgent need up directly. Sharing a cultural legal studies approach with Peters and Giddens, Nainani examines the first season of the recent AppleTV+ series *Severance* (2022–). *Severance* presents an intense world of worker corporatisation, where the individual workers at Lumon Industries have undergone a 'severance' procedure, leading to rigid divisions between their at-work personas and their outside-work lives. Nainani connects the show's prioritising of space (at work/outside work) to critical legal geography, informed by Michel Foucault and Hans Lindahl, to examine the modes of power through which Lumon Industries creates an unchallengeable legal order. Further, he draws parallels between the representations of Lumon Industries in *Severance* and the real-world practices of Amazon, where disposable worker bodies are managed through a combination of access to corporate objects and the spatial features of corporate property. In this way, the imaginary of *Severance* does not prioritise the future but rather provides a cipher for knowing and mapping spatio-legal practices, whereby corporate entities render the world compliant.

This brings us to Chapter 15: Jordan Belor's examination of the adaptation of Philip K Dick's 'Autofac' short story within the 2017–18 UK Channel 4 anthology series *Electric Dreams*.[51] 'Autofac' manifests many familiar Dick tropes: a post-nuclear apocalypse future, a familiar normalcy that hides its truth, the fetishisation of consumption and slippages and indistinction between humans and AI robotic entities. It tells a story of a community

51 Horton (2018) 'Autofac'.

served by an automatic factory (the titular Autofac) and the discovery by members of this community that they are not humans at all, but android consumers manufactured by the Autofac to consume its commercial goods. The Autofac can be seen as a descendant of the digients from *The Lifecycle of Software Objects*, discussed in Chapter 8, which were trained to become the controlling mind and will of their corporation. Belor sees in Autofac a representation of the AI-controlled corporation: one where the corporate purpose of providing profit for shareholders, or benefits of other kinds to human consumers, has shrunk to simply becoming a reproductive machine for specific forms of life. He identifies that the biopolitical essence of the corporation, manifested through Autofac, is based on the control and integrity of data. The collective assemblage of Autofac endures through maintaining data that is the precondition for its endurance. It makes and regulates the 'settlers' who consume its products. Data in 'Autofac' manifests as potentiality in a digitalised world made by tech corporations, which encodes – and indeed legislates – the forms of and potentials for life.

The legal imaginary: Past, present and future

Ultimately, each of the chapters in this volume contributes to an understanding of how the legal imaginary can channel cultural tropes, narratives and memes into law and legality. With our particular focus on science fiction, these chapters establish how, for example, fictitious representations of sovereign entities and space travel form an imagined future that can ground legal analysis in the present. This dynamic and inspirational relationship between the imaginary and time is also present within many of the chapters dealing with the digital: where cultural narratives that anticipate future digital forms ground thinking about how law should respond and what values law should embody when it does respond.

Every chapter in this volume that engages with imaginary futures to inspire reform in the present also witnesses a profound and shared instability – what Sharma terms a 'temporal rift' in Chapter 3. This instability occurs because the imaginary of the future itself happens in the present, and for some science fiction texts, these future imaginaries even exist within our own past. Asimov's initial robot short stories are now over 70 years old, and Philip K Dick's best-known and most critically acclaimed works were published in the late 1960s and early 1970s. There is a real sense of 'yesterday's tomorrow' in these reflections upon the law and policy of today. The anxieties this tomorrow imagined – of enslaved humans with robotic overlords, enslaved robots with human overlords, enslaved robots *and* humans with corporate overlords or even enslaved robots with robotic corporate overlords – emerged from the cultural milieu of fictitious texts that are now a matter of history. For such robot narratives, anxieties around slavery have obvious and deep connections with the enduring legacy of slavery for racial and economic relations in the United States. Imagined narratives of space exploration and exploitation occur within the remote *and* recent history of colonialism on Earth: of corporate-sovereign assemblages extracting resources to the 'core' from a 'periphery' of local communities and environments. The legal imaginary is chronologically complex: past, present and future coalesce.

This is seen particularly in the chapters in Part III. As Peters and Giddens clearly observe, using a contemporary science fiction text about a mega-colossal train in a future frozen and post-apocalyptic world says relatively little about our actual future, but says a great deal about the forms and modes of corporate power we experience in the present.

This should possibly be seen as our ultimate finding when considering science fiction *as* legal imaginary. Within the nexus between law and time is a 'folding', to quote Emily Grabham.[52] This folding is something that resonates deeply with science fiction, with its time-travel narratives.[53] In engaging with science fiction as legal imaginary, the way time becomes folded through the very chapters of this volume itself reveals not only how culture infuses both law and legal thought, but also how law and the practice of thinking about law are, to quote *Doctor Who*, 'wibbly wobbly, timey wimey'.[54] This time-sense is not only located where there is thinking about the project (allegedly empowered but ultimately undermined by positivism) of making laws in the present to deal with future possibilities. It is also essential to law as a fundamental cultural activity. Law is culture within a complex milieu of past, present and future. In other wor(l)ds, such law is nomos.[55]

References

Thalia Anthony, Juanita Sherwood, Harry Blagg and Kieran Tranter (2023) *Unsettling Colonial Automobilities: Criminalisation and Contested Sovereignties*, Emerald.

Renate Brosch (2021) 'Filmic Representations of Eddie Mabo in a Changing Cultural Imaginary' in Geoff Rodoreda and Eva Bischof (eds), *Mabo's Cultural Legacy: History, Literature, Film and Cultural Practice in Contemporary Australia*, Anthem Press, 93.

John G Browning (2014) 'A Long Time Ago, in a Courtroom Far, Far Away, There's No Denying that the Force is All Around Us – Even Judges Refer to George Lucas's Pop Culture Science Fiction Saga' 77 *Texas Bar Journal* 158.

Bree Carlton (2023) 'Heritage, Resistance and Dissonance: Reconstructing Pentridge in a Prison Tourism Theme Park' *International Journal of Heritage Studies* 1. https://doi.org/10.1080/13527258.2023.2284727

Cornelius Castoriadis (1987) *The Imaginary Institution of Society*, Polity Press.

52 Grabham (2016), p 37.
53 Travis (2022).
54 Tranter (2017).
55 Levine (2023), pp 256–57.

Cornelius Castoriadis (1994) 'Radical Imagination and the Social Instituting Imaginary' in Gillian Robinson and John F Rundell (eds), *Rethinking Imagination*, Routledge, 136.
Ted Chiang (2010) *The Lifecycle of Software Objects*, Subterranean Press.
Rosemary J Coombe (1993) 'Cultural and Intellectual Properties: Occupying the Colonial Imagination' 16 *Political and Legal Anthropology Review* 8.
Robert M Cover (1983) 'Nomos and Narrative' 97 *Harvard Law Review* 4.
Karen Crawley and Timothy D Peters (2018) 'Introduction: "Representational Legality"' in Timothy D Peters and Karen Crawley (eds), *Envisioning Legality: Law, Culture and Representation*, Routledge, 1.
Karen Crawley and Kieran Tranter (2019) 'A Maelstrom of Bodies and Emotions and Things: Spectatorial Encounters with the Trial' 32 *International Journal for the Semiotics of Law* 621.
Rebecca Crootof (2015) 'The Killer Robots are Here: Legal and Policy Implications' 36 *Cardozo Law Review* 1837.
Colin Dayan (2011) *The Law is a White Dog: How Legal Rituals Make and Unmake Persons*, Princeton University Press.
Philip K Dick (1972) *Do Androids Dream of Electric Sheep?*, Grafton Books.
Nathan Doherty (2016) 'Hybridized Possibilities: China Miéville's *The Scar* and the Conjuring of Law' 28 *Law & Literature* 233.
Collin M Douglas (2023) 'What We Talk About When We Talk About Killer Robots: The Prospects of an Autonomous Weapons Treaty' 51 *Georgia Journal of International and Comparative Law* 501.
Costas Douzinas and Lynda Nead (1999) 'Introduction' in Costas Douzinas and Lynda Nead (eds), *Law and the Image: The Authority of Art and the Aesthetics of Law*, University of Chicago Press, 1.
David Dyzenhaus (1994) '"Now the Machine Runs Itself": Carl Schmitt on Hobbes and Kelsen' 16 *Cardozo Law Review* 1.
Luis Eslava (2018) 'Dense Struggle: On Ghosts, Law, and the Global Order' in Andreas Philippopoulos-Mihalopoulos (ed), *Routledge Handbook of Law and Theory*, Routledge, 15.
Michael Frank (2017) *The Cultural Imaginary of Terrorism in Public Discourse, Literature and Film: Narrating Terror*, Routledge.
Lon L Fuller (1958) 'Positivism and Fidelity to Law: A Reply to Professor Hart' 71 *Harvard Law Review* 630.
Moira Gatens and Genevieve Lloyd (1999) *Collective Imaginings: Spinoza, Past and Present*, Routledge.
Vincent Goding and Kieran Tranter (2021) '"The Machine Runs Itself": Law is Technology and Australian Embryo and Human Cloning Law' 30 *Griffith Law Review* 240.
Vincent Goding and Kieran Tranter (2023) 'The Robot and Human Futures: Visualising Autonomy in Law and Science Fiction' 34 *Law and Critique* 315.
Peter Goodrich (2013) *Legal Emblems and the Art of Law: Obiter Depicta as the Vision of Government*, Cambridge University Press.
Emily Grabham (2016) *Brewing Legal Times: Things, Form, and the Enactment of Law*, University of Toronto Press.
Anna Grear (2020) 'Legal Imaginaries and the Anthropocene: "Of" and "for"' 31 *Law and Critique* 351.

Alex Green, Mitchell Travis and Kieran Tranter (eds) (2024a) *Cultural Legal Studies of Science Fiction*, Routledge.

Alex Green, Mitchell Travis and Kieran Tranter (2024b) 'The Collapse and the Spiral: Law, Culture and Science Fiction' in Alex Green, Mitchell Travis and Kieran Tranter (eds), *Cultural Legal Studies of Science Fiction*, Routledge, 1–14.

James Greene Jr (2022) *A Convenient Parallel Dimension: How Ghostbusters Slimed Us Forever*, Rowman & Littlefield.

HLA Hart (1958) 'Positivism and the Separation of Law and Morals' 71 *Harvard Law Review* 593.

Patrick Horton (2022) 'Carceral Spectres: Hyperincarceration and the Haunting of Aboriginal Life' 33 *The Australian Journal of Anthropology* 35.

Peter Horton (2018) 'Autofac' *Electric Dreams*, Season 1, Episode 8(Channel 4, United Kingdom, 5 March).

Daniel Hourigan (2013) 'Breach! The Law's *Jouissance* in Miéville's *The City & The City*' 9 *Law, Culture and the Humanities* 156.

Daniel Hourigan (2018) 'On the Possibility of Legal Form in Miéville's Speculative Fictions' 30 *Law & Literature* 167.

Christoffer Kølvraa and Bernhard Forchtner (2019) 'Cultural Imaginaries of the Extreme Right: An Introduction' 53 *Patterns of Prejudice* 227.

Pia Kontos et al (2020) 'Raising the Curtain on Stigma Associated with Dementia: Fostering a New Cultural Imaginary for a More Inclusive Society' 30 *Critical Public Health* 91.

Uma Kothari (2020) 'Colonial Imaginaries, Colonized Places' in Tim Edensor, Ares Kalandides and Uma Kothari (eds), *The Routledge Handbook of Place*, Routledge, 88.

Samuel J Levine (2023) 'Law and Redemption: Expounding and Expanding Robert Cover's Nomos and Narrative' 34 *Yale Journal of Law and the Humanities* 253.

Alex B Long (2011) 'The Freewheelin' Judiciary: A Bob Dylan Anthology' 38 *Fordham Urban Law Journal* 1363.

Tom Lynch (2014) '"Nothing but Land": Women's Narratives, Gardens, and the Settler-Colonial Imaginary in the US West and Australian Outback' 48 *Western American Literature* 374.

William P MacNeil (2007) *Lex Populi: The Jurisprudence of Popular Culture*, Stanford University Press.

Lynn Mather et al (1995) '"The Passenger Decides on the Destination and I Decide on the Route": Are Divorce Lawyers "Expensive Cab Drivers?"' 9 *International Journal of Law and the Family* 286.

Christopher Benjamin Menadue, Kirsti Giselsson and David Guez (2020) 'An Empirical Revision of the Definition of Science Fiction: It is All in the Techne …' *Sage Open*. https://doi.org/10.1177/2158244020963057

China Miéville (2009) *The City and the City*, Del Rey.

Gary Minda (1995) *Postmodern Legal Movements: Law and Jurisprudence at Century's End*, New York University Press.

Christian Moraru (2011) *Cosmodernism: American Narrative, Late Globalization, and the New Cultural Imaginary*, University of Michigan Press.

Linda Mulcahy (2011) *Legal Architecture: Justice, Due Process and the Place of Law*, Routledge.

Jennifer C Nash (2006) 'Bearing Witness to Ghosts: Notes on Theorizing Pornography, Race, and Law' 21 *Wisconsin Women's Law Journal* 47.
Philippe Nonet (1990) 'What is Positive Law?' 100 *Yale Law Journal* 667.
Timothy D Peters (2022) *A Theological Jurisprudence of Speculative Cinema: Superheroes, Science Fictions and Fantasies of Modern Law*, Edinburgh University Press.
Lachlan Robb and Kieran Tranter (2023) 'Hype and Cultural Imaginary in Law and Technology' in Bartosz Brożek, Olia Kanevskaia and Przemysław Pałka (eds), *Research Handbook of Law and Technology*, Edward Elgar, 128.
Michael Robertson and Kieran Tranter (2007) 'Grounding Legal Ethics Learning in Social Scientific Studies of Lawyers at Work' 9 *Legal Ethics* 211.
Kim Stanley Robinson (1992) *Red Mars*, Spectra.
Kim Stanley Robinson (1993) *Green Mars*, Spectra.
Kim Stanley Robinson (1996) *Blue Mars*, Spectra.
Lachlan Ross (2018) 'The Mad Animal: On Castoriadis' Radical Imagination and the Social Imaginary' 146 *Thesis Eleven* 71.
John Rundell (2001) 'Imaginary Turns in Critical Theory: Imagining Subjects in Tension' 2 *Critical Horizons* 61.
Austin Sarat and William L Felstiner (1995) *Divorce Lawyers and Their Clients: Power and Meaning in the Legal Process*, Oxford University Press.
Robert Scheerer (1989) *The Measure of Man, Star Trek: The Next Generation*, Paramount Television.
Carl Schmitt (1985) *Political Theology: Four Chapters on the Concept of Sovereignty*, MIT Press.
River Seager (2023) 'Newtypes, Angels, and Human Instrumentality: The Mecha Genre and its Apocalyptic Bodies' 4 *The Journal of Anime and Manga Studies* 219.
Richard K Sherwin (2000) *When Law Goes Pop: The Vanishing Line Between Law and Popular Culture*, University of Chicago Press.
Richard K Sherwin (2011) *Visualizing Law in the Age of the Digital Baroque*, Routledge.
Steven Soderbergh (2002) *Solaris*, 20th Century Fox.
Neal Stephenson (1992) *Snow Crash*, Bantam.
Cass Sunstein R (2016) *The World According to Star Wars*, Dey Street Books.
John B Thompson (1982) 'Ideology and the Social Imaginary: An Appraisal of Castoriadis and Lefort' 11 *Theory and Society* 659.
Kieran Tranter (2011) 'The Speculative Jurisdiction: The Science Fictionality of Law and Technology' 20 *Griffith Law Review* 817.
Kieran Tranter (2017) 'Law, the Digital and Time: The Legal Emblems of *Doctor Who*' 30 *International Journal for the Semiotics of Law* 515.
Kieran Tranter (2018) *Living in Technical Legality: Science Fiction and Law as Technology*, University of Edinburgh Press.
Mitchell Travis (2022) 'Jurisprudence, Temporality and Science Fiction' 4 *Law, Technology and Humans* 5.
Matthew P Unger (2023) 'Winter's Topography, Law, and the Colonial Legal Imaginary in British Columbia' 26 *Space and Culture* 618.
Honni Van Rijswijk (2018) 'Archiving the Northern Territory Intervention in Law and in the Literary Counter-Imaginary' in Katherine Biber and Trish Luker (eds), *Evidence and the Archive: Ethics, Aesthetics and Emotion*, Routledge, 129.

Majid Yar (2014) *The Cultural Imaginary of the Internet: Virtual Utopias and Dystopias*, Palgrave Macmillan.

June Yip (2004) *Envisioning Taiwan: Fiction, Cinema, and the Nation in the Cultural Imaginary*, Duke University Press.

Part I

Law of space(s)

Chapter 2

Towards an ~~im~~possible polis

Legal imagination and state continuity

Alex Green

Introduction: Two cities, two states

Thomas Baty once quipped that, 'International law, it is generally agreed, has something to do with states'.[1] Good jokes should not need explaining; however, in this case, it helps to do so. By opening *The Canons of International Law* in this manner, Baty draws attention to the controversial question of international law itself: to its contested content and its ambiguous nature. Statehood functions so well in his joke because, naturally, we *all* know what states are, right? Their ubiquitous presence within our lives, their structural influence upon us, and their grand institutional structures make them an obvious foil to the elusive, largely non-coercive,[2] and decentralised international legal order. We might not know what international law is, but at least we know what states are, and it is generally agreed that international law has at least something to do with them: clever stuff.

Clever but dead wrong. Statehood is deeply contested and controversial – especially within international law – which Baty themself goes on to acknowledge and elaborate upon.[3] Elsewhere, I have argued that statehood occasions some of the most controversial questions that international lawyers face and that prevailing approaches to the subject are woefully inadequate to grapple with them.[4] In this chapter, I continue that argument in a somewhat different vein. What concerns me now is primarily the law of state continuity: those principles that govern when and how established states remain in existence through time, notwithstanding whatever vicissitudes might befall them. My primary complaint is that prevailing approaches (within both international legal practice and scholarship) tempt some rather unattractive conclusions and that dominant modes of legal reasoning are ill-equipped to avoid or

1 Baty (1930), p 1.
2 Cf. Miéville (2006), p 119.
3 Miéville (2006), pp 6–28.
4 Green (2024a), pp 1–12, 223–36.

DOI: 10.4324/9781003412274-3

overcome them.[5] At bottom, the law of state continuity suffers from a deficit of legal imagination. My prescribed cure is for international lawyers to flex their imaginative muscles more strenuously, drawing upon speculative fiction by way of inspiration and example.

The text I use in this chapter is China Miéville's *The City & The City*, a 'weird fiction' novel set within the fictional and geographically overlapping city-states of Besźel and Ul Qoma.[6] The bizarre yet plausible geographical and jurisdictional circumstances of these cities are important within my argument because they function as 'intuition pumps' for my contention that international lawyers can and should be more imaginative when it comes to both statehood itself and state continuity.[7] The next section outlines the significance of this novel for our understanding of the state within contemporary international law. I contend that international lawyers – perhaps because of the political controversy surrounding statehood – are trained in various ways to 'unsee' political communities that do not fit the contemporary legal mould. The third section of the chapter turns to the law of state continuity itself, focusing on the unique existential threats faced by Small Island Developing States (SIDS) in light of human-caused climate change. After outlining the dangers posed by rising sea levels, I explain the complicity of prevailing legal approaches to state continuity in the unjust treatment that such states receive. Finally, I present some alternative positions to these 'austere' approaches, drawing upon some creative legal reasoning and the intuitive nudge provided by *The City & The City* itself.

Weirder than fiction: 'Unseeable' communities in international law

China Miéville is no stranger to the structural injustices of international law, having written his doctoral thesis on that topic. Indeed, in the resulting *Between Equal Rights: A Marxist Theory of International Law*, he contends that 'it is possible to accept that international law is law, that it is always part of the international political process, and yet argue that it cannot and will not

5 I have made similar arguments elsewhere; see Green (2021); Green (2023a).

6 Like other broad genres, 'weird fiction' is difficult to define. Miéville comments, 'I don't think you can distinguish science fiction, fantasy and horror with any rigour, as the writers around the magazine Weird Tales early in the last century (Lovecraft in particular) illustrated most sharply. So I use the term "weird fiction" for all fantastic literature – fantasy, SF, horror and all the stuff that won't fit neatly into slots'. *Guardian* (2002); for an excellent historical characterisation of the early movement, see Machin (2018), pp 6–24.

7 An 'intuition pump' is an imagined hypothetical 'designed to focus the reader's attention on "the important" features, and to deflect the reader from bogging down in hard-to-follow details' (Dennett (1984), p 12). For more on the value of (science) fiction as a source of intuition pumps within legal and political theory, see Green (2022).

act to further a "just world order"'.[8] We differ on this point, largely due to our respective understandings of the concept of law. For Miéville, any invocation of the legal form is necessarily a form of violence because it (re)produces the capitalist commodity form and enforces it coercively.[9] On my view, although law *may* have such features, it is fundamentally a moral phenomenon, linked at least to the *pursuit* of justice.[10] Notwithstanding such points of disagreement, Miéville's legal background provides his literary work with extraordinary sophistication on constitutional and jurisdictional matters. Although *The City & The City* is a work of weird fiction, and deliberately alien in its setting as a result, the detail with which Besźel and Ul Qoma are constructed gives them an immediate plausibility, particularly to the international lawyer. In this section, I outline the salient parts of this setting (which is far more important to my argument than the plot itself) and demonstrate how particular concepts therein provide an apt lens for analysing the concept of statehood in international law.

Fiction: Besźel and Ul Qoma

Superficially, *The City & The City* is a crime procedural, taking place initially within Besźel, which occupies a 'curl of coastline' from 'a port hiding a few kilometres up the river to shelter from the pirates of the shore'.[11] This coastline, the blurb enticingly hints, is 'somewhere at the edge of Europe'. Within the narrative, Besźel is very much 'at the edge of Europe', and not just geographically: both culturally and jurisdictionally, Miéville's fictional world occupies the outermost penumbra of Westphalian statehood.

This is because, as alluded to above, the physical space of Besźel overlaps with that of another city. Ul Qoma, which is also a separate state, exists alongside, on top of and below Besźel, separated not by walls or gates but by a practice of legally enforced 'unseeing', whereby citizens of both polities are forbidden from interacting with, acknowledging or responding to events within the 'other' city.[12] The two states are almost totally 'grosstopically' convergent,[13] to use Miéville's phrase, but are worlds apart by virtue of their mutual unseeing. Streets falling within both cities, in that they possess separate names and separate legal and cultural identities but identical spatial and

8 Miéville (2006), p 25.
9 Miéville (2006), pp 302, 316.
10 For the clearest articulation of my own view, albeit in the domestic case, see Green and Hendry (2022) and Green and Hendry (2024); for my views on legal reasoning at the international level, see Green (2024a), pp 1–12, 223–36.
11 Miéville (2009), p 51.
12 Miéville (2009), p 14. This and the following citations are largely illustrative, the relevant customs, conventions and concepts being revealed slowly by Miéville as the narrative unfolds.
13 Miéville (2009), pp 51–53, 161.

physical features, are referred to as 'toplegangers',[14] with intersecting areas being 'crosshatched'.[15] The single legally traversable border between Besźel and Ul Qoma consists of shared checkpoints under 'Copula Hall', the seat of government for both states.[16] Should there be any unlawful 'seeing' of the 'other' city – or, worse, illegal interaction between the two – the crime of 'breach' occurs.[17] The response is immediate, with a clandestine extra-governmental agency also called 'Breach' swooping in to remove the culprits, who are never seen or heard from again.[18]

This bizarre socio-jurisdictional arrangement is made plausible in Miéville's text through a clever combination of legal and cultural detail alongside empathic narration. On the one hand, we are given considerable information both about ordinary life within Besźel and Ul Qoma and about the crime of breach itself. On the other, we experience this shared space through the world-weary eyes of Inspector Tyador Borlú, whose jaded but nonetheless dogged personality promotes immediate investment and immersion. To take a few examples, Chapter 2 presents the following:

> A common form of establishment, for much of Besźel's history, had been the *DoplirCaffé*: one Muslim and one Jewish coffeehouse, rented side by side, each with its own counter and kitchen, halal and kosher, sharing a single name, sign, and sprawl of tables, the dividing wall removed. Mixed groups would come, greet the two proprietors, sit together, separating on communitarian lines only long enough to order their permitted food from the relevant side, or ostentatiously from either and both in the case of freethinkers. Whether the *DoplirCaffé* was one establishment or two depended on who was asking: to a property tax collector, it was always one.[19]

14 Miéville (2009), pp 159, 172.

15 Miéville (2009), pp 225–26. This terminology is reminiscent of, and perhaps was even inspired by, the real-life village of Baarle, which sits at the border of the Netherlands and the Kingdom of Belgium. The territory of Baarle is divided into a patchwork of Dutch (Baarle-Hertog) and Belgian (Baarle-Nassau), which encompass seven and 16 enclaves, respectively, of Dutch and Belgian territory *within* the other state's territorial space. Baarle even includes a quadripoint shared by two of these enclaves. In an amusingly similar vein to the fictional *DoplirCaffés* discussed below, the Dutch and Belgian enclaves sometimes bisect pubs or bars and come with different legally mandated closing times, which can result in the moving of chairs from one 'half' of the establishment to another so that drinking can continue. For more on the fascinating history of Baarle, see Brekelmans (1965).

16 Miéville (2009), pp 85–87, 155–66.

17 Miéville (2009), pp 44–45, 134–35.

18 Miéville (2009), pp 285–87.

19 Miéville (2009), p 26.

Passages rich in such cultural detail populate the text.[20] Here is another, from Chapter 8:

> Most vermin are interstitial. It is very hard to prove that the shy cold-weather lizards in the cracks of Besź walls can live in Besźel only, as frequently claimed: certainly they die if exported to Ul Qoma (even more gently than by children's hands), but they tend to do so in Besź captivity as well. Pigeons, mice, wolves, bats live in both cities, are crosshatched animals. But by unspoken tradition, the majority of the local wolves – mean, bony things long-since adapted to urban scavenging – are generally if nebulously considered Besź: it is only those few of respectable size and none-too-vile pelt, the same notion held, that are Ul Qoman. Many citizens of Besźel avoid transgressing this – entirely unnecessary and invented – categorical boundary by never referring to wolves.[21]

The notion that discriminating amongst the local fauna is 'unnecessary and invented' but that the practice of 'unseeing' itself is not, lends humour but also plausibility to Inspector Borlú's narration, in much the same way as the *DoplirCaffé* owners' manoeuvring around the taxman. We can see ourselves in the people of Besźel and Ul Qoma, so we naturally come to believe that we would be capable of living there. This sense of plausibility is heightened by the behaviour of Tyador Borlú himself, who commits a small and undetectable act of breach at the end of Chapter 4 (by deliberately 'seeing' an elevated Ul Qoman railway line, complete with passing train cars and startled passengers, as the foreign train speeds anonymously past his bedroom window).[22]

Clever writing aside, the plausibility of mutual unseeing as a means for both jurisdictional and ontological separation is borne out by our own lives. As argued by Douglas Guilfoyle:

> Given a moment's thought this is less implausible than many speculative fiction premises. Most of us engage daily in the practice of unseeing things in our urban environment we find inconvenient to acknowledge: the homeless, the mentally disturbed, those collecting for charity, etc.[23]

Although Guilfoyle is essentially correct, he puts the point too mildly. At the root of 'unseeing' – whether in Miéville's fictional variant or in our own

20 Miéville also includes many clever incidental observations on seeming minutiae, such as how tourists from the United States manage to fly to both cities, notwithstanding the jurisdictional complexities (2009, p 88), or the tests that incoming tourists must take in order to avoid breach (2009, pp 92–93).

21 Miéville (2009), p 112.

22 Miéville (2009), p 49.

23 Guilfoyle (2016), p 196.

practices – is existential fear. We simply must ignore what we cannot face without unseating the basis of our own existence, whether that existential threat is physical or normative. The COVID-19 pandemic taught us the extremes to which some people will go in denying evident danger, simply so their worldviews can be confirmed.[24] Similarly, our refusal to 'see' the homeless stems from our dread of acknowledging the structural injustices that construct destitution: injustices in which we are all participants, whether knowingly or otherwise, and of which many of us are beneficiaries. That others suffer due to our indifference undermines the fiction that each of us *must*, in our heart of hearts, be a fundamentally good person. The realisation that we might not be is devastating. As such, being forced to 'see' deconstructs us at the ethical level, a fact evocatively captured by the final lines of Wilfred Owen's 'Mental Cases':

> – Thus their hands are plucking at each other;
> Picking at the rope-knouts of their scourging;
> Snatching after us who smote them, brother,
> Pawing us who dealt them war and madness.[25]

So it is, albeit in a less visceral manner, with Beszél and Ul Qoma. The crime of breach is so serious – and the agency Breach so irresistible – because acknowledgement of the other city would deconstruct the sovereignty, and so the very existence, of the acknowledging state.[26] How can the Besź or Ul Qoman governments truly rule, how can their respective peoples have 'produced equality by organisation',[27] if the 'curl of coastline' upon which both states sit is subject to no true monopoly upon coercive force? If we accept such Weberian characterisations of the state, according to which statehood is defined in terms of successful monopolies of such force within a particular territory,[28] then the coexistence of Beszél and Ul Qoma creates a false negative. Since both states successfully claim a monopoly on legitimate coercion within the same space, neither of them can really do so. One cannot, after all, have two identical monopolies operating at the same time. To acknowledge the shared existence of Beszél and Ul Qoma is therefore to deny it: the existence of states implies a territorial control that such 'grosstopical' convergence rules out.

24 See, for example: Agius et al (2020); Thagard (2021).
25 Owen (1920), p 8. I have avoided adding emphasis here; when I read the poem, I read it upon the first 'us'.
26 Miéville (2009), pp 83–84.
27 Arendt (1958), p 301.
28 Weber (1991), p 78.

From this perspective, fear of 'breach' is the fear of a paradox that refutes an existence maintained through custom, convention and law. As James Crawford and Simon Olleson observe, 'Although they seem real enough to their citizens (and, normally, to others), states are juridical abstractions'.[29] This abstract nature makes the existence of states dependent upon the ongoing practices of private individuals, state representatives and legal experts alike. *The City & The City* illustrates how the socially (including legally) constructed nature of both statehood and territory renders them precarious. In Besźel and Ul Qoma, the criminality of breach is explicable through the fear that the ongoing practices necessary to constitute independent statehood might stop, destroying both states in the process. By contrast, the Besź and Ul Qoman fear of the agency Breach sits more obviously at the core of the uncanny. It merits fear because it is a power behind and above that of both states in a way that,[30] at least on a Weberian understanding of statehood, no power can ever be.[31] All this evinces not just the conceptual depth and plausibility of *The City & The City* but also its usefulness as a lens through which to analyse the idea of statehood in international law. It is to this, and in particular to international legal practices of 'unseeing', that I now turn.

Fact: Recognition, 'effectiveness' and Indigenous peoples

The criteria for the existence of states in international law are deeply controversial. In other work, I have developed a discrete understanding of the law that governs state creation; however, I need not rehearse that argument here.[32] For present purposes, it suffices to say that the two most commonly held views are that states exist for the purposes of international law either to the extent that other states formally recognise their existence or insofar as they are 'effective' in a particular sense.[33] On the first view, the pre-eminence of 'seeing' and 'unseeing' is clear. Formal recognition (or its absence) is the primary means through which established states acknowledge (or deny) the existence of new communities. The State of Israel, among others, unsees the State of Palestine in an attempt to ensure its (alleged) non-existence: an example of non-recognition that is both historically complex and uniquely

29 Crawford and Olleson (2014), p 453.

30 Miéville (2009), pp 83–84, 372.

31 That Breach eventually turns out to be benevolent perhaps hints at a belief on Miéville's part that one should 'always keep a-hold of Nurse; For fear of finding something worse' (Belloc 1907). An alternative reading is that the whole enterprise is largely pointless: the control that Breach exerts is not truly malicious because it is control itself, rather than some ulterior motive or independent end, that matters to law (Miéville 2006), pp 144–53.

32 Green (2024a).

33 This is typically put in terms of recognition being either 'constitutive' of statehood or merely a 'declaratory' act; see the classic discussion in Lauterpacht (1947), pp 1–78.

politically charged. (Indeed, my analysis of Besź and Ul Qoman 'unseeing' somewhat captures why the non-recognition of Palestine may seem existentially imperative to Israel.)

On the second view, recognition has the same expressive effect but lacks legal potency. Instead, new states arise when they have satisfied independently grounded legal criteria. These criteria of 'effectiveness', referenced within Article 1 of the 1933 Montevideo Convention on the Rights and Duties of States,[34] include the existence of a permanent population, a determinate territory, and a government that guarantees 'some degree of maintenance of law and order and the establishment of basic institutions'.[35] Nonetheless, this conception of effectiveness, which ties statehood to stable territorial governance in a largely Weberian mode, can usefully be interpreted as a general standard for the seeing and unseeing of political communities by international law itself. In this subsection, I detail some famous and controversial cases in which putative states were 'unseen' by the international community, before considering the position of Indigenous peoples as a class of communities that are routinely excluded from statehood.

Two famous cases of the former sort are the collective non-recognition of Southern Rhodesia and the Turkish Republic of Northern Cyprus. Collective non-recognition is a particularly active form of 'unseeing': the coordinated refusal on the part of the international community to treat changing political circumstances as having their intended legal effect – whether that be an alteration in government, the annexation of territory or the creation of a new state. It is characteristically undertaken via the United Nations Security Council – for instance, through Resolutions 217 (1965), 253 (1968) and 277 (1970) in the case of Southern Rhodesia,[36] and 541 (1983) and 550 (1984) in the case of Northern Cyprus.[37] In both cases, the process of attempted state creation met with organised non-recognition. The Turkish Republic of Northern Cyprus emerged in 1974 under a Turkish Cypriot administration with military support from the Republic of Turkey.[38] Some 211,000 Greek Cypriots were displaced from the North, with those who remained facing severe restrictions upon their liberty, most notably in terms of freedom of movement.[39] Turkey's use of force was almost universally accepted to have violated Article 2(4) of the United Nations Charter.

34 See also *Deutsche Continental Gas-Gesellschaft v Polish State* (1929) 9 Recueil TAM 336.

35 Crawford (2007), p 59.

36 Security Council resolution 217 (1965), 20 November 1965; Security Council resolution 253 (1968), 29 May 1968; Security Council resolution 277 (1970), 18 March 1970.

37 Security Council resolution 541 (1983), 18 November 1983; Security Council resolution 550 (1984), 11 May 1984.

38 *Loizidou and Cyprus (intervening) v Turkey*, Merits [1996] ECHR 70, paras 16–23.

39 *Cyprus v Turkey*, Merits, App no 25781/94, (2002) ECHR 2001-IV, paras 28–48 (this was held by the Court to violate Article 8 of the European Convention on Human Rights; see paras 165–176).

Southern Rhodesia declared independence from the United Kingdom on 11 November 1965 under the moniker 'Rhodesia'.[40] Controlled by a white minority and unopposed militarily by the United Kingdom, it was condemned by the Security Council and the United Nations General Assembly for its racial segregation and widespread ethnic discrimination.[41] Crucially, despite both swiftly becoming 'effective' in the sense described above, the international refusal to recognise either entity was essentially total. Southern Rhodesia no longer exists, following the 1979 Lancaster House Agreement and the resulting independence of the Republic of Zimbabwe on 18 April 1980. To this day, only Turkey recognises Northern Cyprus.

More contemporary examples include the Donetsk People's Republic and the Luhansk People's Republic, which declared independence from Ukraine on 7 and 27 April 2014 respectively.[42] After initial military conflicts, in which the Russian Federation allegedly played an important role,[43] 'static war' persisted between Ukraine and these two entities until Russia invaded on 25 February 2022.[44] The international community was almost unanimous in its response: to date, no states except the Syrian Arab Republic and the Democratic People's Republic of North Korea have joined Russia in recognising either entity.[45] On 25 February 2022, Russia vetoed a Security Council resolution that would, among other things, have demanded the reversal of Russian recognition.[46] On 2 March 2023, the General Assembly adopted a resolution with largely the same terms.[47] Despite Russian arguments that its military action and recognition of Donetsk and Luhansk were justified under Article 51 of the UN Charter and the 1948 Genocide Convention,[48] international opinion remains firmly antagonistic to both claims.

40 Dugard (1987), pp 90–98.

41 General Assembly resolution 2022 (XX), 5 November 1965; General Assembly resolution 2024 (XX), 11 November 1965.

42 BBC News (2014).

43 Jensen (2017), pp 3–6.

44 On 21 February, Russia formally recognised both entities: Executive Order No 71. On the Recognition of the Donetsk People's Republic, 21 February 2023 (in Russian: http://publication.pravo.gov.ru/Document/View/0001202202220002); Executive Order No 72, On the Recognition of the Lugansk People's Republic, 21 February 2023 (in Russian: http://publication.pravo.gov.ru/Document/View/0001202202220001).

45 Security Council Verbatim Record, 21 February 2022, S/PV.8970.

46 United Nations (2022).

47 General Assembly resolution, 'Aggression Against Ukraine' (A/RES/ES-11/1), 2 March 2022, paras 2–6; see also General Assembly resolution 377A(V), 3 November 1950.

48 Allegations of genocide as a trigger for intervention were made by President Vladimir Putin on 24 February 2022: http://en.kremlin.ru/events/president/news/67843. This argument appears now to be less common, likely due to International Court of Justice proceedings currently being brought by Ukraine; see Application Instituting Proceedings, 26 February 2022, *Allegations of Genocide Under the Convention on the Prevention and Punishment of the Crime of Genocide (Ukraine v Russian Federation)*, 2022 General List No 182. For the official position of Russia on Article 51, see Security Council Verbatim Record, 21 February 2022, S/PV.8970, 11.

In all four cases, the 'unseeing' effected by collective non-recognition is most commonly explained with reference to the violation of various peremptory norms of international law.[49] In the case of Northern Cyprus, these were the norm against the unlawful threat or use of force, reflected in Article 2(4) of the UN Charter, and the mass violation of human rights occasioning the denial of collective self-determination to the non-Turkish population of that territory.[50] In Southern Rhodesia, the relevant norm was the prohibition upon all forms of racial discrimination, occasioning a similar denial of collective self-determination for the non-white population.[51] In the Donbas, the norm in question was once again the unlawful use of force.[52] The prevailing opinion is that these norms are so fundamental to the international legal order that no intended legal effects should result from their breach, at least not so as to benefit the entity that stands in violation.[53] Political communities that arise via breach of such peremptory norms must be 'unseen' because acknowledging their legal existence would plunge international law into an identity crisis similar to those discussed in the previous subsection. In this case, failing to effect non-recognition would be performatively to admit that mere violence can trump fundamental legal principle, and therefore that international law is little more than a rhetorical veneer upon military *faits accomplis*.

Another ongoing and somewhat anomalous case concerns the Republic of Somaliland, which purported to secede from what is now the Federal Republic of Somalia on 17 May 1991.[54] At that time, civil war had plunged Somalia into prolonged anarchy.[55] By contrast, Somaliland swiftly became relatively stable, continuously satisfying the standard criteria of effectiveness to a far greater extent.[56] Indeed, Rowan Nicholson observes that its

49 The International Law Commission defines peremptory norms in the following terms. 'Peremptory norms of general international law (*jus cogens*) reflect and protect fundamental values of the international community. They are universally applicable and are hierarchically superior to other rules of international law' (Conclusion 2); and 'A peremptory norm of general international law (*jus cogens*) is a norm accepted and recognized by the international community of States as a whole as a norm from which no derogation is permitted and which can be modified only by a subsequent norm of general international law having the same character' (Conclusion 3). See International Law Commission (2022a), para 43.

50 Crawford (2007), pp 133–34, 143–47.

51 Crawford (2007), pp 128–31.

52 Weller (2022).

53 Nicholson (2019a), pp 147–48, 160–70; but see pp 175–87.

54 Metz (1993), pp 169–70; Crawford (2007), pp 412–13.

55 Pegg (1998), pp 85–97.

56 For instance: Report of the Secretary-General on the Situation in Somalia, S/2000/1211, 19 December 2000, para 34; Report of the Secretary-General on the Situation in Somalia, S/2001/963, 11 October 2001, paras 18–19; Report of the Secretary-General on the Situation in Somalia, S/2002/198, 21 February 2002, para 28; *Hagi-Salad v Ashcroft*, Judgment of 30 October 2003, 4 UE 4952/96.A (Hesse Administrative Court, Kassel).

'parent state "virtually and substantially abandoned the struggle for supremacy" (which generally indicates that a unilateral secession entity has become effective)'.[57] Nonetheless, Somalia continues to receive foreign recognition, whereas Somaliland has received none.[58] The motive behind this universal unseeing is harder to diagnose than in the cases of Southern Rhodesia, Northern Cyprus or the Donbas republics, where violation of the relevant peremptory norms readily explains the impossibility of international law permitting state creation. Elsewhere, I have argued that the refusal to recognise Somaliland is something of an embedded mistake.[59] Whatever the case, and whatever judgements of *realpolitik* sit behind the unseeing of Somaliland, it illustrates that the international community is fully prepared to ignore the existence of political communities that otherwise satisfy orthodox understandings of statehood.

This willingness to unsee political communities is perhaps most evident in relation to Indigenous peoples, whose statehood was historically denied and subordinated by European colonial powers. Although it has manifested in several ways since the so-called Age of Discovery, the nature of this existential denial is most evocatively captured by Irene Watson in relation to the colonisation of what is now the Commonwealth of Australia:

> Muldarbi law said that the Australian continent was clothed with a blanket of terra nullius of the land, law and people. The Nunga subject in law was deemed not to exist. We were instead defined as British subjects, but subjects without the legal status of British subjects. Nunga laws thereby became covered by the rules and regulations, part of the muldarbi's colonial project of genocide.[60]

The normative power of unseeing is nowhere clearer: genocide cannot be perpetrated against non-existent communities, making the European colonial project's unseeing of Aboriginal Australians the most desperate and total form of ethical self-preservation imaginable. Just as you and I preserve the illusion of our ethical selves by unseeing the destitute and downtrodden, so Europe preserved its illusions of justice and entitlement by manufacturing a false 'destruction of nothing'. But its ethical self-destruction was nonetheless inescapable: by unseeing in order to excuse, genocide was multiplied rather than avoided. To deny the status of our victims is, at least figuratively,

57 Nicholson (2019a), p 190, citing Harcourt (1863), p 9.
58 Crawford (2007), p 415.
59 Green (2024a), pp 102–38.
60 Watson (2015), p 17.

already to destroy them; it adds, as it were, an ultimate insult to the ultimate injury.[61]

Initial practices of unseeing Indigenous peoples were all the more problematic given that they were almost certainly spurious *vis-à-vis* international law at all material times. As Nicholson convincingly argues, even under the strict application of the intertemporal principle,[62] the territories colonised by European states were almost certainly sovereign, even if they did not fit contemporary conceptions of statehood.[63] This holds because, before the consolidation of the modern state system, sovereignty in the sense of 'the jurisdiction of the nation in her territories' was not the exclusive province of states.[64] To put this in terms of what we now call 'effectiveness', we might borrow from the phrasing of Francisco de Vitoria, who averred in relation to the Indigenous peoples of what is now America that 'they have polities which are orderly arranged'[65] and 'undoubtedly [they] had true dominion in both public and private matters'.[66]

But notwithstanding an enduring consensus that 'les hommes de toutes races … doivent être considérés comme égaux en droit',[67] international law still invites self-contradiction by maintaining categorical distinctions between peoples through the concept of statehood. Even the briefest glance at Articles 2 to 27 of the United Nations *Declaration on the Rights of Indigenous Peoples* discloses a list of entitlements that falls far short of statehood.[68] Article 8, for example, stipulates that all Indigenous individuals have the right to a nationality but not to a nationality exclusive to their own people or emanating from their own state – that would be an attribute of Indigenous sovereignty, which international law continues to deny.

Although manifestly unjust, this continued denial is unfortunately typical. Even within the accepted boundaries of statehood, peoples within the Global South continue to be categorised as 'other'. This has been achieved, as Antony Anghie avers, through the idea of 'development', which 'transform[s] cultural differences into economic differences … [and] translate[s] the categories of civilization and non-civilization into the categories of the advanced and backward'.[69] Whatever the instrumental importance of the right to

61 For the importance of status and the wrongfulness of its denial, see Nagel (1995).
62 *Island of Palmas (Netherlands v United States of America) (Award)* (1928) 2 RIAA 829, 845.
63 Nicholson (2019b).
64 Nicholson (2019b), p 500, citing Vattel (2008); see also Nicholson (2019b), pp 524–25.
65 de Victoria (1917), p 127.
66 de Victoria (1917), p 151.
67 Bonfils and Fauchille (1905), pp 310–11. My translation: 'Men of all races … must be considered equal before the law'.
68 General Assembly resolution 61/295, 13 September 2007 (A/RES/61/295), Annex.
69 Anghie (2012), p 204.

development, this conceptual architecture nonetheless invites belief that 'the "primitive" ... must be managed and controlled in the interests of preserving the modern and universal'.[70] In this way, even though Indigenous or economically unproductive (at least from a capitalist perspective) elements of postcolonial states are not quite 'unseen', they are nonetheless perceived through a lens that places them outside the conceptual core of 'statehood proper'. Their manifestation, although not so existentially threatening to prevailing conceptions of statehood that they require unseeing, nonetheless appears to be sufficiently embarrassing to international law that they must be constructed as somehow on the road to European-style 'perfection'.[71]

State continuity and legal imagination: Towards an impossible polis

The previous section concerned statehood as it is and has been. This section, as befits a study emphasising the value of speculative fiction, considers statehood as it might be. I focus particularly on the question of state continuity: under what conditions individual states endure and when they instead become extinct. State continuity is conceptually close to the connected matter of state identity over time; however, it is nonetheless distinct.[72] It is feasible for states to be legally identical with a historical forebear but not continuous with it, as demonstrated by the example of Syria, which merged with the Republic of Egypt in 1958 to form the United Arab Republic.[73] After seceding from that entity in 1961, 'Syria' was swiftly and universally recognised as identical to the pre-1958 entity that shared its name. Similarly, the South African Republic underwent a period of extinction between 1877 and 1881, only to emerge and be recognised as identical to its nominal predecessor.[74] What might explain such cases is an interesting question but not one of immediate concern here. Instead, I shall focus on the requirements for unbroken or unceasing statehood notwithstanding otherwise disruptive events. I am particularly concerned with the existential threats currently posed to SIDS by human-caused climate change. Dominant modes of international legal reasoning, it seems to me, unduly compound the existential threats faced by these communities. My argument in what remains of this chapter is that

70 Anghie (2012), p 207; see also Pahuja (2011), Chapters 3 and 5.

71 For further criticism of this conceptual framework, see Green (2023b), pp 205–06.

72 Cf Marek (1954), pp 5–6.

73 Scharf (1995), p 37.

74 The South African Republic existed between 1852 and 1877, then again between 1881 and 1900. As Crawford notes, Article X of the Pretoria Convention, 3 August 1881, 72 BFSP 900, and Articles X and VIII of the London Convention, 27 February 1884, 75 BFSP 5, 'clearly treat [the South African Republic] as the same State during both periods.' See Crawford (2007), p 690.

this need not be so and that fictional works like *The City & The City* help to illuminate why.

Apocalypse now: SIDS and sea-level rise

SIDS are uniquely threatened by climate change.[75] As global warming causes sea levels to rise, many low-lying and archipelagic landmasses will become either completely uninhabitable or wholly submerged. Tuvalu, which mostly comprises atolls sitting under three metres above mean sea level, may become uninhabitable as early as the mid-twenty-first century.[76] Anticipation of this has prompted a flurry of international political action by SIDS, many of which have taken a significant lead in developing the global response to climate change.[77] For example, on 6 August 2021, the Member States of the Pacific Islands Forum adopted the *Declaration on Preserving Maritime Zones in the Face of Climate Change-related Sea-Level Rise*, which held that

> once having, in accordance with the [United Nations] Convention [on the Law of the Sea], established and notified our maritime zones to the Secretary-General of the United Nations, we intend to maintain these zones without reduction, notwithstanding climate change-related sea-level rise.[78]

Set against this are some generally accepted propositions of international law that cut entirely in the other direction. Elsewhere, I have characterised the complete set of these generally accepted propositions as the 'austere view' of state continuity.[79] They can be found reflected in statements like those of Crawford that 'statehood implies exclusive control over some territory, small or large',[80] Lassa Oppenheim that 'a State without a territory is not possible'[81] or Philip Jessup that 'one cannot contemplate a State as a kind of disembodied spirit'.[82] The essence of the austere view is that states cannot exist without inhabitable land-based territory, such that the total loss

75 Green (2023a), p 81; Purcell (2019), p 229; Mitra and Sanghi (2023); Stewart (2023); Wong (2013); Jain (2014); Bílková (2016).

76 Storlazzi et al (2018).

77 Long (2022), pp 144–50; Corbett et al (2021), pp 87–100.

78 The signatory states and territories were Australia, the Cook Islands, the Federated States of Micronesia, the Republic of Fiji, French Polynesia, the Republic of Kiribati, the Republic of Nauru, New Caledonia, New Zealand, Niue, the Republic of Palau, the Independent State of Papua New Guinea, the Republic of the Marshall Islands, the Independent State of Samoa, the Solomon Islands, the Kingdom of Tonga, Tuvalu and Vanuatu.

79 Green (2023a), pp 82–83.

80 Crawford (2007), pp 48, 671.

81 Oppenheim (1955), p 451.

82 UN Security Council Official Record, 383rd mtg, UN Doc S/PV.383 (2 December 1948) 11.

of such territory necessitates the extinction of that state. In this sense, it is an expression of the view that states must be 'effective' in the sense of maintaining a particular form of territorial governance: a form adopted within Europe (albeit not exclusively) and exported via colonialism.[83] It is backwards-looking, locating statehood solely within its past manifestations. As Malcolm Shaw notes, some version of this view is at least as old as Plato, although it was not always predominant.[84] More recently, within my own jurisdiction, the austere view has been tacitly confirmed by the House of Lords' recent International Relations and Defence Committee report on the United Nations Convention on the Law of the Sea.[85] It has also raised its head within the recent debates on international law and sea-level rise conducted by the International Law Commission (ILC), to which I now turn.

The International Law Commission, the austere view and the limits of legal positivism

Two documents are particularly salient: the second issues paper on sea-level rise and international law, which largely set the terms for current debates on statehood;[86] and the report of the ILC for its 73rd session, which contains the recently recorded debates on that issue.[87] Within the second issues paper, three broad categories of response to the existential threat of rising sea levels were considered: first, reliance upon a strong presumption of state continuity, notwithstanding territorial loss;[88] second, the maintenance of international legal personality without territory;[89] and third, various practical modalities that otherwise accept the legal inevitability of extinction.[90] Some comments on each of these will be instructive. First, as regards the presumption of state continuity, some ILC members suggested in debate that relying upon it 'could result in complex practical difficulties' where inhabitable land is wholly absent.[91] Furthermore, in more conceptual terms, recorded debate emphasised that

> the principle of continuity of statehood [is] temporary, [and] aimed at allowing a State to be protected in the absence of a normal situation, as, for example, in the event of military occupation of a territory or internal

83 Anghie (2012), pp 98–100.
84 Shaw (2009), pp 61–63.
85 International Relations and Defence Committee (2021–2022), paras 117–26.
86 International Law Commission (2022b), pp 21–56.
87 International Law Commission (2022c), pp 332–41.
88 International Law Commission (2022b), pp 46–48.
89 International Law Commission (2022b), p 48.
90 International Law Commission (2022b), pp 49–56.
91 International Law Commission (2022c), p 335, para 213.

violence, referred to in paragraphs 192 and 193 of the second issues paper. Further, it was observed that the inundation of a territory or complete absence thereof could not be compared to a change in a territory, and that the presumption of continuity could be envisaged only where a territory and population existed.[92]

Here, the austere view establishes the fundamental requirement of 'effective' territorial governance, against which the presumption of continuing statehood can only ever be an interim exception. Therefore, contrary to Vaughan Lowe's assertion that the 'road to statehood is a one-way street',[93] some voices within the ILC debate mooted that although statehood should be presumed to continue, this presumption is not and cannot be irrebuttable.

Second, turning to the suggestion that international legal personality can be maintained without territory, this would have the advantage of enabling 'both the active and the passive right of legation [that is, the capacity for formal diplomatic relations], and would [maintain] treaty-making capacity'.[94] However, the only current example of an entity benefiting from an arrangement of this kind is the Sovereign Order of Malta, which is not a state. Moreover, the major historical example relied upon in the second issues paper, the Holy See between 1870 and 1929,[95] concerned (at least in retrospect) a temporary and politically contrived loss of territory, which may render it inapplicable to permanent and physical losses of inhabitable land, such as those faced by SIDS.[96] Indeed, some members of the ILC went so far as to suggest that neither example was helpful at all, even if they were broadly analogous.[97]

Ultimately, as the Sovereign Order of Malta itself demonstrates, international legal personality is not equivalent to statehood. The latter entails a discrete normative place within the international community, secured by a particular status within international law that not all legal persons enjoy. Only states, for example, can be Members of the United Nations,[98] with partially recognised and contested entities, if they are admitted at all, being consigned to 'non-Member Permanent Observer State' status.[99] Although that status has significant value, it is far from full membership. Palestine, for

92 International Law Commission (2022c), p 333, para 204.
93 Lowe (2007), p 165.
94 International Law Commission (2022b), p 48, para 197.
95 International Law Commission (2022b), pp 29–33.
96 Both negative points were noted in recorded debate: International Law Commission (2022c), p 334, para 207.
97 International Law Commission (2022c), p 335, para 213.
98 United Nations Charter 1945, Art 4.
99 General Assembly resolution 67/19, 29 November 2012, A/RES/67/19; for a detailed analysis of this position, see Sakran (2022), Chapter 3.

instance, may participate in UN conferences and bring matters to the attention of the General Assembly or Security Council, but has no voting power.[100] Moreover, perhaps the greatest benefit accruing to Palestine *qua* Observer State – the capacity to accede to any multilateral treaties deposited with the Secretary-General of the UN – is currently moot for SIDS, who already enjoy that right as uncontroversially established states.[101]

Perhaps more importantly, although non-states can sometimes have 'nationals' in the sense of individuals with passports that are recognised for visa purposes by at least some established states, nationality itself is traditionally defined as a 'politico-legal term denoting membership of a State'.[102] The Republic of China (Taiwan), for instance, issues passports that are recognised by both the United Kingdom and the United States (which contrastingly both refuse to recognise passports from Northern Cyprus). Special domestic legislation and bilateral agreements are required for such arrangements to function, taking place as they do outside formal diplomatic relations.[103] Over and above the issue of passports, any loss of capacity on the part of SIDS to ground discrete nationalities would render their erstwhile populations stateless, robbing them of even the formal possibility of consular or diplomatic protection.[104] Considering the poor record of the international community *vis-à-vis* protecting stateless persons – a particularly vulnerable set of the globally 'unseen' – the likely negative consequences of losing statehood are considerable.[105]

The third category of recommendation in the second issues paper is more fatalistic. The alternative modalities considered, whether utilised alone or in combination, avoid the practical problems of state extinction largely by accepting it as inevitable and, in some instances at least, accelerating it. For instance, the establishment of confederations or federations,[106] or the option of unifying with other states,[107] both contemplate trading away independent statehood in order to forestall the statelessness of diasporic populations.[108] Even the option of adopting instrumental associations between two or more formally independent states, in the mode of Cook Islands and New

100 *Report of the Secretary-General: Status of Palestine in the United Nations*, 8 March 2013, UN Doc A/67/738, paras 6–7.
101 *Summary of the Practice of the Secretary-General as Depository of Multilateral Treaties*, UN Doc ST/LEG/7/Rev.1, para 82 (1992).
102 Weis (1979), p 3.
103 Grossman (2001), p 861.
104 International Law Commission (2006).
105 Conklin (2014), pp 113–17, 126–34.
106 International Law Commission (2022b), pp 50–52, paras 206–15.
107 International Law Commission (2022b), p 52, para 216.
108 This was effectively conceded within the debate: International Law Commission (2022c), p 334, paras 207–08.

Zealand,[109] amounts to little more than an underwriting of citizenship in the event that statehood lapses. The austere view of state continuity apparently runs just as deep as do the practices of 'unseeing' highlighted above.

None of this is particularly encouraging from the perspective of state continuity, even though several members of the ILC were broadly in favour of statehood being legally resilient, at least in principle. Although the value of enduring statehood as such has been questioned,[110] the evidence overwhelmingly suggests that SIDS wish to maintain their current legal status.[111] The Independent State of Papua New Guinea, for example, described statehood as 'a threshold issue', since only states can generate maritime zones.[112] This feeling of genuine and pressing concern was echoed, for instance, by various delegates at the Pacific Island Forum's 2023 Regional Conference on Preserving Statehood and the Protection of Persons.[113]

A central problem, as alluded to above, is that dominant 'positivist' modes of international legal reasoning,[114] exemplified by the ILC's own mode of engagement,[115] are predominantly backwards looking.[116] As a mode of normative analysis, positivism is not just entrenched within our past practices but also exhausted by them. Such radically conservative temporality, which would be dismissed as illogical within any other intellectual discipline, is well documented as entrenching historical injustice.[117] Moreover, as alluded to above in relation to the Sovereign Order of Malta and the Holy See, it results in an overreliance upon even the most tenuously connected instances of past practice and a resistance to imagining new possibilities, forestalling any real opportunity for progress.[118] Sea-level rise presents a challenge to state continuity that is unprecedented within recorded history. It requires, if anything, new 'prefigurative theor[ies]' of statehood, whereby the law of state

109 International Law Commission (2022b), p 50, para 205.
110 Sharon (2021), pp 1061–65.
111 International Law Commission (2022b), pp 10–12, paras 23–43; p 40, paras 162–63; pp 46-47, paras 184–88.
112 UN General Assembly (2018), p 5, para 36.
113 For example, Minchin (2023); Kofe (2023).
114 Gardener (2001).
115 International Law Commission (2022b), p 20, paras 68–71. The ILC's attachment to positivism can almost certainly be explained by its ongoing but understandable caution *vis-à-vis* its dual objective of promoting 'the progressive development of international law and its codification' (Article 1, *Statute of the International Law Commission*, General Assembly resolution 174 (II) of 21 November 1947; as amended by resolutions 485 (V) of 12 December 1950, 984 (X) of 3 December 1955, 985 (X) of 3 December 1955 and 36/39 of 18 November 1981). See, for example, Voulgaris (2022); Oral (2019).
116 Travis (2022), p 6.
117 MacKinnon (1989), p 238.
118 For this reason, progress within international law tends to be 'politically' driven, rather than advanced through legal reasoning; see Carter (2008), p 51.

continuity is treated not just as a set of conventional or customary rules but as a means for moral and political advancement.[119] In other work, I suggest that a return to the 'Grotian' mode of legal reasoning,[120] as advocated by those such as Hersch Lauterpacht,[121] would ameliorate these problems to at least some degree.[122] In what follows, I make a different claim: that greater attention to the legal imaginary, supported by resort to speculative fiction, may also help to future-proof international law.

Imagining plausible alternatives: Making continuity possible

Within *The City & The City*, neither Beszél nor Ul Qoma has an 'ordinary' relationship with land. They are both land-based, in a sense, but are as much constituted by cultural and legal convention as they are by lines on a map. Indeed, to both the Besź and Ul Qomans, any land wholly encompassed within the 'other' city definitionally speaking cannot be inhabitable, since to inhabit it would be to acknowledge its existence and thereby commit the crime of breach. Moreover, if we consider the position of Breach itself, whose members exist 'in the interstice' and 'debate among many other things the question of *where* it is that [they] live' [my emphasis],[123] we see yet another community with a tenuous connection to inhabitable land. Even though Beszél and Ul Qoma are clearly not utopian, *The City & The City* is no dystopian parable either: it lacks the social degeneration and sense of hopelessness typical of such narratives.[124] Ultimately, if we can imagine non-ideal, atypical, but nonetheless *possible* states like Beszél and Ul Qoma, why not imagine states with no relationship to inhabitable land at all?

There are at least two ways in which we might do this, legally speaking – at least if we can dispense with the extreme fidelity to past practice required by legal positivism and are prepared to be far more expansive in our interpretive and analogical reasoning. First, it need not follow from the fact that states require territory that this territory must be land-based. Maritime territory has long been recognised under international law, even though it is always 'anchored' by some identifiable area of inhabitable land, and defined with reference to it, on the basis that 'the land dominates the sea'.[125] But this

119 Davies (2017), p 16–19.
120 Schwarzenberger (1941), p 154.
121 Lauterpacht (1946), p 5.
122 Green (2024a) pp 1–12; Green (2023a), pp 83–88; Green (2024b) pp 3, 30.
123 Miéville (2009), p 373.
124 Schmeink (2016), p 67; Zaki (1990), p 244.
125 *North Sea Continental Shelf (Federal Republic of Germany v Denmark; Federal Republic of Germany v Netherlands, Judgment*, ICJ Reports 1969, p 3, para 96; Ja (2014); Cf. Purcell (2019), pp 44–48.

principle belongs to the law of the sea, not the law of statehood. Moreover, it is derived from a particular conception of 'effectiveness' concomitant with the austere view. This conception, as Ntina Tzouvala demonstrates, is both European and capitalist, emphasising the 'territorialisation of relations of power, state monopoly over legitimate violence through the pacification of society, judicialisation of social relations through legal reform and codification so that laws supported core market functions'.[126] On this conception, only inhabitable land counts because, within the nineteenth-century social and technological context within which it was developed, only such land was sufficiently productive.

Were this conception to be dismissed, or at least found to be non-exhaustive, then the possibility of fully autonomous maritime territories, perhaps tied to the *historical* existence of once inhabitable land, would remain open.[127] One possibility is for landmasses rendered unviable by climate change to be granted *sui generis* legal status as 'submerged land territories',[128] in line with the prevailing emphasis upon territorial stability found within general international law.[129] Further authority for moving beyond traditional land-based conceptions of effectiveness also exists within established practice, albeit via analogous implication. In the *Western Sahara* advisory opinion, the International Court of Justice held that, notwithstanding the nomadic nature of the peoples within Rio de Oro and Saguia el-Hamra, that territory could not be considered *terra nullius*.[130] Two points are of note here.[131] First, the court held that 'State practice of the relevant period indicates that territories inhabited by tribes or peoples having a social and political organization were not regarded as *terrae nullius*',[132] and that 'at the time of colonization Western Sahara was inhabited by peoples which, if nomadic, were socially and politically organized in tribes and under chiefs competent to represent them'.[133] Second, when considering various competing title claims over that territory, the court noted the

> very special characteristics which, at the time of colonization by Spain, largely determined the way of life and social and political organization of the peoples inhabiting [Rio de Oro and Saguia el-Hamra]. In consequence, the legal régime of Western Sahara, including its legal relations

126 Tzouvala (2020), p 111.
127 Green (2024b), pp 12–16.
128 I am grateful to Mathias Forteau for raising this point.
129 Miron (2022), pp 106–08.
130 *Western Sahara, Advisory Opinion*, ICJ Reports 1975, p 12, para 81.
131 Green (2024b), pp 27–28.
132 *Western Sahara*, para 80.
133 *Western Sahara*, para 81.

with neighbouring territories, cannot properly be appreciated without reference to these special characteristics.[134]

This is salient for two reasons. First, it suggests that, under certain circumstances, nomadic peoples generate territorial title over the lands through which they travel, satisfying the requirement of 'effectiveness' notwithstanding their non-settled status. Second, it demonstrates that when ascertaining effective control, the physical geography of the relevant territory must be considered. The latter principle is also aired within the *Legal Status of Eastern Greenland* judgment, which referenced 'the Arctic and inaccessible character of the uncolonized parts of the country' when identifying the initial extent of Danish title.[135] That case also established that, where territorial title is uncontested by another state, the standard for evincing effective control will be lower.[136]

Combining these points, SIDS that lose their inhabitable land may arguably be entitled to an autonomous and unaltered maritime territory for four reasons. First, the extent of that territory could be delineated without reference to land,[137] via the maritime zones established and notified to the UN Secretary-General, particularly following the 2021 Pacific Forum declaration cited above.[138] Second, it would effectively be impossible for any other state to establish a countervailing claim to that territory. The more likely point in opposition – that submerged or uninhabitable islands will transform into a portion of the high seas – cannot trigger the heightened scrutiny upon 'effective control' that *Eastern Greenland* indicates arises only in cases where conflicting territorial title is alleged. Third, territory including land submerged due to human-caused climate change might be said to possess special characteristics analogous to the Arctic or Sahara deserts. Fourth, it is wholly conceivable that SIDS might demonstrate both an 'intention and will to act as sovereign, and some actual exercise or display of such authority', which is sufficient *vis-à-vis* those special characteristics.[139]

The relevant analogies are as follows. First, land that has been rendered uninhabitable due to rising sea levels exhibits a hostility to terrestrial plant

134 *Western Sahara*, para 87.

135 *Legal Status of Eastern Greenland, Denmark v Norway, Judgment*, PCIJ Series A/B No 53, pp 50–51.

136 *Eastern Greenland*, p 46.

137 Some support for this might be found in International Law Commission (2022c) p 332, para 196, which avers 'a territory that became fully submerged because of sea-level rise should not be considered a non-existent territory'. However, that paragraph also contests that 'the existence of land territory had been a deeply rooted aspect of statehood', which makes its overall thrust somewhat unclear.

138 Supra note 79 and the adjoining text.

139 *Eastern Greenland*, p 46.

and animal life similar to that found within some desert areas. Humans can and do live at sea for extended periods of time, as evidenced by maritime 'micronations' like the Principality of Sealand,[140] which suggests that, as with extreme desert environments, 'uninhabitability' in the traditional sense is no absolute physical bar. Second, it would be logistically possible for SIDS to exercise control over any persisting maritime territories in a manner analogous to the control that nomadic peoples exercise over desert territories, whether by launching from artificial islands or from other permanent structures upon their erstwhile landmasses.[141] In *Western Sahara*, the court referenced the 'more or less regular routes' between 'perennial water holes' and 'recognized burial grounds',[142] which served to anchor the territorial control of those nomadic peoples. When we add to this the seafaring nomadism of peoples such as the Sama-Bajau,[143] this analogy becomes all the more plausible.

Suggestions such as these require imagining different forms of statehood, divorced from settled relationships with densely populated land. They disrupt understandings of 'effectiveness' tied to historically European social models and so lead us away from international legal orthodoxy. Nonetheless, none of the heterodox imaginings I have suggested are wholly without foundation in international practice, as I have sought to demonstrate. We are dealing now with matters of degree, the acceptance of which turns on the open-mindedness of international lawyers and state representatives.

Moving even further into the imaginary, a different and more radical strategy would be to jettison the idea of territory itself. Historically, many states have persisted without effective governments and with severely reduced populations, whether due to civil war or belligerent occupation.[144] Although there are obvious logical differences between the loss of control over territory and the absence of territory itself,[145] the notion that states might persist without territory is not entirely without conceptual precedent. For instance, Tuvalu recently announced that it intends to create a virtual space within which its culture and politics can continue to be practised.[146] Prime Minister Natano even went so far as to characterise this initiative as 'our digital nation', which 'will provide an online presence that can replace our physical presence and

140 Hobbs (2021); Hobbs and Williams (2022), pp 20–81.

141 Possible uses for these structures were considered by the ILC: International Law Commission (2022b), pp 43–44, paras 166–74; but see the doubts raised in International Law Commission (2022c), p 334, para 205.

142 *Western Sahara*, para 87.

143 Jubilado (2010); Jubilado et al (2010).

144 Crawford (2007), pp 678, 688–90.

145 International Law Commission (2022c), p 335, para 213.

146 Jonas (2022).

allow us to continue to function as a state'.[147] Indeed, some scholars have averred losses of cultural identity and political connectedness to be a central danger faced by SIDS, should their statehood lapse.[148] Reconstructing political communities within cyberspace may well prevent these losses, which some have (perhaps prematurely) characterised as inevitable.[149]

Initiatives like Tuvalu's digital nation will require international recognition and support if they are to have any implications for state continuity. However, they nonetheless suggest interesting possibilities for how statehood itself might change as technology progresses. Speculative fiction contains many similar imaginings, most memorably within tales like *The Matrix*,[150] *The Thirteenth Floor*[151] and *Neuromancer*.[152] Even contemporary video games with massively multiplayer online elements indicate the potential for genuine communities to develop and persist online.[153] Indeed, such cyber-social potential may go some way to dispelling the objection that one cannot conceive of 'population' without territory, since all populations must be populations *of* somewhere.[154] Given that we can imagine cultural and political communities without physical locations, why not imagine discrete polities without lines on a map?

Conclusion: The statehood of tomorrow?

Even if we had the option, probably very few of us would opt to live what would no doubt be logistically complex lives within communities like Beszél or Ul Qoma. However, we can certainly *imagine* doing so. For all its weirdness, the setting presented within *The City & The City* has true authenticity. We can identify ourselves in the Besź or Ul Qoman practices of unseeing, both as individuals and (or so I have argued) as lawyers. Moreover, the jurisdictional arrangements that constitute Miéville's fictional world feel *possible* to us: something that goes a long way towards explaining the engaging nature of the narrative within which they are portrayed.

In this chapter, I used *The City & The City* to argue two things: first, that international law shares Besź and Ul Qoman practices of unseeing, through which it discriminates between (and often against) various forms of political community by assigning statehood to some but not to others; and second, that

147 Jonas (2022).
148 Wong (2013), pp 349–50; see also Lixinski et al (2022).
149 Sharon (2021), p 1062.
150 Lana Wachowski and Lilly Wachowski, *The Matrix* (Warner Bros. Pictures, United States, 1999).
151 Josef Rusnak, *The Thirteenth Floor* (Columbia Pictures, United States, 1999).
152 William Gibson, *Neuromancer* (1984).
153 Poor and Skoric (2014); Strimling and Frey (2020).
154 Sharon (2021), p 1062.

the very plausibility of Besźel and Ul Qoma themselves acts as an intuition pump, highlighting the lack of legal imagination currently being exercised within the law of state continuity as it applies to sea-level rise. We should try harder to imagine modes of statehood that contemporary international law, or at least orthodox interpretations of that law, deem to be impossible. This is no mere academic exercise, as I have attempted to show, because the inability to conceive of statehood other than in orthodox terms has serious existential, practical and expressive implications for SIDS.

The foregoing discussion disclosed a number of ways to imagine statehood differently, although these were by no means exhaustive. We might add other possibilities, such as the potential for states to arise on Mars or the Moon notwithstanding Article II of the Outer Space Treaty,[155] or that of 'Refugee Nation', which in some iterations is proposed to be created on artificial islands in international waters,[156] notwithstanding the orthodox view that such islands cannot establish or extend maritime entitlements.[157] Within speculative fiction, there are also several examples where statehood is not territorial but vehicular, such as the Aeldari Craftworlds of *Warhammer 40,000*,[158] the Colonial Fleet in *Battlestar Galactica*[159] and the 'atolls' of *Waterworld*.[160] Set alongside initiatives such as Tuvalu's digital nation, these possibilities disclose diverse conceptions of statehood, which international law currently struggles to admit. But human-caused climate change has placed us at something of a Westphalian moment,[161] where we will soon be forced by geographical change to revisit our understandings of the state in much the same way that political change forced a revision of connected concepts in the mid-seventeenth century. What precisely the future will hold is unclear; however, reading speculative fiction carefully, and with an open mind concerning our current practices, may well prevent us from becoming too surprised.

155 *Treaty on the Principles of Governing the Activities of States in the Exploration and Use of Outer Space, including the Moon and Other Celestial Bodies*, Art II, Annex to General Assembly resolution 2222(XXI), 19 December 1966. This article reads: 'Outer space, including the Moon and other celestial bodies, is not subject to national appropriation by claim of sovereignty, by means of use or occupation, or by any other means'; see also Collis (2017).

156 Adam Taylor, 'A Silicon Valley Mogul Wants to Solve the Global Refugee Crisis by Creating a New Country', *Washington Post*, 23 July 2015.

157 Articles 60 and 121(3), *United Nations Convention on the Law of the Sea*, Montego Bay, 10 December 1982, 1833 UNTS 3; Purcell (n 76) 18–19; cf. Saunders (2021).

158 Games Workshop, *Codex: Aeldari* (Games Workshop 2022) 11–14.

159 *Battlestar Galactica* (Universal Studio Group, United States, 2004–09).

160 Kevin Reynolds, *Waterworld* (Universal Pictures, United States, 1995).

161 Boucher (2001).

References

Hannah Arendt (1958) *The Origins of Totalitarianism*, Meridian Books.

Christine Agius, Annika Rosamond and Catarina Kinnvall (2020) 'Populism, Ontological Insecurity and Gendered Nationalism: Masculinity, Climate Denial and COVID-19' 21 *Politics, Religion & Ideology* 432.

Antony Anghie (2012) *Imperialism, Sovereignty, and the Making of International Law*, Cambridge University Press.

Sundhya Pahuja (2011) *Decolonising International Law: Development, Economic Growth and the Politics of Universality*, Cambridge University Press.

Thomas Baty (1930) *The Canons of International Law*, J. Murray.

BBC News (2014) 'Ukraine Crisis: Protesters Declare Donetsk "Republic"', 7 April 2014, https://www.bbc.co.uk/news/world-europe-26919928.

Hilaire Belloc (1907) 'Jim: Who Ran Away from His Nurse, and was Eaten by a Lion' in Edward Gorey (Ed.) *Cautionary Tales for Children*, Eveleigh Nash.

Veronika Bílková (2016) 'A State Without Territory?' 47 *Netherlands Yearboook of International Law* 19.

Henri Bonfils and Paul Fauchille (1905) *Manuel de droit international public (Droit des gens)*, 4th ed, Arthur Rousseau.

David Boucher (2001) 'Resurrecting Pufendorf and Capturing the Westphalian Moment' 27 *Review of International Studies* 557.

FA Brekelmans (1965) *De Belgische enclaves in Nederland: bijdragen tot de rechtsgeschiedenis van Baarle-Hertog en Baarle-Nassau*, Stichting Brabants Historisch Contact.

Barry Carter (2008) 'Making Progress in International Institutions and Law' in Russell Miller and Rebecca Bratspies (eds), *Progress in International Law*, Brill, 51.

Christy Collis (2017) 'Territories Beyond Possession? Antarctica and Outer Space' 7 *The Polar Journal* 287.

William Conklin (2014) *Statelessness: The Enigma of the International Community*, Hart.

Jack Corbett, Xu Yi-Chong and Patrick Weller (2021) *International Organizations and Small States: Participation, Legitimacy and Vulnerability*, Bristol University Press.

James Crawford (2007) *The Creation of States in International Law*, Oxford University Press.

James Crawford and Simon Olleson (2014) 'The Character and Forms of International Responsibility' in Malcom Evans (ed), *International Law*, 4th ed, Oxford University Press, 211.

Margaret Davies (2017) *Law Unlimited: Materialism, Pluralism, and Legal Theory*, Routledge.

Daniel Dennett (1984) *Elbow Room: The Varieties of Free Will Worth Wanting*, MIT Press.

John Dugard (1987) *Recognition and the United Nations*, Grotius.

John Gardener (2001) 'Legal Positivism: 5½ Myths' 46 *American Journal of Jurisprudence* 199.

Alex Green (2021) 'The Precarious Rationality of International Law: Critiquing the International Rule of Recognition' 22 *German Law Journal* 1613.

Alex Green (2022) 'The Importance of Dystopian Hypotheticals: Towards an Ethical Turn in Liberal Political Philosophy' 4 *Law, Technology and Humans* 60.

Alex Green (2023a) '*The Creation of States* as a Cardinal Point: James Crawford's Contribution to International Legal Scholarship' 40 *Australian Year Book of International Law* 67.

Alex Green (2023b) 'A Political Theory of State Equality' 14 *Transnational Legal Theory* 178.

Alex Green (2024a) *Statehood as Political Community: International Law and the Emergence of New States*, Cambridge University Press.

Alex Green (2024b) 'Three Reconstructions of "Effectiveness": Some Implications for State Continuity and Sea-Level Rise' *Oxford Journal of Legal Studies* 44(2),20.

Alex Green and Jennifer Hendry (2022) '*Ad Hominem* Criminalisation and the Rule of Law: The Egalitarian Case Against Knife Crime Prevention Orders' 42 *Oxford Journal of Legal Studies* 634.

Alex Green and Jennifer Hendry (2024) *Legal Pluralism: New Trajectories in Law*, Routledge.

Andrew Grossman (2001) 'Nationality and the Unrecognised State' 50 *International and Comparative Law Quarterly* 849.

The Guardian (2002) 'China Miéville's Top 10 Weird Fiction Books' 16 May, https://www.theguardian.com/books/2002/may/16/fiction.bestbooks

Douglas Guilfoyle (2016) 'Reading *The City & the City* as an International Lawyer: Reflections on Territoriality, Jurisdiction and Transnationality' 4 *London Review of International Law* 195.

William Harcourt (1863) *Letters by Historicus on Some Questions of International Law*, Macmillan.

Harry Hobbs (2021) 'Micronations: A Lacuna in the Law' 19 *International Journal of Constitutional Law* 71.

Harry Hobbs and George Williams (2022) *Micronations and the Search for Sovereignty*, Oxford University Press.

International Law Commission (2006) *Draft Articles on Diplomatic Protection*, UN Doc A/RES/61/35.

International Law Commission (2022a) *Draft Conclusions on Identification and Legal Consequences of Peremptory Norms of General International Law (Jus Cogens)*, UN Doc A/77/10.

International Law Commission (2022b) *Second Issues Paper on Sea-level Rise in Relation to International Law*, UN Doc A/CN.4/752.

International Law Commission (2022c) *Report of the International Law Commission on the Work of Its Seventy-third Session*, UN Doc A/77/10.

International Relations and Defence Committee (2021–22) *UNCLOS: The Law of the Sea in the 21st Century* (House of Lords Paper No 159, 2nd Report of Session 2021–22), International Relations and Defence Committee.

Tom Long (2022) *A Small State's Guide to Influence in World Politics*, Oxford University Press.

Simon Kofe (2023) 'Keynote Address, Tuvalu Foreign Affairs Minister Simon Kofe to Regional Conference on Statehood, Protection of Persons Affected by Sea Level Rise, 27 March 2023', https://www.forumsec.org/2023/03/27/remarks-keynote-address-tuvalu-foreign-affairs-minister-simon-kofe-to-regional-conference-on-statehood-protection-of-persons-affected-by-sea-level-rise

Bing Bing Ja (2014) 'The Principle of the Domination of the Land Over the Sea: A Historical Perspective on the Adaptability of the Law of the Sea to New Challenges' 57 *German Yearbook of International Law* 1.
Abhimanyu George Jain (2014) 'The 21st Century Atlantis: The International Law of Statehood and Climate Change Induced Loss of Territory' *50 Stanford Journal of International Law* 1.
Donald Jensen (2017) *Moscow in the Donbas: Command, Control, Crime and the Minsk Peace Process*, NATO Defence College 1.
Natalie Jonas (2022) 'As Tuvalu Succumbs to Rising Sea Levels, the Island Nation Wants to be the First Virtue Country' *Salon*, 3 December 2022, https://www.salon.com/2022/12/03/as-tuvalu-succumbs-to-rising-sea-levels-the-island-nation-wants-to-be-the-first-virtual-country
Rodney Jubilado (2010) 'On Cultural Fluidity: The Sama-Bajau of the Sulu-Sulawesi Seas' 32 *Kunapipi* 89.
Rodney Jubilado, Hanafi Hussin and Maria Manueli (2010) 'The Sama-Bajaus of the Sulu-Sulawesi Seas: Perspectives from Linguistics and Culture' 15 *Jati* 83.
Hersch Lauterpacht (1946) 'The Grotian Tradition in International Law' 23 *British Yearbook of International Law* l.
Hersch Lauterpacht (1947) *Recognition of States in International Law*, Cambridge University Press.
Lucas Lixinski, Jane McAdam and Patricia Tupou (2022) 'Ocean Cultures, the Anthropocene and International Law: Cultural Heritage and Mobility Law as Imaginative Gateways' 23 *Melbourne Journal of International Law* 1.
Vaughan Lowe (2007) *International Law*, Oxford University Press.
James Machin (2018) *Weird Fiction in Britain, 1880–1939*, Palgrave Macmillan.
Catherine MacKinnon (1989) *Towards a Feminist Theory of the State*, Harvard University Press.
Krystina Marek (1954) *The Identity and Continuity of States in International Law*, Librairie E. Droz.
Ryan Mitra and Samskriti Sanghi (2023) 'The Small Island States in the Indo-Pacific: Sovereignty Lost?' 31 *Asia Pacific Law Review* 428.
Helen Metz (1993) *Somalia: A Country Study*, 4th ed, Library of Congress.
China Miéville (2006) *Between Equal Rights: A Marxist Theory of International Law*, Pluto Press.
China Miéville (2009) *The City & The City*, Pan.
Stuart Minchin (2023) (Director General of The Pacific Community), 'Remarks Official Opening of the 2023 Regional Conference on Preserving Statehood and Protecting Persons: Legal Options and Institutional Responses to the Impacts of Sea-Level Rise' 27 March, https://www.forumsec.org/2023/03/27/35754
Alina Miron (2022) 'Les conséquences de l'élévation du niveau des mers sur le tracé des lignes de base' in V Boré Eveno (ed), *Elévation du niveau de la mer et droit international. De l'adaptation à l'action*, Pedone 106.
Thomas Nagel (1995) 'Personal Rights and Public Space' 24 *Philosophy & Public Affairs* 83.
Rowan Nicholson (2019a) *Statehood and the State-like in International Law*, Oxford University Press.
Rowan Nicholson (2019b) 'Was the Colonisation of Australia an Invasion of Sovereign Territory?' 20 *Melbourne Journal of International Law* 493.

Nilufer Oral (2019) 'The International Law Commission and the Progressive Development and Codification of Principles of International Environmental Law' 13 *Florida International University Law Review* 1075.

Lassa Oppenheim (1955) *International Law, Vol. 1*, 8th ed, D. McKay.

Wilfred Owen (1920) *Poems*, Chatto & Windus.

Scott Pegg (1998) *International Society and the De Facto State*, Ashgate.

Nathaniel Poor and Marko Skoric (2014) 'Death of a Guild, Birth of a Network: Online Community Ties Within and Beyond Code' 9 *Games and Culture* 182.

Kate Purcell (2019) *Geographical Change and the Law of the Sea*, Oxford University Press.

Shadi Sakran (2022) *The Legal Consequences of Limited Statehood: Palestine in Multilateral Frameworks*, Routledge.

Michael Scharf (1995) 'Musical Chairs: The Dissolution of States and Membership in the United Nations' 28 *Cornell International Law Journal* 29.

Lars Schmeink (2016) *Biopunk Dystopias: Genetic Engineering, Society and Science Fiction*, Liverpool University Press.

Georg Schwarzenberger (1941) *Power Politics: An Introduction to the Study of International Relations and Post-War Planning*, Jonathan Cape.

Imogen Saunders (2021) 'Artificial Islands and Territory in International Law' 52 *Vanderbilt Journal of Transnational Law* 643.

Ori Sharon (2021) 'To Be or Not to Be: State Extinction Through Climate Change' 51 *Environmental Law* 1041.

Malcolm Shaw (2009) 'Territory in International Law' 13 *Netherlands Journal of International Law* 61.

Melissa Stewart (2023) 'The Cascading Consequences of Sinking States' 59(2) *Stanford Journal of International Law* 130.

Curt Storlazzi, Stephen Gingerich, AP van Dongeren, Olivia Cheriton, Peter Swarzenski, Ellen Quataert, Clifford Voss, Donald Field, Hariharasubramanian Annamalai, Greg Pinak and Robert McCall (2018) 'Most Atolls will be Uninhabitable by the Mid-21st Century Because of Sea-level Rise Exacerbating Wave-driven Flooding' 4 *Science Advances* 1.

Pontus Strimling and Seth Frey (2020) 'Emergent Cultural Differences in Online Communities' Norms of Fairness' 15 *Games and Culture* 394.

Paul Thagard (2021) 'The Cognitive Science of COVID-19: Acceptance, Denial, and Belief Change' 195 *Methods* 92.

Mitchell Travis (2022) 'Temporality and Science Fiction' 4 *Law, Technology and Humans* 5.

Ntina Tzouvala (2020) *Capitalism as Civilisation: A History of International Law*, Cambridge University Press.

United Nations (2022) 'Security Council Fails to Adopt Draft Resolution on Ending Ukraine Crisis, as Russian Federation Wields Veto' *Press Release*, 25 February, SC/14808, https://press.un.org/en/2022/sc14808.doc.htm

UN General Assembly (2018) *Sixth Committee: Summary Record of the 23rd Meeting*, UN Doc A/C.6/73/SR.23.

Emer de Vattel (2008) *The Law of Nations, or, Principles of the Law of Nature, Applied to the Conduct and Affairs of Nations and Sovereigns, with Three Early Essays on the Origin and Nature of Natural Law and on Luxury*, Béla Kapossy and Richard Whatmore (eds), Liberty Fund.

Francisco de Victoria (1917) *De Indis et de Ivre Belli Relectiones*, Ernest Nys (ed), John Pawley Bate (trans), Carnegie Institution of Washington.
Nikolas Voulgaris (2022) 'The International Law Commission and Politics: Taking the Science Out of International Law's Progressive Development' 33 *European Journal of International Law* 761.
Irene Watson (2015) *Aboriginal Peoples, Colonialism and International Law: Raw Law*, Routledge.
Max Weber (1991) 'Politics as Vocation' in HH Gerth and C Wright Mills (eds), *From Max Weber: Essays in Sociology*, Routledge.
Paul Weis (1979) *Nationality and Statelessness in International Law*, 2nd ed, Brill.
Marc Weller (2022) 'Russia's Recognition of the "Separatist Republics" in Ukraine was Manifestly Unlawful' *EJIL:Talk!*, 9 March 2022, https://www.ejiltalk.org/russias-recognition-of-the-separatist-republics-in-ukraine-was-manifestly-unlawful
Derek Wong (2013) 'Sovereignty Sunk? The Position of 'Sinking States' at International Law' 14 *Melbourne Journal of International Law* 346.
Hoda Zaki (1990) 'Utopia, Dystopia and Ideology in the Science Fiction of Octavia Butler' 17 *Science Fiction Studies* 239.
William Gibson (1984) *Neuromancer* Victor Gollancz, London.

Chapter 3

Playing Loki? International law, decision-making and intertemporality through the Marvel multiverse

Kritika Sharma

Introduction

Perhaps questioning whether international judges can equate to the Norse god of evil or Marvel's vision of the trickster god of mischief Loki Laufeyson seems out of place. Rather, is it simply out of *time*? This chapter focuses on the link between how time is perceived and dealt with in the Marvel and DC Comics franchises and uses this as a cipher to analyse judicial decision-making within international law. In identifying the two approaches to time and temporality (those of Marvel and DC) with those of the A and B series of time, this chapter looks at how reading these approaches into an analysis of international judicial decision-making can unlock a vast resource of legal tools, particularly for better understanding this decision-making process. Drawing from a more B series-styled understanding of time, located within the Marvel multiverse, this chapter argues that leaning on the treatment of time in Marvel's *Loki* could prove to be particularly mnemonic for analysing judicial decision-making in international law. This, as this chapter highlights, is owed to the coexistence of multiple temporalities (or 'intertemporality') within the Marvel multiverse. Not only do multiple timelines persist within the Marvel multiverse, showcased stunningly through *Loki*'s particular focus on time, but elements from different timelines also interact with each other within this (not always) peaceful coexistence. All these issues are poignantly exposed and accentuated in the Marvel Cinematic Universe (MCU)'s television series adaptation of *Loki*[1] who, along with another (time) variant of himself, leads to the dissolution of an artificially constructed linear timeline, the 'sacred timeline'. Using this example and the varying manifestations of intertemporality within *Loki*, this chapter aims to challenge perceived notions of objective and linear temporalities in international judicial decision-making by highlighting that these are artificially constructed, and the

1 Herron (2021) *Loki*.

DOI: 10.4324/9781003412274-4

linearity is a work of legal fiction. This chapter instead suggests how adopting a more non-linear approach towards decision-making allows for a better understanding of the infinite possibilities that exist within the international judicial decision-making process. It argues that focusing on the temporal positioning of *the judges* themselves, and embracing the coexistence of multiple temporalities within which international judges are situated, would allow for a better understanding of this decision-making process.

Intertemporality in this chapter is understood as the coexistence of multiple temporalities, arguably non-linear in their varying forms.[2] As a theme, intertemporality runs through both worlds, that of Marvel as well as international law. Through this chapter, I argue that intertemporality and its various manifestations reveal themselves in multiple forms throughout both Marvel comics and the MCU, as well as in international law, both in academic work and judicial decision-making. However, it is approached differently in both worlds. While Marvel's *Loki* (as well as science fiction more generally) openly embraces intertemporality, with all the chaos[3] it often brings with it, there is an apparent expectation *vis-à-vis* judges in international law to position themselves temporally at a particular point in time, on the basis of the law and rules they are bound by.[4] Acknowledging this tendency, I then look at concrete examples from the International Court of Justice (ICJ) and the International Criminal Court (ICC) to demonstrate that the supposed linear temporality within judicial decision-making has been artificially created. In fact, the two cases (*Chagos* and the *Situation in Afghanistan*) discussed in the chapter aim to demonstrate how it is not only rules that can time-travel,[5] but judges too. The chapter argues that a key aspect of this is the ability, as well as the approach – ranging from activism to reluctance – of the Courts to include within their decisions a consideration of the *impact* these decisions might have, and thus their ability to travel to and from the future in this respect.

2 See Grabham (2016), 23, who looks at the 'more than one-ness' of time – especially *vis-à-vis* legal temporalities.

3 Leaning on chaos theory, it has been argued that 'time does not always flow according to a line ... not according to a plan but, rather, according to an extraordinarily complex mixture, as though it reflected stopping points, ruptures, deep wells, chimneys of thunderous acceleration, rendings, gaps – all sown at random, at least in a visible disorder ... Once you understand this, it's not hard to accept the fact that time doesn't always develop according to a line and thus things that are very close can exist in culture, but the line makes them appear very distant from one another'. Grabham (2016), p 25.

4 For literature that looks at 'time in interpretation and application of international law from a variety of angles', see Merkouris (2022), p 196, fn 5.

5 See, for example, Merkouris (2022).

On the perception of time and the Marvel and DC multiverses

This chapter draws on the division of the A series and B series of the conception or understanding of time, also alluded to as the 'tensed and tenseless view of time'.[6] The division into A and B series of time in accordance with MacTaggart's theory appears to be based largely on the assumption that the conception of time involves 'a series of positions'.[7] The ways these positions relate to each other appear to effectively divide these two categories. In the A series, the series of positions appears to be spread across the future and the past, being connected through the present. In the B series, this distinction or division into past, present and future is replaced with a focus on events and a measure of the position of events as being either earlier than, simultaneous with or after certain events.

The focus of the A series on the distinction of time into the past, present and future is denied by the B series. Instead, in the B series, it is the focus on events and their relationships with one another as being earlier than, after or simultaneous with that replaces the A series's focus on 'the apparent transition from future to past through the present', which for the A series is considered as 'the fundamental characteristic of time and an objective feature of reality in some way or another'.[8]

The basis of the two series, A and B, appears to have been widely accepted, as reflected in the A and B view on time.[9] These ontologies of time can be seen as underlining different ways of thinking about time, such as presentism, which develops on an A-series form of thinking about time, and eternalism, grounded in more of a B-series manner of thinking about time.[10]

Noting Aristotle's definition of time as 'the amount of movement from before to after', and referring to the view that 'this idea must be associated with an idea of causality', it has been observed that 'it is necessary law of our sensibility and therefore a condition of all perception that preceding Time necessarily determines what follows'.[11] Eco states that

'This idea has been maintained even by relativistic physics, not in the study of the transcendental conditions of the perceptions, but in the definition of the nature of time in terms of cosmological objectivity, in such a way that time would appear as the *order of causal chains*.'[12] This corresponds to a description of a historical seriality in time as opposed to a cosmological

6 See Ingthorsson (1998), p 287.
7 See Ingthorsson (1998), p 287.
8 See Ingthorsson (1998), p 287.
9 See, for example, Banfi (2017), pp 1–3.
10 See, for example, Banfi (2017), pp 1–2.
11 See Eco (1979), p 932.
12 See Eco (1979), p 932.

seriality in time. The former (historical seriality) has been used to describe the overall serial continuity in Marvel comics as opposed to the more mythical and oneiric seriality in most DC comics.[13] Broadly, this maintains the division in treatment of time between the Marvel and DC franchises into the A and B series. Serra notes that:

> The historical approach organizes events relating to our past into a causative series. Events of the past are consecutively viewed then as the result of some other, earlier events. The historical consciousness always presupposes a reference to some preceding situation – but not the initial one! – which, in turn, is causally related to yet another, even earlier, preceding situation, and so on.[14]

Contrary to this approach, it has been observed that DC comics – such as in the case of Superman – present a 'massive bombardment of events which are no longer tied together by any strand of logic, whose interaction is ruled no longer by any necessity, the reader, without realizing it, of course, loses the notion of temporal progression', and that

> Superman happens to live in an imaginary universe in which, as opposed to ours, causal chains are not open (A provokes B, B provokes C, C provokes D, and so on, *ad infinitum*), but closed (A provokes B, B provokes C, C provokes D, and D provokes A), and it no longer makes [sense] to talk about temporal progression on the basis of which we usually describe the happenings of the macrocosm.[15]

Thus, the seriality in DC comics – other than some of its series, such as 'Crisis on Infinite Earths' (1985–86) – has largely been said to follow a cyclic seriality instead of the continuity essentially adhered to by Marvel comics. This emphasis on events rather than a serial continuity can also be seen in DC's *multiverse*-focused[16] comics and cinematic ventures, such as *The Flash*.[17] In this, after Barry Allen (The Flash) unleashes a cascade of altered outcomes and consequences by travelling back in time and changing how events have transpired, Batman explains to him and his accidentally created double how the multiverse is like a bowl of spaghetti created through branched events that diverge from the original events that transpired but intersect at certain fixed positions. This focus on fixed events that stay constant, causal loops, as

13 See, for example, Serra (2016), pp 646–59.
14 See Serra (2016), pp 647–48. Serra cites Uspenskij (1987), p 21.
15 See Serra (2016), p 647, who cites Eco (1979), pp 115–16.
16 See, for example, Fox (1961) *The Flash*.
17 See Muschietti (2023) *The Flash*.

Batman explains, as well as temporal paradoxes, highlights the latent temporal temperament within DC comics that largely diverges from that of Marvel comics.

The Marvel multiverse instead maintains its allegiance to a serial continuity, often also visible through a rich contextual history collected over time by its characters.[18] Thus, while adhering largely to a B series-styled approach towards time and temporality, the treatment of time in the Marvel multiverse continues to develop in a manner that *goes further* from a strict reading of this ontology. Specifically with respect to the multiverse, it becomes clear to viewers of the MCU's more multiverse-oriented ventures (and comic readers, of course) that not only does the Marvel multiverse entail parallel universes that coexist alongside each other like a stack of oblong pancakes, but, along with its infinite possibilities, it brings with it the possibility of interaction between elements from these parallel universes and, as a result, parallel timelines. *Loki* provides a textbook example of this by presenting viewers, right from Episode 1, with an explanation of the multiple timelines that once existed as a result of the multiverse, and how the Time-Keepers brought peace to these warring and competing timelines by agreeing upon a single timeline: the sacred timeline. The next section explores this aspect of intertemporality in the Marvel multiverse and *Loki*, and the idea of infinite possibilities and choices.

Time in Marvel and infinite possibilities

One area where the Marvel multiverse[19] and the realm of international law diverge, at least *prima facie*, is in their treatment of time. Undoubtedly, and to varying degrees and in diverse situations, international law and the judicial institutions that apply it and are established under it often engage with the question of time, or *the intertemporal problem*. While predominantly associated with the determination of applicable law, issues arising from the relationship between time and international law, and its development and application, are just as prevalent. The focus of this chapter, however, remains the interpretation of international law *vis-à-vis* judicial decision-making and determining *where* on the timeline the international judicial decision-makers sit and why. It has been observed, for instance, how 'time is not an objective property or determination of things in themselves, but rather a medium or

18 See Sharma (2022), pp 90–91 on how 'the continuity in Marvel comics facilitates the development of a context and an arc in these characters' histories and personalities', in the context of making alternative storylines play out in certain ways, placing limits on counterfactual thinking.

19 See, for example, Everett (1939) *Motion Picture Funnies Weekly*.

mode of ordering which finds its true home only in the context of *human* experience'.[20]

It has been observed how international law and its conceptual structure have been presented as temporally neutral, or even as atemporal.[21] However, unlike such a stance towards temporal objectivity or neutrality – or perhaps even artificially constructed linearity – time is a rampant theme in the Marvel multiverse. This is both in the case of the comics and their adaptation within the MCU. Time, it cannot be understated, works differently in the Marvel multiverse. As stated above, this is because the comics are set in a multiverse; as a result, parallel timelines and parallel universes operate alongside each other. Also, while these alternative timelines exist in parallel and are set alongside each other, several elements of interaction prevail among them. This results in alternate storylines that give life to alternate outcomes for the characters involved and result in varying and rapidly multiplying consequences. It also allows for situations where elements from the past, present and future interact with each other and often work against or in concert with one another. *Spider-Man* set the stage for this,[22] as did *The Avengers* through the Infinity Saga.[23] Other movies and series that followed have further explored this theme by focusing on the multiverse, including *Doctor Strange*,[24] *WandaVision* [25] and *Ant Man*.[26] However, none has revolved so squarely around the pervasiveness of time and intertemporality as the TV adaptation of *Loki* that follows the trickster god as he has been charged with crimes against the sacred timeline.[27]

In Episode 1, 'Glorious Purpose', the god of mischief was brought before the Time Variance Authority (TVA) for his crimes, for his role in New York, on the basis that while the Avengers' mission in New York 'was meant to happen', his escape was not. Thus, once being brought into the custody of the TVA, Miss Minutes (essentially the TVA's interactive announcement system) sets out the following:

> Long ago, there was a vast multiversal war. Countless unique timelines battled each other for supremacy, nearly resulting in the total destruction of … well, everything. But then, the all-knowing Time-Keepers emerged, bringing peace by reorganizing the multiverse into a single timeline, the

20 See, for instance, Tranter (2018), p 71. Tranter also refers to moments in *Dune* where 'time is experienced in a human context'.
21 Polackova Van der Ploeg (2022), p 6.
22 Watts (2021) *Spider-Man: No Way Home*.
23 See, for instance, Russo (2019) *Avengers: Endgame*.
24 Raimi (2022) *Doctor Strange in the Multiverse of Madness*.
25 Shakman (2021) *WandaVision*.
26 Reed (2023) *Ant-Man and the Wasp: Quantumania*.
27 Herron (2021) *Loki*.

> Sacred Timeline. Now, the Time-Keepers protect and preserve the proper flow of time for everyone and everything.[28]

She goes on to tell the god of mischief that, however,

> sometimes, people like you veer off the path the Time-Keepers created. We call those Variants. Maybe you started an uprising, or were just late for work. Whatever it was, stepping off your path created a nexus event, which, left unchecked, could branch off into madness, leading to another multiversal war. But, don't worry, to make sure that doesn't happen, the Time-Keepers created the TVA and all its incredible workers. The TVA stepped in to fix your mistake and set time back on its predetermined path. Now that your actions have left you without a place on the timeline, you must stand trial for your offences. So sit tight, and we'll get you in front of a judge in no time.[29]

She then ends with the slogan, 'For all time', to which everyone responds, 'Always'.[30] The series therefore commences with this introduction to the TVA, which appears to be headed by the Time-Keepers, custodians or guardians of the sacred timeline, equipped with the powers to maintain this timeline and fix any divergence from it. Embedded in the basis of multiple coexisting timelines, and fraught with a consequential multiversal war driven by competing timelines, the Time-Keepers oversaw the union of these timelines into the sacred timeline. Essentially, this meant an agreement to adhere to a single unified timeline. Thus, similar to a perceived temporal linearity in international judicial decision-making with which an adjudicator is said to operate, the sacred timeline is linear and unified through fiction, artificially construed. The TVA and its workers are therefore instructed to detect any variation from adherence to the sacred timeline. This usually occurs when an individual or a being acts in a way that diverges from how they were *meant to*, from their predetermined path that aligns with the sacred timeline. The variation then results in a branching of the timeline. The TVA then apprehends the variant, trims the timeline and *fixes it* by ensuring everything goes according to plan – or, more accurately, according to time. Thus, Loki, a variant, soon realises that he isn't in fact the only Loki variant and quickly gets involved in a TVA operation to apprehend another Loki variant who calls herself Sylvie.[31] What becomes clear quite rapidly, through

28 Herron (2021) 'Glorious Purpose'.
29 Herron (2021) 'Glorious Purpose'.
30 Herron (2021) 'Glorious Purpose'.
31 Herron (2021) 'The Variant'.

the several Loki variants[32] that seemingly exist as a result of deviating from their predetermined paths, is that with each act there lies a reservoir of infinite possibilities, only one of which is predetermined in accordance with the sacred timeline, with the rest resulting in their decision-maker falling under the province of the TVA. So, with variants that are basically variations from a predetermined linear temporal path, and the possibility of travelling both across timelines as well as to different points of each timeline, *Loki* initially highlights an approach towards intertemporality that is often missing from analyses of how judicial decision-making is conducted at international courts and tribunals. This approach towards temporality marks the first set of episodes from Season 1 of Loki.

The next block of episodes of Season 1, however – particularly the last episode, 'For All Time. Always.' – exposes the artificiality of this constructed singular timeline and reveals instead 'He Who Remains', also known to Marvel fans as Kang the Conqueror,[33] who appears to have put the entire facade into place.[34] Having worked on this mirage of sorts to place some order into the chaos that multiversal war had created, Kang is the brain behind the TVA and its work, and has taken it upon himself to protect this order to prevent his own variants from various other timelines competing for power and throwing them all back into the throes of multiversal war. He explains to both Loki and Sylvie how it is impossible for them to kill him since he knows all that has happened and *can* happen. He says, 'I know it all. And I've seen it all. Everything you guys did on Lamentis, I saw. All the stuff the TVA didn't know about, I knew'.[35] The imagery from this episode also deserves highlighting, particularly the scene where Kang is seen going through all the possible scripts and variations of what could have happened and what happened on different parallel timelines simultaneously. This could be linked to the image of judges within international law going through possible variations of each of their decisions to see what outcome that might lead to. Kang then reveals that their thinking they had broken out of his scheme was also predetermined by him, as he responds to Sylvie when she says, 'We broke out of your little game. That's how we got here'. Kang tells her, 'No, wrong. Every step you took to get here, Lamentis, the Void, I paved the road. You … You just walked down it. And I have the rest, uh right here'. He says, holding up a script, 'Everything that's uh … going to happen. There's only one way this can go'.

32 Several of these variants are revealed in the episode 'Journey into Mystery'. See Herron (2021) 'Journey into Mystery'.
33 See, for example, Lee (1964) *Avengers*, Vol 1 No 8.
34 Herron (2021) 'For All Time. Always'.
35 Herron (2021) 'For All Time. Always'.

Thus, the role of Kang the Conqueror shines a different light on the idea of infinite choices.[36] This appears to cast a shadow on this idea, capping the several permutation combinations at a finite amount, through the role of Kang who has seen them all. However, even this is simply a variable, as seen at the end of the episode when Sylvie diverges from Kang's script (presumably, but unconfirmed) and kills him. As a result, the two Lokis are responsible for freeing the timeline back into multiple timelines.

Tying into the theme of knowing all that was, is, and could be, the Marvel multiverse houses another species of beings with windows into the parallel worlds that exist and into possible storylines and timelines. This is the role of the Watcher. This role, as is made particularly clear through Marvel's *What If...?* series, highlights how in the Marvel multiverse[37] time and space are 'more than just a linear path' and instead present a 'prism of endless possibility, where a single choice can branch out into infinite realities, creating alternate worlds from the ones you know'.[38] The Watcher who narrates the *What If...?* series thus effectively demonstrates that there are infinite possibilities and potential outcomes for every decision, leading to cascading effects and multiplying consequences. The *What If...?* series essentially takes known storylines involving known characters from the Marvel multiverse, such as the Hulk, Thor, the Fantastic Four, the Submariner and Spider-Man, among others, and puts a spin on their original storyline.[39] Each of these alternate outcomes exists in alternative timelines, demonstrating the non-singularity of a timeline and the possibility of infinite choices for each decision, with its own set or sets of repercussions and impact. Therefore, what is highlighted through *Loki* as Marvel's embrace of intertemporality, in a manner that is non-linear and pluralistic, is reinforced through several other Marvel enterprises such as in *What If...?*. The next section looks at whether this has been or can be read into international judicial decision-making. It does this by first looking at how international law and its temporalities are analysed or constructed, then by looking at examples of cases where the approach of international courts goes outside of what appears to be an artificially constructed temporal linearity.

36 Herron (2021) 'For All Time. Always'.

37 Andrews (2021) *What If...?*

38 Andrews (2021) 'What If... Captain Carter Were the First Avenger?'.

39 For instance, the Avengers are never formed on the basis that Bruce Banner continues to think like himself and not like the Hulk while transforming into the green monster; the Chameleon no longer plays a role as a supervillain and rival against Spider-Man; Jane Foster picks up Thor's hammer; Thor, being an only child, throws a large intergalactic party wreaking havoc; and Agent Carter, instead of Steve Rogers, becomes the first super soldier.

Time in international adjudication and infinite possibilities

International law and time: Perceived neutrality or atemporality?

Issues concerning time and international law have increasingly come into sharper focus within international legal scholarship. Most of this has focused on intertemporal problems and doctrines to address or avoid them up to a point.

Polackova Van der Ploeg and Pasquet acknowledge that, 'in contrast to other scholarly fields with well-identifiable and developed studies of time, international law has been characterized by a lack of focused attention to the relationship between time and international law'.[40] Observing that 'there has been a conspicuous discrepancy between practitioners' and doctrinal scholarship's preoccupation with the mechanics of temporal rules and an absence of more foundational considerations of understandings, manifestations, uses and implications of time in international law', they note that, 'in fact, the conceptual structure of international law would often seem to be presented as essentially atemporal-temporally neutral'.[41] Merkouris, for instance, notes that:

> Legal science and, for our purposes, international law is no stranger to the complexities and the problems that the passage of time can produce. The principle of *tempus regit actum,* the principle of contemporaneity, and intertemporal law are but a few manifestations of the approaches that have emerged through practice in order to respond to the inherent difficulties of deciding in the present on matters of the near or far removed past.[42]

However, while considerable space has been dedicated to the intertemporal *problem* and corresponding doctrines aimed at addressing it, comparatively less space has been devoted to the temporal inclination or proclivity of judicial decision-makers themselves.

The intertemporal problem or solution?

Intertemporal law has been said to focus 'on the temporal applicability of a norm' and 'if legal interaction of any kind took place in the distant past and in the meantime the relevant legal rules have evolved or even changed, the question of whether the old or the current law is to be applied'.[43] Moreover,

40 Polackova Van der Ploeg (2022), p 6.
41 Polackova Van der Ploeg (2022), p 6.
42 Merkouris (2022), p 196.
43 Kotzur (2008), para 1.

it has been acknowledged that 'possible tensions between a contemporaneous and a present-day understanding of the language used need to be balanced when interpreting treaties or other agreements'.[44]

The intertemporal rule, as far as international law is concerned, has also been described as 'a result of the universalization of international law', based on an understanding that 'the more universal legal standards became, the more important was an appropriate balance between legal stability and legal flexibility'.[45] Perhaps it should also be noted here that scholars have acknowledged that 'legal stability as a form of legal certainty is an element of "rule of law" thinking'.[46] Kotzur, for example, observes how, 'despite all stability and objectivity, all law is man-made and thus a living instrument following the changes and evolutionary, sometimes also revolutionary, moments in human life'.[47] Kotzur describes the doctrine of intertemporal law as 'an important guarantor of stability', stating that 'titles validly created in the past and trustfully relied on by the Parties cannot simply be outlawed by subsequent developments', or 'otherwise chaos would prevail and an international legal system based on the rule of law would lack the constitutive element of legal certainty'.[48] Thus, to a large extent, the question appears to concern stability, certainty and trust.

Huber is said to have expounded the doctrine of intertemporal law, stating that 'a juridical fact must be appreciated in the light of the law contemporary with it, and not the law in force at the time when the dispute in regard to it arises or falls to be settled'.[49] Distinguishing between the creation and existence of rights, Huber states that

> the same principle which subjects the acts creative of a right to the law in force at the time the right arises, demands that the existence of the right, in other words its continued manifestation, shall follow the conditions required by the evolution.[50]

It has been argued that instead of being viewed as adversative, the two elements of contemporaneous application of the law and flexibility based on the evolution of the law ought to be considered as complementary.[51] Essentially while the first strand of this doctrine requires that 'the legality of an act be judged by the law in force at the time the act occurs', the second strand asks

44 Kotzur (2008), para 3.
45 Kotzur (2008), para 4.
46 Kotzur (2008), para 4.
47 Kotzur (2008), para 4.
48 Kotzur (2008), para 14.
49 Kotzur (2008), para 6.
50 Kotzur (2008), para 6.
51 Kotzur (2008), para 6.

for a change in the law to essentially be taken into consideration.[52] Largely, it is the second strand that has been subject to controversy compared with the first, which is widely accepted.[53]

As mentioned earlier, however, the intertemporal doctrine chiefly appears to be aimed at addressing an 'intertemporal *problem*'. The *Institut de Droit International* (IDI), in its resolution on 'The Intertemporal Problem in Public International Law', states that:

Unless otherwise indicated, the temporal sphere of application of any norm of public international law shall be determined in accordance with the general principle of law by which any fact, action or situation must be assessed in the light of the rules that are contemporaneous with it.[54]

However, perhaps this is where drawing on the treatment of time in the Marvel multiverse, or for that matter even the DC multiverse, could unlock access to a larger reservoir of legal tools that might aid judges in either addressing or acknowledging their temporal placement. The idea that judges situate themselves at a particular point in time, as decided by the constraints of applicable law and rules of interpretation, should be tempered with an acknowledgement that this constructs an artificial sense of linearity that could bear little resemblance to anything other than legal fiction. In fact, even a preliminary survey of decisions among international courts and tribunals highlights that courts are operating in a manner that treats temporality as being more non-linear than appears to have been formally acknowledged. Two examples of where judges at international courts and tribunals have *time-travelled* are discussed in the next section.

If rules can time-travel can judges do so too? On infinite possibilities

Discussing how the law on the interpretation of treaties could at times be anachronistic, in an account on 'Time-Traveling Rules of Interpretation: Of "Time-Will" and "Time-Bubbles"' in *International Law and Time,* Merkouris talks of how rules time-travel. Merkouris does this in order to deconstruct the 'practice of going back in the past to interpret a treaty, and in doing so to look for guidance to the rules of interpretation formulated in the future'.[55] Perhaps that paves the way for further questioning of how, if rules *could* travel through time, why ought not judges be able to time-travel too? On at least two occasions, possibly several others, judges at international

52 Wheatley (2021), p 1.
53 Wheatley (2021), p 1.
54 Kotzur (2008), para 9.
55 This is done to demonstrate that 'this practice is logically, methodologically and normatively incorrect, and full of contradictory elements'; see Merkouris (2022), pp 196–97.

courts and tribunals have in fact travelled through time. These are through the advisory opinion of the International Court of Justice in *Chagos* and the International Criminal Court's decision through its Pre-Trial Chamber in the *Situation in Afghanistan.*

The first of these cases looks at time-travelling and intertemporality from the more classical case of the intertemporal problem[56] and delineation of applicable law, while the second invokes intertemporality in a manner that falls outside of the classical scope of the intertemporal problem. For this reason, the focus of this chapter lies predominantly on the latter.

In the *Chagos* advisory opinion, the court was asked essentially to *look back*, and answer whether 'the process of decolonialization of Mauritius' had been lawfully completed when Mauritius was granted independence in 1968, following the separation of the *Chagos* Archipelago from Mauritius, and having regard to international law, including obligations reflected in General Assembly resolutions 1514 (XV) of 14 December 1960, 2066 (XX) of 16 December 1965, 2232 (XXI) of 20 December 1966 and 2357 (XXII) of 19 December 1967.

Essentially, the court had to look at whether this had been considered unlawful at that point in time in the past, which the United Kingdom argued it was not, 'because international lawyers would not have recognised the existence of the right of peoples to self-determination *at that time*'.[57] Seated in the *present*, the judges of the court determined, as Wheatley notes, that the 'self-determination norm crystallised with the adoption of the 1960 General Assembly resolution 1514 (XV), and that its customary status was confirmed with the adoption of the 1970 Declaration on Friendly Relations', so the separation of the Archipelago had been unlawful at that point in time.[58] Wheatley argues that this decision would have been difficult to envisage in the 1960s.[59] Therefore, what has a significant impact on the determination of when a rule of customary law has crystallised is *where along the timeline* the judges are seated. In this case, the approach of the United Kingdom has been described as focusing on specific events in how it conceives of the notion of time, aligning with the B series described above. The notion of time in these arguments describes time in terms of its relation to events – that is, being either earlier than, later than or simultaneous with fixed events that do not change over time and are thus tenseless.[60] In this regard, this category conforms with how time is engaged with in the DC multiverse, including the fixed intervals to

56 Wheatley (2021), p 484.
57 Wheatley (2021), p 484.
58 Wheatley (2021), p 485.
59 Wheatley (2021), p 485.
60 On the concept of 'timelessness', for instance, see Tranter (2017), p 519, referring to a state where 'the ordering and relations of the represented species of law [are] temporally locked'.

which Batman refers, for instance in *The Flash* – while he explains the theory of the multiverse as it stands in the DC realm. In contrast, the ICJ's opinion, according to the argument advanced by Wheatley, reflects the logic of the A series, whereby the passage of time was integral in assisting the court to determine with the benefit of hindsight (akin to that of the Watcher, or Kang the Conqueror and other participants in the world of *Loki*) that the norm of self-determination had in fact crystallised via the adoption of the 1960 .[61] The court's approach was thus more in line with Marvel's treatment of time, adhering to a more B series-styled temporality. Thus, the court travelled not only from the past to the present but from 'now' (in 2019) to the past and then back, before ultimately turning to the future. The turn to the future can be observed in the court's statement that the United Kingdom 'has an obligation to bring to an end its administration of the Chagos Archipelago as rapidly as possible, and that all Member States must co-operate with the United Nations to complete the decolonization of Mauritius'.[62]

Another instance of time travel by an international court is the decision rendered by the Pre-Trial Chamber of the ICC, refusing the Prosecutor's request to open an investigation into the situation of Afghanistan.[63] While this decision was overturned by the Appeals Chamber,[64] its analysis – which amounted to a significant amount of time travel, particularly into the future – was not addressed by the Appeals Chamber and remains an interesting case study for understanding the temporal inclination of the Pre-Trial Chamber. The Pre-Trial Chamber ventured into this time travel when, after finding that the jurisdictional requirements and admissibility requirements for allowing such a request had been met, it decided to determine whether such an investigation would not be in the interests of justice.[65] It decided that it was not, in fact, in the interests of justice for the investigation to be opened. While the Appeals Chamber held that the Pre-Trial Chamber erred in conducting an

61 See Wheatley (2021), p 486, stating in particular that the reason for which the court could determine as such, in spite of this having been difficult to do in the 1960s, was that 'the ICJ was judging the issue with the benefit of hindsight, in a certain knowledge that the General Assembly had confirmed the existence of the self-determination norm in 1970, with the adoption of the Declaration on Friendly Relations'.

62 *Legal Consequences of the Separation of the Chagos Archipelago from Mauritius in 1965, Advisory Opinion, ICJ Reports 2019*, p 95, para 182.

63 See *Situation in the Islamic Republic of Afghanistan, Decision Pursuant to Article 15 of the Rome Statute on the Authorisation of an Investigation into the Situation in the Republic of Afghanistan* [2019] ICC-02/17-33.

64 *Situation in the Islamic Republic of Afghanistan, Judgment on the Appeal Against the Decision on the Authorisation of an Investigation into the Situation in the Islamic Republic of Afghanistan* [2020] ICC-02/17-138.

65 See *Situation in the Islamic Republic of Afghanistan, Decision Pursuant to Article 15 of the Rome Statute on the Authorisation of an Investigation into the Situation in the Republic of Afghanistan* [2019] ICC-02/17-33, para 87.

analysis of whether or not the interest of justice requirements had been met,[66] the Pre-Trial Chamber's analysis of this was particularly interesting in terms of its treatment of time. Specifically, its own temporal placement within the context, which saw the Pre-Trial Chamber travel not only back into time – common for an international criminal court or tribunal[67] – but also into the future, predicted how the course of such an investigation might go. In particular, for its analysis of whether it was not in the interests of justice to allow an investigation into the situation, the Pre-Trial Chamber found that:

> The following factors appear to be particularly relevant: (i) the significant time elapsed between the alleged crimes and the Request; (ii) the scarce cooperation obtained by the Prosecutor throughout this time, even for the limited purposes of a preliminary examination, as such based on information rather than evidence; (iii) the likelihood that both relevant evidence and potential relevant suspects might still be available and within reach of the Prosecution's investigative efforts and activities at this stage.[68]

Thus, looking at the time elapsed and the lack of cooperation in the past, the Chamber not only travels back in time but also relies on the past to construct the future to analyse *the likelihood* that 'both relevant evidence and potential relevant suspects might still be available', and goes on to speculate that in light of the situation thus far, 'coupled with the complexity and volatility of the political climate still surrounding the Afghan scenario', this makes 'it extremely difficult to gauge the prospects of securing meaningful cooperation from relevant authorities for the future, whether in respect of investigations or of surrender of suspects'.[69] To a certain extent, this demonstrates that, should the adjudicator be positioned so as to factor in considerations *vis-à-vis* the future, these would arguably be constructed through a 'projection of future events based on reflection of past events'.[70]

66 See *Situation in the Islamic Republic of Afghanistan, Judgment on the appeal against the decision on the authorisation of an investigation into the situation in the Islamic Republic of Afghanistan*, [2020] ICC-02/17-138, para 46.

67 See, for instance, on time and international criminal law, Waters (2022), pp 99–109.

68 *Situation in the Islamic Republic of Afghanistan, Decision Pursuant to Article 15 of the Rome Statute on the Authorisation of an Investigation into the Situation in the Republic of Afghanistan* [2019] ICC-02/17-33, para 91.

69 See *Situation in the Islamic Republic of Afghanistan, Decision Pursuant to Article 15 of the Rome Statute on the Authorisation of an Investigation into the Situation in the Republic of Afghanistan* [2019] ICC-02/17-33, para 94.

70 Tranter refers to this 'prudence' as 'a function of a thinking being in time'. See Tranter (2018), pp 71–72.

The Pre-Trial Chamber of the ICC also effectively ventured into its own projection of the allocation of resources by the Prosecutor and review of the economy of such an investigation. Specifically, it stated that:

> In the foreseeable absence of additional resources for the coming years in the Court's budget, authorising the investigation would therefore result in the Prosecution having to reallocate its financial and human resources; in light of the limited amount of such resources, this will go to the detriment of other scenarios (be it preliminary examinations, investigations or cases) which appear to have more realistic prospects to lead to trials and thus effectively foster the interests of justice, possibly compromising their chances for success.[71]

Thus, despite finding that the requirements for jurisdiction and admissibility had been met to authorise an investigation, the Pre-Trial Chamber was of the view that such authorisation would not be in the interests of justice because of the low prospects of a successful investigation.[72] Thus the Chamber travelled into the past, projected its findings into a future investigation that it then decided in the present ought not to be conducted in light of the unlikelihood of its chances of a successful completion. In doing this, the Chamber's methodology resembled that employed in *Loki* by the officers of the TVA, and the imagery presented in Episode 6, where Kang shows Loki and Sylvie how he went through everything that could have happened until that moment,[73] demonstrating once again that perhaps leaning in on Marvel's and *Loki*'s stance towards intertemporality while analysing international judicial decision-making might prove to be a particularly useful cipher. The next section develops this approach further as the *Loki* model.

The Loki model

The two examples above demonstrate that, in practice, any temporal neutrality or linearity that might be attributed to judicial decision-makers, including at international courts and tribunals in particular, can only be artificial. In fact, as is visible in these two cases listed above, the temporal alignment of the judges in these instances is not that far from the temporal approach found within the Marvel multiverse. As mentioned above, the example of

71 See *Situation in the Islamic Republic of Afghanistan, Decision Pursuant to Article 15 of the Rome Statute on the Authorisation of an Investigation into the Situation in the Republic of Afghanistan*, [2019] ICC-02/17-33, para 95.

72 See *Situation in the Islamic Republic of Afghanistan, Decision Pursuant to Article 15 of the Rome Statute on the Authorisation of an Investigation into the Situation in the Republic of Afghanistan* [2019] ICC-02/17-33, para 96.

73 Herron (2021) 'For All Time. Always'.

the ICC Pre-Trial Chamber depicts how the judges of the Chamber engaged in the kind of time travel that is rather commonplace in several *Loki* episodes, with a fluidity across different timelines and in a manner also akin to a time loop of sorts.[74] The latter was particularly the case when the court projected into the future through a heavy reliance on the past. The subsections below develop components of a *Loki* model, embracing and acknowledging that adjudicators find themselves placed within a space of intertemporality, rather than constructing an artificial linearity *vis-à-vis* their own temporal placement. The essence of this model may already exist within the judicial decision-making sphere at these courts and tribunals; however, an explicit acknowledgement and perhaps endorsement thereof may possibly add further clarity and transparency to the manner in which we understand the judicial decision-making process and the decisions themselves. In particular, this approach towards intertemporality, one that is rampant in each of the scenes of *Loki*, finds its space in the work of judges at international courts and tribunals, where judges take into consideration the *impact* of their judgments. This happens indirectly in the *Chagos* opinion in view of its nature as an advisory opinion itself and directly in the *Afghanistan* decision, where the judges venture into an analysis of the financial repercussions of a decision to allow the investigation and a projected view of how such an authorised investigation would play out.

Temporal narratives and imagery: Towards intertemporality

While the judges in both cases time-travelled in a manner adherent to the B series and visible throughout the Marvel multiverse, a key point of divergence is the absence of an acknowledgement of this approach and resultant intertemporality. An acknowledgement, for instance, would have led the ICC Pre-Trial Chamber to recognise that its projection into the future and envisaged outcome was *one* out of an infinite collection of possible futures,[75] thus exposing the contingencies underlying such decision-making. Narratives of an intertemporal *problem* still appear to dominate the time and international judicial decision-making conversation – unlike the case of the *Loki* model, where instead this intertemporality is embraced. Different temporal elements from different times are allowed, if not almost encouraged, to coexist. It is

74 See also the concept of the folding or percolating of time. Grabham (2016), pp 25, 36, for instance, argues that 'the "extraordinarily complex mixture" that we might wish to trace in analysing law and time, instead of acting as a backdrop to human action, is constantly percolating, folding in on itself'. Grabham thus uses the 'idea of "folding" to analyse the materialization of *legal* temporalities', adopting an approach that engages 'with topographical concepts of time in analysing law and legality'.

75 See also Grabham (2018), p 11 on the possibility to 'return to observe and follow law's own recursivity and to remain open to unpredictable legal futures'.

this acceptance or possibly acknowledgement that is absent in international judicial decision-making. Embracing the coexistence of various timelines in the act of judicial decision-making allows for greater transparency in the choices taken and available at the time these decisions were made. Projects such as the feminist judgments (which themselves bear a remarkable similarity to methodological devices used in Marvel comics, including the *What If...?* series) have demonstrated with astounding clarity how decision-making involves a series of choices, and that these decisions can be taken differently and result in different outcomes based on the how these choices are exercised.[76]

Loki, or Kang the Conqueror?

Adopting the *Loki* model and rereading international judicial decisions using this lens allow us to borrow from science fiction, tools and methodologies that are often closed off to this field based on an inherent system of limitations. This approach would cater to an analysis of the temporal *inclination*, or placement, perhaps, of judges at these international courts and tribunals with greater clarity, given that characters within the Marvel multiverse (particularly *Loki*) are not constrained by the demands of temporal neutrality or linearity. However, even if one were to embrace intertemporality in the exercise of the international judicial decision-making function, what form would this take? Would the international judge assume the role of He Who Remains (Kang the Conqueror) and unify the multiple timelines into a singular, linear, sacred timeline based on an agreement of sorts and an artificially constructed system of authority to keep it in place and trim any deviations from it? This could happen through adopting the perception of atemporality and neutrality and denying the existence of a temporal stance altogether. Or perhaps instead, as argued throughout this chapter, it might be more beneficial for the international judge – equivalent to Loki – to dismantle the artificially constructed sacred timeline to reveal the multiple courses of time suppressed under it and unleash the infinite courses of time and space that include the chances of an outbreak of multiversal war. Of course, these are not the only two forms in which the *Loki* model could be manifested through the role of the international judge. As becomes clear towards the end of Season 1, the two Lokis 'crack open the multiverse', bringing Watchers to the forefront. Watchers, who are mystical beings allocated the role of observing all the universes – all that was, is, and will be, along with windows into the parallel worlds of what could be – provide a third form of applying the *Loki* model to understanding the temporal placement of the international judge. For instance, in *What If...?* the Watcher is heard saying, 'For, none save a

76 See, for example, Hodson (2019); Grey (2021); see also Sharma (2022).

watcher can truly know what could have happened,'[77] and, 'I observe all that transpires here. And I do not, cannot, will not interfere.'[78] Tasked with observation, but barred from interference, could this be the international judge's role with time? However, in considering that, it is crucial to recall that throughout the comics as well as within the MCU, the Watcher has on occasion broken his oath.

Conclusion

The realms of Marvel comics and international judicial decision-making have much more in common than initially meets the eye. This is also the case for the treatment of time and the temporal situation of the international judge along the timeline(s) constructed through applicable law. Rereading international judicial decisions and analysing the decision-making process at these courts and tribunals with a science-fiction lens (here, one modelled after the god of mischief) allows for a wider and possibly more transparent understanding of the temporal alignment of judges within the decision-making process. However, the objective here has been to demonstrate how leaning on temporal models depicted within science fiction through Marvel comics (and the MCU) provides a fruitful methodological tool for critique and analysis of these processes and decisions. Analysing whether the stance of the international judge *vis-à-vis* time aligns with the trickster god himself or conforms instead to the role of the Conqueror (Kang – He Who Remains) or instead ventures into the domain of the Watcher, all-knowing, all-seeing, bound by observation, barred from interference, yet somehow effectuating change, allows for the unlocking of additional methodological tools for critique and analysis. Possibly there is more to embracing this intertemporality, and calling it what it is, and therefore effectively trying not to 'impose linear legal timeframes on non-linear experiences'.[79] Perhaps there is value in Mobius's statement that 'existence is chaos. Nothing makes any sense, so we try to make some sense of it'.[80]

References

Secondary sources

Luca Banfi (2017) 'A-Theory or B-Theory of Time? An Aristotelian Answer' 1 *Critical Reflections*, https://scholar.uwindsor.ca/cgi/viewcontent.cgi?article=1119&context=essaysofsignificance

77 Thomas (2021) *What If...?*, 7.
78 Andrews (2021) 'What If ... Captain Carter Were the First Avenger?'.
79 Grabham (2018), p 11.
80 Herron (2021) 'For All Time. Always'.

Umberto Eco (1979) *The Role of the Reader: Explorations in the Semiotics of Texts*, Indiana University Press.

Bill Everett (1939) *Motion Picture Funnies Weekly*, Funnies Inc, Vol 1 #1.

Gardner Fox (1961) *The Flash*, Vol 1#123, DC Comics.

Emily Grabham (2016) *Brewing Legal Times: Things, Form, and the Enactment of Law*, University of Toronto Press.

Emily Grabham and Siân M Beynon-Jones (2018) 'Introduction' in Siân M Beynon-Jones and Emily Grabham (eds), *Law and Time*, Routledge, 1.

Rosemary Grey, Kcasey McLoughlin and Louise Chappell (2021) 'Gender and Judging at the International Criminal Court: Lessons from "Feminist Judgment Projects"' 34 *Leiden Journal of International Law* 247.

Loveday Hodson and Troy Lavers (eds) (2019) *Feminist Judgments in International Law*, Hart.

Rögnvaldur Ingthorsson (1998) 'MacTaggart and the Unreality of Time' 9 *Axiomathes* 287.

Markus Kotzur (2008) 'Intertemporal Law' in Rüdiger Wolfrum (ed), *Max Planck Encyclopedia of Public International Law*, https://opil.ouplaw.com/display/10.1093/law:epil/9780199231690/law-9780199231690-e1433

Stan Lee (1964) *Avengers*, Vol 1#8, Marvel Comics.

Panos Merkouris (2022) 'Time-Traveling Rules of Interpretation: Of "Time-Will" and "Time-Bubbles"' in Klara Polackova Van der Ploeg, Luca Pasquet and León Castellanos-Jankiewicz (eds), *International Law and Time: Narratives and Techniques*, Springer, 195.

Klara Polackova Van der Ploeg and Luca Pasquet (2022) 'The Multifaceted Notion of Time in International Law' in Klara Polackova Van der Ploeg, Luca Pasquet and León Castellanos-Jankiewicz (eds), *International Law and Time: Narratives and Techniques*, Springer, 1.

Marcello Serra (2016) 'Historical and Mythical Time in the Marvel and DC Series' 49 *Journal of Popular Culture* 646.

Kritika Sharma (2022) 'What if Feminist Judgments were Written on Earth 616?' 4 *Law Technology and Humans* 81.

Roy Thomas (2021) *What If? The Original Marvel Series Omnibus*, Vol. 1, Marvel Comics.

Kieran Tranter (2017) 'Law, the Digital and Time: The Legal Emblems of *Doctor Who*' 30 *International Journal for the Semiotics of Law* 515.

Kieran Tranter (2018) *Living in Technical Legality: Science Fiction and Law as Technology*, Edinburgh University Press.

Boris Uspenskij (1987) *Storia e semiotica*, Bompiani.

Timothy William Waters (2022) 'Digressing Towards Justice: International Criminal Law's Narrative of Moral Transit Through Violence' in Klara Polackova Van der Ploeg, Luca Pasquet and León Castellanos-Jankiewicz (eds) *International Law and Time: Narratives and Techniques*, Springer, 99.

Steven Wheatley (2021) 'Revisiting the Doctrine of Intertemporal Law' 41 *Oxford Journal of Legal Studies* 484.

Primary legal sources

Legal Consequences of the Separation of the Chagos Archipelago from Mauritius in 1965, Advisory Opinion, I.C.J. Reports 2019, p 95.

Situation in the Islamic Republic of Afghanistan, decision pursuant to Article 15 of the Rome Statute on the Authorisation of an Investigation into the Situation in the Republic of Afghanistan, 12 April 2019, ICC-02/17-33.

Situation in the Islamic Republic of Afghanistan, judgment on the appeal against the decision on the authorisation of an investigation into the situation in the Islamic Republic of Afghanistan, 5 March 2020, ICC-02/17-138.

Films and television programs

Bryan Andrews (2021) *What If ...?* Marvel Studios.

Bryan Andrews (2021) , 'What If ... Captain Carter Were the First Avenger?' *What If ...?* Season 1, Episode 1 ((Marvel Studios, United States, 11 August).

Kate Herron (2021) 'Glorious Purpose' *Loki*, Season 1, Episode 1, (Marvel Studios,United States, 9 June).

Kate Herron (2021) 'Journey into Mystery' *Loki*, Season 1, Episode 5, (Marvel Studios, United States, 7 July).

Kate Herron (2021) 'For All Time. Always' *Loki*, Season 1, Episode 6, (Marvel Studios, United States, 14 July).

Andy Muschietti (2023) *The Flash (*Warner Bros. Pictures, DC Studios, United States, 12 June).

Sam Raimi (2022) *Doctor Strange in the Multiverse of Madness* (Marvel Studios, United States, 2 May).

Peyton Reed (2023) *Ant-Man and the Wasp: Quantumania* (Marvel Studios, Unired States, 6 February).

Anthony Russo and Joe Russo (2019) *Avengers: Endgame* (Marvel Studios, United States, 22 April).

Matt Shakman (2021) *WandaVision* (Marvel Studios, United States, 15 January-5 March).

Jon Watts (2021) *Spider-Man: No Way Home* (Marvel Studios, United States, 17 December).

Chapter 4

Life on the front line

The lives of child soldiers in *Neon Genesis Evangelion*

Emily Muir

Introduction

Discourse on law, war and childhood has grown in scope over the last five years.[1] UNICEF has identified that between 2005 and 2022, more than 105,000 children were verified as being used by parties in conflict.[2] The consequences of war on children urgently need further investigation. Under international humanitarian law, the recruitment of child soldiers is prohibited. Despite this, children continue to be victimised and exploited in armed conflicts. This chapter explores law, war and childhood by referring to *Neon Genesis Evangelion* ('*Evangelion*') as an example of children in armed conflict. It expands on the discussion of children in armed conflict and the discourse on ethics that has become important to the contemporary global climate.[3] It expands on this discussion by exploring the theories of justice that underpin the ideas that allow killing in war: the second limb of just war theory, or *jus in bello*. *Jus in bello* conceptualises three principles that should be met for armed conflict to be ethical and justified: discrimination, proportionality and responsibility. *Jus in bello* looks at conduct during wartime, or the 'right conduct in war'.[4] These principles are established to identify the targets of the armed conflict and protect those who are not (discrimination); determine how much force is morally appropriate (proportionality); and decide who should bear the moral responsibility for the harm caused (responsibility).[5]

This chapter presents this argument in five parts. The first part explores international law and the problems experienced by child soldiers in armed conflicts. The second part contextualises the discussion of *jus in bello* within the narrative of *Evangelion* by introducing the key characters within the text.

1 Dijkstra et al (2022), p 464.
2 United Nations (2023); UNICEF (2022).
3 Dijkstra et al (2022), pp 464–65.
4 Jackson (2011), p 584; Walzer (1977), p 21.
5 Morkevicius (2018), p 200; Toner (2010), p 95; Mayer (2013), p 304.

DOI: 10.4324/9781003412274-5

The third part explores *jus in bello* and its three principles. It demonstrates that although *jus in bello* seeks to establish combatants and non-combatants, as well as place limitations on violence, there are various aspects of *jus in bello* that are still discussed today. The fourth part critiques the principles of discrimination, proportionality and responsibility through the perspective of child soldiers in the narrative of *Evangelion*. The chapter concludes that, although just war theory provides the best rationale for the establishment of war principles, it does not adequately protect vulnerable groups, in particular children, from the harmful effects of armed conflict.

Contemporary discourse on child soldiers and international humanitarian law

According to the principles of just war theory, children are a vulnerable group deserving of protection during wartime.[6] Despite the position that the involvement of children in war constitutes a breach of international law, children continue to be recruited or used in war activities.[7] There are extensive international frameworks and regulations to protect children in and from armed conflict.[8] Despite these frameworks, there are numerous reports that children continue to be involved in armed conflict.[9] The contemporary discourse on child soldiers and international law suggests a new type of warfare exists that involves the use of child soldiers. There are numerous reasons for this development – including the use of irregular forces, which eliminates the distinction between civilians and soldiers. Child soldiers are thus utilised as part of the irregular forces, which are usually led by warlords.[10] There is an identification with ethnic groups, cultures or religions; however, 'conflicts are driven by economic factors' and utilise systematic atrocities such as massacres, mass rape and children as light infantry to force civilians out of the region.[11] Advances in new technologies and warfare strategies enable children to become effective soldiers in modern wars.[12]

Rosen suggests that the reasons for the failure of international humanitarian law to prevent child soldiering lie in the definition of childhood. The

6 Walzer (1977), p 21; United Nations Human Rights Office of the High Commission (2002).
7 McBride (2014), p 5; United Nations (2023); Office of the Special Representative of the Secretary-General for Children and Armed Conflict (2018); Wuilbercq (2021); United Nations Human Rights Office of the High Commission (2002).
8 United Nations (20 November 1989), UN Doc A/44/49; l (25 May 2000) UNTS vol/2173, 222; United Nations General Assembly (1998) Article 8(b) xxvi; International Committee of the Red Cross (1949) Fourth Geneva Convention; Hague Conference (1980), Hague XXVIII.
9 Child Soldiers International (2004); Drumbl (2012), p 137.
10 Schauer and Elbert (2010), pp 312–13.
11 Schauer and Elbert (2010), pp 312–13.
12 Schauer and Elbert (2010), p 315.

definition of children varies within countries, and therefore the frameworks are unable to encapsulate the experience of childhood.[13] McBride focuses on establishing the jurisprudence for the crime of recruiting child soldiers, attributing the increase in children's involvement as child soldiers to modern weaponry.[14] However, the issues are identified as deeper than new methods of warfare and include socioeconomic factors in the analysis of child soldiers and war crimes – for example, drug abuse, children who consent to recruitment and the perception of war as heroic or patriotic.[15] Ultimately, children should be considered protected in armed conflict. By engaging in a discourse on 'what is childhood?' better justice outcomes can be achieved for children.[16] War crimes, like the recruitment of child soldiers, are strongly connected to identity.[17] The child identity is fundamental to access to justice for children in war contexts.

Exploring jus in bello and child soldiering

International humanitarian law consists of the laws that govern war. The frameworks of international humanitarian law are synonymous with just war theory,[18] which has two limbs: *jus ad bellum* and *jus in bello*.[19] The first limb, *jus ad bellum*, consists of six principles, while the second limb, *jus in bello*, has three. These nine principles together are called just war theory. Just war theory attempts to unify the understanding of the justice of war.[20] There are three guiding principles that look at the way war is conducted. This is known as the second limb of the just war theory, or *jus in bello*. First, *jus in bello* attempts to reduce harm by limiting violence to combatants or soldiers through the discrimination principles;[21] second, it reduces harm by considering how much force is appropriate through the principle of proportionality and necessity;[22] and third, the principles seek out where the responsibility lies in the war through the discussion of liability.[23]

The four Geneva Conventions embed some of these theories into international law. The first convention protects the sick and wounded and protects

13 Rosen (2007), p 297.
14 McBride (2014), p 8.
15 McBride (2014), pp 7–8.
16 McBride (2014), p vii.
17 Rosen (2012), pp 1–3; Wessells (2006), p 36; Jiménez (2019).
18 von Elbe (1939), p 671; Luban (2017) p 434.
19 Lang (2013), pp 1–16; Scholz (2011), pp 1146–50; McMahan (2009), pp 3–4.
20 Muir (2023), p 43.
21 Enemark (2013), p 332; Schott (2008), p 128; Davidovic (2018), p 173; May (2007), p 169; Lazar (2015), p 93.
22 Morkevicius (2018), p 206; Cannizzaro, (2014), p 335.
23 Roff (2013), p 354.

medical facilities, while the second protects those who are shipwrecked.[24] The third offers protections to prisoners of war.[25] The fourth convention requires UN member states to punish those who commit crimes such as unlawful killing, torture, serious bodily injury or suffering, unlawful deportation (ethnic cleansing), unlawful confinement and gender-based crimes such as rape and forced prostitution.[26] The fourth convention includes three additional protocols, extending civilian protections to victims of wars against racist regimes, wars of self-determination and internal conflicts.[27] All these conventions intend to place limitations on conduct in war by discriminating between combatants and non-combatants, placing responsibility on states and further discussing proportionate or acceptable conduct in war.[28] Despite these conventions, there is limited recognition of the way war treats children as they tread in the liminal space between innocent and not innocent, victim and combatant.

Some academic literature assists in these definitions. Walzer's *Just and Unjust War* provides an in-depth analysis of the justice and morality of war by examining principles of non-combatants and how they traditionally are given immunity from involvement in warfare.[29] McMahan develops these principles, outlining the 'moral liability to attack' and the differences between 'innocent' and 'non innocent' people in warfare.[30] On the other hand, Fabre's critique of *jus in bello* highlights an emphasis on the rights of combatants at the expense of those of non-combatants.[31] This chapter explores *jus in bello* and contextualises the theory of *jus in bello* from the perspective of child soldiers. *Jus in bello* distinguishes combatants from non-combatants and establishes the difference between the targets in the war and civilians.[32] Prima facie, the involvement of children in armed conflict is a breach of the *jus in bello* principles.[33]

Evangelion more specifically takes a closer look at the targets of armed conflict through its narrative. *Evangelion* critiques the identity of child soldiers, their ability to consent and their responsibility once they have taken up arms. *Evangelion* suggests that there are various reasons why children

24 International Committee of the Red Cross (1949) First Geneva Convention; International Committee of the Red Cross (1949) Second Geneva Convention.
25 International Committee of the Red Cross (1949) Third Geneva Convention.
26 International Committee of the Red Cross (1949) Fourth Geneva Convention.
27 International Committee of the Red Cross (1949) Fourth Geneva Convention.
28 Luban (2017), p 434.
29 Walzer (1977), p 21.
30 McMahan (2009), p 8.
31 Fabre (2013), pp 7–8.
32 Melzer (2014), p 299; French (2018), p 157; McMahan (2008), p 21; Orend (2013), pp 105–59; Ohlin (2018), pp 240–42.
33 Morkevicius (2018), p 205.

consent to being weaponised as part of an armed conflict.[34] These include volunteering, seeking revenge, martyrdom, economic reasons, abduction, fear and family.[35] In *Evangelion*, Shinji is both child and soldier, both non-combatant and combatant. Shinji's position as both someone who should be protected and the person who protects complicates the application of *jus in bello* and demonstrates that the principle continues to fail children globally. The next section of this chapter critiques *jus in bello* by exploring the various factors of a child soldier's life that complicate their access to protection within the cultural imaginary.

Finding friends: An overview of Neon Genesis Evangelion

This chapter engages in a cultural legal analysis of the Japanese anime *Evangelion*. Japanese popular culture offers a wide variety of media for the analysis of legal theory.[36] Cultural legal studies examine how law and popular cultures affect each other,[37] leveraging popular culture to 'question law and justice'.[38] It demonstrates how cultural texts construe law and transform the way the legal system behaves.[39] Analysing cultural artefacts for their value as law aims to demonstrate how 'concepts of law' are 'reflected in, but also refracted by literary texts'.[40] Ultimately, this process leads to 'unexpected insights regarding the underlying value system presented'.[41]

Evangelion has received worldwide critical acclaim.[42] The initial series, which is the focus of this chapter, became celebrated by fans and transformed into a long-running franchise with multiple movie adaptations and merchandise.[43] The anime was produced by Gainax and Tatsunoko Production, written by Hideki Anno and primarily directed by Kazuya Tsurumaki.[44] It comprises 26 episodes and was broadcast in Japan from October 1995 to March 1996.[45] It eventually debuted on Australia's SBS channel in 1999, four

34 Vindevogel et al (2011), p 555; Kurukulasuriya (2003), pp 13–14; De Silva et al (2001), pp 125–34.
35 Vindevogel et al (2011), p 555; Kurukulasuriya (2003), pp 13–14; De Silva et al (2001), pp 125–34.
36 Pearson et al (2018), pp 6–12; Pearson and Tranter (2015), p 825.
37 Muir (2023), p 41.
38 Sharp (2016).
39 Silbey (2002), p 139; Friedman (1989), p 1579; Brown et al (2014); Bainbridge (2006), p 153; Asimow and Mader (2004); Greenfield and Osborn (2006); de Zwart et al (2015); Thornton (2002).
40 MacNeil (2007), p 156.
41 Peters (2015), p 262.
42 Muir (2023), p 44.
43 Galbraith (2012), p 241.
44 Muir (2023), p 43; Malone et al (2010), p 347; Redmond (2007), p 183.
45 Muir (2023), p 43; Andreu and Torrents (2014), p 283; Malone et al (2010), p 348.

years later.[46] The series integrated multiple anime genre tropes and Japanese narrative constructions, which allowed the anime to produce a flexible and diverse narrative.[47]

Beyond its critical acclaim, *Evangelion* provides an excellent base for cultural legal analysis and the representation of warfare and child soldiers due to its significant focus on children. Children have been portrayed in popular culture for millennia. Children's popular culture inhabits the child, both as an audience and within the narrative. Popular culture often tells the story of children's experiences of the world around them.[48] More specifically, 'images and narratives of child wartime heroes are perennial and celebrated'.[49] Children in media are creators of culture and subjects of media,[50] creating stories that are a 'critical point of social contention', where we can reflect on the meaning of childhood.[51] Images of children in Japanese popular culture are equally celebrated. The globally celebrated manga and anime market provides an abundance of child imagery to explore. Interestingly, children's media from the East has a diverse audience.[52] *Evangelion* portrays a 'contemporary repetition of mechanized children in Japanese anime'.[53] It symbolises a 'larger national consciousness through manipulating, metamorphosing, or mutating the bodies of their main characters, first combining them with mechanical properties then freeing them into a conscious non-bodily existence', exploring the significance of the child body and connection to cultural insights of the world today.[54]

Evangelion is the story of a 14-year-old boy named Shinji Ikari who is recruited into a war organisation called NERV by his father, Gendo Ikari. As part of the war organisation, Shinji pilots a robot called an Evangelion ('EVA') and fights Angels, celestial beings who are 'the central military threat to Earth's civilisation'.[55] Shinji is recruited into the organisation with other children,[56] Rei Ayanami and Asuka Langley Soryu.[57] During the series, he lives with Misato Katsuragi, NERV's commander, becoming friends with classmates Toji Suzuhara, Kensuke Aida and Hikari Horaki. Most

46 Muir (2023), p 43; Anime News Network (2022).
47 Muir (2023), p 43; Tsuchiya (2022), pp 360–66.
48 Shepherd (2012), p 147.
49 Muir (2023), p 40; Dong (2012), p 172; Hashimoto (2015), p 12; Bosworth (2011), pp 185–97.
50 Fass (2006), p 8.
51 Fass (2006), pp 202–3.
52 Annett (2014), pp 6–8.
53 Landa (2012), p 16.
54 Landa (2012), p 16.
55 Muir (2023), p 43.
56 The reference to the chosen child soldiers as First Children, Second Children and Third Children within the narrative of *Neon Genesis Evangelion*.
57 Muir (2023), p 43.

importantly, Shinji develops a special relationship with Kaworu Nagisa,[58] who is Shinji's romantic interest and an Angel. This relationship changes the way he connects with individuals and increases his involvement in the Human Instrumentality Project – a project 'designed to obliterate humanity and shape one consciousness'.[59]

The series begins 15 years after the Second Impact, before the Third Impact. These impacts are moments in history when humanity is close to extinction. It is presumed that the First Impact was mostly due to the environmental effect when the Spear of Longinus was embedded within Antarctica. This caused worldwide devastation and eliminated most of humanity. The world then experiences the Second Impact, which was an attack on Earth by the Angels. The United Nations works with NERV, a quasi-military agency, to prevent further attacks from the Angels. The EVAs are used to fight the Angels, prevent the Third Impact and save humanity.

Evangelion can be seen as a discourse on just war theory through the way it represents children as stakeholders in armed conflict.[60] In particular, this representation of the child soldier is common within popular culture – often in magical, alien or mythical warfare, where the children emerge as selfless heroes.[61] Throughout the course of the series, *Evangelion* explores *jus in bello* principles through Shinji and his experiences of armed conflict, love and friendship. Its representations of child soldiers and their placement as heroes complicate the application of *jus in bello* and help to explain why the principle continues to fail children globally.[62] It argues that identity and environment play a key role in the recruitment of child soldiers. These factors are not considered in the traditional structures of just war theory, and new developments in the war context complicate the applications of justice within our current international frameworks. The recruitment of children in armed conflict is considered a war crime by the International Criminal Court.[63] Despite prohibition, children continue to be recruited within real and fictitious conflicts such as the armed conflict represented in *Evangelion*. This chapter analyses the representation of the child characters and uses the reading of *Evangelion* to critique the concepts of legitimate wars.[64]

58 Muir (2023), p 43.
59 Muir (2023), p 44.
60 Muir (2023), p 43.
61 Muir (2023), p 42.
62 Dong (2012), p 172; Hashimoto (2015), p 12; Schott (2008), p 125; McMahan (2009), p 199.
63 Brocklehurst (2005), p 116; United Nations (2023).
64 Vindevogel et al (2011), p 553; Ul Hassan et al (2017), p 1514; Shenoda et al (2018); Shenoda et al (2015); Rieder and Choonara (2012); Park (2010), p 331; Landa (2012); Kurukulasuriya (2003), pp 13–14; Kumar and Multani (2019); Betancourt (2011), pp 307–12; Nickl (2018), pp 82–94; Wolf et al (2011); Gates and Reich (2010), p 25.

The child identity versus the child soldier: When a child is the protected as well as the one who protects

Principle 1: Distinction and necessity

Evangelion explores the way that violence is limited to soldiers and raises a discussion of children as soldiers. The identities, conflicts and positions of children in *Evangelion* are revealed through an analysis of their self-perceptions. This analysis suggests that children are recruited into armed groups through a variety of means, including coercion, misunderstanding of violence, desensitisation to death and the promise of glory or other benefits.[65] *Evangelion* highlights that children experience war differently, and the inner world of a child soldier reveals that the discrimination principle of *jus in bello* fails to effectively exclude children as combatants.[66]

The discrimination principle – or the distinction principle[67] – 'distinguishes combatants from non-combatants in a conflict'.[68] This is to 'preserve to the greatest degree possible the safety and security' of civilians[69] by directing hostilities towards combatants and providing protection to civilians.[70] Essentially, this principle prevents soldiers from 'kill[ing] indiscriminately'.[71] However, this is 'difficult to put into practice' and does not protect civilians from harm.[72] For example, civilians can experience the other effects of war – both social and economic. Further, 'the principle of immunity includes an element of resistance'.[73] This part of the principle indicates that the civilian must 'lack ... a real and direct threat' to combatants.[74] It does not matter whether the civilian is innocent or supports the aggression, or whether the soldier is voluntary or conscripted.[75] If the individual participates and is a threat to another combatant, they are considered to be distinguished from civilians and therefore a soldier of the enemy party.[76] This is particularly a problem for children who are recruited into armed conflict, as the principles

65 Vindevogel et al (2011), p 555; Kurukulasuriya (2003), pp 13–14; De Silva et al (2001), pp 125–34.
66 Wessells (2006), p 31.
67 French (2018), p 152; McMahan (2009), p 12.
68 French (2018), p 152; Lang et al (2013), pp 1–16; Scholz (2011), pp 1146–50; McMahan (2009), pp 3–4.
69 French (2018), p 152; Melzer (2014), p 299; McMahan (2008), p 21; Orend (2013), pp 105–59.
70 French (2018), p 152; McMahan (2008), p 12.
71 French (2018), p 154; Melzer (2014), p 299; McMahan (2008), p 21; Orend (2013), pp 105–59.
72 French (2018), p 153; Schott (2008), p 124.
73 French (2018), p 153; Melzer (2014), p 299; McMahan (2008), p 21; Orend (2013), pp 105–59.
74 French (2018), p 155; McMahan (2008), p 12.
75 French (2018), p 155; Lazar (2017), p 119.
76 Haque (2017), p 59.

suggest that, even for children, once they participate in the hostilities and become a threat, they give up their immunity or civilian status and become a combatant or unjust combatant. This problem is explored through the moral and legal status of the child soldiers in *Evangelion*. The moral status is the recognition that people inherently have a 'rational capacity to make our own choices, for our own reasons' or 'individual rights'.[77] As the children explore their participation in the hostilities with the Angels, their role within the war and their moral status become apparent.[78]

Evangelion explores Shinji's motives for being a pilot in Episodes 1–3. Shinji wants to protect Rei, and he wants his father's approval. In the first episode, Shinji witnesses his fellow pilot, Rei, being injured, and this event prompts him to pilot EVA-01 for the first time.[79] This scene is significant because it shows Shinji's willingness to sacrifice his own safety to protect others. He feels empathy for Rei, who is injured and cannot fight. This empathy becomes the feeling that encourages Shinji to pilot EVA-01 and engage in combat. This is an important scene because Shinji gives up his civilian immunity in the first scene, and we see that his reason for giving up his immunity is to protect someone else. This scene critiques the discrimination principle because it indicates that children will make choices that protect the people around them. Shinji's compassion in this scene demonstrates one of the many reasons why children are recruited into armed conflict.

Shinji also has a personal motive that compels him to be a pilot. The narrative explores Shinji's moral status,[80] which recognises that Shinji has the innate ability to make his own choices for his own reasons – these are his individual rights.[81] These rights can be lost during war because 'if you are sufficiently responsible for an unjustified threat that is serious enough to make killing proportionate, and if killing you is necessary, then you can be liable to be killed'.[82] Shinji has a fundamental right to life and liberty.[83]

Shinji's moral status changes with his motivations for engaging in combat. In Episode 3, an analysis of the *mise en scène*[84] juxtaposes different aspects of Shinji's identity and exploration of his 'rational capacity to make [his] own choices for his own reasons'.[85] In this episode, Shinji goes to live with Misato after his traumatic first battle with an Angel. Lying on his bed, he

77 Lazar (2017), p 119.
78 Rodin and Shue (2008), pp 1–2; Child Soldiers International (2004); Drumbl (2012), p 137.
79 Tsurumaki (1995), '使徒、襲来' ('Angel Attack').
80 Lazar (2017), p 119; French (2018), p 155.
81 Lazar (2017), p 119; Schott (2008), p 124.
82 Lazar (2017), p 119; Rodin and Shue (2008), pp 1–2.
83 Lazar (2017), p 119; McMahan (2008), p 21; Orend (2013), pp 105–59.
84 Gibbs (2012), p 8.
85 Ishidō (1995), '鳴らない, 電話' ('The Silent Phone'); Lazar (2017), p 119.

relives his traumatic experience.[86] The scene is washed with colours of indigo and violet. Shinji is positioned in a corner of the room and displayed from a bird's eye view. In this scene, the audience is directed to investigate Shinji from above. Thus, the audience gets a serious glimpse into Shinji's state of mind as he relives the EVA fight. After his violet-filtered flashbacks, the scene cuts back to indigo, and he asks himself, 'Why am I doing this?' The scene ends with Misato looking in on him and Shinji pretending to be asleep. This scene presents a duality to Shinji by displaying his consciousness in two colours: indigo and violet.[87] The hues are used to enhance the subject and suggest that Shinji is going through an internal conflict and is struggling to find an answer.[88] The next day, Shinji is going through simulation training and, unlike his state of mind the day before, he has become repetitive and his eyes are blank. He locks onto the target and pulls the trigger, speaking in a robotic monotone. The contrast in Shinji's identity reveals two very different Shinjis. In his room, he is very open about his feelings; however, inside the EVA, he responds to commands without emotion, as if disassociated from the experience. This unwillingness to be open with himself and with his guardian illustrates that Shinji is yet to understand his own status and is in denial.[89]

Like Shinji's sense of identity, his motives consistently shift. This is immediately apparent at the end of Episode 4.[90] Toji Suzuhara and Kensuke Aida, Shinji's school friends, leave the lockdown emergency facilities to see the EVA and Angel fight. EVA-01, with Shinji piloting it, is being brutally attacked by the Angel and is on the brink of being defeated. Seeing his friends on the hill in the middle of the battle, and clearly in danger, Shinji snaps out of his repetitive depressive state and a protective instinct kicks in. Shinji opens the EVA unit and his friends enter the unit to find safety. The new feelings of protection spur him on and he re-engages the EVA with the Angel. This scene creates a new sense of friendship and bonds that Shinji relies on as a pilot. Friendship becomes Shinji's motivation to be a good pilot.

Evangelion builds upon Shinji's experiences as a child soldier by creating parallels between Shinji and the other child soldiers. By doing this, *Evangelion* critiques a child's ability to establish self-identity,[91] demonstrating that children rely on their environment to shape their identity. For child soldiers, this means that sections of their identity go unestablished, and the result is involvement in armed conflict. It raises the idea that immunity is held

86 Ishidō (1995), '鳴らない, 電話' ('The Silent Phone').

87 Brown et al (2013), p 5.

88 Watkins (2013), p 233; Belton (2013), p 189.

89 McBride (2014), p 5; Rosen (2012), pp 1–3; Wessells (2006), pp 31–36; Jiménez (2019); Vindevogel et al (2011), p 555; Kurukulasuriya (2003), pp 13–14; De Silva et al (2001), pp 125–34; Issa (2019), p 88.

90 Kaga (1995), '雨、逃げ出した後' ('Rain after Running Away').

91 McBride (2014), p 8.

by civilians and equally should be held by soldiers.[92] More particularly, it introduces the idea that with limitations on 'combatant targetability', further immunities might be extended to child soldiers.[93]

Evangelion demonstrates that child soldiers cannot rely on the principle of civilian immunity. However, it also critiques the involvement of children in war by unpacking the inner moral and legal status of the child soldier, making the argument that children's involvement in armed conflict is more than a question of their civilian involvement. It often relates to how their environment shapes their identity and thus leads to their involvement in armed conflict. The consideration of the distinction principle involves an analysis of identity, particularly the identity of child soldiers, including the environment that leads to the involvement of children in armed conflict.

Principle 2: Proportionality

Proportionality is a fundamental part of the judicial process. It is a part of the rule of law, and a judge uses it to interpret legislation.[94] The principle of proportionality also plays a role in the *jus in bello* principles.[95] It is the test that 'decides whether an act of war will be justified'.[96] The principle of proportionality 'weigh[s] the harms the act of war will cause against its contribution to "the end of victory"'.[97] Through this principle, 'combatants must assess the damage that they will do against' the military advantage and consider whether it is necessary for winning the war.[98] However, proportionality does not prevent harm to human rights, and acts that meet proportionality tests can hurt civilians.[99] *Evangelion* exposes this dilemma within *jus in bello*.

This is reflected in *Evangelion* through Shinji's decision-making process in Episode 24. In this episode, Rei helps Shinji by leading him to Lilith and Kaworu.[100] Kaworu and Shinji have a deep and meaningful relationship. Shinji reveals to Kaworu that his isolation is a result of not having someone who understands him, yet he feels a connection to Kaworu. He has felt connection as friendship with his school friends; however, there is a deeper, more meaningful relationship with Kaworu – so much so that Shinji feels betrayed when Kaworu is revealed as the 17th Angel in Episode 24. Shinji follows Kaworu into Terminal Dogma and is faced with the Angel, Lilith. Kaworu

92 Blum (2010), pp 17–57.
93 Blum (2010), pp 17–57.
94 Beatty (2004), p 160.
95 McMahan (2017), p 132.
96 Tomlin (2020), p 35.
97 Tomlin (2020), p 35.
98 Tomlin (2020), p 36.
99 Haque (2017), pp 191–92.
100 Masayuki (1996), '最後のシ者' ('The Last Cometh').

begins to understand that humans have hope through Shinji. Kaworu asks Shinji to make a choice to kill him and save everyone. Freedom and choice are emphasised in this scene.

A contrast is developed between right actions and weighing up Kaworu's life against humanity. It emphasises that both individuals are important and that 'war is not a rational expression of human freedom, hence war is immoral'.[101] This scene is the first time in the series where an Angel and a human – enemies – reveal their emotions to each other.[102] In this scene, Shinji considers proportionality.[103] He asks himself whether it is worth killing his friend and newfound love. Shinji makes the final transformation into 'a tool to advance the good of others' by deciding to kill Kaworu.[104] However, when weighed up, this act meets the proportionality test: Shinji decides to save humanity. Through the critical analysis of proportionality, this scene demonstrates that there is a moral dilemma. Shinji does not take the path of love and friendship, but that of destruction. This scene symbolises that both sides can weigh up a human right to life and, in most cases, both sides can fail to yield a result that does not harm children.

There are many ways in which a proportionate act in armed conflict can alter the life of a child or, in the case of *Evangelion*, alter the life of a child soldier. Like Shinji, Rei also questions her moral status as a pilot. She believes it is loyalty to Gendo, represented by Rei treasuring keepsakes from Gendo; however, she betrays this loyalty in Episode 23 when she refuses to comply with Gendo's orders and self-destructs her EVA to save Shinji. However, as she develops as a character, she begins to exhibit 'human will'.[105] Rei wakes up at the end of the episode and tells Shinji, 'I think I am the Third'.[106] In this scene, Rei is alluding to being the third Rei clone. Her body dies, her memory is vague, but her feelings pass on to each clone. Rei is yet to understand the shifts in her physical status. Here, Rei weighs up her emotions for Shinji and Gendo and weighs up her loyalty to them. This indicates that emotion plays a role in the consideration of proportionality – even in a soldier who is built for combat.

Rei struggles through a different experience compared with Shinji. She looks at her life through a haze of lost memories and unexplained emotions, which leads her to different conclusions. As a homunculus, her personality seems to metamorphose according to the last recorded mental state she was in before her current body is no longer usable. In her new clone, despite her

101 Schott (2008), p 125.
102 Davidovic (2018), p 173; Bazargan-Forward (2018), p 195.
103 May (2007), p 212.
104 Lazar (2017), p 119.
105 Schott (2008), p 124.
106 Masuo (1996), '涙' ('Tears').

memory loss, her emotional state continues to evolve. In a way, she remembers the impression of her last emotions but cannot fully comprehend why she feels the way she does. Her emotions are 'not transparent to [herself] and [she is] in a relation of self-alienation'.[107] This is explored by reflecting her emotions through an Angel in Episode 23.[108] In this episode, the 16th Angel biofuses with Rei and starts a conversation with her inner self. The Angel mirrors Rei's feelings back to Rei, who finally identifies her emptiness as loneliness and not an inability to identify emotions. Depression and isolation have caused too many emotions to build up inside of her, leaving her emotionally numb and struggling to identify them.[109] This demonstrates that Rei's mental state reflects human emotions and functions, but when her body dies her mental state holds on to her emotional data – though not her memory data.

In this scene, Rei is experiencing a moral dilemma without sufficient information to make her decision. This raises an important critique of the child's state of mind when considering a question like proportionality. A child soldier such as Rei can be placed in a position where they need to weigh up different positions and act, but sometimes child soldiers make decisions without all the data needed to decide.

Through the analysis of the child's identity or state of mind, *Evangelion* demonstrates that a decision on proportionality, from the perspective of a child, will only involve the aspects of their life that they can see and feel, not the wider global picture. The global picture involves the discussion of the child soldier's responsibility. The narrative explores the condition of the child soldier and elaborates on the issue of status within *jus in bello*. When placed in the position of having to decide on a proportionate act within armed conflict, the child soldier may also be morally responsible – or feel morally responsible.

Principle 3: Moral responsibility

Evangelion explores the moral responsibility of the soldier and expands on the discussion of child soldiers by indicating that the child's identity plays a large role in the imagery of the hero. Shinji can be described as the perfect image of a hero as he reflects a number of relevant hero tropes.[110] More specifically, within the *mecha* and *sekai kei* genre constructions, he is shy, gets

107 Schott (2008), p 124.
108 Masuo (1996), '涙' ('Tears').
109 Li et al (2013), pp 5–7.
110 Campbell (2017), p 274; Elkin (1955), p 99.

things wrong and is cowardly.[111] However, he continues to rise to the occasion and even surpass his potential.[112]

Shinji's moral status incorporates these components of heroic imagery. Shinji's moral status is further solidified by drawing Shinji into the Human Instrumentality Project, where all consciousness is absorbed into his mind. Shinji's consciousness is unstable from the grief from killing Kaworu. But as this event unfolds, there is another aspect of the *jus in bello* that is revealed: responsibility.[113] Shinji becomes responsible for the violence by posing a threat to life, extending liability to Shinji as a soldier. Shinji makes the final transformation into 'a tool to advance the good of others' by deciding to kill Kaworu.[114]

The *jus in bello* discussions around responsibility come from the revisionist perspectives of just war theory. Soldiers may have some responsibility for the violence in war; however, that responsibility also moves backwards, from the orders made by a commander all the way to the involvement of the state.[115] Lazar explores the concept of the right to life and the soldier who 'can be responsible for a threat in virtue of posing it oneself, or contributing to it, or even failing to prevent it'.[116] These discussions raise more questions about the status of the soldier.[117] However, on the flipside, there are also discussions of moral responsibility.[118]

The child soldier can be viewed as an unjust combatant and has one of three available excuses that mitigate the circumstances for the responsibility of children in armed conflict.[119] Specifically, McMahan suggests, 'Just combatants should show them mercy, even at the cost of additional risk to themselves, in order to try to allow these already greatly wronged children a chance at life'.[120] Although McMahan makes some identification of the child's circumstances in armed conflict, children are often abducted or forced to participate in armed conflict. *Evangelion* suggests a stronger responsibility on the just combatants – even state bodies to limit the involvement of children in armed conflict. This is suggested by using children conscripted into NERV, because without them the EVA will not be operational. The children link their psychology with the cyborgs, which are linked to specific children

111 Poitras (2008), p 57; Goldberg (2004); Routt (2000), p 29; Broderick (2002), p 11; Howard (2014), p 370.
112 Campbell (2017), p 105.
113 May (2007), p 192.
114 Lazar (2017), p 119; Bazargan-Forward (2018), p 195.
115 Lazar (2017), p 119; Campbell (2017), p 274; Elkin (1955), p 99.
116 Lazar (2017), p 119; Benbaji (2007), p 560.
117 Benbaji (2007), p 559
118 Benbaji (2007), p 560.
119 McMahan (2009), p 200; Lazar (2017), p 119; Benbaji (2007), p 560.
120 McMahan (2009), p 202.

due to their mothers' souls inside the EVA. Only specific children can do this. This places an incredible responsibility on Shinji to provide salvation to all of humanity because only the children can hold the burden of defending humanity.

Evangelion critiques these circumstances through the suggestions of the mother EVA link, especially during the psychological explorations of the children's links to their respective mothers. For example, Asuka's link to her mother slowly becomes hatred, and as she develops into a woman, her identity becomes less linked with that of her mother, and she loses control of her EVA. In comparison, Shinji accepts the role of saviour early in the series and, by killing Kaworu, accepts further responsibility for the fate of humanity, thus highlighting the problematic solution to the world's inability to resolve conflict that burdens children with adult responsibilities. This suggests that adults need to take more responsibility for the harms of armed conflict.

Shinji comes to discover that understanding each other involves facing each person from the other's perspective, embracing friendship and working through whatever differences might be causing friction. There can be multiple realities occurring at the same time. Shinji's communications with himself and others reveal alternative realities that can be made possible through mediation. The narrative recognises that if Shinji failed to fulfil the prophecy and kill the final Angel, he would not be able to reject the project. Unknowingly, Shinji has contributed to killing.[121] Even if the killing seemed unjust, killing his love reveals to him that the Angels are not bad. Shinji, like Kaworu, acts out of 'loyalty and a belief that their cause is just'.[122]

The final scenes of the series suggest that 'some wrongful killing is worse than others' – in other words, if Shinji had not killed the Angels, he would not have been able to protect non-combatants who were affected by the Angels and avoid the catastrophe that came with them.[123] This suggests that 'in all conflicts this clean division between the "just side" and the "unjust side" falls apart'.[124] All souls have rights, and they 'retain those rights'.[125] More typically, the final scene reveals Shinji's struggles for freedom and love.[126] The children in *Evangelion* experience being offered the ability to consent under conditions that force them to pilot EVA. They are unconscious selves at the end of the series through Shinji, which extensively discusses the need to retain individual rights and access to the freedoms that are unavailable to them.

121 McMahan (2009), p 210.
122 Lazar (2017), p 120; Schott (2008), p 124.
123 Lazar (2017), p 120; McMahan (2009), p 210.
124 Lazar (2017), p 120; Schott (2008), p 124.
125 Lazar (2017), p 120.; McMahan (2008), p 21; Orend (2013), pp 105–59.
126 Alfredson (2023), p 310.

Evangelion critiques humanity for giving human rights and freedoms to children while simultaneously denying them access to those rights. Further, the discussion of responsibility suggests that responsibility extends to the world at large[127] to participate in eliminating the circumstances that lead to the involvement of children in armed conflict.

Conclusion

This chapter has argued that the second limb of the just war theory in *Evangelion* develops attentional narratives that can transform understandings of law, war and childhood.[128] *Evangelion* explores the criteria involved in the *jus in bello* principle, such as distinction and necessity, proportionality and responsibility through the imagery of the child in *Evangelion*. This chapter has explored the child's identity and outlined that it is an important factor in the discussion of children in armed conflict. Further, *Evangelion* discussed the inner conflicts of the child's identity and determined that the child's perspectives of proportionality are often limited to what the child can see and feel. For the characters in *Evangelion*, decisions were made based on their feelings of love, friendship and aspects of the self, over wider considerations of the global atmosphere of armed conflict. Through the course of the series, Shinji and the other children critique the *jus in bello* principles as they experience different forms of friendship and love. At the end of the series, Shinji applies his sense of personhood to his confrontation with Kaworu and, through his experience of the Human Instrumentality Project, determines that the world can establish a better understanding of conflict by exploring identities. Finally, *Evangelion* raises an important discussion about the moral responsibility of soldiers and concludes that a larger responsibility should be placed on the world to participate in eliminating the circumstances that lead to the involvement of children in armed conflict. *Evangelion* challenges the understanding of armed conflict by exploring the child's identity and the moral responsibility of leaders, offering an alternative discourse on the *jus in bello* principles.

References

Secondary sources

Lisa S Alfredson (2023) 'Child Soldiers as Contemporary Slaves: A Human Rights Approach' 22 *Journal of Human Rights* 307.

Anime News Network (2022) 'Neon Genesis Evangelion (TV)' 25 February 2022, http://www.animenewsnetwork.com/encyclopedia/anime.php?id=49

127 Arbour (2008), p 448.
128 Schott (2008), p 125.

Sandra Annett (2014) *Anime Fan Communities: Transcultural Flows and Frictions*, Palgrave Macmillan.
Louise Arbour (2008) 'The Responsibility to Protect as a Duty of Care in International Law and Practice' 34 *Review of International Studies* 445.
Michael Asimow and Shannon Mader (2004) *Law and Popular Culture: A Course Book*, Peter Lang.
Jason Bainbridge (2006) 'Lawyers, Justice and the State: The Sliding Signifier of Law in Popular Culture' 15 *Griffith Law Review* 153.
Andreu Ballús and Alba G Torrents (2014) '*Evangelion* as Second Impact: Forever Changing That Which Never Was' 9 *Mechademia: Second Arc* 283.
Saba Bazargan-Forword (2018) 'Weighing Civilian Lives in War: Domestic and Foreign' in Larry May (ed), *The Cambridge Handbook of the Just War*, Cambridge University Press, 168.
David M Beatty (2004) *The Ultimate Rule of Law*, Oxford University Press.
John Belton (2013) 'Color and Meaning in Marnie' in Simon Brown, Sarah Street and Liz Watkins (eds), *Color and the Moving Image: History, Theory, Aesthetics, Archive*. Routledge, 189.
Yitzhak Benbaji (2007) 'The Responsibility of Soldiers and the Ethics of Killing in War' 57 *The Philosophical Quarterly* 558.
Theresa Betancourt (2011) 'Developmental Perspectives on Moral Agency in Former Child Soldiers' 54 *Human Development* 307.
Gabriella Blum (2010) 'The Dispensable Lives of Soldiers' 2 *The Journal of Legal Analysis* 115.
David A Bosworth, (2011) 'David, Jether, and Child Soldiers' 36 *Journal for the Study of the Old Testament* 185.
Helen Brocklehurst (2005) 'Just War? Just Children?' in Mark Evans (ed), *Just War Theory: A Reappraisal*, Edinburg University Press, 114.
Mick Broderick (2002) 'Anime's Apocalypse: *Neon Genesis Evangelion* as Millenarian Mecha' 7 *Intersections: Gender, History and Culture in the Asian Context* 1.
Kathryn Brown, Michael Asimow and David Ray Papke (2014) *Law and Popular Culture International Perspectives*, Cambridge Scholars.
Simon Brown, Sarah Street and Liz Watkins (2013) *Color and the Moving Image: History, Theory, Aesthetics, Archive*, Routledge.
Joseph Campbell (2017) *The Hero with a Thousand Faces*, Yogi Impressions.
Enzo Cannizzaro (2014) 'Proportionality in the Law of Armed Conflict' in Andrew Clapham and Paola Gaeta (eds), *The Oxford Handbook of International Law in Armed Conflict*, Oxford University Press, 332.
Child Soldiers International (2004) *Child Soldiers Global Report 2004 – Nepal*, https://www.amnesty.org/en/wp-content/uploads/2021/08/act760082004en.pdf
Jovana Davidovic (2018) 'Proportionality and Necessity in Bello' in Larry May (ed), *The Cambridge Handbook of the Just War*, Cambridge University Press, 152.
Harendra de Silva, Chris Hobbs and Helga Hanks (2001) 'Conscription of Children in Armed Conflict: A Form of Child Abuse. A Study of 19 Former Child Soldiers' 10 *Child Abuse Review* 125.
Melissa de Zwart, Bernadette Richards and Suzanne Le Mire (2015) *Law and Popular Culture in Australia*, LexisNexis Butterworths.
Hylke Dijkstra, Myriam Dunn Cavelty, Nicole Lenne and YF Revkers (2022) 'War in Ukraine' 43 *Contemporary Security Policy* 464.

Lan Dong (2012) 'Childhood in War and Violence: *Turtles Can Fly* and *The Kite Runner*' in Vibiana Bowman Cvetkovic and Debbie Olson (eds), *Portrayals of Children in Popular Culture: Fleeting Images*, Lexington Books, 169.

Mark A Drumbl (2012) *Reimagining Child Soldiers in International Law and Policy*, Oxford University Press.

Frederick Elkin (1955) 'Popular Hero Symbols and Audience Gratifications' 29 *The Journal of Education Sociology* 97.

Christian Enemark (2013) 'Unmanned Drones and the Ethics of War' in Frits Allhoff, Nicholas G Evans, and Adam Henschke (eds), *Routledge Handbook of Ethics and War: Just War Theory in the 21st Century*, Routledge, 327.

Cecile Fabre (2013) *Cosmopolitan War*, Oxford University Press.

Paula S Fass (2006) *Children of a New World: Society, Culture, and Globalization*, New York University Press.

Shannon French (2018) 'Distinction and Civilian Immunity' in Larry May (ed), *The Cambridge Handbook of the Just War*, Cambridge University Press, 152.

Lawrence Friedman (1989) 'Law, Lawyers and Popular Culture' 98 *Yale Law Journal* 1579.

Patrick W Galbraith (2022) 'The *Evangelion* Boom: On the Explosion of Fan Markets and Lifestyles in Heisei Japan' in Noriko Murai, Jeff Kingston and Tina Burrett (eds), *Japan in the Heisei Era (1989–2019): Multidisciplinary Perspectives*, Routledge, 234.

Scott Gates and Simon Reich (2010) *Child Soldiers in the Age of Fractured States*, University of Pittsburgh Press.

John Edward Gibbs (2012) *Mise-en-Scene: Film Style and Interpretation*, Columbia University Press.

Wendy Goldberg (2004) 'This Isn't Your Mother's Mecha: The Adolescent and Narrative in *Neon Genesis Evangelion*' Popular Culture Association National Conference, New Orleans, https://www.evamonkey.com/writings/goldberg-wendy-this-isnt-your-mothers-mecha-the-adolescent-and-narrative-in-neon-genesis-evangelion.php

Steven Greenfield and Guy Osborn (2006) *Readings in Law and Popular Culture*, Routledge.

Adil Ahmad Haque (2017) 'A Theory of *Jus in Bello* Proportionality' in Jens David Ohlin, Larry May and Claire Finkelstein (eds), *Weighing Lives in War*, Oxford University Press, 188.

Akiko Hashimoto (2015) '"Something Dreadful Happened in the Past": War Stories for Children in Japanese Popular Culture' 13 *The Asia-Pacific Journal* 1.

Christopher Howard (2014) 'The Ethics of *Sekai-kei*: Reading Hiroki Azuma with Slavoj Žižek' 7 *Science Fiction Film and Television* 365.

Layal Issa (2019) 'Avoiding the Third Tragedy: Evaluating Criminal Responsibility of Child Soldiers Under International Law' 34 *Temple International and Comparative Law Journal* 61.

David Michael Jackson (2011) 'Jus in Bello' in Deen K Chatterjee (ed), *Encyclopedia of Global Justice*, Springer, 584.

Ana Maria Jiménez (2019) 'Challenges for the Protection of Child Victims of Recruitment and Use in an Era of Complex Armed Conflicts: The Colombian Case' in Mark A Drumbl and Jastine C Barrett (eds), *Research Handbook on Child Soldiers*, Edward Elgar, 52.

Kamayani Kumar and Angelie Multani (2019) *Childhood Traumas: Narratives and Representations*, Routledge.
Lasanda Kurukulasuriya (2003) 'Child Soldiers Key to Rebuilding Sri Lanka' 16 *Herizons* 13.
Amanda Landa (2012) 'Mechanized Bodies of Adolescence: Weaponized Children, National Allegory and Japanese Anime' 3 *Red Feather Journal* 16.
Anthony F Lang, Cian O'Driscoll and John Williams (2013) 'Introduction: The Just War Tradition and the Practice of Political Authority' in Anthony F Lang, Cian O'Driscoll and John Williams (eds), *Just War: Authority, Tradition, and Practice*, Georgetown University Press, 1.
Seth Lazar (2015) 'Risky Killing and the Ethics of War' 126 *Ethics* 91.
Seth Lazar (2017) 'Evaluating the Revisionist Critique of Just War Theory' 146 *Daedalus* 113.
Carl Li, Mari Nakamura and Martin Roth (2013) 'Japanese Science Fiction in Converging Media: Alienation and *Neon Genesis Evangelion*' 6 *Asiascape*, http://www.asiascape.org/resources/publications/asiascape-ops6.pdf
David Luban (2017) 'Just War Theory and the Laws of War as Nonidentical Twins' 31 *Ethics & International Affairs* 433.
William P MacNeil (2007) *Lex Populi: The Jurisprudence of Popular Culture*, Stanford University Press.
Paul M Malone, Madeline Ashby and Thomas Lamarre (2010) 'Review: Three Faces of Eva' 5 *Mechademia: Second Arc* 345.
Larry May (2007) *War Crimes and Just War*, Cambridge University Press.
Chris Mayer (2013) 'Minimizing Harm to Combatants: Nonlethal Weapons, Combatants' Rights, and State Responsibility' in Frits Allhoff, Nicholas G Evans and Adam Henschke (eds), *Routledge Handbook of Ethics and War: Just War Theory in the 21st Century*, Routledge, 301.
Julie McBride (2014) *The War Crime of Child Soldier Recruitment*, TMC Asser Press.
Jeff McMahan (2008) 'The Morality of War and the Law of War' in David Rodin and Henry Shue (eds), *Just and Unjust Warriors: The Moral and Legal Status of Soldiers*, Oxford University Press, 19.
Jeff McMahan (2009) *Killing in War*, Oxford University Press.
Jeff McMahan (2017) 'Proportionality Defense' in Jens David Ohlin, Larry May and Claire Finkelstein (eds), *Weighing Lives in War*, Oxford University Press, 131.
Nils Melzer (2014) 'The Principle of Distinction Between Civilians and Combatants' in Andrew Clapham and Paola Gaeta (eds), *The Oxford Handbook of International Law in Armed Conflict*, Oxford University Press, 296.
Valerie Morkevičius (2018) *Realist Ethics: Just War Traditions as Power Politics*, Cambridge University Press.
Emily Wati Muir (2023) 'To Face the World Alone or Together: *Jus Ad Bellum* and the Lives of Child Soldiers in Neon Genesis Evangelion' 5 *Law, Technology and Humans* 40.
Benjamin Nickl (2018) 'Through the Eyes of Child Soldiers: On War, Violence and Trauma in Popular Entertainment Fictions' 1 *Close Encounters in War Journal* 82.
Office of the Special Representative of the Secretary-General for Children and Armed Conflict (2018) 'Reintegration of Former Child Soldiers' https://childrenandarmedconflict.un.org/wp-content/uploads/2018/09/Reintergration-brochure-layout.pdf

Jens David Ohlin (2018) 'The Basic Structure of *Jus in Bello*' in Larry May (ed), *The Cambridge Handbook of the Just War*, Cambridge University Press, 234.

Brian Orend (2013) *The Morality of War*, Broadview Press.

Augustine SJ Park (2010) 'Child Soldiers and Distributive Justice: Addressing the Limits of Law?' 53 *Crime, Law and Social Change* 329.

Ashley Pearson, Thomas Giddens and Kieran Tranter (2018) 'Crime Fighting Robots and Duelling Pocket Monsters' in Ashley Pearson, Thomas Giddens and Kieran Tranter (eds), *Law and Justice in Japanese Popular Culture: From Crime Fighting Robots to Duelling Pocket Monsters*, Routledge, 1.

Ashley Pearson and Kieran Tranter (2015) 'Code, Nintendo's Super Mario and Digital Legality' 28 *International Journal for the Semiotics of Law* 825.

Timothy D Peters (2015) 'Reading the Law Made Strange: Cultural Legal Studies, Theology and Speculative Fiction' in Cassandra Sharp and Marrett Leiboff (eds), *Cultural Legal Studies: Law's Popular Cultures and the Metamorphosis of Law*, Routledge, 252.

Gilles Poitras (2008) 'Contemporary Anime in Japanese Popular Culture' in Mark W MacWilliams (ed), *Japanese Visual Culture: Explorations in the World of Manga and Anime*, ME Sharp, 48.

Dennis Redmond (2007) 'Anime and East Asian Culture: *Neon Genesis Evangelion*' 24 *Quarterly Review of Film and Video* 183.

Michael Rieder and Imti Choonara (2012) 'Armed Conflict and Child Health' 97 *Archives of Disease in Childhood* 59.

David Rodin and Henry Shue (2008) 'Introduction' in David Rodin and Henry Shue (eds), *Just and Unjust Warriors: The Moral and Legal Status of Solders*, Oxford University Press, 1.

Heather M Roff (2013) 'Killing in War: Responsibility, Liability and Lethal Autonomous Robots' in Frits Allhoff, Nicholas G Evans and Adam Henschke (eds), *Routledge Handbook of Ethics and War: Just War Theory in the 21st Century*, Routledge, 352.

David M Rosen (2007) 'Child Soldiers, International Humanitarian Law, and the Globalization of Childhood' 109 *American Anthropologist* 296.

David M Rosen (2012) *Child Soldiers: A Reference Handbook*, ABC-CLIO, LLC.

William D Routt (2000) 'Stillness and Style in Neon Genesis Evangelion' 8 *Animation Journal* 28.

Elisabeth Schauer and Thomas Elbert (2010) 'The Psychological Impact of Child Soldiering' in E Martz (ed), *Trauma Rehabilitation After War and Conflict: Community and Individual Perspectives*, Springer, 311.

Sally J Scholz (2011) 'War, Just and Unjust' in Deen K Chatterjee (ed), *Encyclopedia of Global Justice*, Springer, 1146.

Robin May Schott (2008) 'Just War and the Problem of Evil' 23 *Hypatia* 122.

Cassandra Sharp and Marett Leiboff (2016) *Cultural Legal Studies: Law's Popular Cultures and the Metamorphosis of Law*, Routledge.

Sherry Shenoda, Ayesha Kadir and Jeffrey Goldhagen (2015) 'Children and Armed Conflict' 136 *Pediatrics* e309.

Sherry Shenoda, Ayesha Kadir, Shelly Pitterman, Jeffrey Goldhagen, Parminder S Suchdev, Kevin J Chan, Cynthia R Howard, Patrick McGann, Nicole E St Clair, Katherine Yun and Linda A Arnold (2018) 'The Effects of Armed Conflict on Children' 142 *Pediatrics* e2018.

Iris Shepherd (2012) 'Representations of Children in Pixar Films: 1995–2011' in Vibiana Bowman Cvetkovic, and Debbie C Olson (eds), *Portrayals of Children in Popular Culture: Fleeting Images*, Lexington Books, 147.

Jessica Silbey (2002) 'What We Do When We Do Law and Popular Culture?' 27 *Law & Social Inquiry* 139.

Margaret Thornton (2002) *Romancing the Tomes: Popular Culture, Law and Feminism*, Routledge-Cavendish.

Patrick Tomlin (2020) 'Proportionality in War: Revising Revisionism' 131 *Ethics* 34.

Christopher Toner (2010) 'The Logical Structure of Just War Theory' 14 *Journal of Ethics* 81.

Shinsuke Tsuchiya (2022) 'From Acting Out Stories to Telling Stories: Elicitation of Oral Narrative Productions in the Japanese Language Classroom' 56 *Japanese Language and Literature* 355.

Fahim Ul Hassan, Kasi Sekar and Aravind E Raj (2017) 'Healing the Wounds of Conflict: Need for School Mental Health Programs for Children Affected by Armed Conflict in Kashmir' 8 *Indian Journal of Health and Wellbeing* 1510.

UNICEF (2022) 'Children Recruited by Armed Forces or Armed Groups' https://www.unicef.org/protection/children-recruited-by-armed-forces

United Nations (2023) 'Child Recruitment and Use' https://childrenandarmedconflict.un.org/six-grave-violations/child-soldiers

Sofie Vindevogel, Kathleen Coppens, Ilse Derluyn, Marten De Schryver, Gerrit Loots and Eric Broekaert (2011) 'Forced Conscription of Children During Armed Conflict: Experiences of Former Child Soldiers in Northern Uganda' 35 *Child Abuse & Neglect* 551.

Joachim von Elbe (1939) 'The Evolution of the Concept of the Just War in International Law' 33 *The American Journal of International Law* 665.

Michael Walzar (1977) *Just and Unjust Wars: A moral Argument with Historical Illustrations*, Basic Books.

Liz Watkins (2013) 'Herbert G Ponting's Materials and Texts' in Simon Brown, Sarah Street and Liz Watkins (eds), *Color and the Moving Image: History, Theory, Aesthetics, Archive*, Routledge, 23.

Michael Wessells (2006) *Child Soldiers: From Violence to Protection*, Harvard University Press.

Shelby Wolf, Karen Coats, Patricia Enciso and Christine Jenkins (2011) *Handbook of Research on Children's and Young Adult Literature*, Routledge.

Emeline Wuilbercq (2021) 'Factbox: Ten Facts About Child Soldiers Around the World' *Thomas Reuters*, https://www.reuters.com/article/us-global-childsoldiers-factbox-trfn-idUSKBN2AC0CB

International Conventions

Hague Conference on Private International Law (1980) *Hague Convention on the Civil Aspects of International Child Abduction*, https://www.ag.gov.au/families-and-marriage/families/international-family-law-and-children/hague-convention-civil-aspects-international-child-abduction

International Committee of the Red Cross (ICRC) (1949) *Geneva Convention for the Amelioration of the Condition of the Wounded and Sick in Armed Forces in the Field* (First Geneva Convention).

International Committee of the Red Cross (ICRC) (1949) *Geneva Convention for the Amelioration of the Condition of Wounded, Sick and Shipwrecked Members of Armed Forces at Sea (Second Geneva Convention)*, 75 UNTS 85.

International Committee of the Red Cross (ICRC) (1949) *Geneva Convention Relative to the Treatment of Prisoners of War (Third Geneva Convention)*, 75 UNTS 135.

International Committee of the Red Cross (ICRC) (1949) *Geneva Convention Relative to the Protection of Civilian Persons in Time of War (Fourth Geneva Convention)*, 75 UNTS 287.

United Nations (20 November 1989) UN Doc A/44/49 Convention on the Rights of the Child, entered into force on 2 September 1990.

United Nations General Assembly (1998) Rome Statute of the International Criminal Court.

United Nations Human Rights Office of the High Commission (2002), UNTS Vol/ 2173, 222 Optional Protocol to the Convention on the Rights of the Child on the involvement of children in Armed Conflict, 12 February 2002.

Television programs

Hiroyuki Ishidō (dir) (1995) 新世紀エヴァンゲリオン *(Neon Genesis Evangelion)*, "鳴らない, 電話" *(The silent phone)*, TV Tokyo, season 1 episode 3.

Tsuyoshi Kaga (dir) (1995) 新世紀エヴァンゲリオン *(Neon Genesis Evangelion)*, "雨、逃げ出した後" *(Rain after running away)*, TV Tokyo, season 1, episode 4.

Masayuki (dir) (1996) 新世紀エヴァンゲリオン *(Neon Genesis Evangelion)*"最後のシ者" *(The last cometh)*, TV Tokyo, season 1, episode 24.

Shoichi Masuo (dir) (1996) 新世紀エヴァンゲリオン *(Neon Genesis Evangelion)*, "涙" *(Tears)*, TV Tokyo, season 1, episode 23.

Kazuya Tsurumaki (dir) (1995) 新世紀エヴァンゲリオン *(Neon Genesis Evangelion)*,"使徒、襲来" *(Angel attack)*, season 1, episode 1, TV Tokyo.

Chapter 5

Science fiction and interstellar rights and institutions

Erika Techera, Renae Barker and Meredith Blake

Introduction

Law is frequently reactive to problems as they arise, yet international space law is one of the few areas that has historically been more future-focused. The Outer Space Treaty and the Moon Agreement were far ahead of their time in imagining a future filled with commercial space activities and private actors. While the treaties predicted these technological advances, their implementation was still science fiction in the 1960s and 1970s when these treaties were drafted. Shows such as *Star Trek* and *The Jetsons* imagined what future space habitation might look like when the reality was still far out of reach, but their imaginaries are now becoming a reality. Yet relatively little attention was paid to potential challenges associated with human interactions and communities of people living and working in space. Perhaps that was a step too far into the imaginary. Current and near-future human space travel and habitation plans, however, draw sharply into focus the importance of addressing this gap.[1] One aspect that has attracted limited scholarship is the protection of rights and freedoms. Of course, the fields of human and cultural rights have evolved considerably over the last 50 years,[2] reflecting the recognition of fundamental human values; still, there is little doubt that minimum standards set in international legal instruments continue to be broken.[3] There is little doubt that we can, and should, learn from Earth-based experiences to shape the jurisprudence of the future for space activities, yet science fiction also has much that can inform forward-facing developments.

Countless sources in creative writing have portrayed the challenges facing humanity, many of them dystopian in their grim assessment of humanity's flaws. The often sparsely regulated and physically challenging environments

1 For example, commercial space tourism opportunities are now offered by Virgin Galactic, Blue Origin and other companies, and the NASA Artemis mission is planning to return to the Moon in 2025.

2 Baderin and Ssenyonjo (2016).

3 Harvey (2015), pp 46–47.

DOI: 10.4324/9781003412274-6

of the jungle (*Heart of Darkness*),[4] desert islands (*Lord of the Flies*)[5] and the contexts of viral contagion (*Blindness*)[6] and medical research (*The People in the Trees*)[7] are associated with fictional worlds where, untethered by rules and norms, people do awful things to each other. Other science fiction, explored further in this chapter, depicts idealistic futures filled with evolved technologies, species and societies. The question is how to prevent the former and facilitate the latter. It is in this context that we explore the application of human and cultural rights and religious freedoms in space.

The prospect of an ongoing presence of humanity in space brings with it difficult questions about how to properly regulate human interactions, given the unique challenges posed by harsh and remote environments. Space undoubtedly represents such an environment.[8] Moving out of home Earth exposes humans to a profoundly foreign environment in which new norms around interactions with others must be forged. Science fiction depicts alternative universes in which chaos often seems to reign, or utopian societies flourish. Reality lives somewhere in the middle of these extremes, yet it is from extremes that we can ultimately learn the most valuable lessons. We argue that human history and the fictional creations of novelists and filmmakers clearly highlight the threats to, and imagined futures of, human equality and dignity which space poses. This draws sharply into focus the relevance of human and cultural rights and freedoms, and the values at the heart of the United Nations Declaration of Human Rights.[9] We see living and working in space as replete with these threats, but also providing opportunities to tackle the challenges facing humanity while avoiding a repetition of past atrocities. Rather than merely minimising the risk that reality will mimic science fiction dystopias, we must find ways to make off-world societies more just. While it is tempting to consider future human dealings with technology or alien life forms, here we restrict ourselves to human-to-human interactions, and in particular to the provision of individual rights and freedoms necessary for peaceful and successful space travel and habitation. Given the dependence of human societies on normative order – associated with both informal

4 Conrad (1899).
5 Golding (1954).
6 Saramago (1995)
7 Yanagihara (2013).
8 Galvez-Pol et al (2021).
9 Universal Declaration on Human Rights (1948) (UDHR), Preamble: 'Whereas recognition of the inherent dignity and of the equal and inalienable rights of all members of the human family is the foundation of freedom, justice and peace in the world. Whereas disregard and contempt for human rights have resulted in barbarous acts which have outraged the conscience of mankind, and the advent of a world in which human beings shall enjoy freedom of speech and belief and freedom from fear and want has been proclaimed as the highest aspiration of the common people'.

rules and formal legal regulation[10] – these issues should be of fundamental concern.

We seek to contribute to scholarship on the development of innovative laws for space travel and habitation, drawing upon futures envisaged in science fiction. We focus on science fiction for two purposes. The first is to provide conceptions of space futures that give the 'speculative grounding' for situations that might arise. In doing so, science fiction provides some support for our suggested Prime Directive solution.[11] The second is because science fiction provides some justification for the facilitative role that we argue law can play in space futures. Law has both a regulatory and facilitative role. The regulatory role is demonstrated by current international space treaties, which provide global rules for outer space, as well as domestic laws that implement these treaties and create national systems for a range of activities including permitting launches and returns and providing a framework for liability. US domestic law also plays a facilitative role by creating the environment to encourage investment in private space industries and the development of commercial space resource exploration and exploitation. International space law once provided a facilitative role but no longer does so, given the rapid pace of change. We argue that international law can play this role again, in the context of human space travel and habitation associated with living and working in space.

This chapter draws on selected film and television case studies as vehicles to identify potential problems and prospective solutions, and so to reimagine future space law. *Gattaca* and *Solaris* raise questions as to the motives behind space travel and habitation, as well as the prospect of lawlessness where science might operate unfettered from earthbound constraints. These films also question what are assumed to be universal human values as they explore the consequences of ignoring human rights in extreme environments and situations that were not envisaged during the drafting of current Earth-based human rights regimes. The space-based future of human rights is extended using *Babylon 5* to emphasise potential freedom of religion and belief (FoRB) in a hostile and potentially lethal environment. Where even access to oxygen cannot be taken for granted, the 'necessity'[12] to keep people alive in a hostile environment has the potential to be used as a trump card allowing for the wide-scale abrogation of human rights in the name of survival.[13] In considering the implications of these examples drawn from science fiction, we consider near-future human space travel and settlements – be they based on

10 Note Hobbes' view that laws are needed to 'tie their hands from rapine and revenge'; Hobbes (2008).

11 Tranter (2011).

12 See International Covenant on Civil and Political Rights (1966) (ICCPR), Art 18(3).

13 For a decision of other formulations of limitations of FoRB, see Barker (2024).

the Moon, other celestial bodies or artificial satellites orbiting Earth. The science fiction examples upon which we draw are based at various points along imagined future human histories, from *Gattaca*, which is set effectively in the present day, through to *Babylon 5*, set in 2257–62.[14] Despite their disparate time periods, they provide regulatory insights that can be used to inform the jurisprudence of the future. In seeking solutions, we draw upon the fictional institutions and governance arrangements in *Star Trek* to advance the future governance of humans in space. We pose the novel idea of a 'Prime Directive', incorporating both a positive duty to protect others from distress as well as a right to be protected oneself. This advance in current space and human rights law seeks to drive both individual and collective action in and for space futures.

The chapter commences by providing an overview of current global space law relevant to issues of human rights, freedoms and values. The sections that follow explore two critical challenges missing from current frameworks: religious freedoms and human rights. The final section explores one idea for the future that is drawn from science fiction, but also seeks to overcome some limitations of contemporary earthbound governance.

A brief overview of space law

Early global efforts to develop principles for outer space began with the establishment of the UN Office for Outer Space Affairs (UNOOSA) in 1958 to promote peaceful cooperation in outer space. When the UN Committee on the Peaceful Uses of Outer Space (UNCOPUOS) was formed in 1959, UNOOSA became the secretariat for it. UNCOPUOS continues to assist the UN General Assembly (UNGA) by developing policies related to outer space on behalf of UN member states. The establishment of such bodies was forward-facing, an example of law being future-facing, as the first human being to travel in space was still three years away.[15]

In 1963, a UNGA Resolution set out fundamental legal principles on the peaceful uses of outer space; this was later 'hardened' into the Outer Space Treaty (OST).[16] This binding legal instrument incorporates critical principles focused on peace, cooperation, and mutual assistance, drawing from very real Earth-based concerns of the time. This instrument remains relevant today, and has been broadly endorsed by the international community. Its principles include that outer space is the province of all humankind, and

14 Referred to in the series as 'the dawn of the third age of mankind'.

15 Yuri Gagarin became the first human in space in 1961.

16 Declaration of Legal Principles Governing the Activities of States in the Exploration and Use of Outer Space (1962) and the Outer Space Treaty (1967) (OST).

exploration and use of outer space shall be for the benefit of all countries.[17] Importantly, outer space – including the Moon – cannot be nationally appropriated.[18] Activities must be carried out in accordance with international law, and peace and security are to be maintained.[19] Relevantly, Article I[2] provides:

> Outer space, including the Moon and other celestial bodies, shall be free for exploration and use by all States *without discrimination of any kind, on a basis of equality and in accordance with international law*, and there shall be free access to all areas of celestial bodies.[20]

Whether these protections extend to individual rights is debatable, and it is more likely that they envisage freedom of access and exploration for all nations. Only limited guidance is provided by Article III, which requires state parties to

> carry on activities in the exploration and use of outer space, including the Moon and other celestial bodies, in accordance with international law including the Charter of the United Nations in the interest of maintaining international peace and security and promoting international co-operation and understanding.[21]

Also important is Article V, which provides that astronauts (which are undefined) are to be considered 'envoys of mankind' with agreed protections afforded to them. Whether the term 'astronaut' includes non-military trained, non-governmental personnel remains a matter of debate.[22] Cooperation and mutual assistance are underscored, with due regard (again undefined) to be given to the corresponding rights of other nations.[23] Presumably, this would extend to the protection and regulation of nationals who may be engaged in outer space activities. The treaty has attracted 109 signatories, including all of the space-faring nations. Even the most recent space governance developments continue to refer to, and endorse, the OST, cementing its place as central to future space governance.[24]

17 OST Art I.
18 OST Art II.
19 OST Arts II and III.
20 OST Art I[2]. Emphasis added.
21 OST Art III.
22 See Kumer (2020). Although beyond the scope of this chapter, the phrase 'envoy of mankind' points to a belief, common to science fiction, that humankind will meet other intelligent life as it ventures into space.
23 OST Art IX.
24 NASA, *The Artemis Accords* (2020).

The four subsequent legal instruments all build upon the foundation provided by the OST, with each instrument explicitly underlining this in the Preamble and/or text, before expanding upon specific aspects: rescue, liability and registration. The Rescue Agreement was adopted in 1968 and sets out obligations for the rescue and return of astronauts (still undefined) who have suffered an accident, are in distress or have unintentionally landed in foreign areas.[25] The Liability Convention (1972) expands upon the international responsibility and liability provisions in the OST.[26] Damage is defined as including personal injury, and therefore could accommodate mental distress[27] associated with restrictions on religious or other freedoms.[28] The Registration Convention (1975) establishes an international register of space objects and details of who must submit information and what must be provided.[29] As we will argue more fully below, the provisions in the Rescue Convention and Liability Convention relating to distress could form the foundation of a future space-based human rights regime founded on our proposed 'Prime Directive'. However, we note that this will require a subtle shift in emphasis and grammar from a mere right to be protected from distress, and states being liable for that distress, to individuals and states having positive obligations to prevent distress from occurring at all.

The final instrument adopted during this phase of space law development was the Moon Agreement (1979).[30] By now, science fiction was beginning to turn into reality with the first crewed landing on the Moon in 1969. Yet the Moon Agreement still contains legal provisions for what was science fiction, looking to future uses of the Moon. The Moon Agreement reaffirmed that the Moon 'shall be used by all State Parties exclusively for peaceful purposes' and shall be the 'province of all mankind'.[31] Peaceful purposes remain undefined, but could provide a foundation for recognition of religious, cultural and other human rights, although the onus would be placed on states to legislate for these. Interestingly, Article 4 was quite forward-looking in stating that exploration and use should be for the benefit of everyone – 'present and future'; albeit without exploring 'benefit' further. Although the principle of intergenerational equity 'is a rather new addition to the bundle of principles governing environmental issues', as Atapattu notes, 'it is at the heart of many

25 Agreement on the rescue of astronauts, the return of astronauts and the return of objects launched into outer space (1968) (Rescue Agreement).
26 Convention on the international liability for damage caused by space objects (1972) (Liability Convention).
27 We note that damages for 'mere distress' are often not recoverable in domestic law.
28 Liability Convention Art I(a).
29 Convention on registration of objects launched into outer space (1974) (Registration Convention).
30 Moon Agreement Art 1.
31 Moon Agreement Arts 2–4.

ancient legal traditions'.[32] Additional provisions include the requirement to safeguard the 'life and health of persons on the Moon', who are all to be considered astronauts.[33] This implies that astronauts are a subset of humans that may be living or working on the Moon, and thereby extends the protections afforded to them. The more controversial aspects of the Moon Agreement surround the efforts to go further than the OST in declaring the Moon and its natural resources to be the common heritage of humankind, with a regime to be developed to assess, manage and share benefits.[34] The international regime, including detailed procedures for the exploitation of lunar resources, has not emerged.[35]

The Moon Agreement was the last international treaty developed for outer space. Despite offering sensible ways forward, the treaty did not gain much international support. Although it remains in force, it is essentially of little effect in terms of setting standards for future activities on the Moon. It has been followed by decades of soft law in the form of declarations, recommendations and guidelines.[36] Some binding instruments have been adopted in narrow areas, but the vast majority of instruments of broad application are non-binding, and no detailed soft law for the rights of human participants in space travel and settlements has emerged.

Although space-faring nations adopted domestic legislation early,[37] the last 20 years have seen significant activity as they reformed their law to meet current and future needs.[38] In addition, other nations wishing to be space-faring and/or grow a space industry have also developed legal regimes.[39] These laws focus on national interests, in some cases including creating an environment to attract overseas investment and industry activity. The diversity is illustrated by the Australian and US legal approaches. Australian legislation

32 Atapattu (2019), p 170.

33 Moon Agreement Art 10.

34 Moon Agreement Art 11(1).

35 While beyond the scope of this chapter, science fiction dealing with the use of the moon and the perils of unregulated resource extraction could be employed to develop governance frameworks that help avoid such dystopian futures.

36 For example, the Declaration on International Cooperation in the Exploration and Use of Outer Space, Taking into Particular Account the Needs of Developing Countries (1996), the UNCOPUOS Space Debris Mitigation Guidelines (2007), Guidelines for the Long-term Sustainability of Outer Space Activities (2019) and the Recommendations on National Legislation Relevant to the Peaceful Exploration and Use of Outer Space (2013).

37 For example, the United States established NASA in 1958.

38 For example, Australia and the United States reformed their laws in 2018 and 2015, respectively. Australia's amended laws were preceded by the establishment of the Australian Space Agency, and include a licensing, permitting and liability regime to support space launches and returns. The US amendments seek to advance national interests in the commercial space industry by creating a regulatory context for investment and authorising commercial exploration and exploitation of space resources.

39 Luxembourg and New Zealand have both adopted space laws in the last five years.

focuses on permitting launches and returns from its territory,[40] whereas the US law goes much further in authorising commercial resource extraction on the Moon.[41] While elements of imagined futures remain in these national laws, the scope is much more limited to those which governments can see occurring within their lifetimes, or perhaps those of their children.

This diversity of domestic laws leads to fragmentation, causes complexity and uncertainty and could result in a race to the bottom. UNCOPUOS has sought to assist nations in harmonising laws, at least in relation to the implementation of current international law, through its Resolution on Recommendations on National Legislation Relevant to the Peaceful Exploration and Use of Outer Space.[42] In addition, the International Law Association has adopted the Sofia Guidelines for a Model Law on National Space Legislation[43] to further this assistance. Neither of these documents refers to religion or culture, human rights or values. Such issues must be addressed from the very beginning of human habitation in space, as they speak to the core of what it means to be human in a way that the regulation of the technical aspects of space travel and habitation cannot and does not.

In looking to the future and the rapidly evolving space ambitions of various nations, the potential inadequacy of international space law has not been lost on the global community. UNOOSA hosted the UNISPACE+50 conference in 2018, which included thematic priorities, one of which focused on law.[44] No specific reference was made, however, to the topics focused upon in this chapter. In addition, the *Space 2030 Agenda* (adopted in 2021) encourages UNCOPUOS 'to continue to coordinate efforts to … complement existing international space law, when appropriate, to respond to emerging issues'.[45] It was also recognised that studying 'legal and institutional initiatives' is needed 'to ensure that international space law is a relevant part of global space governance in the 21st century' and to find ways to 'strengthen the Legal Subcommittee … to promote the progressive development of international space law' and to identify 'areas that may require additional regulation'.[46] What emerges remains to be seen, but there is no indication that human rights-related matters will be a focus.

Beyond public international law and the institutions that support it, the International Space Station (ISS) provides us with an example of a successful

40 Space (Launches and Returns) Act (2018).

41 Commercial Space Launch Competitiveness Act (2015).

42 UNGA Resolution, *Recommendations on National Legislation Relevant to the Peaceful Exploration and Use of Outer Space* (2013).

43 UNCOPUOS (2013).

44 UNOOSA (nd).

45 UNGA Resolution, *The 'Space2030' Agenda: Space as a Driver of Sustainable Development* (2021), para 12.

46 UNOOSA (undated).

multinational collaboration, facilitated by the ISS Agreement.[47] Yet this Agreement provides no relevant provisions regarding human rights. One of the latest multilateral agreements to be adopted (albeit not a UN instrument) is the Artemis Accords.[48] Relevantly, they affirm the first four space treaties but not the Moon Agreement. In addition, Section 3 confirms that space should be used exclusively for peaceful purposes in accordance with international law, and Section 6 extends emergency assistance to all 'personnel' who may be in distress in outer space. The Accords include no definitions to enable a clearer understanding of 'distress'.

Finally, there are a number of civil society organisations focused on the Moon and ensuring safe and sustainable future activities. These include the Open Lunar Foundation,[49] the Moon Village Association,[50] For All Moonkind[51] and the Secure World Foundation,[52] as well as policy solutions through the Moon Dialogs.[53] Each of these bodies has a different membership and mandate, and while none provides a source of law, they demonstrate that the future of space law is of interest to stakeholders beyond state actors. Several of these NGOs have addressed the issue of space governance. For All Moonkind released a *Recommended Framework and Key Elements for Peaceful and Sustainable Lunar Activities* in 2022.[54] Several chapters envisage governance developments including the prevention of human rights violations:

> Human interactions on the Moon are governed by international treaties, national legislations and other international norms, among which the principle of international cooperation and protection of human rights are the most important. As a lunar community develops and lunar stakeholders and activities increase, it will be important to prevent emergencies and disasters, disputes, and human rights violations. Achieving this requires appropriate regulation of human interactions.[55]

47 International Space Station Agreement (1998).

48 The Accords were not prepared under the auspices of any UN body but were drafted by the US NASA and have since been signed by multiple nations. They provide shared principles for safe and peaceful future space operations based, largely on existing international space law, with some additions such as a commitment to interoperability and protection of heritage: NASA, Artemis Accords (2020).

49 Open Lunar Foundation, https://www.openlunar.org.

50 Moon Village Association, https://moonvillageassociation.org.

51 For All Moonkind, https://www.forallmoonkind.org.

52 Secure World Foundation, https://swfound.org.

53 Moon Dialogs, https://www.moondialogs.org.

54 For All Moonkind (2022).

55 For All Moonkind (2022), Chapter 11, p 47.

What underlies the solution is international human rights law, given that it exists on Earth, with no further detail or elaboration provided.[56] The newly released Moon Dialogs' *Lunar Policy Handbook* includes a whole section on governance, but the contents do not extend beyond existing space law, with a strong focus on the role of nation-states.[57] Extraterrestrial governance institutions do not feature in these documents.

In conclusion, the OST provides some comfort that basic human rights were intended to apply in space via the operation of Articles I[2] and III of the OST.[58] In particular, Article III requires state parties, *inter alia*, to 'carry on activities in the exploration and use of outer space … in accordance with international law'.[59] However, this ignores the reality that international human rights laws observed on Earth may need to be added to, or modified, for application in space.[60] The right to breathable air is one rather poignant example that is not historically needed on Earth,[61] which would be a very real concern for future space dwellers.[62] Indeed, without such rights, future space settlements will arguably be prone to tyrannical regimes, due to the harsh nature of the surrounding environment.[63] In addition, recent space governance developments, which have largely been domestic, and the lack of attention paid to these very human issues at the international level, implies that they are matters best left to national governments on the assumption that people travelling, living or working in space will remain citizens of nations on Earth.[64] Off-world citizenship is not envisaged, nor are gaps or difficulties that may be encountered in implementing, complying with and/or enforcing Earth laws in space.

Space, science fiction and the challenge to humanity's values

The context of space has been used by filmmakers to expose the fragility of fundamental human values; in doing so, it raises existential questions about humanity. Two films from science fiction are particularly notable in demonstrating this idea and helping to show the role that governance can and should play in modern and real-life human engagement with space. Even

56 For All Moonkind (2022), p 49.
57 Moon Dialogs (2023).
58 Ripoll (2021), p 163.
59 OST Art III.
60 See Cowley (2019), pp 334–35.
61 Although, given modern pollution and environmental degradation, such a right may well have contemporary significance on Earth.
62 See Cowley (2019), p 335; Stevens (2015).
63 Cockell (2015), p 3.
64 Ripoll (2021), p 168.

critics of the view that liberal institutional frameworks can overcome destructive human frailties admit that liberal political philosophy is motivated by fundamentally humane concerns.[65] In addition to autonomy, liberals also champion the basic dignity of every person, the equal status of all people and the value of authentic personal choices.

One film that uses space as the backdrop to question the values of humanity – and therefore the rules and laws around our interactions with others – is *Solaris* (2002), based on Stanislaw Lem's 1961 novel.[66] In the film, the main protagonist, Dr Chris Kelvin (played by George Clooney) is a clinical psychologist approached by a corporation that operates a space station orbiting the planet Solaris. His task is to investigate unusual occurrences on the station, although these are not revealed in detail. On arrival at the station, Kelvin finds that one of his friends working there has committed suicide and that other members of the crew have died or disappeared. He begins dreaming about his dead wife Rheya (who committed suicide), encountering her on several occasions. He later learns that replicas of the crew's loved ones have been appearing at the station, and that the Rheya he has been encountering is one of these replicas. The bizarre events cause Kelvin to ponder the effect of the space travel and experiences at Solaris on his Earthly assumptions and behaviours:

> Earth. Even the word sounded strange to me now ... unfamiliar. How long had I been gone? How long had I been back? Did it matter? I tried to find the rhythm of the world where I used to live. I followed the current. I was silent, attentive, I made a conscious effort to smile, nod, stand, and perform the millions of gestures that constitute life on earth. I studied these gestures until they became reflexes again. But I was haunted by the idea that I remembered her wrong, and somehow I was wrong about everything. [67]

His experience also raises the question of whether the norms and rules associated with Earth apply in this foreign environment. Dr Helen Gordon, one of the two remaining crew members, creates a device that can permanently destroy the replicas as a means of preserving the human presence on the station. Kelvin questions the basis of the use of the device:

65 Green (2022), p 74, where he contends that liberal institutional structures lack 'ethical muscle'.

66 Soderbergh (2002) *Solaris* (to be distinguished from Tarkovsky's 1972 *Solaris*).

67 Soderbergh (2002) *Solaris*.

Chris Kelvin: What about your visitor, the one you're so ready to destroy without hesitation? Who is it? What is it? Does it feel? Can it touch? Does it speak?

Dr Helen Gordon: We are in a situation that is beyond morality. [68]

Her comment reflects the potential void of behavioural and decisional norms associated with this strange environment,[69] and the perceived absence of a moral compass this exchange is consistent with the film's questioning of the motives for space travel and habitation, specifically whether living in space is both necessary to and aligned with the preservation of humanity:

Gibarian: We don't want to conquer space at all. We want to expand Earth endlessly. We don't want other worlds; we want a mirror. We seek contact and will never achieve it. We are in the foolish position of a man striving for a goal he fears and doesn't want. Man needs man![70]

Current space governance appears to support this science fiction 'mirror'. The international space laws draw heavily on the law of the sea and other Earthly legal frameworks with no legal innovations that address humanity's assumption of species superiority. Indeed, it is a common trope of science fiction literature and film to show humans as somehow exceptional, compared with other civilisations encountered in outer space.[71] This 'speciesism',[72] which characterises the liberal democratic tradition informing human rights instruments, has been equated with racism and 'leads to behaviour that challenges our future on this planet'.[73] It is contended that this can be redressed in the conception of an evolved society participating in space travel and habitation. Our point is that humanity can learn from its history, as well as science fiction literature, and embrace a higher level of behavioural norms – one that is more inclusive and respectful of diversity.

The film *Gattaca*[74] depicts a future society in which eugenics is commonly practised to produce children with desired physical and intellectual traits – the 'Valids'. Access to space travel is 'selective' in the sense that the 'In-Valids' (those born outside the eugenics programme and generally associated with 'faulty' DNA) are not permitted to engage in professional employment, which

68 Soderbergh (2002) *Solaris*.
69 See Bohlander (2021).
70 Soderbergh (2002) *Solaris*. This idea of man's dependence upon man is discussed in relation to AI governance, specifically the role of international human rights law: see Su (2022).
71 Vint (2008), p 257.
72 Wolfe (2022).
73 Swartz and Mischler (2023).
74 Niccol (1997) *Gattaca*.

is reserved for Valids. In that way, eugenics is linked to the gateway to all the possibilities that space brings with it, compounding the discrimination that is intrinsic to the eugenics programs and the corresponding societal structures. The chief character, Vincent Freeman, is born an In-Valid, with poor eyesight and heart issues, and a predicted lifespan of 30 years. Vincent has never accepted his genetic destiny and is determined to become a crew member on a space expedition to a Saturn moon. He bitterly explains his fate: 'I belonged to a new underclass, no longer determined by social status or the colour of your skin. No, we now have discrimination down to a science'.

This raises the question of the characterisation of discrimination. Under Earth laws, we cannot discriminate on grounds of 'irrelevant' characteristics (eg race) but we can on relevant ones (eg qualification).[75] In space, where life is constantly at risk, what is relevant versus irrelevant becomes blurred when a human's very genetic make-up, strengths and weaknesses may put their life, and the lives of others, in jeopardy. Even gender may become relevant, for example, to prevent the conception of babies in space, while differences in culture, race or religion may similarly be discarded in order to minimise risk of conflict. By way of example, could a genetic predisposition to obesity preclude selection for space travel?[76]

Vincent pushes back against the discriminatory regulatory regime in *Gattaca*, appealing to the notion of universality:

> Blood has no nationality.
>
> For someone who was never meant for this world, I must confess I'm suddenly having a hard time leaving it. Of course, they say every atom in our bodies was once part of a star. Maybe I'm not leaving ... maybe I'm going home.[77]

However, ultimately it is individual moral judgement that proves determinative, demonstrating perhaps the importance of individual human ethics to the preservation of humanity.[78] Vincent engages an illegal DNA broker to provide him with blood and urine samples from a Valid, assuming the identity of Jerome, an Olympic athlete who suffered paralysis in an accident. He evades detection of his In-Valid status in his new job as a computer programmer, and after submitting false genetic samples is selected as a finalist for a place on the crew. Ultimately, however, Vincent is able to embark on his space career not through any change in the discriminatory regime or adherence to

75 Rees et al (2018), p 86.

76 For evidence of existing genetic discrimination see Tiller et al (2020).

77 Niccol (1997) *Gattaca*.

78 Green (2022) contends that liberal political philosophy needs to refocus upon the importance of individual ethical behaviour.

fundamental values, but rather through the exercise of individual discretion. The doctor overseeing background checks for the space mission knowingly changes Vincent's test results because of his son's admiration for Vincent. It is therefore not his manufactured and false genetic perfection, but rather independent human intervention that gives him his dream of space travel. Again, this emphasises the centrality of individual ethical behaviour in countering the discriminatory regime. It demonstrates that top-down morally flawed regulation can be countered by the individual's own moral compass, and in this sense is aligned with the notion of a Prime Directive that involves both a collective and an individual morally driven response.

Both films raise the issue of governance around human engagement with space, in several ways. One issue concerns the basis of accessing space travel, another the motive behind space travel and habitation. They also raise the prospect of lawlessness, or at least the exposition of morally corrupt behaviour, when human existence is stripped bare of its protective legal and social infrastructure. Both films reference the potential for science to operate unfettered of usual constraints, with ethically problematic consequences.[79] These issues raise important questions about how best to regulate human travel and habitation in space, particularly the risk that is posed to key human values of respect for dignity, personal autonomy and equal treatment. Arguably, it is the protection of these key values that is linked to the maintenance of a humane world.[80]

These particular values are the subject of protections under numerous international, transnational and domestic human rights legal instruments. The Universal Declaration on Human Rights (UDHR) is the foundational legal instrument that responded to the atrocities that characterised World War II. It prescribes a 'common standard of achievement for all peoples and nations' and requires states to recognise all humans as being 'born free and equal in dignity and rights', regardless of 'nationality, place of residence, gender, national or ethnic origin, colour, religion, language, or any other status'.[81] The UDHR set the tone for further international, transnational and domestic instruments protecting political and civil liberties.[82] However, the UDHR and subsequent human rights instruments look backwards to avoid repeating the atrocities of the past. Examples such as *Solaris and Gattaca*, and others discussed in this chapter, expose the issues confronting humanity that space travel and habitation raise, but also suggest the potential for a

79 A theme pursued in a range of literary sources including Yanagihara (2013) *The People in the Trees* and Shelley (1818/1965) *Frankenstein*.

80 Papamichael and Partis-Jennings (2016).

81 UDHR.

82 For example, the ICCPR, and the European Convention on Human Rights.

future based upon rules that incorporate human rights and responsibilities in the new, relatively uncharted frontier of space travel and habitation.

These science fiction films demonstrate the frailties of humanity, particularly those associated with beliefs that some humans are 'better' than others. Arguably, human rights protections, based in the universal value of human dignity, work to address these frailties. Dworkin, for example, argues that there is a 'unity of value' based in a conception of human dignity that brings together accounts of ethics, morality and politics.[83] The films, however, show that these frailties lurk beneath the surface, ready to emerge where societal structures become weakened through systemic racism or human habitation in remote and harsh environments. The questioning of what it is to be human in *Solaris*, through the 'duplicate' Rheya, confronts the idea that there is something uniquely 'human' underpinning interactions and relationships. *Gattaca* exposes the darker side of the search for human perfection using medical science, and in this sense also raises the question of what it is to be human. Both films use space as the medium for exploring this question – *Gattaca* through access to space travel and *Solaris* through living in space.

Travel to and habitation in space have therefore already been identified with deep questions about human identity and values, and indicate the importance of regulatory structures to the maintenance of our understanding of humankind. Respect for the values of human dignity, equality and autonomy is either actively challenged or absent, and brings into sharp relief the role of protective legal mechanisms as a way of preserving these values through the suppression of baser human instincts. Yet, as the next section will show, the transposition of Earthly human rights to the space context is not unproblematic.

Religion, culture and human rights

FoRB is often described as the oldest human right.[84] Whether or not this is true, it is still a central human right finding numerous expressions in international,[85] transnational[86] and domestic law.[87] As one Australian High Court judge has put it, 'Freedom of religion, the paradigm freedom of conscience, is the essence of a free society'.[88] As such, it is an ideal case study

83 Dworkin (2011).

84 Kirby (2009), p 4; Durham (1994), p 618; and Hill (2020), p 150.

85 See, for example, UDHR; ICCPR; Convention on the Rights of the Child (1989) (CRC).

86 See, for example, Convention for the Protection of Human Rights and Fundamental Freedoms (1950), Art 9.

87 See, for example, US Constitution, Amendment I; Australian Constitution, s 116; Canadian Constitution Act (1982), Pt. 1 cl. 11, being Schedule B in Canada Act, (1982) (UK); Constitution of the Republic of South Africa (1996), Chapter 2, s 15.

88 *Church of the New Faith v Commissioner of Pay-Roll Tax (Vic)* (1983) 154 CLR 120.

through which to examine in detail the issues raised above and the challenges posed to human rights by space travel and habitation.

Babylon 5[89] is an apt science fiction TV show through which to explore future governance implications for religion in space. The show does not shy away from exploring religious themes and ideas – even if, as McCarron asserts, the ideal religion presented by *Babylon 5* is closer to humanism or an 'atheistic religion'.[90] One particularly poignant episode is 'Parliament of Dreams'. In the closing scene, station commander Jeffrey Sinclair demonstrates humanity's religion as part of the station-wide festival, via showcasing its diversity. He introduces the assembled alien dignitaries to a parade of religious leaders and practitioners, including, *inter alia*, a Roman Catholic priest, a Buddhist monk, an Orthodox Jewish Rabbi and a Taoist, along with 12 other named religions and cultures and several other that are seen but not named as the episode ends. This highlights an area of human experience that will need to be accommodated in the creation of governance structures for future space travel and settlements – the diversity of religious belief and expression.[91]

The *Parliament of Dreams* also presents a related yet contrasting issue. In the opening scene, the station's head of security, Michael Garibaldi, confronts an alien religious pilgrim insisting that he give up a knife-like object. The pilgrim objects stating, 'You don't understand. This is my ceremonial blade. I am a pilgrim here for the sacred day of Chu'dag'. In typical Garibaldi fashion, the head of security retorts, 'I don't care if you're the Easter Bunny. You're not bringing this onto the station'. The incident parallels current issues around religious freedom and religious or sacred objects and symbols that may, if misused, pose a security threat, with the most obvious, and best-known, example being the Sikh Kirpan.[92] This incident in the opening scene, when contrasted with the closing scene, highlights two related issues for the governance of future space settlements: first, how will the diversity of religious experiences and practices be accommodated in a confined space station or settlement; and second, how will religious practices, beliefs or objects that pose a risk to the 'safety, order, health or morals of the fundamental rights and freedoms of others'[93] in the settlement or station be regulated or controlled?

89 The show takes its name from the biblical story of the Tower of Babel, see Genesis 11: 1–19.

90 McCarron (1998), p 141.

91 This contrasts with the earlier presentation of the station's other main alien groups, the Narn, Centauri and the Minbari who each presented a single celebration or event as their contribution to the festival. The Vorlons did not take part in the festival.

92 See, for example, recent debate about the wearing of the Kirpan in Australian schools: Barker (2021, 2023).

93 ICCPR Art 18(3).

While some have argued that religion will not and should not be relevant for space travel[94] and habitation, or that secular space travellers should be selected over those with religious conviction,[95] religious belief and practice already have a long association with space exploration. The first American astronaut to walk in space, Ed White II, carried with him three religious symbols: a Star of David, a crucifix and a St Christopher medal. Many astronauts since have carried other symbols of faith as part of their personal preference kits.[96] It is therefore reasonable to assume that future space workers and settlers will bring their existing religion with them as others have done throughout Earth's history.[97] For example, the English brought Christianity and the Church of England to Australia – whether or not this resulted in the short-lived establishment of that church in Australia is still debated by academics.[98] Inevitably, the practice of religion may need to be adapted to accommodate the very different conditions found in a near-future space settlement or space station. Experience has shown this is possible in practice as well as in theoretical and theological deliberation on the topic.[99] However, some religious rituals, such as the lighting of a candle or the burning of incense – practices common to several religions including Catholicism and Buddhism – may be dangerous in a confined context where inhospitable or lethal environments are literally millimetres away. The result may well be a certain amount of self-selection in those who choose to travel to and live or work in space, as those whose religious practices cannot be accommodated easily may choose not to live or work in space. However, from the perspective of this chapter, that is less important than the question of explicit and deliberate selection by those organising the space activity or settlement, as the potential for exclusion raises issues of governance in the form of the applicable human rights regime. If a future is possible where we discriminate on the basis of genetics, as depicted in *Gattaca*, how much more is this possible in relation to religion or culture, which is subjective and often divisive?

Some commentators, such as Cohen, have already argued that future space settlements or stations could, or even should, select secular participants; however, this ignores the very real issue of the human right to the FoRB.[100] Excluding future space settlement inhabitants on the basis of the presence or absence of their religious beliefs or practice fundamentally undermines this

94 Oviedo (2019), p 217; Murray (2021), p 276.
95 Cohan (2013), p 104.
96 See Mersch (2013).
97 Murray (2021), p 271; Impey (2021), p 249.
98 See Barker (2016).
99 See Murray (2021), pp 274–76; Cohan (2013), pp 104–5.
100 Cohan (2013), p 104.

important human right – which, in international law, cannot be derogated from, even in times of national emergency.[101]

The first place to look for the answer to this problem is the existing international human right's framework governing both the exploration of space and human rights. As outlined above, FoRB is already enshrined in international, supranational and domestic law, as such any extension of those laws to future space travel and settlements could incorporate existing FoRB and other human rights provisions. However, as already discussed, this ignores the need to update existing human rights for application in space travel and settlements.

In his brief overview of the human rights that may require modification before they can be applied to space habitation, Cowley suggests that FoRB, if it is desirable to include at all, may well need to be modified.[102] We would disagree with his offhand remark that perhaps FoRB could be jettisoned in any future declaration of human rights in space. However, we acknowledge that the right, and more particularly its limitations, will need to be re-examined. As Crowley observes, in space habitations, 'relatively little dissent could be tolerated, since the implications of any acts of sabotage of, or threats to destroy, basic life support systems would be so much more far-reaching than on Earth'. However, this is precisely why we argue that religious belief and practice, cultural rights and human rights more broadly must be considered at the early formation of the governance of near-future space settlements and not left to be considered after more technical and scientific aspects of future missions have been sorted out.[103]

The resolution of these issues in the governance of future space settlements and stations before they occur is essential. As hinted at above, and highlighted in the opening scenes of *Babylon 5*'s 'Parliament of Dreams' episode, some religious practices may in fact pose a real risk to a future space station or settlement. International, supranational and domestic law protecting FoRB already envisages limiting the exercise of FoRB in certain circumstances. For example, Article 18(3) of the International Covenant on Civil and Political Rights (ICCPR) permits the manifestation of religion or belief to be limited, where necessary, 'to protect public safety, order, health or morals or the fundamental rights and freedoms of others'.[104] Determining when it may be appropriate to limit FoRB and the necessary preconditions to doing so is not easy. Different jurisdictions have come up with different tests to determine the issue. In future space travel, or on a settlement or station, where resting from work during a prescribed sabbath may not just be

101 ICCPR Art 4(2).
102 Cowley (2019), p 335.
103 Oviedo (2019), pp 217–18.
104 ICCPR, Art 18(3).

inconvenient for those around you but may also put the safety of your fellow inhabitants at risk if necessary tasks for survival go undone, the threshold to determine whether a restriction is in fact necessary is likely to be much lower than that accepted on Earth. Even if the threshold is not in fact lowered, then at the very least it is likely to be more readily met, leading to more frequent abrogation of human rights despite the existence of the UDHR or other human rights instruments.

Future governance

The above sections highlight the risks of leaving a regulatory vacuum where specific issues we have raised have not presented themselves on Earth in the same ways, or where the current solutions on Earth are inadequate or potentially inapplicable to future space habitation. The implication is that existing human rights regimes can simply be applied to space travel and settlement, despite the fact that these regimes have not overcome the problems on Earth that they were designed to address. While we accept that institutions and rules are not the entire solution and should not be focused upon to the exclusion of the 'human element',[105] we believe governance arrangements have a role to play given the extreme environments that are likely to give rise to novel social conditions. If so, then gaps could be filled by new or amended laws, or left to allow organic, bottom-up and bespoke arrangements to emerge.

In seeking to confront the challenge, where can we turn? There is no doubt that international space and human rights laws, created on Earth and for Earth-based human societies, provide a solid foundation – but will this be fit for purpose in space? Both the OST and HR law provide actionable rights, fundamental principles and standards. Clearly, these rights and principles do play a role in raising the bar of human behaviour. This is not always through enforcement, but rather through the expectation that once written these standards will be complied with. Yet we frequently fail to meet these standards. Furthermore, as minimum standards they include no aspirational goal to elevate our responsibilities. This may not be the role of the current international human rights regime, but we suggest that as humanity moves out into space it should be. By limiting ourselves to minimum standards, we have no loftier goal to hold in tension with our decisions and actions. If human rights standards alone remain that goal, then the bar is too low. Breaches of them are non-negotiable and, as noted above, there are gaps and deficiencies when it comes to space travel and settlements. We argue that the human rights regime is not yet ready for space futures.

There are fundamental limitations of both international and domestic law that could inhibit developments to achieve a loftier standard for the

105 Green (2022), p 60.

space context. For example, international law is the domain of nation-states, and other actors are excluded from participating at the global level, including corporations and private industry which are likely to dominate in space futures.[106] Furthermore, the principle of sovereignty is central, and by requiring domestic implementation of international law, national interests and approaches are favoured. In the absence of a global policing and justice agency, international law is also difficult to enforce. Relying purely on domestic law to provide for humans in space may be problematic given the likelihood of multinational crews, as well as shared facilities and services, raising jurisdictional issues and diverse domestic regulations. Given these limitations of international and domestic law, it is international law that can provide a uniform standard to be applied to all people travelling to or living and working in space. Developing a new international instrument may result in fragmentation of space and/or human rights law. Yet, if the political will to develop such a standard does not exist, the global gap will remain, with domestic jurisdictions likely to provide differing approaches.

No current international space law developments appear to suggest alternate legal systems or novel rules for human space futures. It is in this context that we turn to science fiction for ideas. We draw upon interesting possibilities in *Star Trek* to highlight fictional universes that themselves draw upon western cultural contexts to frame futurist challenges while also providing fictional ways to overcome them. *Star Trek's* 'Starfleet', for example, at its simplest, fills the gap for interstellar law enforcement in a way that has not been achieved by the United Nations on Earth. *Star Trek*'s Starfleet is an arm of the United Federation of Planets, a somewhat utopian governance regime, albeit drawing heavily on the United Nations and US Constitution. Notably, the appearance of weaknesses in later movies and TV series were, as with examples highlighted above, overcome through individuals acting in accordance with their ethical beliefs demonstrating the potential value of an individual duty.[107]

In searching for ways forward for space governance that pragmatically accept the dominance of governance institutions and rules, while also seeking to address the very human elements explored earlier, we again turn to *Star Trek* for a possibility. Here we suggest the adoption of a 'Prime Directive', which dates to the original TV series.[108] Creator Gene Roddenberry's

106 Although the OST does make limited reference to non-state actors in Article VI: 'States Parties ... shall bear international responsibility for national activities in outer spaces ... whether such activities are carried on by governmental agencies or by non-governmental entities ... The activities of non-governmental entities in outer space ... shall require authorization and continuing supervision by the appropriate State Party to the Treaty.'

107 See Green (2022), p 69.

108 *Star Trek* (1968) 'The Omega Glory'; see Peltz (2003), p 640.

aversion to the Vietnam War[109] led to this non-interventionist General Order #1, which prohibits Starfleet members from interfering with the development of alien cultures.[110] The non-interventionist command has been the subject of much literature,[111] but it is not the specific content of the Prime Directive that we suggest has value here, but rather the idea of such a vehicle. Just as the creator of *Star Trek's* Prime Directive sought to reflect and prevent atrocities on Earth in his fictional universe,[112] so too do we seek to avoid replicating past horrors. Nevertheless, 'an uncompromising ethical rule can create more problems than it solves'.[113] Smith points out the questionable moral choices forced by a strict application of *Star Trek*'s Prime Directive, as well as the multiplicity of examples where the Directive is ignored or bent, often with questionable moral outcomes. As 'it turns out, the Prime Directive is neither the primary concern nor an inviolable directive'.[114] However, in tracing the evolution of the Prime Directive from a commandment to an aspirational principle,[115] our point is made. Our Prime Directive should not be seen as a fixed rule, but rather combines a rights-based approach and an ideal to aspire to, and one against which to measure our success or failure. In this respect, it is aligned with approaches from virtue ethics that identify key character traits as integral to moral assessment. It can therefore incorporate, for example, empathy as well as respect for personal autonomy.[116] When characters in *Star Trek* fail to uphold the Prime Directive, the audience is able to judge this action against an aspirational standard that is well known. Its application may not always be perfect, but it does provide a yardstick to guide ethical decision-making and ultimately governance.[117]

For our purposes, in relation to human space futures and the challenges outlined, such a Directive would not relate only to a failure to intervene in human rights violations but would rather create both a positive and negative duty – a conscious positive action as well as a negative obligation to refrain from acting. In doing so it would play a regulatory role that both harnesses the power of individual behaviour and creates a collective backstop.

109 Peltz (2003).
110 *Star Trek*, Original Series (1966–69).
111 See, for example, Peltz (2003); Joseph and Carton (1992); Scharf and Roberts (1994); Richards (1997).
112 See also Peltz (2003), p 640.
113 Smith (2016), p 199.
114 Peltz (2003), p 635.
115 See Peltz (2003), p 647; although he refers to commentators finding it akin to a constitutional principle that returns to Green's fundamental point about a liberalist focus on constitutions, rules and institutions.
116 Hursthouse (2016).
117 See Smith (2016), pp 199–202.

Avoidance of distress is the Prime Directive of all envoys of humankind

The word 'distress' appears in several international space treaties[118] and draws heavily on the law of the sea. Rather than the obligation being only to render assistance and search and rescue those in distress, it should be to avoid distress altogether. This could encompass positive and negative obligations, being a shield to prevent others from being distressed, as well as refraining from acting in a way to cause such distress. While fantasy rather than science fiction, the *Eragon* book series highlights the subtle difference and profound impact of such an approach. In the series, the protagonist Eragon gives a blessing to a child in Elvish that was meant to be 'may luck and happiness follow you and may you *be* shielded from misfortune'. However, due to his poor grasp of Elvish, he instead says, 'May luck and happiness follow you and may you *be a* shield from misfortune' (emphasis added). This small grammatical change had a profound impact on the child, who was forced to grow up magically in order to be able to fulfil the obligations of the blessing to shield others from misfortune.

Existing human rights frameworks, even if successfully adapted and adopted for space travel and habitation, act only as a shield from distress for individuals, structured around a defined set of predetermined rights. They are a minimum standard and inevitably focused on the rights of the individual rather than on their responsibilities to humanity. Our Prime Directive for space travel and habitation proposes a subtle grammatical shift to aspire to not only be shielded from distress but also to seek to shield others. A negative duty is created: to refrain from causing distress. This is combined with the positive duty to act to protect others from distress. In turn, an individual would also have the right to be protected from distress. This combination of positive and negative duties is a progression of current international human rights and space law. The obligation could also expand upon current law by defining distress widely to include physical, economic, mental, psychological, emotional and cultural distress. Furthermore, making all space travellers and settlers envoys of humankind, and providing them with a Prime Directive, could be the key to move beyond self-interest and, to extend the metaphor from *Eragon* further, to grow up more rapidly to a more evolved or utopian society. In doing so, we can learn from both the utopian and dystopian futures presented to us in science fiction.

The Prime Directive can drive individual and collective action in and for space futures. Peltz finds that *Star Trek*'s Prime Directive is inherently violable and aspirational, and 'can never be fully realized on Earth'.[119] Yet perhaps

118 See, for example, Rescue Agreement, Artemis Accords, etc.
119 Peltz (2003), p 636.

if it is applied in space, for what is likely to be a small group of people at first, it could eventually influence Earthly human rights governance through the advancing of human values.

Conclusion

Given the current commercial space tourism opportunities and the imminent prospect of humans returning to the Moon, it is timely to explore the international legal regimes that can, could or should apply to space travel and habitation. We have a moral imperative to recognise inherent human weaknesses and to address them through space governance arrangements. Legal reality (as experienced here on Earth) provides multiple examples that demonstrate our preoccupation with self-interest at the expense of others. The science fiction imaginaries explored highlight the threats to human values that space futures might hold, but also provide some potential ways forward. We offer one such suggestion, a Prime Directive, involving the application of a positive duty to prevent distress and a right to be protected from distress: an obligation to shield and a right to be shielded by others.

Another way to understand our Prime Directive is to contrast the conclusions of Lord Atkins in *Donoghue v Stevenson*[120] with his source material in the Bible. Lord Atkins famously asked, 'Who, then, in law is my neighbour?', ultimately concluding that, 'You must take reasonable care to avoid acts or omissions which you can reasonably foresee would be likely to injure your neighbour'. In our Prime Directive, we would argue that humanity must move from merely 'avoid[ing] acts or omissions' to actively acting to assist those in distress – or, as Leviticus puts it, a person must 'not stand idly by when the blood of your neighbour is at stake'.[121]

We have demonstrated that human rights regimes on Earth cannot simply be extended into space. International space and human rights laws both emerged from the atrocities of World War II, and we should not wait for some future horror to propel us to act. If we cannot protect basic dignity, non-discrimination and freedom of religion in space, then all human rights are arguably up for negotiation, and potentially violation, in the name of survival.

References

Samudu Atapattu (2019) 'Intergenerational Equity and Children's Rights' in Clair Fenton-Glynn (ed), *Children's Rights and Sustainable Development: Interpretating the UNCRC for Future Generations*, Cambridge University Press, 167–191.

120 *Donoghue v Stevenson (1932) AC 562*

121 Leviticus 19:16.

Mashood A Baderin and Manisuli Ssenyonjo (2016) 'Development of International Human Rights Law Before and After the UDHR' in Manisuli Ssenyonjo and Mashood A Baderin (eds), *International Human Rights Law: Six Decades After the UDHR and Beyond*, Routledge, 3–27.

Renae Barker (2016) *State and Religion: The Australian Story*, Routledge.

Renae Barker (2021) 'A Religious Symbol, Not a Knife: At the Heart of the NSW Kirpan Ban is a Battle to Define Secularism' *The Conversation*, 26 May 2021, https://theconversation.com/a-religious-symbol-not-a-knife-at-the-heart-of-the-nsw-kirpan-ban-is-a-battle-to-define-secularism-161413

Renae Barker (2023) 'Why a Queensland Court Overturned a Ban on Religious Knives in Schools' *The Conversation*, 10 August 2023, https://theconversation.com/why-a-queensland-court-overturned-a-ban-on-religious-knives-in-schools-211042

Renae Barker (2024) 'Rejecting Security: A Comparative Analysis of the Rejection of Security, Public Safety and Public Order Concerns as a Ground for Restricting Freedom of Religion in Religious Dress Cases' in Tania Pagotto, Joshua M Roose and GP Marcar (eds), *Security, Religion, and the Rule of Law: International Perspectives*, Routledge, 151–171.

Michael Bohlander (2021) 'Joining the "Galactic Club": What Price Admission? A Hypothetical Case Study of the Impact of Human Rights on a Future Accession of Humanity to Interstellar Civilisation Networks' 132 *Futures* 102801. https://doi.org/10.1016/j.futures.2021.102801

Charles S Cockell (2015) 'Introduction: Human Governance and Liberty Beyond Earth' in Charles S Cockell (ed), *Human Governance Beyond Earth: Implications for Freedom*, Springer, 1.

Jonathan D Cohan (2013) 'Spaceflight and the Separation of Church and State' 11 *Astropolotics* 100.

Robert Cowley (2019) 'Yes, We Earthlings Should Colonize Mars if Martian Rights Can be Upheld' 17 *Theology and Science* 332.

W Cole Durham (1994) 'Freedom of Religion: The United States Model' 42 *The American Journal of Comparative Law* 617.

Ronald Dworkin (2011) *Justice for Hedgehogs*, Harvard University Press.

For All Moonkind (2022) 'Recommended Framework and key Elements for Peaceful and Sustainable Lunar Activities' https://moonvillageassociation.org/download/recommended-framework-and-key-elements-for-peaceful-and-sustainable-lunar-activities

Alejandro Galvez-Pol, Marcos Nadal and James M Kilner (2021) 'Emotional Representations of Space Vary as a Function of Peoples' Affect and Interoceptive Sensibility' 11 *Scientific Reports* 16150, https://doi.org/10.1038/s41598-021-95081-9

Alex Green (2022) 'The Importance of Dystopian Hypotheticals: Towards an Ethical Turn in Liberal Political Philosophy' 4 *Law, Technology and Humans* 60.

Colin Harvey (2015) 'Time for Reform? Refugees, Asylum-Seekers and Protection Under International Human Rights Law' 34 *Refugee Survey Quarterly* 43.

Mark Hill (2020) 'Historical Hinterlands for Religious Freedom in the United Kingdom' 33 *Studies in Christian Ethics* 147.

Thomas Hobbes (2008) *Leviathan*, JCA Gaskin (ed), Oxford University Press.

Rosalind Hursthouse (2016) *On Virtue Ethics*, 6th ed, Routledge.

Christopher D Impey (2021) 'Science and Faith Off-Earth' in Margaret Boone Rappaport and Konrad Szocik (eds), *The Human Factor in the Settlement of the Moon*, Springer, 245.

Paul Joseph and Sharon Carton (1992) 'The Law of the Federation: Images of Law, Lawyers, and the Legal System in *Star Trek: The Next Generation*' 24 *University of Toledo Law Review* 43.

Michael Kirby (2009) 'Law, Human Rights and Religion – of Genocide, Sexuality and Apostasy' 9 *The Macquarie Law Review* 3.

Vijay Kumer (2020) 'Viewpoint Research "Envoys of Mankind" in the Era of Commercial Human Spaceflight' 18 *The International Journal of Space Politics & Policy* 144.

Kevin McCarron (1998) 'Religion, Philosophy, and the End of History' in Edward James and Farah Mendlesohn (eds), *The Parliament of Dreams: Conferring on Babylon 5*, Science Fiction Foundation, 131.

Carol Mersch (2013) 'Religion, Space Exploration, and Secular Society' 11 *Astropolitics* 65.

Moon Dialogs (2023) 'Lunar Policy Handbook' https://www.moondialogs.org/lunar-policy-handbook

Gerald F Murray (2021) 'Religion in a Lunar Settlement: An Anthropological Assessment' in Margaret Boone Rappaport and Konrad Szocik (eds), *The Human Factor in the Settlement of the Moon*, Springer, 269.

Luis Oviedo (2019) 'Religion for a Spatial Colony: Raising the Right Question' in Konrad Sxocik (ed), *The Human Factor in a Mission to Mars*, Springer, 217.

Andres Papamichael and Hannah Partis-Jennings (2016) 'Why Common Humanity? Framing the Responsibility as a Common Response' 53 *International Politics* 83.

Richard J Peltz (2003) 'On a Wagon Train to Afghanistan: Limitations on *Star Trek*'s Prime Directive' 25 *University of Arkansas at Little Rock Law Review* 635.

Neil Rees, Simon Rice and Dominique Allen (2018) *Australian Anti-discrimination & Equal Opportunity Law*, Federation Press.

Thomas Richards (1997) *The Meaning of Star Trek*, Doubleday.

José Antonio Jurado Ripoll (2021) 'International Treaties and the Future of the Nation-State Concept on the Moon' in Margaret Boone Rappaport and Konrad Szocik (eds), *The Human Factor in the Settlement of the Moon*, Springer, 161.

Michael P Scharf and Lawrence D Roberts (1994) 'The Interstellar Relations of the Federation: International Law and *Star Trek: The Next Generation*' 25 *University of Toledo Law Review* 577.

Mary Shelley (1818/1965) *Frankenstein: Or the Modern Prometheus* Signet, New York

Kelly C Smith (2016) 'The Curious Case of the Martian Microbes: Marionmania, Intrinsic Value and the Prime Directive' in James SJ Schwartz and Tony Milligan (eds), *The Ethics of Space Exploration*, Springer, 195.

Adam H Stevens (2015) 'The Price of Air' in Charles S Cockell (ed) *Human Governance Beyond Earth: Implications for Freedom*, Springer, 51.

Anna Su (2022) 'The Promise and Perils of International Human Rights Law for AI Governance' 4 *Law, Technology and Humans* 166.

B Swartz and B Mischler (eds) (2023) *Speciesism in Biology and Culture: How Human Exceptionalism is Pushing Planetary Boundaries*, Springer.

Andrei Tarkovsky (1972) *Solaris* Mosfilm

Jane Tiller, Susan Morris, Toni Rice, Krystal Barter, Moeen Riaz, Louise Keogh, Martin B Delatycki, Margaret Otlowski and Paul Lacaze (2020) 'Genetic Discrimination by Australian Insurance Companies: A Survey of Consumer Experiences' 28 *European Journal of Human Genetics* 108.

Kieran Tranter (2011) 'The Speculative Jurisdiction: The Science Fictionality of Law and Technology' 20 *Griffith Law Review* 817.

Sherryl Vint (2008) '*Babylon 5*: Our First, Best Hope for Mature Science Fiction Television' in JP Telotte (ed), *The Essential Science Fiction Television Reader*, University Press of Kentucky, 247.

Katharine Wolfe (2022) 'Can Critiques of "Speciesism" be Disentangled from Ableism?' 16 May, https://blog.apaonline.org/2022/05/16/can-critiques-of-speciesism-be-disentangled-from-ableism%EF%BF%BC

Treaties and international agreements

Agreement on the Rescue of Astronauts, the Return of Astronauts and the Return of objects Launched into Outer Space (adopted 22 April 1968, entered into force 3 December 1968) 672 UNTS 119 (Rescue Agreement).

Convention for the Protection of Human Rights and Fundamental Freedoms (adopted 4 November 1950) 213 UNTS 221.

Convention on the International Liability for Damage Caused by Space Objects (adopted 29 March 1972, entered into force 1 September 1972) 961 UNTS 187 (Liability Convention).

Convention on Registration of Objects Launched into Outer Space (adopted 12 November 1974, entered into force 15 September 1976) 1023 UNTS 15 (Registration Convention).

Convention on the Rights of the Child (adopted 20 November 1989) 1577 UNTS 3.

Declaration of Legal Principles Governing the Activities of States in the Exploration and Use of Outer Space (UNGA Resolution 1962 (XVIII)).

International Covenant on Civil and Political Rights (adopted 19 December 1966, entered into force 23 March 1976) 999 UNTS 171 (ICCPR).

International Space Station Agreement (1998), https://www.state.gov/wp-content/uploads/2019/02/12927-Multilateral-Space-Space-Station-1.29.1998.pdf

NASA (2020) 'The Artemis Accords' https://www.nasa.gov/specials/artemis-accords/index.html

Outer Space Treaty (adopted 27 January 1967, entered into force 10 October 1967) 610 UNTS 205 (OST).

UNCOPUOS, Information on the Activities of International Intergovernmental and Non-governmental Organizations Relating to Space Law (26 March 2013, A/AC.105/C.2/2013/CRP.6) https://www.unoosa.org/pdf/limited/c2/AC105_C2_2013_CRP06E.pdf

UNGA Resolution, Recommendations on National Legislation Relevant to the Peaceful Exploration and Use of Outer Space (16 December 2013, A/RES/68/74) https://www.unoosa.org/pdf/gares/A_RES_68_074E.pdf

UNGA Resolution, The 'Space2030' Agenda: Space as a Driver of Sustainable Development (28 October 2021, A/RES/76/3)

Universal Declaration on Human Rights (adopted 10 December 1948) 217 A(III) (UNGA) (UDHR).
UNOOSA (nd) UNISPACE +50, 'Thematic Priorities' https://www.unoosa.org/documents/pdf/unispace/plus50/thematic_priorities_booklet.pdf

Domestic legislation

Commercial Space Launch Competitiveness Act (2015) (US)
Space (Launches and Returns) Act (2018) (Australia)

Cases

Church of the New Faith v Commissioner of Pay-Roll Tax (Vic) (1983) 154 CLR 120
Donoghue v Stevenson [1932] AC 562

Foundations

For All Moonkind, https://www.forallmoonkind.org
Moon Dialogs, https://www.moondialogs.org
Moon Village Association, https://moonvillageassociation.org
Open Lunar Foundation, https://www.openlunar.org
Secure World Foundation, https://swfound.org

Books, films and television programs

Joseph Conrad (1899) *Heart of Darkness*.
William Golding (1954) *Lord of the Flies*, Penguin.
Vincent McEveety *Star Trek* (1966–69) Original Series.
Andrew Niccol (1997) *Gattaca*, Columbia Pictures.
José Saramago (1995) *Blindness*, Mariner Books.
Steven Soderbergh (2002) *Solaris*, Twentieth Century Fox/Lighthouse Entertainment.
Vincent McEveety *Star Trek* (1968) 'The Omega Glory' *TV Episode 23*, Original Series.
Hanya Yanagihara (2013) *The People in the Trees*, Doubleday.

Chapter 6

International law in outer space

Protecting against 'evil' corporate actors

Stacey Henderson and Melissa de Zwart

Introduction

The predicted future experiences of humans living beyond Earth have captured the imaginations of generations. Covering the spectrum from utopian to dystopian, science fiction provides an opportunity to explore what the future may look like for humanity beyond Earth. In imagining the future for humans living in space, science fiction may help us to prevent a dystopian nightmare and offer an opportunity to create a better future of sustained human presence in space. In this chapter, we first outline current plans for sustained human presence in outer space by government space agencies and private companies. We then draw on Kim Stanley Robinson's *Mars* trilogy to explore the fictional dominance of corporate space actors controlling every aspect of human presence on Mars for the benefit of shareholders on Earth,[1] and on James SA Corey's *The Expanse* novel series[2] to examine the role of evil corporate actors exploiting and experimenting on inhabitants of space habitats for corporate gain. Having established the potential for corporate actors to contribute to, and actively cause, significant harm to humans living in space, we interrogate whether international space law can adequately protect humans living in space against a dystopian future dominated by malevolent corporate actors.

Plans for sustained human presence in outer space

In 1911, Konstantin Tsiolkovsky – often referred to as the 'father of rocketry' – wrote, 'Humanity will not remain on the earth forever, but in pursuit of light and space it will at first timidly penetrate beyond the limits of the atmosphere, and then conquer all the space around the sun'.[3]

1 Robinson (1992, 1993, 1996).
2 Corey (2012).
3 Letter from Konstantin Tsiolkovsky to Boris Vorobiev dated 12 August 1911, reproduced in Hall and Shayler (2001).

DOI: 10.4324/9781003412274-7

Turning this prediction into reality, the US National Aeronautics and Space Administration (NASA) has a long history of planned crewed missions to the Moon, Mars and beyond, including 'colonisation' studies. NASA's Artemis project includes plans for the Artemis Base Camp,[4] an inhabited base near the Moon's South Pole, as well as Gateway, an inhabited space station in orbit around the Moon.[5] Other national space agencies also have human habitation of the Moon firmly in their sights. The China National Space Administration (CNSA) and Russian State Space Corporation (Roscosmos) have plans for the International Lunar Research Station, an inhabited experimental research facility on the surface of the Moon, intended to be operational in the 2030s.[6]

Mars, too, has captured the attention of space agencies as a possible human habitation location beyond Earth. In 1960, NASA held a Mars expedition study, focusing on propulsion mechanisms and orbital trajectories required for a return mission to Mars. This study went on to form the basis of the lunar landings during the Apollo missions.[7] In 1984, the Case for Mars II Conference, which was partly funded by NASA, included discussions about a permanent Mars base that would serve as a precursor to permanent human habitation of the red planet.[8] In 2004, then President Bush proclaimed in his 'Vision for Space Exploration' that crewed missions to Mars were an important part of the United States' objective to 'extend human presence across the solar system'.[9] The NASA Transition Authorisation Act of 2017 explicitly mentioned the 'requirements of future exploration and utilisation activities leading to human habitation on the surface of Mars'[10] and 'the long-term goal of human missions near or on the surface of Mars in the 2030s'.[11] The Artemis project led by NASA will see the return of humans to the Moon, with the aim that what is learned 'on and around the Moon to take the next giant leap: sending the first astronauts to Mars'.[12] NASA predicts that crewed missions to Mars – even initial missions – will be for more extended periods of time than previous Moon missions, with mission durations estimated to be between 30 and 550 days.[13] In 2017, the United Arab Emirates unveiled

4 Shekhtman (2021).
5 European Space Agency.
6 China National Space Administration (2021).
7 Portree (2001), p 5.
8 Portree (2001), p 63.
9 Bush (2004).
10 *NASA Transition Authorisation Act of 2017*, Pub L No 115-10, Section 414(b), 131 Stat 18, 34.
11 *NASA Transition Authorisation Act of 2017*, Pub L No 115-10, 432(b)(2)(A), 131 Stat 18, 39.
12 NASA (nd).
13 Jet Propulsion Laboratory (2005), p 8; Hoffman (2001).

its Mars 2117 project, which plans to 'establish the first inhabitable human settlement in Mars by 2117'.[14]

Private space companies are also planning to establish human habitats beyond Earth, including on other planets and in orbits. In 2016, Elon Musk announced SpaceX's Interplanetary Transport System as part of the ultimate goal of 'making humans a multi-planetary species'.[15] SpaceX envisages up to 1000 spacecraft leaving Earth every 26 months, enabling a permanent human presence on Mars of one million people within 40 to 100 years.[16] In January 2020, Musk tweeted that he expects 100,000 people to travel regularly between Earth and Mars, at an expected cost of between US$100,000 and US$500,000, with loans available for those who cannot afford the ticket cost up front.[17] The cost of the flight to Mars would be repaid by working in the SpaceX Mars city,[18] an initiative that has been criticised as the introduction of indentured servitude on Mars.[19] Indentured servitude on Earth is bad enough, but when you are dependent on someone else for the very air that you breathe, the potential for grave abuses and suffering increases exponentially. Instead of inhabiting another planet, Blue Origin's Jeff Bezos plans to develop 'space colonies' – human habitats in orbit that replicate Earth's weather and gravitational pull, holding as many as a million people and incorporating 'rivers and forests and wildlife'.[20] Again, these habitats will be like 'corporate towns', where citizens are subject to the laws and regulations imposed by the corporate operator.[21] While this provides scope for creating new opportunities and improved ways of living, it also reduces citizenship from a social contract to a commercial contract,[22] which may be both one-sided and practically difficult to enforce in a domain without a traditional sovereign.

Technological advances mean human habitation of space is now closer to becoming a reality than ever before. With space agencies and private space companies working towards sustained human presence in space, it is imperative that we consider the likely experiences of, and risks to, humans living in space habitats. As noted above, many of the most ambitious plans for space come from the corporate sector rather than national space agencies. Indeed, national space agencies have become increasingly reliant on the commercial sector for core space functions, including launch, resupply and return

14 United Arab Emirates Federal Ministry (2019).
15 SpaceX (2018).
16 SpaceX (2018).
17 Musk (2020).
18 Brown (2020).
19 Musk (2020).
20 Avery (2021).
21 Patterson (2022).
22 Boucher and Kelly (1994).

of astronauts.[23] The International Space Station (ISS), long an exemplar of international cooperation in space, is due to be decommissioned by the end of this decade and certain modules will be transitioned to a commercial space station operated by Axiom.[24] In the next part of this chapter, we draw upon Kim Stanley Robinson's *Mars* trilogy, James SA Corey's *The Expanse* novel series and the National Geographic *Mars* series, which melds fact and fiction, to explore what the future may look like for humans living beyond Earth.

Lessons from science fiction

The texts explored in this chapter present a dystopian vision of what the future of sustained human presence in space may be like. The common theme in this dystopia is the role of the corporate actor and the impact that corporate conduct has on humans living beyond Earth. Whether by deliberate action or unintended consequence in pursuit of profit, it is clear from these texts that corporate actors are imagined to significantly impact the futures and experiences of humans living on other planets. The question that this chapter seeks to explore is whether existing international space law can help to protect those inhabitants of future space settlements from such a nightmarish future.

Kim Stanley Robinson's *Mars* trilogy explores the terraforming[25] and habitation of Mars by the 'First Hundred' human settlers and their descendants. The first novel in the trilogy, *Red Mars*,[26] begins with the First Hundred hoping to establish a small scientific research station,[27] but the real motives of those responsible for sending the mission to Mars are soon revealed. The mission to settle Mars is driven by mega-corporations on Earth, referred to as 'transnats', and their desire to terraform Mars and exploit rich mineral deposits on Mars for profit.[28] The scientific motives for the mission to Mars are secondary to the lust for profits.

Debates between members of the First Hundred about whether Mars should be rapidly terraformed or preserved in an undisturbed state lead to an ideological split between the members of the First Hundred,[29] with the 'Greens', in favour of terraforming, led by Saxifrage Russell on one side,[30] and the 'Reds', in favour of preserving Mars in its original state, led by Ann

23 National Aeronautics and Space Administration (2019).
24 Howell (2017).
25 Terraforming ('Earth-shaping') is the hypothetical process of deliberately changing the environment of a celestial body to make it more like Earth.
26 Robinson (1992).
27 Robinson (1992), pp 61, 94–159.
28 Robinson (1992), p 442.
29 Robinson (1992), pp 39–40, 91.
30 Robinson (1992), pp 89–92, 169, 177–78.

Clayborne on the other.[31] The scientific interests of the First Hundred are displaced by the hypercapitalist motives of the 'transnats', enormous corporations that exert influence on the 'United Nations Office for Martian Affairs' (UNOMA) and push for exploitation of the resources on Mars with no consideration of the risks that may pose to inhabitants of the red planet.[32] Eventually the transnats replace entire governments on Earth and the economic motives behind the terraforming and exploitation of Mars are more starkly revealed. UNOMA bureaucrat and German millionaire Helmut Bronski violates a Mars Treaty by allowing a transnat, Armscor, to begin prospecting on Mars.[33] John Boone, the first human to set foot on Mars and unofficial leader of the First Hundred, responds to the destruction wrought by heavy mining operations at Bradbury Point:

> John shook his head. That afternoon they drove for an hour back to the habitat, past raw pits and slag heaps, toward the distant plume of the refineries on the other sides of the habitat mesa. He was used to seeing the land torn up for building purposes, but this ... It was amazing what a few hundred people could do ... wreaking such havoc just to strip away metals, destined for Earth's insatiable demand.[34]

In *Green Mars*,[35] Ann Clayborne observes 'the planet ... melting under her feet. Disintegrated. Reduced to mush in some Terran cartel's mining venture'.[36] This echoes plans for in situ resource utilisation and the exploitation of space resources currently being pursued by space agencies and private space companies, including through the NASA-led Artemis project[37] and the China- and Russia-led International Lunar Research Station.[38] While frequently characterised as being the best way for humanity to acquire fuel, drinkable water, and breathable air as humans venture further into the solar system,[39] the financial lure of the promise of potentially enormous profits to be derived from space mining cannot be ignored. As Robinson warns us in the *Mars* trilogy, the corporate desire to acquire profit can lead to incredible destruction, violent conflict and suffering.

A revolution is eventually launched against the occupying corporations, which is quickly crushed by the willingness of the Earth-aligned transnat

31 Robinson (1992), pp 133, 141, 268; Robinson (1993), p 155; Robinson (1996), p 298.
32 Robinson (1996), p 602.
33 Robinson (1992), pp 271, 277.
34 Robinson (1992), pp 276–77.
35 Robinson (1993).
36 Robinson (1993), p 128.
37 National Aeronautics and Space Administration (nd).
38 Pultarova (2021).
39 Meurisse and Carpenter (2020).

troops to use extreme violence to annihilate any opposition.[40] The vulnerability of life on a planet without a habitable atmosphere is starkly highlighted, with biospheres ripped open and destroyed, and inhabitants left to find refuge or perish.[41] Even the hero 'First Martian' John Boone perishes due to oxygen deprivation, having been beaten and left unconscious beyond the safety of a human habitat.[42] The *Mars* trilogy's predictions about the power of corporations and the risks posed to humans by corporate actions deliver an even starker warning now than they did in the 1990s, when the novels were written. With the increasing technological dominance of corporate actors in space and the planned human settlement of space by private space companies, the potential risks to future inhabitants of corporate space settlements are greater than ever. The *Mars* trilogy warns us that the corporate desire for profit frequently comes at the expense of the weak and vulnerable.

Similarly, in *The Expanse* series by James SA Corey (the pseudonym of authors Daniel Abraham and Ty Franck), corporate actors play a crucial role in shaping the politics, economy and social dynamics of the universe in which the series is set. Earth and Mars corporations control the vast majority of commercialised resources, including water, air, food and minerals, whereas 'Belter'[43] corporations control trade routes. The vulnerability of humans in space is highlighted early in the first novel, *Leviathan Wakes*,[44] which opens with the ice-hauler, *Canterbury*, responding to a distress signal from a mysterious stricken vessel after some debate amongst the crew about the obligation to render assistance:[45]

> The law of the solar system was unequivocal. In an environment as hostile to life as space, the aid and goodwill of your fellow humans wasn't optional. The emergency signal, just by existing, obligated the nearest ship to stop and render aid – which didn't mean the law was universally followed.[46]

The extreme vulnerability of humans in space is a repeated theme in the novels, with the reliance on others for every aspect of survival – even air to breathe – impacting the social dynamics of space habitats.[47] For example,

40 Robinson (1992), p 470.
41 Robinson (1992), p 477.
42 Robinson (1992), pp 17–18.
43 'Belters' are the 'working class' who live and work in the asteroid belt between Mars and Jupiter or the moons of outer planets, mining resources for the inhabitants of Earth and Mars.
44 Corey (2012).
45 Corey (2012), pp 13–16.
46 Corey (2012), p 14.
47 Corey (2012), p 61.

Detective Miller observes in the context of policing on Ceres, the dwarf planet that makes up almost one-third of the mass of our solar system's asteroid belt, that:

> Sometimes people fell out airlocks. Sometimes evidence vanished from the lockers. It wasn't so much that it was right or wrong as that it was justified. You spent your life in a stone bubble with your food, your water, your *air* shipped in from places so distant you could barely find them with a telescope, and a certain moral flexibility was necessary.[48]

Against this backdrop, the impact of corporate actors on the lives of those living in space habitats is explored. Corporations such as 'Protogen' are portrayed as prioritising profits over human lives and the wellbeing of inhabitants, even conducting unethical experiments on inhabitants of space stations in their attempts to control and weaponise a mysterious alien biological substance, known as the 'protomolecule'.[49] Protogen even goes to the extent of instigating a war between Earth and Mars to benefit shareholder interests, maximise profit and seek corporate advantage.[50] Corporate actors in *The Expanse* series are portrayed as sinister and largely uncontrollable, with the ability to manipulate governments[51] highlighting the potential risks of allowing unchecked corporate power to exist in space:

> 'Protogen, protomolecule', Holden said. 'They had no idea what it does, but they slapped their label on it like they'd made it. They found an alien weapon, and all they could think to do was *brand* it'.[52]

The question is whether existing international space law can adequately protect inhabitants of future space settlements against the excesses of such malevolent corporate actors and their unclear and unarticulated motivations.

International space law and the prevention of a dystopian future

International space law never contemplated sustained human habitation beyond the Earth. The existing international space law regime was created at a time when very few states had space capabilities, let alone private or commercial actors. There are five international space law treaties: the Treaty

48 Corey (2012), p 24.
49 Corey (2012), p 296.
50 Corey (2012), pp 342–46.
51 Corey (2012), p 410.
52 Corey (2012), p 345.

on Principles Governing the Activities of States in the Exploration and Use of Outer Space, including the Moon and Other Celestial Bodies ('Outer Space Treaty');[53] the Agreement on the Rescue of Astronauts, the Return of Astronauts and the Return of Objects Launched into Outer Space ('Rescue and Return Agreement');[54] the Convention on International Liability for Damage Caused by Space Objects ('Liability Convention');[55] the Convention on Registration of Objects Launched into Outer Space ('Registration Convention');[56] and the Agreement Governing the Activities of States on the Moon and Other Celestial Bodies ('Moon Agreement'),[57] as well as soft law instruments. The Outer Space Treaty provides the legal foundation for all activities in outer space. In contrast, the Moon Agreement is the least significant of the space law treaties, and is sometimes considered to be a failed treaty due to its low level of ratifications. None of the major space-faring states is a party to the Moon Agreement, despite having been involved in its negotiation. At the time of writing, the Moon Agreement has only 17 states parties, following Saudi Arabia's withdrawal on 5 January 2024.[58]

Space law has been described by Frans von der Dunk as 'all law that actually one way or another, follows humans into outer space'.[59] The applicability of international law, including the Charter, was recognized as a guiding principle by the United Nations Committee on the Peaceful Uses of Outer Space even before negotiations for the Outer Space Treaty had commenced.[60] Article III of the Outer Space Treaty explicitly confirms that international law generally applies to space as a domain. Article III provides that:

> States Parties to the Treaty shall carry on activities in the exploration and use of outer space, including the Moon and other celestial bodies, in accordance with international law, including the Charter of the United Nations, in the interest of maintaining international peace and security and promoting international cooperation and understanding.

This means that international space law includes the space law treaties and international law more generally, including treaties and customary international law, and general principles of law.[61] This broad understanding of what law applies in space may provide a pathway to regulating the excesses of

53 Outer Space Treaty (1967).
54 Rescue and Return Agreement (1968).
55 Liability Convention (1972).
56 Registration Convention (1976).
57 Moon Agreement (1984).
58 Saudi Arabia (2023).
59 Von der Dunk (2020), p 1.
60 United Nations General Assembly (1961) resolution 1721 (XVI).
61 Statute of the International Court of Justice (1946) Art 36.

corporate actors in space and protecting inhabitants of future space settlements beyond the Earth.

Given the Cold War origins of the Outer Space Treaty, and the fact that only states were regarded as being capable of undertaking space activities at the time the treaty was negotiated, the Outer Space Treaty provides little guidance with respect to sustained human presence in space or the regulation of corporate actors. The provisions of the Outer Space Treaty were intended to maintain balance and transparency to ensure continued access to space by the Cold War superpowers, the United States and the Soviet Union.[62] The later space law treaties build upon the foundation of the Outer Space Treaty and reflect an interest by non-space-faring and developing states in being able to access the growing benefits of access to the space environment.[63] Existing space laws and policies are far more concerned with regulating space activities connected to Earth-based actors – for example, launches from Earth,[64] promoting domestic space industries[65] or the return of space objects to their state of registry[66] – than with the regulation of corporate actors and future humans in space. However, the principles contained in existing international space law treaties provide a strong foundation for the development of future laws specific to humans in space and the conduct of corporate actors.

All current space-faring states are party to the Outer Space Treaty. Article I allows states parties to 'use' outer space, which at first glance would include the use by humans of other planets as a place to live, provided the habitat was operated for the 'benefit and interests of all countries'. However, the Outer Space Treaty also provides that outer space 'shall be the province of all [hu]mankind'[67] and that 'outer space, including the Moon and other celestial bodies, is not subject to national appropriation by claim of sovereignty, by means of use or occupation, or by any other means'.[68]

The principle of non-appropriation in Article II of the Outer Space Treaty is arguably a principle of customary international law, having received widespread acceptance and representing state practice for more than 50 years.[69] As customary international law, the principle of non-appropriation applies to all states, not just those that are a party to the Outer Space Treaty. Further, the operation of Article VI of the Outer Space Treaty means that

62 United Nations General Assembly (1961) resolution 1721 (XVI); United Nations General Assembly (1966) A/AC.105/C.2/SR.57.

63 United Nations General Assembly (1963) A/C.1/PV.1342; United Nations General Assembly (1967) A/PV.1640.

64 Space (Launches and Returns) Act (2018).

65 Australian Department of Industry, Science and Resources (2019).

66 Outer Space Treaty (1967) Art V; Rescue and Return Agreement (1968).

67 Outer Space Treaty (1967) Art I.

68 Outer Space Treaty (1967) Art II.

69 Fitzmaurice and Henderson (2019).

every space activity is ultimately a national space activity for which a state may be responsible. This means that no one, be they state, corporate actor or individual, can exercise legal control over any part of outer space, including celestial bodies, as if it were their legal territory. While the term 'celestial bodies' is not defined in any of the space law treaties, the International Astronomical Union adopted definitions in 2006 that recognise the following as 'celestial bodies': the Sun; the planets; the Moon of Earth and the moons of other planets; near-Earth objects; dwarf planets; trans-Neptunian objects; asteroids; comets; and Kuiper belt objects.[70]

While there is disagreement about whether the principle of non-appropriation also extends to appropriation of resources extracted from celestial bodies,[71] the principle of non-appropriation clearly precludes any possibility of states expanding their territory through planetary exploration and the establishment of extraterrestrial human habitats. Article VI of the Outer Space Treaty ultimately makes a state internationally responsible for the activities of its private space corporations through the obligation to authorise and continuously supervise space activities. Article VI provides that:

> States Parties to the Treaty shall bear international responsibility for national activities in outer space, including the Moon and other celestial bodies, whether such activities are carried on by governmental agencies or by non-governmental entities, and for assuring that national activities are carried out in conformity with the provisions set forth in the present Treaty. The activities of non-governmental entities in outer space, including the Moon and other celestial bodies, shall require authorization and continuing supervision by the appropriate State Party to the Treaty.[72]

This means states are required to ensure that corporations are prevented from appropriation of celestial bodies and exercising exclusive control over any part of outer space. However, as the *Mars* trilogy and *The Expanse* series both warn, mega-corporations may grow so large and powerful that they can exert influence over governments, which would reduce the protection offered by the anticipated state oversight of corporate space activities provided by existing licensing regimes.[73] For example, in *Red Mars*, Frank Chalmers is prepared to renegotiate the (fictional) Mars Treaty, described as having been based 'on the old Outer Space Treaty', noting further that 'was the first mistake, because the Outer Space Treaty was in fact a very fragile arrangement

70 International Astronautical Union (2006).

71 See, for example, Tronchetti (2015), p 769; Brearly (2006); Tennen (2016).

72 Outer Space Treaty (1967) Art VI.

73 See, for example, USA (1998); Belgium (2005); Netherlands (2007); France (2008); Space (Launches and Returns) Act (2018).

and so the Mars Treaty is too'.[74] Further, the absence of sovereignty leaves open both the possibility of *de facto* control over a celestial body being exercised by the first claimant and the difficulty of any state being able to exercise actual control over such claims – legitimate or not.[75]

The potential for corporate behaviour in space to pose a real risk to both humans and the space environment is something that requires consideration now, as we are on the verge of both human and robotic missions to space becoming more feasible.[76] For example, Musk's vision for the SpaceX Mars city involves a servant class, easily controlled by restricting access to air, water and food while they repay an amount that the company decides will satisfy their debt. In the absence of any oversight mechanisms, there is a greater risk that humans in space habitats may fall victim to corporate exploitation. While it might seem far-fetched now (being presented as a somewhat tongue-in-cheek option), alarm bells should already be ringing in relation to the potential erosion for norms sadly only recently established on Earth to be eroded in space, such as laws against slavery.[77] As the *Mars* trilogy makes especially stark, this potential ambiguity regarding the practical ability to exercise jurisdiction – through enforcement, laws, courts and so on – also creates significant risks for the preservation of the planetary environment.[78]

Article V of the Outer Space Treaty provides that state parties must regard astronauts as 'envoys of [hu]mankind' and 'render them all possible assistance in the event of accident, distress, or emergency landing'.[79] Article V goes on to provide that 'in carrying on activities in outer space and on celestial bodies, the astronauts of one State Party shall render all possible assistance to the astronauts of other State Parties'.[80] This is further expanded in the Rescue and Return Agreement, which extends the obligation to rescue and provide assistance to 'personnel of a spacecraft'.[81] The Moon Agreement takes the rescue obligation even further, with Article 10 providing that:

1. States Parties shall adopt all practicable measures to safeguard the life and health of persons on the Moon. For this purpose they shall regard any person on the Moon as an astronaut within the meaning of article V of the Treaty on Principles Governing the Activities of States in the Exploration and Use of Outer Space, including the Moon and Other

74 Robinson (1992), p 341.
75 De Zwart (2016).
76 National Aeronautics and Space Administration (2022).
77 International Covenant on Civil and Political Rights (1966) Art 8; Australia, Modern Slavery Act (2018).
78 Discussed further below.
79 Outer Space Treaty (1967) Art V.
80 Outer Space Treaty (1967) Art V.
81 Rescue and Return Agreement (1968) Art 2.

Celestial Bodies and as part of the personnel of a spacecraft within the meaning of the Agreement on the Rescue of Astronauts, the Return of Astronauts and the Return of Objects Launched into Outer Space.

2. States Parties shall offer shelter in their stations, installation, vehicles and other facilities to persons in distress on the Moon.[82]

It is this obligation to rescue that is being debated in the initial stages of *Leviathan Wakes*, during discussions of whether or not the spacecraft *Canterbury* must respond to the *Scopuli*'s distress call or whether the crew could simply ignore it and continue on their way.[83]

None of the space law treaties defines 'astronaut'[84] or 'personnel of a spacecraft',[85] and it remains unsettled at law whether all inhabitants of space habitats would be considered to be 'astronauts' or 'personnel of a spacecraft', and thus be entitled to this protection.[86] For example, would tourists to a private space station be entitled to assistance and to be rescued under the obligation to assist in the Outer Space Treaty and the Rescue and Return Agreement, or does their status as tourists mean that they fall outside the category of persons entitled to protection? What of humans born in space settlements? The terms 'astronaut' and 'personnel of a spacecraft' might suggest that individuals falling within these categories have had some specialised training or have an operational role in the mission. The Principles Regarding Processes and Criteria for Selection, Assignment, Training and Certification of ISS (Expedition and Visiting) Crewmembers for the International Space Station distinguish between a professional astronaut (or cosmonaut) and a spaceflight participant,[87] which would support the interpretation of 'astronaut' and 'personnel of a spacecraft' as requiring something more than mere presence in space. One implication of this interpretation for humans living permanently off-Earth is that there may be no obligation on others to rescue them or render assistance in the event of an emergency, such as a shortage of oxygen, food, fuel or water.

An excellent example of this is provided in the National Geographic television series *Mars*, where a commercial mining enterprise, Lukrum, establishes a base on Mars with insufficient water. They immediately make a demand for water from the scientific base, noting that their request cannot be refused on the basis of the provisions of the Outer Space Treaty.[88] The commander

82 Moon Agreement (1984) Art 10.
83 Corey (2012), p 14.
84 Outer Space Treaty (1967) Art V.
85 Rescue and Return Agreement (1968).
86 Lyall (2010); Fitzmaurice and Henderson (2019).
87 'Principles Regarding Processes and Criteria for Selection, Assignment, Training and Certification of ISS (Expedition and Visiting) Crewmembers' (2001).
88 National Geographic (2018).

of the scientific base responds that they should have ensured that they had enough supplies with them to be self-sufficient. However, as *Leviathan Wakes* reminds us, 'In an environment as hostile to life as space, the aid and goodwill of your fellow humans wasn't optional'.[89] Thus the Lukrum demands are reluctantly met by the scientific base. The law needs to respond to the potential gap in the obligation to rescue and assist to ensure that all humans in space are entitled to protection and to be rescued in the event of an emergency.

The treatment of humans living in future space habitats is something that will require further consideration before humans are living in such habitats, especially to the extent that they are controlled by corporate entities. In the *Mars* trilogy, we see heavy-handed tactics and extreme violence being used against inhabitants by Earth-aligned transnat troops in their efforts to quell dissent.[90] Further, in *The Expanse* series, we see civilian spacecraft targeted and vapourised,[91] and violent tactics by corporate mercenaries on Eros against civilians as they were being herded into radiation shelters to be infected with the protomolecule.[92] As noted above, appeals to laws are misplaced in contexts absent enforcement mechanisms:

> Some idiot was shouting at one of the so-called cops: he was a lawyer; he was getting all of this on video; whoever was responsible was going to be in big trouble. Miller watched a bunch of people start to gather around the confrontation. The guy in the riot gear listened, nodded, and shot the lawyer once in the kneecap.[93]

While international humanitarian law[94] and international human rights law[95] may assist – and clearly apply in space – the risk is still that corporate actors so far from Earth may not feel any need to temper their behaviour and may consider that they are beyond the reach of any legal consequences.

Communications between space habitats and Earth, and between space habitats, is another area where the law will need to evolve in order to provide

89 Corey (2012), p 14.

90 Robinson (1992, p 477), Part 7: Senzeni Na, which witnesses the brutal retaliation against the Mars uprising, beginning with the death of rebel leader Arkady, who bursts into flame as his town shield is punctured, followed by the death of thousands: 'It was not hard to destroy Martian towns. No harder than breaking a window or popping a balloon.'

91 Corey (2012), p 54.

92 Corey (2012), p 289.

93 Corey (2012), pp 293–94.

94 International humanitarian law includes the principles of distinction, precautions and proportionality. These may all provide protection for civilians in the event of an international or non-international armed conflict in space.

95 The right to life seems of particular relevance.

greater protection for inhabitants. After all, in the event of distress or emergency in a space habitat, there must be a means of calling for help. Cutting off communication with those outside a space habitat where gross abuses are being perpetrated would be a logical tactic for evil corporate actors trying to hide what they are doing from scrutiny. Even the International Space Station does not have any rules in the Intergovernmental Agreement,[96] or associated Code of Conduct,[97] allowing or limiting communications with Earth, and both are silent on the rights of astronauts to communicate with Earth. NASA allows its astronauts on the ISS to contact their families, seemingly whenever they wish to do so outside of their required working hours. However, this may be due to advances in technology making communication between the ISS and Earth cheaper and easier, and not something that is protected by law.

The international legal framework that governs rights of communication largely stems from human rights law.[98] Although it remains somewhat open to debate regarding just which parts of international law generally apply in outer space,[99] it is generally accepted that human rights can apply in space.[100] However, human rights law does not contain a right to communication in and of itself. Yet it is the ability to communicate that will be important in the context of space habitats, in an environment where humans cannot survive without assistance, where communication is essential for connection to humanity, where humans are reliant on others for every breath and where being able to communicate and seek assistance may be crucial to survival. In the future, regulation of communications in space could include priority access to means of communication or spectrum for space habitats to facilitate emergency communications. Hamelink and Hoffmann advocate for the recognition of a right to communicate, which they argue should be understood in terms of protection of the enabling environment to facilitate relational communications, with communication processes to be recognised as a human need and firmly protected by law.[101] If it is the enabling environment that facilitates communication that is to be protected, this will include protection of infrastructure on Earth as well as that in space – protection for everything that enables communication.

The positive legal obligation for states to avoid harmful contamination contained in Article IX of the Outer Space Treaty is also relevant to the

96 Intergovernmental Agreement (1998).
97 Code of Conduct for the International Space Station Crew (2000).
98 Universal Declaration of Human Rights (1948); International Covenant on Civil and Political Rights (1966); International Covenant on Economic, Social and Cultural Rights (1966).
99 See, for example, von der Dunk (2021).
100 See, for example, Freeland and Ireland-Piper (2022).
101 Hamelink and Hoffmann (2008).

protection of humans from reckless and ill-intentioned corporate actors. Article IX provides in part that:

> In the exploration and use of outer space, including the Moon and other celestial bodies, States Parties to the Treaty shall be guided by the principle of cooperation and mutual assistance and shall conduct all their activities in outer space, including the Moon and other celestial bodies, with due regard to the corresponding interests of all other States Parties to the Treaty. States Parties to the Treaty shall pursue studies of outer space, including the Moon and other celestial bodies, and conduct exploration of them so as to avoid their harmful contamination and also adverse changes in the environment of the Earth resulting from the introduction of extraterrestrial matter and, where necessary, shall adopt appropriate measures for this purpose.[102]

Harmful contamination is not defined within the space law treaties, which leaves the term open to interpretation. Taking a holistic approach to the interpretation of 'harmful contamination', consistent with the interpretive approach provided for in the Vienna Convention on the Law of Treaties,[103] the use of the term 'shall' denotes a binding legal obligation. It has been suggested to be 'all possible kinds, forms or instances of harmful interference in outer space, deliberate or unintentional alike'.[104] At the heart of the *Mars* trilogy are the irreconcilable attitudes of the Mars settlers, the various Earth-based governments and corporate actors to terraforming. Many of the terraforming activities, such as radiation contamination, alteration of the atmosphere and installation of solar mirrors, would be considered 'harmful contamination' of the Mars environment,[105] albeit undertaken to make the planet more amenable to human habitation. The release of the protomolecule by corporate actors seeking to weaponise and monetise it in *The Expanse* series seems a particularly clear situation of harmful contamination of the space environment, as are the destructive mining operations of Mars in the *Mars* trilogy.

With states reluctant to enter into new multilateral treaties, the more progressive initiatives in the development of space law have come through the implementation of international law through bilateral or multilateral cooperative agreements – for example, the Artemis Accords, announced by NASA in 2020 as a 'shared vision for principles, grounded in the Outer Space Treaty of 1967, to create a safe and transparent environment which

102 Outer Space Treaty (1967) Art IX.
103 Vienna Convention on the Law of Treaties (1969) Art 31.
104 Marchisio (2009), p 176.
105 De Zwart et al (2021).

facilitates exploration, science, and commercial activities for all of humanity to enjoy'.[106] Involvement in NASA's Artemis project is contingent on national space agencies accepting and adhering to the Artemis Accords, a series of principles that form the basis of agreements between NASA and national space agencies. Australia is one of the few states that are party to the Moon Agreement as well as being signatories to the Artemis Accords. With 42 signatories as of 31 May 2024, there are more signatories to the Accords than the Moon Agreement, making the Accords significant for the interpretation and evolution of space law.

The Accords contain principles that fall roughly into two categories: existing norms that are broadly repetitive of the provisions of the Outer Space Treaty;[107] and those that extend well beyond its provisions and attempt to establish new norms of behaviour.[108] Falling somewhere between these two extremes are principles dealing with the creation of international standards to ensure interoperability of space systems,[109] the protection of lunar heritage[110] and agreement to adhere to the UN Space Debris Mitigation Guidelines.[111]

Several of the principles of the Artemis Accords will be important in the context of sustained human presence in space. Interoperability of systems,[112] for instance, will be critical to ensure safe and robust space exploration, as well as to ensure that space stations can be repaired and crew members rescued. The Artemis project contemplates that states will participate through their national space agencies, but also that specific tasks and activities may be undertaken by commercial providers.[113] The engagement of a broad range of commercial entities may require the use of commercial off-the-shelf technology to reduce the cost of manufacture, use and replacement.[114] There is therefore a requirement for the development of standards to ensure interoperability and for new laws and regulations relevant to safety, efficiency and cost, and to ensure that corporate actors are not cutting costs in order to maximise their profits at the expense of human safety. Given the geopolitical tensions between countries with current and planned space habitats, new international law may be required to ensure maximum protection of inhabitants of space habitats, regardless of whether they are space agencies

106 National Aeronautics and Space Administration (2020).
107 See, for example, National Aeronautics and Space Administration (2020) Sections 3 and 6.
108 See, for example, National Aeronautics and Space Administration (2020) 11(7)–(11) 'safety zones'.
109 National Aeronautics and Space Administration (2020) Section 5.
110 National Aeronautics and Space Administration (2020) Section 9.
111 National Aeronautics and Space Administration (2020) Section 12.
112 National Aeronautics and Space Administration (2020) Section 5.
113 National Aeronautics and Space Administration (2020) Section 2.
114 De Zwart (2021).

or private space stations, and regardless of the nationality or astronaut status of inhabitants.[115]

On Earth, there is increasing recognition of the need for corporations to adopt and act according to principles of corporate social responsibility and to endorse projects such as the UN Sustainable Development Goals.[116] It is hoped that stakeholders, including governments, customers, partners and shareholders, will demand that corporations maintain sustainable and responsible principles to maintain a social licence to operate, but it cannot be guaranteed once these entities operate beyond Earth.[117]

Conclusion

Writing in 1995, Heidi Keefe captured the relationship between science fiction and the space colonialisation:

> We are standing at the threshold of a new era. Human colonisation on other planets is no longer science fiction. It can be science fact ... If humanity is to continue for another million years, our future lies in boldly going where no-one else has gone before.[118]

As we move towards a future as a multiplanetary species, international space law will need to strike a balance between encouraging the activities of corporations 'with positive and honourable motives'[119] and preventing malevolent corporate actors from exploiting and harming humans in space. The protective capacity of law must be utilised to ensure that humans living beyond Earth are adequately protected from suffering caused by corporate greed and do not suffer harm from deliberate action or as an unintended consequence of the pursuit of profits.

While existing space law provides a good foundation for sustained human presence in space, it may not be sufficient to adequately protect humans living beyond Earth from harm caused by corporate actors. Some obligations in respect of inhabited space stations may now be customary international law – for instance, the obligation to rescue an astronaut in distress – but further developments in the law are necessary to ensure clarity of responsibilities and obligations and to maximise protection for humans beyond Earth. We must heed the warnings from science fiction about the risks that flow from

115 Freeland (2010).
116 De Zwart et al (2023).
117 De Zwart et al (2023).
118 Keefe (1995), p 346.
119 Von der Dunk et al (2004), p 150.

allowing corporate greed to flourish unrestrained at the expense of those living among the stars.

References

Secondary sources

Dan Avery (2021) 'Blue Origin Founder Jeff Bezos Says That People will be BORN in Space Centuries from Now and will Visit Earth on Vacation "the Way You Visit Yellowstone National Park"' *Daily Mail*, 13 November, https://www.dailymail.co.uk/sciencetech/article-10196631/Jeff-Bezos-predicts-people-born-space-visit-Earth-vacation.html

David Boucher and Paul J Kelly (1994) *The Social Contract from Hobbes to Rawls*, Routledge

Andrew Brearly (2006) 'Mining the Moon: Owning the Night Sky?' 4 *Astropolitics* 59

Mike Brown (2020) 'SpaceX Mars City: Elon Musk Reveals How You Will Pay for Your Trip' *Inverse*, 21 January, https://www.inverse.com/article/62390-spacex-mars-city-elon-musk-reveals-how-you-will-pay-for-your-trip

George W Bush (2004) 'A Renewed Spirit of Discovery: The President's Vision for US Space Exploration' *Media Release*, January.

China National Space Administration (2021) *International Lunar Research Station: Guide for Partnership*, http://www.cnsa.gov.cn/english/n6465652/n6465653/c6812150/content.html

James SA Corey (2012) *Leviathan Wakes*, Orbit Books.

Melissa de Zwart (2016) *Google in Space? How will Space Governance Accommodate Non-State Actors?* RUMLAE, https://ssrn.com/abstract=2809409

Melissa de Zwart (2021) 'To the Moon and Beyond: The Artemis Accords and the Evolution of Space Law' in Melissa de Zwart and Stacey Henderson (eds), *Commercial and Military Uses of Outer Space*, Springer, 65.

Francesco de Zwart, Stacey Henderson and John Culton (2023) 'CSR/ESG in Commercial Space Operations and the Artemis Accords' in Melissa de Zwart, Stacey Henderson, John Culton, Deborah Turnbull and Amit Srivastava (eds), *Human Uses of Outer Space: Return to the Moon*, Springer, 109.

Melissa de Zwart, Stacey Henderson and Rachel Neef (2021) 'The Principle of "Harmful Contamination" Applied to Human Missions to Mars' 45 *Journal of Space Law* 276.

Joshua Fitzmaurice and Stacey Henderson (2019) 'On the Legality of Mars Colonisation' 40 *Adelaide Law Review* 841.

Steven Freeland (2010) 'Fly Me to the Moon: How will International Law Cope with Commercial Space Tourism?' 11 *Melbourne Journal of International Law* 90.

Steven Freeland and Danielle Ireland-Piper (2022) 'Space Law, Human Rights and Corporate Accountability' 26 *UCLA Journal of International Law and Foreign Affairs* 1.

Rex Hall and David Shayler (2001) *The Rocket Men: Vostok & Voskhod – the First Soviet Manned Space-flights*, Springer.

Cees J Hamelink and Julia Hoffmann (2008) 'The State of the Right to Communicate' 7 *Global Media Journal* 14.

Stephen J Hoffman (ed) (2001) *The Mars Surface Reference Mission: A Description of Human And Robotic Surface Activities*, NASA, https://space.nss.org/wp-content/uploads/2001-NASA-Mars-Surface-Reference-Mission.pdf

Elizabeth Howell (2017) 'A Private Space Station Might be Born from the ISS' https://www.space.com/35454-international-space-station-retire-private-axiom-orbit-commercialization.html

Jet Propulsion Laboratory, National Aeronautics and Space Administration (2005) 'Planetary Protection and Contamination Control Technologies for Future Space Science Missions' https://solarsystem.nasa.gov/resources/294/planetary-protection-and-contamination-control-technologies-for-futurespace-science-missions

Heidi Keefe (1995) 'Making the Final Frontier Feasible: A Critical Look at the Current Body of Outer Space Law' 11 *Computer & High Technology Law Journal* 345.

Francis Lyall (2010) 'Who is an Astronaut? The Inadequacy of Current International Law' 66 *Acta Astronautica* 1613.

Sergio Marchisio (2009) 'Article IX' in Stephen Hobe, Bernhard Schmidt-Tedd and Kai-Uwe Schrogl (Eds.) *Cologne Commentary on Space Law: Outer Space Treaty (Volume 1)*, 176.

Alexandre Meurisse and James Carpenter (2020) 'Past, Present and Future Rationale for Space Resource Utilisation' 182 *Planetary and Space Science* 104853.

National Geographic, *Mars* (2018) Season 2, Episode 1 'We Are Not Alone'.

Catherine F Patterson (2022) 'Governing Poverty and Disorder: Corporate Towns and Social Policy' in Catherine F Patterson (ed), *Urban Government and the Early Stuart State*, Cambridge University Press 1–13. https://doi.org/10.1016/j.pss.2020.104853

David SF Portree (2001) *Humans to Mars: Fifty Years of Mission Planning, 1950–2000*, NASA History Office.

Tereza Pultarova (2021) 'Russia, China Reveal Moon Base Roadmap but No Plans for Astronaut Trips Yet' https://www.space.com/china-russia-international-lunar-research-station

Kim Stanley Robinson (1992) *Red Mars*, Random House.

Kim Stanley Robinson (1993) *Green Mars*, Random House.

Kim Stanley Robinson (1996) *Blue Mars*, Random House.

Lonnie Shekhtman (2021) 'NASA's Artemis Base Camp on the Moon will Need Light, Water, Elevation' 28 January, https://www.nasa.gov/feature/goddard/2021/nasa-s-artemis-base-camp-on-the-moon-will-need-light-water-elevation

Leslie I Tennen (2016) 'Enterprise Rights and the Legal Regime for Exploitation of Outer Space Resources' 47 *University of the Pacific Law Review* 281.

Fabio Tronchetti (2015) 'Legal Aspects of Space Resource Utilisation' in Frans von der Dunk and Fabio Tronchetti (eds), *Handbook of Space Law*, Edward Elgar, 501.

Frans von der Dunk (2020) *Advanced Introduction to Space Law*, Edward Elgar.

Frans von der Dunk (2021) 'Armed Conflicts in Outer Space: Which Law Applies?' 97 *International Law Studies* 188.

Frans von der Dunk et al (2004) 'Surreal Estate: Addressing the Issue of "Immovable Property Rights on the Moon"' 20 *Space Policy* 149.

International agreements and legislation

Agreement among the Government of Canada, Governments of Member States of the European Space Agency, the Government of Japan, the Government of the Russian Federation, and the Government of the United States of America concerning Cooperation on the Civil International Space Station, Washington, done 29 January 1998, entered into force 27 March 2001. Space Law – Basic Legal Documents, D.II.4 ('Intergovernmental Agreement').

Agreement Governing the Activities of States on the Moon and Other Celestial Bodies, opened for signature 18 December 1979 (entered into force 11 July 1984) ('Moon Agreement').

Agreement on the Rescue of Astronauts, the Return of Astronauts and the Return of Objects Launched into Outer Space, opened for signature 22 April 1968 (entered into force 3 December 1968) ('Rescue and Return Agreement').

Code of Conduct for International Space Station Crew (2000).

Convention on International Liability for Damage Caused by Space Objects, opened for signature 29 March 1972 (entered into force 1 September 1972) ('Liability Convention').

Convention on Registration of Objects Launched into Outer Space, opened for signature 14 January 1975 (entered into force 15 September 1976) ('Registration Convention').

International Astronautical Union (2006) Definition of a Planet in the Solar System, RES/B5, 24 August 2006.

International Covenant on Civil and Political Rights, opened for signature 16 December 1966 (entered into force 23 March 1976).

International Covenant on Economic, Social and Cultural Rights, opened for signature 16 December 1966 (entered into force 3 January 1976).

National Aeronautics and Space Administration (2020) The Artemis Accords: Principles for Cooperation in the Civil Exploration and Use of the Moon, Mars, Comets, and Asteroids for Peaceful Purposes (13 October 2020).

Principles Regarding Processes and Criteria for Selection, Assignment, Training and Certification of ISS (Expedition and Visiting) Crewmembers' (2001) ISS Multilateral Crew Operations Panel (Web Page, November 2001), https://spaceref.com/status-report/principles-regarding-processes-and-criteria-for-selection-assignment-training-and-certification-of-iss-expedition-and-visiting-crewmembers

Saudi Arabia (2023) 'Agreement Governing the Activities of States on the Moon and Other Celestial Bodies: Withdrawal' 5 January, https://treaties.un.org/doc/Publication/CN/2023/CN.4.2023-Eng.pdf

Statute of the International Court of Justice (1946) UKTS 67.

Treaty on Principles Governing the Activities of States in the Exploration and Use of Outer Space, including the Moon and Other Celestial Bodies, opened for signature 27 January 1967 (entered into force 10 October 1967) ('Outer Space Treaty').

United Nations General Assembly (1961) Resolution 1721 (XVI) International Cooperation in the Peaceful Uses of Outer Space, 1085th plenary meeting (adopted 20 December 1961).

United Nations General Assembly (1963) A/C.1/PV.1342 (2 December 1963).

United Nations General Assembly (1966) Summary Record of the Fifty-Seventh Meeting, A/AC.105/C.2/SR.57 (20 October 1966).

United Nations General Assembly (1967) A/PV.1640 (19 December 1967)
Universal Declaration of Human Rights (1948) UNGA Res 217 A(III) (adopted 10 December 1948).
Vienna Convention on the Law of Treaties, opened for signature 23 May 1969 (entered into force 27 January 1980).
Legislation – Australia
Department of Industry, Science and Resources (2019) Australia's Civil Space Strategy 2019–2028.
Modern Slavery Act 2018 (Cth).
Space (Launches and Returns) Act 2018 (Cth).
Legislation – Belgium
Law on the Activities of Launching, Flight Operations or Guidance of Space Objects (2005).
Legislation – France
Loi n°2008-518 de 3 juin 2008 relative aux operations spatiales (2008).
Legislation – Netherlands
Wet ruimtevaartactiviteiten 2007 (Space Activities Act).
Legislation – United States
Commercial Space Launch Act (1998).
NASA Transition Authorisation Act of 2017, Pub L No 115-10, 131 Stat 18.

Web pages

Elon Musk (2020) Twitter, 17 January, https://twitter.com/elonmusk/status/1217991853615677440
European Space Agency, 'Gateway' (web page), https://www.esa.int/Science_Exploration/Human_and_Robotic_Exploration/Exploration/Gateway
National Aeronautics and Space Administration (2019) Commercial Resupply Services (web page), https://www.nasa.gov/mission_pages/station/structure/launch/overview.html
National Aeronautics and Space Administration (2022) Solar System Exploration (web page), https://solarsystem.nasa.gov/missions/?order=launch_date+desc&per_page=50&page=0&search=&fs=&fc=33&ft=&dp=&category=33
National Aeronautics and Space Administration (nd) Artemis (web page), https://www.nasa.gov/specials/artemis
SpaceX (2018) 'Making Humans a Multiplanetary Species' (web page), 20 December, http://www.spacex.com/mars
United Arab Emirates Federal Ministry (2019) 'Mars 2117 Project' (web page), 24 September, https://government.uae/en/more/uae -future/203 0-2117

Chapter 7

Society is just people, and the law is just their club rules

What utopian science fiction can teach us about legal vulnerability and exploitation in off-world human settlements

Evie Kendal

Introduction

The field of law and literature is said to have the power to 'illuminate our way to the future', but scholars like Bruce L Rockwood note that popular literature is often disregarded in favour of canonical texts, leaving a vast 'unmined' potential in the widely read genre of science fiction.[1] He claims this is despite the fact that science fiction 'has come to play an ever more important role in shaping the metaphors of everyday life, including those we use to view law and society'.[2] When science fiction *is* brought into academic debate, it is often to explore the social implications of emerging technologies, or sometimes to ridicule opposing views of science or philosophy. Nevertheless, as a genre including utopian fiction, with its focus on world-building and alternative 'quasi-human' societies,[3] science fiction is a rich source of cultural knowledge about past, present and potential future socio-legal systems.

This chapter considers how human vulnerability in the harsh environment of space is depicted in science fiction, with a particular focus on occupational health and safety for off-world workers, human rights and incarceration on other planets. As the potential pool of texts is stratospherically large, the sample will be limited to specific episodes of long-running science fiction television series that focus on off-world mining or incarceration, or both. Representatives from some of the most influential space-based science fiction franchises have been prioritised, as they are the examples with which the general public and science fiction fandom are most likely to be familiar. The chapter will begin by considering how legal world-building functions in science fiction before exploring specific textual depictions of human

1 Rockwood (1999), pp 267–68.
2 Rockwood (1999), p 269.
3 Suvin (1973).

DOI: 10.4324/9781003412274-8

vulnerability and exploitation, and the fictional legal systems that promote these. It will conclude with a discussion of what lessons we might learn from science fiction when designing new off-world human settlements.

Science fiction legal world-building

Damien Trentesaux et al note that science fiction is where writers can push known science and technology to their limits and then try to 'extrapolate consequences'.[4] For many, the potential consequences of new technologies include safety concerns, job losses, changes to interpersonal relationships and even legal punishments, including for intentional misuse or unforeseen harm. Science fiction provides a site to test out not only alternative socio-technical realities but hypothetical legal systems as well. With its focus on creating better realities, Mike Nellis claims it is surprising that 'there has been little mainstream penological interest in utopian thought', especially when one of the main foci is eliminating crime and anti-social behaviours.[5] Ironically, such attempts often succeed in creating the most powerful dystopian narratives found in the science fiction genre. As examples, Nellis first considers *Minority Report*, where technology is used for 'preventing or pre-empting crime', leading to changes to how illegal activity is defined and the policing of human thoughts, and secondly correctional interventions, such as Philip K. Dick's concept of the wearable 'tattletale' device that provides tracking data for convicted felons.[6] In their stories, these technologies revolutionise sentencing, and while the former is an extreme deviation from current legal practice, Nellis notes that the latter predicted ankle monitors. Thus, when such devices were developed in the real world, there was already a source of knowledge on how they might function. As Jorge L Contreras writes, science fiction

> is an ideal medium in which to consider how the law can and should develop in the face of technological change. Lawyers, judges and law professors thrive on hypothetical scenarios. Within the context of a science fiction story, an author can postulate a law or rule that responds to a scientific or technological discovery in a way that extends far beyond the classroom thought experiment … Science fiction offers the ultimate legal hypothetical. It is not only analytical, as a government report or law review article can be, but also emotive. It portrays characters living with the consequences of different regulatory and legal regimes. And if the characters are believable, and the legal rules are plausible, then 'experience', as it is,

4 Trentesaux et al (2021), p 247.
5 Nellis (2013), p 164.
6 Nellis (2013), p 169.

> can be simulated where none existed before. Works of science fiction thus serve as extended thought experiments, the best of which achieve character empathy that can give purchase to policy arguments and analysis.[7]

However, Contreras's view that the legal systems depicted in science fiction must be 'plausible' to be instructive is not shared by other legal commentators. Christine Corcos et al provide compelling opposition, noting that while the science in science fiction is often held to punishingly high standards for plausibility by fans, the hypothetical legal systems are not:

> The same *strictures* which apply to the presentation of the hard and social sciences with regard to science fiction worlds do not seem to apply in the area of law, so that we have in the same story scrupulously accurate (or at least not violently *inaccurate*) portrayals of science and psychology, and wildly distorted views of law, based on what its author believes would be the acceptable norms governing her imaginary society.[8]

One possible reason accounting for the contradiction could be that science fiction is explicitly *science* fiction, not *legal* fiction, and that any applicability to legal thinking is coincidental. However, given its focus on world-building and the creation of alternative societies that all require some method of law enforcement, this explanation is unsatisfying. Camilla A Hrdy and Daniel H Brean provide an interesting discussion of the different standards of evidence required for technological 'enablement' between patent law and science fiction that perhaps suggests an alternative. The former requires that a 'person having ordinary skill in the art' could 'actually practice the invention by reading the disclosures revealed in the patent'.[9] In other words, the patent will not be issued unless the invention can reasonably be manufactured and used based on the applicant's description. However, the latter is not focused on what could reasonably be produced today, but rather what might plausibly be extrapolated given the current state of science and technology. Importantly, these authors note that a 'key feature of Sci Fi Enablement is that it is not judged with the benefit of hindsight', which is why Mary Shelley's *Frankenstein* did not fail this criterion even after it was determined her proposed method of reanimating a corpse was scientifically impossible.[10] It was a plausible scientific speculation at the time; therefore, it demonstrates science fiction technological enablement. What matters here is patent law is decided by judges, while science fiction enablement is decided by what

7 Contreras (2022), pp 72–73.
8 Corcos et al (1999), pp 1045–46.
9 Hrdy and Brean (2021), p 400.
10 Hrdy and Brean (2021), p 405.

Hrdy and Brean label the 'fan of ordinary skill in the art'.[11] Such a person has already been primed by exposure to other works of science fiction to suspend their disbelief when reading about alien planets, futuristic weapons and alternate histories. However, there are limits to this based on the fan's lived experience of real-world science and technology that dictate how much exposition is required to justify the author's deviations.

For example, a fan knows that gravity exists on Earth, and while they are willing to accept a future Earth without it, the change must be justified. Anything less is unacceptable 'hand-waving'.[12] More precisely, the fan expects the laws of physics to apply consistently wherever and whenever they are, so violations of this expectation demand substantial explanation. However, the fan does not expect legal systems within their sphere of experience to be even vaguely consistent. An alien planet where all people with purple hair are summarily executed makes about as much sense as some of the draconian laws in effect in different jurisdictions around the world. The law is constantly changing depending on when and where you are, and these changes may not have predictable patterns or consistent explanations. More importantly, it is generally accepted that when you visit another jurisdiction, its laws will apply to you whether or not you know or understand them. In Suvinian terms, a scientific or technological 'novum' in science fiction must be 'validated by cognitive logic',[13] but the truth and widespread acceptance of vastly inconsistent legal systems make departures from the known a much less demanding cognitive leap.

So, if it is not in imagining plausible legal hypotheticals, what contributions do science fiction legal systems make? Their first role is to make discussion of complex legal phenomena accessible to the public. According to Kieran Tranter, 'Science fiction is the "mythform" of the present, forming a storehouse of images, narrative and tropes through which the present imagines itself and its future'.[14] Contreras notes that these images provide a surrogate 'experience' for legal professionals,[15] but they also do the same for general audiences. These 'what if' experiments so adept at exposing the public to new sociotechnological futures, and influencing their expectations of emerging developments,[16] do the same for possible legal futures. Second, and perhaps most importantly, they can also humanise potential victims through narrative empathy. Kritika Sharma's comparison of alternative feminist legal judgments and the Marvel *What If…?* comic series demonstrates how both

11 Hrdy and Brean (2021), p 401.
12 Hrdy and Brean (2021), p 406.
13 Suvin (1979), p 45.
14 Tranter (2019), p 119.
15 Contreras (2022), pp 72–73.
16 Azagra-Caro et al (2021), p 1890.

these thought experiments lean 'on the use of counterfactuals'.[17] They get us to consider what should be by exploring – even the extremes – of what could be. When considering how the distance and isolation of space exacerbate human vulnerability, these extremes include possible futures where employers or law enforcement can withhold the basics of survival from non-compliant workers and citizens, even to the point of restricting their air. In the textual examples to be discussed in this chapter, controlling air, food, water and gravity is a means by which authority is exerted over political dissidents, prisoners and labourers. Science fiction is the genre best placed to explore these dystopian visions of the future, considering legal issues from within a human (or human-like) context, such that ethico-legal issues can be viewed in a more holistic way, focused on the implications for the people involved.

Another contribution that science fiction legal systems can provide is useful comparisons with real legal systems. Cara Linley's article, '"Do You Really Need That?": Legal Thinking and the Law of Necessity in Post-apocalyptic Fiction', is a good example, highlighting that the implausibility of any given system of law arising in a post-apocalyptic future need not affect its relevance in considering real-world analogies.[18] She uses various fictional representations of the law of necessity doctrine worked out ad hoc in worlds where all law has been abandoned and scavengers are focused solely on survival. We may not live in such a lawless reality, but Linley draws direct comparisons with the lack of legislative guidance faced by many in the justice system when dealing with hoarders during the COVID-19 global pandemic. Hoarders may have felt justified in their actions because they really were facing a personal crisis; however, as Linley notes, 'claims of necessity appear to be commonly understood as an individualized claim which becomes an issue where there is a state of affairs which affects a large percentage, or even the whole, of a population', as in the case of COVID-19.[19] Similarly, in post-apocalyptic fiction, protagonists are commonly seen searching for scarce resources, but when they uncover a valuable cache, they rarely consider the needs of the next scavenger. The audience is often also positioned to disregard any claims of this hypothetical other. Applying a critical lens to resource distribution methods in post-apocalyptic fiction can therefore highlight weaknesses in our real-world crisis-management systems.

Finally, science fiction also allows for safe experimentation with legal systems that challenge the status quo – permitting application to real-world scenarios without didactically demanding it. A common case study is the use of artificial intelligence (AI) systems in science fiction, which various scholars

17 Sharma (2022), p 91.
18 Linley (2022), p 29.
19 Linley (2022), p 29.

link to pervasive public fears about this technology in the real world.[20] Fear of lost jobs, automation and victimisation manifest in various ways in science fiction, with these stories not only suggesting possible methods of legal recourse but also feeding concerns within the legal profession regarding the increased automation of justice and law.[21] Assumptions about how law can and should evolve as a result of AI developments can thus be explored in science fiction at the same time as legal scholarship. Folúkẹ́ Adébísí claims science fiction provides a space for legal discussion to break free from the entrenched 'biases, prejudices, and proclivities' of law as 'embedded in society', with its inherently colonial aspects:[22]

> Ultimately, law reveals itself as a colonial discipline because, within it, bodies and space-time have been revalued and redefined to meet the needs of enclosure, propertymaking and capital accumulation – and not the protection of life ... To question the presumptions upon which the world-making of Euro-modern legal knowledge is based, the tools adopted must have the capacity to bend the rules of the law's assumed 'naturals' with impunity. Science fiction provides us with just such a prospect.[23]

In this way, specific issues can be isolated and analysed outside of the contexts in which we typically find them. Such abstraction may make these conversations more palatable and less threatening for people on opposing sides of an issue.

It is exactly Adébísí's focus on law protecting capitalism over human life that forms the basis of the case studies to be considered throughout the remaining sections of this chapter, with a particular focus on off-world mining and labour prisons, and the science fiction legal systems supporting them. These examples demonstrate just some of the potential areas where science fiction can guide legal discussions and public engagement with legal issues, while retaining its entertainment value. Witnessing the exploitation and abuse of characters with which we have been positioned to identify helps to elucidate potential threats to human rights and safety in off-world settlements. Especially in situations where profits are likely to be prioritised over safety, necessity might be used to justify the exploitation of minorities to provide fuel and resources for the majority while the need to maintain a fragile order and social cohesion for species survival may be used as a defence for undermining individual liberty. The next section will explore science-fictional depictions of exploitative and unsafe working conditions in off-world

20 Rockwood (1999), p 274; Burgess (2022), p 125.
21 Coade (2019), p 43.
22 Adébísí (2022), p 28.
23 Adébísí (2022), pp 28–29.

mining before considering how science fiction can contribute to discussions regarding protecting worker rights far beyond the reach of earthbound regulatory bodies.

Occupational health and safety for space miners in science fiction

Our discussion of off-world mining occupational health and safety (OHS) begins at the pergium production station of Janus 6 in the *Star Trek* episode 'The Devil in the Dark' (1967).[24] With five guards already dead before the action begins and another killed soon thereafter, it is clear that the station's manager will not be winning any workplace safety awards. In fact, the 'monster' tunnelling through the rocks at the station is responsible for at least 50 deaths, and after it sabotages the main circulating pump of the station's reactor, Captain James T Kirk (played by William Shatner) notes that everyone at the facility faces 'death by asphyxiation or death by radiation poisoning'. Regardless of this threat, and the increasing body count whenever the monster appears, abandoning the station is never considered, with countless imperatives to get production going again lest 12 planets lose the power source for their life-support systems. There is no doubt that the lives of these others are given more weight than those of the station's guards or miners. The equipment providing heat, light and air for the mining colony is also described as 'outdated' and 'antiquated', with no replacement parts despite being essential to the miners' survival. Yet all we hear is Kirk declaring, 'We must have that pergium!' and, 'It is vitally important that we get this installation back into operation'. Even when science officer Commander Spock (Leonard Nimoy) discovers that the monster is a sentient, silicon-based life form that he says it would be a 'crime against science' to destroy, Kirk still orders that it be shot on sight, whether or not it attacks first. Absolutely nothing is considered more important than mining that fuel.

This example is presented in sharp contrast to the more recent *Star Trek: Strange New Worlds* episode 'Lost in Translation' (2023),[25] where it is discovered that mining deuterium within a specific nebula was torturing and killing an alien species the ship could not detect. While the Kirk we find in 'The Devil in the Dark' only considers the interests of the silicon-based Horta species when it becomes clear they can exploit its tunnelling abilities to make the facility 'a thousand times more profitable' and the miners 'embarrassingly rich', the character's more recent iteration in 'Lost in Translation' (played by Paul Wesley) is instrumental in helping communications officer Ensign Uhura (Celia Rose Gooding) convince Captain Pike (Anson Mount) to destroy the

24 Pevney (1967) 'Devil in the Dark'.
25 Liu (2023) 'Lost in Translation'.

fuel refinery to protect the aliens. Before this, Pike had also prioritised the mining activity even over essential maintenance needed on his own vessel, the flagship *Enterprise*. Rather than an inspiring speech about valuing other forms of life, Pike ultimately states, 'Well, Starfleet can build a new gas station someplace else. One where there isn't anything living in the deuterium'. This is noteworthy because throughout the episode we have learned how toxic the substance is, and about the hallucinogenic effects of deuterium poisoning. At no point are these safety concerns considered for workers maintaining the fuel refineries. In both episodes, the right of Starfleet to extract minerals from celestial bodies is also never questioned.

It is not always the fuel itself or some external beast that is threatening the wellbeing of off-world miners in science fiction. In 'Dulcinea', the pilot episode of *The Expanse* (2015),[26] environmental threats are secondary to political discrimination as the cause of death and disability for the asteroid belt miners, or 'Belters'. Growing up in low gravity leaves these humans with weak lungs and bones, but there are treatments available to mitigate these hazards for those wealthy enough to access them. Belters, however, are mostly considered second-class citizens. The series opens by describing the political tensions between UN-controlled Earth and the independent military power, Mars. But as one Belter agitator protests, whether the Ceres mining station on which the Belters live is controlled by Earth or Mars is irrelevant, because 'to them, we will always be slaves. That's all we are to the Earthers and Dusters. They built their solar system on our backs, spilled the blood of a million of our brothers. But in their eyes, we're not even human anymore'. This quote explores two common preoccupations in utopian science fiction: posthumanism and the diverging of the human species into bioenhanced 'haves' and 'have-nots'. 'Dulcinea' also dramatises the dystopian hypothetical – what if your boss controlled your air?

Charles S Cockell claims space is inherently 'tyranny-prone', as it represents an environment where governments or employers could theoretically withhold oxygen for non-compliance.[27] In the Belt, we are told that 'air and water are more precious than gold', and that Earth and Mars have stripped what might have been 'enough water for 1000 generations' to hoard the resource for themselves. As the Belter protestor tells us, 'the immense wealth and resources that flow through our gates were never meant for us', but whenever they complain about their conditions, their air and water are 'held back'. We also see the vulnerability of miners who rely on the mining company for medical care when workplace injuries occur, with one ice miner losing an arm at the beginning of the episode and then worrying his employer will cheat him out of the quality prosthetic to which his years of service

26 McDonough (2015) 'Dulcinea'.
27 Cockell (2022), p viii.

entitle him. Similarly, repairs to the mining ship are neglected because from the company's perspective it is cheaper to 'settle up with a few widows' than to improve the safety of the vessel.

This also explains why business owners on Ceres choose to pay bribes to avoid safety inspections. The lead character, Detective Miller (Thomas Jane), succinctly describes the legal situation that allows such disregard for occupational health and safety regulations when he tells his rookie partner there are 'no laws in Ceres. Just cops'. By this stage in the episode, we have already seen him take a bribe, beat up a suspect and agree to kidnap a woman as a 'favour' to a 'stakeholder'. We have also seen a UN official participate in the gravity-based torture of a suspected Belter terrorist.

In the real world, we have billionaire SpaceX CEO Elon Musk provocatively declaring that his planned Mars colony will not recognise Earth-based law.[28] *The Expanse*'s Wild West of prospecting, safety violations and exploitation depicts one potential future resulting from such a lack of predetermined guidelines. Even when there are 'statutes' the characters in the series are meant to follow, the distance from any enforcement agency means corruption is rife. For example, the obligation to render aid to another ship in distress – presumably modelled on existing 'rule of rescue' policies in maritime and space law[29] – is initially ignored by a crew seeking an 'on-time bonus' for cargo delivery. The only way protagonist Jim Holden (Steven Strait) can force the issue is to log the distress call with HQ so the company will be legally 'on the hook' for failing to investigate.

Even imagining a scenario where any real off-world mining colonies could be tightly regulated for safety standards, it would still be the case that space itself would be a hostile environment for human survival. When it comes to science fiction mining colonies, we have various examples where human greed and the urge to subjugate miners for profit only exacerbate an already unsafe natural environment. In *Andromeda*'s 'So Burn the Untamed Lands' (2004),[30] for example, the air surrounding a quartz crystal mine is toxic, causing skin lesions and burns, as well as neurological damage to the species forced to work in them. The crystals are a valuable power source, and the owner of the mines, Cutter (Matthew Bennett), defends his exploitation of the miners by saying, 'I count on them to dig, they count on me for food and a decent place to live. In return, I look after the families, so it's a perfect social contract'. However, anyone familiar with this philosophy will recognise that this arrangement is the exact opposite of an appropriate social contract, instead allowing one person to extract benefits from a system to which

28 Liberatore (2020).

29 UNOOSA (1967), 2345 (XXII). Agreement on the Rescue of Astronauts, the Return of Astronauts and the Return of Objects Launched into Outer Space.

30 Montesi (2004) 'So Burned the Untamed Lands'.

they have not contributed while everyone else suffers. Cutter has a well-paid and loyal security workforce keeping the 'workers in line', but *Andromeda*'s hero, Captain Dylan Hunt (Kevin Sorbo), declares that the miners 'deserve a better life', eventually evacuating them from the planet with the promise that he will take them somewhere where they can make a living 'without sacrificing [their] health and sanity'.

Stargate SG-1's 'First Commandment' (1997)[31] is another example where the world of the mining colony is the source of occupational injury, with Jonas (William Russ), a delusional officer masquerading as a deity on a foreign planet, forcing local cave dwellers to labour under a toxic sun to build him a temple. The caves on the planet are the only safe place away from the sun's radiation for the humans who were originally abducted and brought to the planet as slave miners. Jonas justifies sacrificing the lives of the labourers to the 'sun sickness' by appealing to a 'greater good' defence focused on how much better the lives of the cave dwellers will be once they no longer live underground in 'squalor' like a 'third world country in a bottle', with their burgeoning population and a lack of appropriate dwellings to accommodate them. *Farscape*'s 'Home on the Remains' (2000)[32] has an even more graphic depiction of life within a mining facility, with nogelti crystal miners living inside the rotting corpse of the planet-sized space-dwelling Budong. Here, miners may strike it rich if they find a vein of crystals to mine, but also risk bumping into one of the creature's toxic pustules, whereupon they die a painful death, covered in burning acid. The society living in the Budong is self-organised – mostly thieves and mercenaries motivated entirely by crystal trade – but unsurprisingly falls victim to an unscrupulous leader who starts killing off successful miners to steal their bounty. Thus, these ungoverned space communities become an illustration of the adage 'no honour among thieves'. As with many of the other episodes sampled here, nothing is more important than finding and claiming mineral treasures, with personal and public safety – not to mention friendship and loyalty – taking a back seat to the drive for profit.

These examples all share certain similarities, including that off-world workers are susceptible to exploitation due to their isolation from other human societies and the desperate need for resource extraction to promote settler survival in an environment where all fundamental needs must be met artificially. However, from a socio-legal perspective, each text displays a different method of organising work in off-world societies, and different norms for establishing property rights. Life on the Budong is anarchy, whereas Ceres is highly regulated – at least on paper. Nogelti crystal miners operate under a 'finders keepers' model, while Belters are comparable to sweatshop workers

31 Berry (1997) 'First Commandment'.
32 Woods (200) 'Home on the Remains'.

on Earth, engaged in alienated labour to generate wealth for the elite. But in both cases, greed and safety shortcuts lead to worker injury and death. Jonas and Cutter also serve as a reminder that in the vastness of space, dictators are likely to arise, and curbing their power will pose a significant challenge for any incorporated law enforcement organisation. Perhaps most interestingly, even in the most 'progressive' example above ('Lost in Translation'), the existence of mining and its intrinsic risks to human health and safety is taken for granted. These examples also demonstrate that the ethico-legal question of who (if anyone) has a legitimate claim to the natural resources of space is often elided in science fiction narratives, as will be explored next.

Who owns minerals mined in space?

Worker safety is often subjugated to the interests of cost-cutting, time-saving and ultimately profit-generation for off-world mining facilities. However, OHS issues are not the only legal concerns exposed by science fiction miners. There are also issues of private versus public ownership and national appropriation to consider. The validity of mining, salvage operations and post-apocalyptic scavenging is rarely questioned in science fiction; however, in the real world these are all controversial legal issues – especially in the space environment. Regarding the former, Garcia-del-Real et al state:

> According to the Outer Space Treaty (United Nations, 1967), countries are not allowed to claim sovereignty over any space body. If, for instance, a country plants a flag on an asteroid or planet, it could not declare it as its property. There is something missing in the Outer Space Treaty, however, since it does not specify anything regarding mineral resources that could be found in celestial bodies.[33]

Other legal scholars look to the Outer Space Treaty's (OST) demand that space be treated as 'the province of mankind' to challenge private claims to natural resources in space. Brian M Hoffstadt notes that this idea is often thought to derive from the ancient Roman idea of *res communis* – that is, the right to 'free access and use – but not rights of ownership – to the shared property of the community'.[34] Nevertheless, the United States and Luxembourg were the first to issue private asteroid mining licences in 2015 and 2016, respectively, with various other countries planning to follow suit.[35] More recently, Martin Svec has argued that 'the lack of a comprehensive legal framework and the consequent legal uncertainty surrounding

33 Garcia-del-Real et al (2020), p 43.
34 Hoffstadt (1994), p 587.
35 Garcia-del-Real et al (2020), p 44.

legality and conditions under which space resources can be utilised represent a significant barrier for private investors'.[36] He further notes that the Moon Agreement is the 'only international treaty explicitly addressing space mining', but has only been ratified by 18 states.[37] The so-called norms of customary international law and OST principles on which we would usually rely to regulate such an issue, yield contradictory guidance depending on how space resources are classified.[38]

Regarding the issue of salvage, with the ever-increasing volume of space junk threatening the usability of some of our most valuable orbits, the need to improve orbital debris mitigation and remediation strategies is currently receiving a lot of attention in space ethics and law. One contributing factor is the inconsistency between space and maritime law with regard to liability and salvage. Article 7 of the OST has been read to bestow perpetual ownership and responsibility over space objects, leaving no avenue for non-consensual removal by third parties, even when the asset would generally be considered abandoned and/or poses a threat to the environment.[39] Arpit Gupta is one of several scholars calling for the application of maritime legal regulations to salvage operations in space, and further for legal differentiation between 'space objects' and 'space debris' to facilitate this process.[40] Such an intervention could both legalise and incentivise orbital clean-up activities. The short-lived science fiction series *Firefly*[41] depicts a possible future of space piracy if formal international agreements for off-world salvage are not drawn up to improve the efficacy and safety of such operations.

There are many science fiction stories that deal with ownership of space resources, including products of space mining. While they are diverse, there is a common pattern that can be identified through these samples that aligns with Adébísí's concerns about the way law often prioritises private business interests over human life.[42] Two particularly egregious examples involve fictional mining corporations claiming ownership over regions of space where humans or aliens have established colonies, and seeking to exercise a legal right to destroy their homes – namely, *Doctor Who*'s 'Colony in Space' (1971)[43] and *Star Trek: Voyager*'s 'Homestead' (2001).[44] In the first, our intrepid Gallifreyan, the Doctor, finds himself in the middle of a territory dispute when a planet is mistakenly classified as both 'suitable for colonisation'

36 Svec (2022), p 1.
37 Svec (2022), p 1.
38 Svec (2022), p 1.
39 Gupta (2019), p 241.
40 Gupta (2019), p 230.
41 Solomon (2002) 'Out of Gas'.
42 Adébísí (2022), p 28.
43 Briant (1971) 'Colony in Space'.
44 Burton (2001) 'Homestead'.

and as a duralinium mining site, with its mineral rights assigned to the private mining corporation IMC. Earth is described by one of the colonists as having 'no room to move, polluted air, not a blade of grass left on the planet and a government that locks you up if you think for yourself', but Earth's need for 'all the minerals we can find' is used to defend IMC's right to gut this other world, leaving it uninhabitable. When the Doctor (Jon Pertwee) asks one of the colonists whether there are laws to deal with such matters, he is told that a complaint can be made to Earth's government, but by the time it goes through the system the planet will be 'useless' and reduced to a 'galactic slagheap'. This mirrors real-world concerns about the enforceability of any laws in space that involve Earth-based regulators, including those surrounding OHS conditions for space workers. In response to IMC's claims, the Doctor suggests the 'one hundred thousand million' humans they supposedly represent may do better moving from Earth to similar planets, to a colony 'where they can live like human beings, not battery hens'. The IMC representative remains unswayed and merely reiterates that their job is to find minerals for Earth's population. As with previous examples discussed in this chapter, mining profits are the highest priority. At the conclusion of the episode, the Adjudicator's judgment has been sought, and if they side with the mining corporation the colonists will have to leave or be classified as outlaws.

Illegally continuing to occupy their own home is also the solution opted for by the Talaxian refugees in 'Homestead', whose colony is threatened with destruction by another species that uses explosives to extract ore from the asteroids they have been licensed to mine. When Captain Kathryn Janeway (Kate Mulgrew) tries to negotiate to save the Talaxians' colony, the miners claim the 'operation isn't worth the expense' if they exclude that region of the asteroid field, as it allegedly contains 30 per cent of the total ore. Even when it is explained that the colonists will not be able to evacuate in time and that a rescue mission for several of *Voyager*'s crew members is also ongoing, the miners insist they cannot pause their operation because they are on a 'strict deadline'. This point is made again when it is suggested that maybe the colonists could compensate them for the lost mining profits by providing geothermal energy substitutes, with Commander Nocona (John Kenton Shull) noting it would take time to make the technology compatible with their systems and, 'We have quotas to meet, we don't have time for that'. Generating capital and meeting quotas are again placed above the survival needs of others. At no point in either story is it suggested the inhabitants have a claim on the mineral resources themselves, by nature of living on the relevant celestial bodies. This is similar to Kirk's unwillingness to consider that the Horta species may have a right to the resources of their own home planet in 'The Devil in the Dark'.

In both 'Colony in Space' and 'Homestead', the law supports the miners, while justice would seem to support the colonists. Even though the laws are recognised to be unjust in both cases, in the first instance the Doctor appeals to have his companion pardoned for trespass at one point because they were not aware of the alien planet's laws, while in the second the risk of violating Starfleet's 'Prime Directive' on non-interference in other cultures means *Voyager*'s security officer, Tuvok (Tim Russ), initially states that he cannot be involved in helping the Talaxians defend their home. Both assume that under usual circumstances local laws should be respected, even when they conflict with the ethical and legal norms of the visitors. As noted earlier, this aligns with various audience expectations regarding entering different jurisdictions.

The future Prime Directive is also subtly referenced in 'Marauders' (*Star Trek: Enterprise*, 2002),[45] when the crew members of the first *Enterprise* visit a deuterium mining planet, only to discover the miners will not do business with them. On further investigation, they learn that the facility is being shaken down by violent Klingons who claim the best fuel for themselves, leaving the miners to eke out a living mining the 'deep strata' reserves, whose impurities require extensive refining to render them usable. It is also revealed the Klingons have killed and injured some of the miners. Captain Jonathan Archer (Scott Bakula) recognises that their technologically advanced Vulcan allies would not approve of interfering in another culture, but his Vulcan science officer, T'Pol (Jolene Blalock), agrees with his assessment that the marauding Klingons do not constitute a 'culture', so protecting the vulnerable miners against them is permissible. Two very interesting issues arise in this episode that are relevant to our discussion here. The first is the implication that had these marauders answered to the Klingon 'High Council', the crew of the *Enterprise* would not have been justified in protesting their abuse of the miners. The same behaviours used to defend counter-violence would then cease to provide grounds for retaliation: once established, such actions are sanctioned by internal laws, no matter how unjust or discriminatory. The second is the acceptance that the deuterium fields are not safe to go near, coupled with the expectation that the miners will nevertheless continue to work there and provide fuel for trade. The *Enterprise* crew show no scruples in accepting deuterium in exchange for their assistance, despite the risky working conditions involved in its extraction. It appears that the rights they are willing to help the miners defend are simply those that would allow them to keep risking their health and safety to meet their quotas. Unlike Hunt from *Andromeda*, Archer apparently does not consider that the miners might 'deserve a better life' that includes the promotion of occupational health.

As in the previous section, mining and human (or alien) suffering caused by mining are taken for granted in these off-world fictional societies. These examples also depict various methods for assigning property rights and pursuing restitution when such rights are violated; however, the perspective that

45 Vejar (2002) 'Marauders'.

space resources are not subject to appropriation is rarely entertained, despite this being a common interpretation of the relevant sections of the OST. But even when ownership can clearly be established, a common theme in the above examples is that enforcement of these rules often depends on systems so distant from the colony as to be effectively useless for providing legal remedy. This is perhaps one of the most action-guiding elements when considering the contribution science fiction can make to establishing ethico-legal systems and norms for off-world societies in the real world, which will be discussed next.

How can we protect the health and safety of real off-world workers?

By depicting how off-world workers might be exploited, science fiction elucidates some possible avenues for ethico-legal protection. The obsession with fuel at any cost seen in so many of the examples described above suggests that labour contracts will need to be tightly regulated to avoid overwork and unsafe conditions. Given the complexities of monitoring these from such a long distance, local regulators may need to be established off-world to oversee operations.[46] This prioritisation of mining for fuel is not only seen in fiction but is also evident in economic systems around the world that provide unparalleled subsidies and tax-minimisation options for mining companies, regardless of their impact on the environment and human health, often justifying this by appeals to broad social benefit.[47] Limiting the 'greater good' arguments in language and policies pertaining to space mining may therefore be necessary to avoid a repeat of this situation in the off-world setting. The next section will further consider how prioritising resource extraction over human rights could also lead to various rights violations, such as slavery and a lack of due process.

For a more direct OHS example, Rockwood notes that labour disputes form a key plot point in the series *Babylon 5*, with a major strike only being resolved once Commander Jeffrey Sinclair (Michael O'Hare) uses a liberal legal interpretation of the order 'by any means necessary' to redistribute military resources among the civilian workforce.[48] The episode of the same name (1994)[49] also highlights the extreme vulnerability of both space workers (in terms of conditions and safety) and their industries (related to labour disruptions, freight delays and lost assets). Here, necessity is once more the key theme driving employers and governments to demand that workers submit to

46 Kendal (2021), p 15.
47 Bogdanski (2011), p 324.
48 Rockwood (1999), p 272.
49 Johnston (1994) 'By Any Means Necessary'.

unsafe conditions. This again suggests significant forethought and regulation will be required to ensure smooth operations for such commercial ventures in the real world. It also demonstrates the geopolitical tensions present when mixing military and non-military workforces from different jurisdictions, a concern noted in the literature regarding the potential for multi-nation, dual-purpose facilities operating on the Moon.[50] How inconsistent labour laws on Earth might impact off-world employment conditions for citizens from multiple countries is also worth considering here.

Finally, although the *Star Wars* franchise's *Andor* is included in this chapter mostly for the upcoming discussion of prison labour, the justification that humanoid prisoners 'are cheaper than droids' for providing manual labour is also relevant in the broader space labour context. For riskier jobs that can be automated, future OHS standards may dictate that humans are not to be recruited into these roles, even if they are cheaper. This is an example where automation may promote human workers' interests, as opposed to the instances in science fiction where AI is seen as a threat to human welfare.[51] This brings us to our next related consideration: how science fiction narratives explore issues of human rights in space, including for vulnerable and confined populations, such as prisoners. As will be shown, many prison systems in science fiction overlap with labour camps, with similar safety concerns as those seen in the commercial sector.

Human rights violations and the space penal colony in science fiction

A more serious complication when dealing with inconsistent laws across different jurisdictions relates to how we should approach violations of human rights, and whether these justify undermining the sovereignty of other states. In science fiction stories, such questions must also consider the intrinsic rights of potential alien species. Regarding one of the most broadly accepted human rights violations, the fan database TVTropes.com claims that in science fiction:

> While the Cool Starship of the series has fully automated food dispensers, and artificial intelligence and nanotechnology are realities, indentured servitude and slavery of sapient beings is still widespread, and the most common slave occupation by far in The Future (TM) is the lowly miner.[52]

50 Stewart and Rappaport (2021), p 11.

51 Burgess (2022), p 125.

52 TVTropes.com (2023), 'We Will Use Manual Labour in the Future.'

An example can be found in the new *Doctor Who* series episode, 'The Impossible Planet' (2006),[53] where a species known as the Ood are considered a 'basic slave race' supposedly 'born' for work in the mines. They are variably referred to in the episode as 'slaves', 'cattle' or 'livestock', and characters justify their treatment of them by claiming it is what they want, and that they are too stupid to look after themselves otherwise.

Enslaved miners in science fiction may also be completing prison sentences, including for trumped-up charges specifically intended to increase the supply of labourers. There are also other types of forced labour represented in science fiction prison systems, as well as non-labour penal colonies that would nonetheless violate numerous human rights conventions, including for being what TVTropes label a 'Deadly Environment Prison'.[54] Such prisons may be located in areas of toxic exposure (including, but not limited to mines) or make escape impossible due to treacherous terrain or other physical hazards. The Deadly Environment Prison often minimises costs by reducing the need for a large security force. Some science fiction penal colonies also avoid prison breaks through their remote location or one-way transportation systems.

As *Star Trek*'s Prime Directive and similar regulations from other science fiction franchises demonstrate, respecting local law and custom is a common requirement in science fiction, even when the laws are generally considered unfair, harsh or arbitrary. For example, when discussing the lifelong incarceration of the SG-1 team on the prison planet Hadante, in the episode 'Prisoners' (*Stargate: SG-1*, 1998),[55] legal advisers tell their superior, General George Hammond (Don S Davis), 'SG-1 broke the law ... We don't have to agree with their laws but we may have to respect them'. Hammond later appeals to the justices who sentenced the team for unwittingly aiding a convicted prisoner, claiming their zero-tolerance stance on crime and guilt by association was unjust. Meanwhile, on Hadante, archaeologist Daniel Jackson (Michael Shanks) compares sending all prisoners on a one-way trip through the Stargate to the British sending their criminals to the Botany Bay penal colony in Australia in the eighteenth and nineteenth centuries. Previously, Jackson had also tried to assure the authorities that the team had 'no desire to interfere with [their] legal system'. Interfering does indeed prove to be problematic, as mounting their own escape necessitates collaborating with a fellow prisoner scientist, whom we later learn was imprisoned for genocide. Regardless, once the team is safely returned, there is no attempt to intervene on behalf of any of the other prisoners.

53 Strong (2006) 'The Impossible Planet'.
54 TVTropes.com (2023), 'Deadly Environment Prison.'
55 Warry-Smith (1998) 'Prisoners'.

While Hammond's appeal on behalf of SG-1 is at least heard (despite the fact that it is established 'there is no return from Hadante for anyone'), when Captain Hunt is sentenced to life imprisonment for sedition on a penal colony in the *Andromeda* episode, 'A Rose in the Ashes' (2000),[56] his request to access an appeals process is considered 'very funny' by the AI Deputy. Like Hadante, there is no release from Helios 9, or 'Hell 9' as the prisoners call it; however, 'A Rose in the Ashes' takes it a step further by arbitrarily detaining all the children of convicted prisoners too. When Hunt meets Kae-Lee (Claudette Mink), who was born on the prison planet, she explains that according to their legal system, if your parents were criminals, you are 'born guilty' due to the belief criminality is genetic: 'hardwired ... diagnosable and inherited'. Control of the prisoners is managed through access to food, with the planet being terraformed specifically to prevent the growth of edible vegetation, and escape is prevented due to a network of deadly drones that attack anyone trying to approach or leave the prison planet. Thus, Hell 9 incorporates multiple Deadly Environment Prison elements. More importantly, the fact that children are imprisoned, neglected and tortured for misbehaviour for their entire lives due to their parents' crimes represents a major violation of their rights. This is both facilitated and arguably necessitated by the one-way transport design of the prison transfer system.

Remoteness and limited access to the penal colony also allow the legal system of Olesia to functionally execute all its criminals by sending them into the path of the Wraith – a species that feeds on humans – in the *Stargate: Atlantis* episode 'Condemned' (2005).[57] While the Magistrate (Alan C Peterson) initially claims only the 'most violent prisoners' are sent to the island where the Stargate is located to 'satiate' the Wraith, it is soon discovered that prison population numbers are artificially inflated by sending all criminals to the colony, regardless of their crime, and unfairly convicting anyone threatening to expose the system of 'unspecified violations'. The arrangement, ostensibly made to protect the advanced civilisation of Olesia from uncontrolled Wraith 'cullings', is considered by Atlantis's leader, Dr Elizabeth Weir (Torri Higginson), to be 'cruel and unusual punishment', prompting local recruit Teyla Emmagan (Rachel Luttrell) to ask, 'Do you kill all your violent criminals on Earth?' The (proudly Canadian) Dr Rodney McKay (David Hewlett) responds, 'Certain countries, yes', leaving the (all-American) Commander John Sheppard (Joe Flanigan) to deflect the conversation, asking. 'Do we need to get into this right now?' This is undoubtedly a reference to the United States' continued use of the death penalty, which many consider a violation of human rights. McKay goes so far as to refer to the penal colony as Olesia's own 'Alcatraz', while other members of the Atlantis crew question whether

56 Warry-Smith (2000) 'A Rose in the Ashes'.
57 DeLuise (2005) 'Condemned'.

they should do trade deals with a population whose ethics are inconsistent with their own. Cathartic relief is provided when the Magistrate, after promising a Wraith collaborator he had 'put in measures to augment the population on the island', ultimately ends up as a meal himself.

The intentional inflation of prison populations for dubious gains, including through providing for-profit prison labour, is something of which some real-world prison systems are similarly accused.[58] The issue is also well-dramatised in a four-episode story arc in *Andor* ('Announcement', 2022; 'Narkina 5', 2022; 'Nobody's Listening', 2022; and 'One Way Out', 2022).[59] Protagonist Cassian Andor (Diego Luna) is given a six-year sentence for an alleged crime that the sentencing official notes would have carried a six-month term prior to the 'change of guidelines' aimed at increasing the prison-labour workforce involved in manufacturing parts for the under-construction Death Star. Judged 'labour worthy' and sent to the 'factory facility' on Narkina 5, Andor works 12-hour shifts where different groups of prisoners are forced to compete in terms of productivity. A fellow prisoner says their food rations are impacted by the results: 'Top table gets flavour, last table gets fried' – referring to the electrified tunqstoid floor that sends painful shocks to the inmates, who are required to always be barefoot. Andor continues to protest his innocence, claiming he did 'nothing', but the response from a cellmate is just, 'A lot of that going around lately'. The other prisoners are also shocked to learn that claims their sentences were all doubled due to rebel activity are suspect, as Andor has never heard of this on the outside.

On Narkina 5, inmates are considered disposable, suicide is 'not discouraged' and new labourers are rapidly found to replace any who die. Entire floors of prisoners are sometimes killed to maintain the secret that none of the prisoners are ever actually released; they are just moved to other labour facilities. The electrified floor is only one of the Deadly Environment Prison elements of Narkina 5, as it is later discovered that the prison is located in the middle of a vast ocean, so even if prisoners escape, most of them drown. The focus on prisoners being barefoot in a situation where their feet are the focal point of torture is particularly chilling throughout the story arc, and it is clear that most of the citizens on other worlds are not aware of the corruption within the justice system or the conditions of the labour prison. An important enabler for the large prison population is the sophisticated technology employed, with Andor estimating only 100 security staff are guarding 5000 men. This is an example of science fiction exploring how legal systems might engage new technological interventions, with Adébísí claiming the genre provides 'a major site for contemplating possibilities for the emergence

58 Galinato and Rohla (2020).

59 Caron (2022) 'Announcement'; Haynes (2002) 'Narkina 5'; Haynes (2022) 'Nobody's Listening'; Haynes (2022) 'One Way Out'.

of dystopias and utopias … and rais[ing] questions that can only be answered outside the confines of the strict boundaries of legal writing'.[60]

As in the case of feeding prisoners to life-sucking aliens, the use of torture to control prisoners would be classified as 'cruel and unusual punishment', thereby violating their fundamental human rights. All the examples in this section illustrate that both off-world miners and prisoners are vulnerable to abuse, and prisoners on mining planets are doubly so. This is typically exacerbated by the remoteness of space, costs and practicalities of transportation, a lack of regulatory oversight, and the imperative of having fuel (or, in the case of *Andor*, space weaponry) to survive. But in highlighting these issues in fictional scenarios, science fiction also provides an opportunity to start the conversation regarding human rights protection in reality. In his article, 'Do Androids Dream of Electric Free Speech?', Chip Stewart claims that legal scholars are 'able to do things that judges and lawyers do not have to do … look forward to future disputes, ones that don't exist yet but are almost certainly going to arise'.[61] For this activity, science fiction can provide the groundwork for imagining possible future legal issues, and a playground for applying existing and theoretical legal frameworks to these new possibilities. For possible future off-world societies, such speculations can augment lessons learned from history, as will be our final point of discussion here.

Real-world penal colonies

The question of whether space may provide a new location to warehouse Earth's prisoners is often asked online, with varying levels of seriousness.[62] History, including the use of Botany Bay as a penal colony, suggests legal systems may one day entertain this possibility in earnest, although practical and ethical obstacles may prove insurmountable. Nevertheless, it is worth considering what the genre of science fiction might recommend for such a proposal. In the above examples, this might be summarised in one word: don't. In most cases, the only characters in favour of harsh penal colonies in space-based fictions are the established sociopaths, such as *Andromeda*'s violent, Nietzschean character Tyr Anasazi (Keith Hamilton Cobb), who declares that permanently removing criminals from the gene pool is in society's interests. However, assuming a blanket warning against such systems was disregarded, science fiction penal colony narratives do outline some possible mitigation strategies to minimise potential abuse. These include guaranteeing that an appeals system would have the authority and logistical support to release prisoners – no one-way transfer systems or irremediable lifelong

60 Adébísí (2022), p 27.
61 Stewart (2014), p 438.
62 Weigel (2020).

sentences permitted. The need for close regulation to prevent prisoner abuse is also clear. It is also important to note that even if Earth prisoners are never sent off-world, if human settlements are formed in space, then these may choose to develop their own incarceration systems to deal with anti-social behaviours. Independent colonies may be faced with similar challenges to those seen in the outer-planet systems of *Firefly* or *Farscape* – essentially a Wild West situation where 'might is right'. They may fall victim to marauders, such as those plaguing the deuterium miners in *Star Trek: Enterprise*, or dictators like Jonas from *Stargate* or Cutter from *Andromeda*, who willingly sacrifice citizens to maintain their own power. Establishing any sense of law and order may require the development of bespoke justice systems for space-dwelling communities. Nevertheless, the increased vulnerability of prisoners in such systems warrants close examination, with the various corruption threats identified in science fiction legal systems providing some insight into where things might go wrong.

Conclusion: What lessons can we apply in the real world?

When it comes to deciding whether or not we should establish penal colonies, humanity already has lessons from the real Botany Bay to learn from. We similarly already know what happens when mining corporations are not sufficiently regulated, including for occupational health and safety standards. So, what contribution can an episode like 'Prisoners' (*Stargate SG-1*, 1998) or 'Dulcinea' (*The Expanse*, 2015) make to these discussions? As noted at the start of this chapter, plausibility is rarely demanded of a science fiction legal system, and thus it is unlikely that audiences will attempt to model real-world legal solutions on those depicted in science fiction. However, what the tropes discussed above can achieve is the illustration of the sheer magnitude of the vulnerability of future human workers and prisoners in space. When considering how hostile the space environment is to human survival, any off-world employment may fall under the category of a 'Deadly Environment Prison', under conditions of capitalism. As the 'Narkina 5' story arc in *Andor* also demonstrates, allowing the creation of off-world incarceration facilities will make it all the easier to conceal prison conditions from public and regulatory scrutiny. The epigraph at the start of 'A Rose in the Ashes' (*Andromeda*, 2000) rings true: 'The truest measure of a society is how it treats its elderly, its pets and its prisoners'.[63] In the sample of texts considered in this chapter, the vulnerabilities of labourers (including migrant workers), the aged, the sick and the incarcerated are all exacerbated by the remoteness of space.

63 The episode attributes this quote to its fictional text, *Keeper of the Way Vision of Faith VII* (CY 9891).

Dennis Livingston claims that science fiction is a 'laboratory of the imagination' that has a 'presumptive impact on the society from which it emerges'.[64] It provides a shared language to reflect on the world we live in, as well as the ethical, legal and social implications of alternative futures. Further, Livingston notes that science fiction encourages us to consider 'where we are or should be going as a society'.[65] This includes how we want to build future human societies in space. If we want to avoid the harsh working and discipline conditions seen in 'Nobody's Listening' (*Andor*, 2022), for example, we need to not only start listening to labourers and prisoners in the real world about how we can improve their health and safety but also draw on the rich history of thought experimentation we have available to us on these topics in utopian science fiction. We need to use our imagination, and empathy, to dream up better – *eu*topian – worlds. And then we need to work to bring them into reality.

References

Secondary sources

Folúké Adébísí (2022) 'Black/African Science Fiction and the Quest for Racial Justice Through Legal Knowledge: How Can We Unsettle Euro-modern Time and Temporality in Our Teaching?' 4 *Law, Technology and Humans* 24.

Joaquín M Azagra-Caro, Laura González-Salmerón and Pedro Marques (2021) 'Fiction Lagging Behind or Non-fiction Defending the Indefensible?' 46 *The Journal of Technology Transfer* 1889.

John A Bogdanski (2011) 'Reflections on the Environmental Impacts of Federal Tax Subsidies for Oil, Gas, and Timber Production' 15 *Lewis & Clark Law Review* 323.

Paul Burgess (2022) 'The Rule of Law, Science Fiction and Fears of Artificial Intelligence' 4 *Law, Technology and Humans* 124.

Melissa Coade (2019) 'Those in Favour Say AI' 53 *Law Society Journal* 41.

Charles S Cockell (2022) *Interplanetary Liberty: Building Free Societies in the Cosmos*, Oxford University Press.

Jorge L Contreras (2022) 'Science Fiction and the Law: A New Wigmorian Bibliography' 13 *Harvard Journal of Sports and Entertainment Law* 65.

Christine Corcos, Isabel Corcos and Brian A Stockhoff (1999) 'Double-Take: A Second Look at Cloning, Science Fiction and Law' 59 *Louisiana Law Review* 1041.

Gregmar I Galinato and Ryne Rohla (2020) 'Do Privately-Owned Prisons Increase Incarceration Rates?' 67 *Labour Economics* 101908.

Jose Garcia-del-Real, George Barakos and Helmut Mischo (2020) 'Space Mining is the Industry of the Future … Or Maybe the Present?' 72 *Mining Engineering* 40.

64 Livingston (1982), pp 281–82.
65 Livingston (1982), p 282.

Arpit Gupta (2019) 'Regulating Space Debris as Separate from Space Objects' 41 *University of Pennsylvania Journal of International Law* 223.
Brian M Hoffstadt (1994) 'Moving the Heavens: Lunar Mining and the Common Heritage of Mankind in the Moon Treaty' 42 *UCLA Law Review* 575.
Camilla A Hrdy and Daniel H Brean (2021) 'Enabling Science Fiction' 27 *Michigan Technology Law Review* 399.
Evie Kendal (2021) 'Environmental and Occupational Ethics in Early Lunar Populations: Establishing Guidelines for Future Off-World Settlements' in Margaret Boone Rappaport and Konrad Szocik (eds), *The Human Factor in the Settlement of the Moon: An Interdisciplinary Approach*, Springer, 233.
Stacey Liberatore (2020) 'SpaceX Declares Independence: Elon Musk's Firm Says They will Not Recognize Earth Law in Planned Mars Colony and Says "Free Planet" will Adopt "Self Governing Principles"' *Daily Mail*, 31 October, https://www.dailymail.co.uk/sciencetech/article-8897601/Elon-Musks-SpaceX-says-not-recognize-Earth-laws-planned-Mars-colony.html
Cara Linley (2022) '"Do You Really Need That?": Legal Thinking and the Law of Necessity in Post-apocalyptic Fiction' 51 *Foundation* 22.
Dennis Livingston (1982) 'The Biology of Utopia: Science Fiction Perspectives on Ectogenesis' in Helen B Holmes, Betty B Hoskins and Michael Gross (eds), *The Custom-made Child? Women-centred Perspectives*, Humana Press, 281.
Mike Nellis (2013) 'Techno-utopianism, Science Fiction and Penal Innovation: The Case of Electronically Monitored Control' in Margaret Malloch and Bill Munro (eds), *Crime, Critique and Utopia*, Palgrave Macmillan, 164.
Bruce L Rockwood (1999) 'New Possibilities' 23 *Legal Studies Forum* 267.
Kritika Sharma (2022) 'What if Feminist Judgments Were Written on Earth 616? A Tale of Feminism and Science Fiction' 4 *Law, Technology and Humans* 81.
Darko Suvin (1973) 'Defining the Literary Genre of Utopia: Some Historical Semantics, Some Genology, A Proposal, and a Plea' 6 *Studies in the Literary Imagination* 121.
Darko Suvin (1979) *Metamorphoses of Science Fiction: On the Poetics and History of a Literary Genre*, Yale University Press.
Chip Stewart (2014) 'Do Androids Dream of Electric Free Speech? Visions of the Future of Copyright, Privacy and the First Amendment in Science Fiction' 19 *Communication Law and Policy* 433.
Richard A Stewart and Margaret Boone Rappaport (2021) 'The Military on the Moon: Geopolitical, Diplomatic, and Environmental Implications' in Margaret Boone Rappaport and Konrad Szocik (eds), *The Human Factor in the Settlement of the Moon: An Interdisciplinary Approach*, Springer, 173.
Martin Svec (2022) 'Outer Space, an Area Recognised as *Res Communis Omnium*: Limits of National Space Mining Law' 60 *Space Policy* 101473.
Kieran Tranter (2019) '*Die Buribunken* as Science Fiction: The Self and Informational Existence' 28 *Griffith Law Review* 118.
Damien Trentesaux, Raphaël Rault, Emmanuel Caillaud and Arnaud Huftier (2021) 'Ethics of Autonomous Intelligent Systems in the Human Society: Cross Views from Science, Law and Science-Fiction' in Theodor Borangiu, Damien Trentesaux, Paulo Leitão, Olivier Cardin and Samir Lamouris (eds), *Service-Oriented, Holonic and Multi-Agent Manufacturing Systems for Industry of the Future: Proceedings of SOHOMA 2020*, Springer, 246.

TVTropes.com (2023) 'Deadly Environment Prison' https://tvtropes.org/pmwiki/pmwiki.php/Main/DeadlyEnvironmentPrison

TVTropes.com (2023) 'We will Use Manual Labour in the Future' https://tvtropes.org/pmwiki/pmwiki.php/Main/WeWillUseManualLaborInTheFuture

United Nations Office for Outer Space Affairs (UNOOSA) (1967) *Treaty on Principles Governing the Activities of States in the Exploration and Use of Outer Space, Including the Moon and Other Celestial Bodies*, United Nations.

UNOOSA (1967) *2345 (XXII). Agreement on the Rescue of Astronauts, the Return of Astronauts and the Return of Objects Launched into Outer Space*, United Nations.

Brandon Weigel (2020) 'Review 21: Solitary. If Prisoners Were Used to Colonize Mars' *Medium*, 17 October, https://medium.com/sci-fi-movie-reviews/review-21-solitary-25a635020ca5

Films and television shows

Dennis Berry (dir) (1997) 'First Commandment' *Stargate: SG-1* The Bridge Studios, 22 August.

Michael E Briant (dir) (1971) 'Colony in Space' *Doctor Who*, BBC, 10 April.

LeVar Burton (dir) (2001) 'Homestead' *Paramount*, 9 May.

Benjamin Caron (dir) (2022) 'Announcement' *Andor*, Disney, 19 October.

Peter DeLuise (dir) (2005) 'Condemned' *Stargate: Atlantis*, Pegasus Productions, 12 August.

Toby Haynes (dir) (2022) 'Narkina 5' *Andor*, Disney, 26 October.

Toby Haynes (dir) (2022) 'Nobody's Listening' *Andor*, Disney, 2 November.

Toby Haynes (dir) (2022) 'One Way Out' *Andor*, Disney, 9 November.

Jim Johnston (dir) (1994) 'By Any Means Necessary' *Babylon 5*, Warner Bros, 11 May.

Dan Liu (dir) (2023) 'Lost in Translation' *Star Trek: Strange New Worlds*, Paramount, 20 July.

Terry McDonough (dir) (2015) 'Dulcinea' *The Expanse*, Syfy, 15 November.

Jorge Montesi (dir) (2004) 'So Burn the Untamed Lands' *Andromeda*, Andromeda V Productions, 12 November.

Joseph Pevney (dir) (1967) 'The Devil in the Dark' *Star Trek: The Original Series*, Paramount, 9 March.

David Solomon (dir) (2002) 'Out of Gas' *Firefly*, Mutant Enemy, 25 October.

James Strong (dir) (2006) 'The Impossible Planet' *Doctor Who 2005*, BBC, 17 November.

Michael Vejar (dir) (2002) 'Marauders' *Star Trek: Enterprise*, Paramount, 30 October.

David Warry-Smith (dir) (1998) 'Prisoners' *Stargate: SG-1*, Double Secret Productions, 10 July.

David Warry-Smith (dir) (2000) 'A Rose in the Ashes' *Andromeda*, BLT Productions, 27 November.

Rowan Woods (dir) (2000) 'Home on the Remains' *Farscape*, Jim Henson Productions, 16 June.

Part II

Dealing with the digital

Chapter 8

Artificial intelligences and legal persons as rule of law subjects in *The Lifecycle of Software Objects*

Paul Burgess and Daniel Chia Matallana

Introduction

In common with the rest of the book, this chapter explores the contribution of science fiction to legal scholarship. More specifically, we use the sociotechnical imaginaries of jurisprudence within Chiang's novella *The Lifecycle of Software Objects* to consider the legal personality of artificial intelligence (AI) and its relationship with the concept of the rule of law. Building on Tranter's notion of technical legality and MacNeil's approach to reading jurisprudentially, this chapter investigates how science fiction can provide a deeper understanding of legal personality and how the law should engage with a technological society.[1] Our methodological approach involves several key steps. First, we identify the legal and jurisprudential motifs inherent within the traditional science fiction tropes as manifested in this single novella. We then critically examine the fundamental legal concepts in connection with the themes presented in Chiang's fictional world. Next, we interrogate how these jurisprudential concerns are mediated in narrative. Finally, using the provocative and imaginary tools of science fiction, we aim to speculate about the jurisprudential challenges that confront legal theory within the narrative.

The rule of law is a foundational concept across many nations that oppose the arbitrary application of power. It is universally seen as positive.[2] This chapter builds on a literature, stemming from primary sources more than 2000 years old, that considers the meaning of the concept – which has varied over time and is continually being developed.[3] In this chapter, we commence with an aggregated characterisation of popular views of the concept – which we expand as we go – and project that idea into the future. We apply these characterisations to Chiang's science fiction vision to consider how the concept of the rule of law may operate, or may need to operate, if its protections are to continue.

1 Tranter (2018); MacNeil (2009).
2 Krygier (2011).
3 Burgess (2017a).

DOI: 10.4324/9781003412274-10

As Chiang's entities are inventions of science fiction and are a product of technology, they are not an entity to which legal personhood has previously been granted. The fact that a particular technology does not exist is not a reason not to consider the potential problems or solutions that may relate to that entity. This approach has been related to forms of artificial intelligence, artificial inventors and technologies that may enhance democracy and the rule of law.[4] We use this imaginary scenario to consider the impact that the rule of law may have in relation to such an entity. This has merit beyond mere academic speculation; considering these issues can, for example, provide a foundation on which to structure policy responses should technology catch up to the science fiction vision. The realities of realising science fiction, whether utopian or dystopian, can be instructive.[5]

The various tropes that Chiang introduces – relating to artificial entities' ability to deal with property, act as a director of a company or consent to sex – replicate ideas that have been raised in other science fiction accounts. Their inclusion within a single novella does, however, afford a unique opportunity. This allows the ideas advocated by both Tranter and McNeil, respectively relating to the need for a comprehensive understanding between technology and the law and the need to seek out legal concepts to read science fiction jurisprudentially, to be applied to a single source text.[6] The three tropes afford a unique opportunity to explore the rule of law and legal personhood in a single science fiction universe.

In considering the nature, character and importance of science fiction as a sociotechnical imaginary with reference to the novella, we shed light on the relationship between legal personality and the rule of law. The conclusion that we offer can be simply stated: there is an intimate relationship between legal personality and the rule of law, and changes to the entities that are granted legal personality may drastically change their protection under the rule of law. To reach this conclusion we adopt a simple structure. In the next section, we briefly consider the meaning of the rule of law and legal personhood. We then explore the content and context of Chiang's social imaginary. In the fourth section, we consider the ways in which the rule of law may protect digient-like entities. In the final section, we provide a brief conclusion.

The rule of law and legal personhood

In what follows, we briefly set out the rationale for how we will conceive of these ideas for this chapter. While there are a variety of accounts that have

4 Abbott (2020); Novelli et al (2022); Chesterman (2021); Chen and Burgess (2019); Burgess (2021).

5 Tranter (2002); Beebe (1998).

6 Tranter (2018); MacNeil (2009).

existed or been accepted for both the rule of law and legal personhood, we ultimately adopt more contemporary views of the ideas.

The general principle of the rule of law is easily stated: it opposes the arbitrary application of power. Beyond this general statement, the concept's content becomes contested.[7] Conceptions of the rule of law are often framed around lists of requirements or rules that should be adhered to or can be identified in a rule of law state. These lists may include desiderata such as predictability, stability or transparency in the law-making process; they may also include the need for thicker ideas such as the facilitation of human rights. As a contested concept, no two conceptions are precisely alike.

The adoption of a single conception – even a popular conception such as those provided by thinkers like Fuller or Raz – may be criticised for either cherry-picking or may mean any conclusions drawn are non-generalisable. For this reason, we first set out some of the most popular rule of law ideas to initially set out an aggregated uncontroversial form of the concept. We then expand upon specific ideas in the context of Chiang's novella.

The rule of law has traditionally been taken to be a concept that opposes the application of power by the state. The accounts provided by Aristotle, Locke, Dicey, Hayek, Fuller and Raz – thinkers previously described as the 'usual suspects' of the rule of law – each provides a solution to a problem that stems from the state-based exercise of power.[8] While each solution is different, points of similarity beyond the state-centric nature of the accounts can be seen. For example, their accounts all reflect an element of predictability and procedural clarity.[9]

The usual suspects' accounts are all relatively old. (Raz's account is the most recent, at a little under 50 years old.) In the last 20 years, a different form of conception has emerged in which the arbitrary power requirement has been extended to private applications of power or even *any* application of arbitrary power.[10] While differing fundamentally from the usual suspects' state-based ideas, the new conceptions have still been accepted as rule of law ideas.

The various forms make analytical precision in a chapter like this difficult. To proceed, even initially, more precision is required. At this initial point, we take a wide idea of the rule of law's meaning that takes account of the newer conceptions. This approach avoids controversy regarding the adoption of specific conceptions or approaches. We take the rule of law to be a concept that opposes the arbitrary application of power – regardless of the source of

7 Waldron (2002); Burgess (2017a).
8 Burgess (2017a).
9 Burgess (2017b).
10 Krygier (2011); King (2018); Sempill (2017); Bhatt et al (2021).

the arbitrary exercise of that power.[11] This provides a broadly accepted statement of the concept. In the sections that follow, we build from this broad idea and explore more specific rule of law conceptions to point out some nuances relating to the source.

The idea of legal personality also requires analytical precision. We will ultimately embrace Kurki's bundle theory. As this is a departure from conventional views, we will first critically assess orthodox theories of legal personality. This examination aims to elucidate how deeply entrenched humanist principles within western legal theory pose challenges to the evolution of the personhood paradigm, which is hindered by more than just the perceived arbitrariness of the legal system.

The law's anthropocentric view of legal persons, as Pietrzykowski explains, has informed the most traditional and sometimes accepted theories of legal personality.[12] The centrality of humanism in philosophy serves as the foundation for the western legal system and the paradigm of personhood, which 'treats legal order as an institution subordinated and dedicated exclusively to the interests of the human being'.[13] It is from this understanding that the more orthodox definition of legal personality has been adapted. This notion asserts that legal persons are frequently stated as having the ability to hold rights and duties.[14] Humans are clearly capable of being legal persons by virtue of their being human – but the status of being a legal person can be extended to non-human beings.[15]

The uniqueness of human beings in which humanism has influenced philosophical and legal endeavours assumes that only humans have dignity, while other species have a merely instrumental value. This humanistic essence of legal personhood founded the orthodox understanding. Human dignity means that humans should be morally and legally subjects of the law, and not objects serving the interest of others. Granting legal personality to other entities is based on the need to grant humans the protection of their interests, in the case of the so-called fiction theory.[16] This states that it is the law, by the construction of a fiction, that grants the status of personhood to other non-human entities – a proper and predictable form of organisation that ensures the fulfilment of their desires to cooperate among them.[17] An obvious example is the limited liability company. This form of legal personhood has also been applied to idols, animals and trees.[18] Further extensions – for

11 This is broadly similar to Krygier (2011).
12 Pietrzykowski (2018).
13 Pietrzykowski (2018), p 28.
14 Solum (1992).
15 Teubner (2006).
16 Pietrzykowski (2018).
17 Pietrzykowski (2018), p 32.
18 Solaiman (2017); Cupp (2009); Teubner (2006).

example, in the application of personhood to novel beings that exist only online or have been spontaneously formed on the internet – have also been contemplated.[19]

The categories of entities to which legal personhood has been attributed could be aggregated in a number of different ways. They could relate to having a physical presence in the world (humans, animals, trees and so on) or not (legal company); they could relate to being an entity to which personhood is attributed by *default* (humans) or not (animals or other entities); or they could relate to entities that we created for the sole purpose of being imbued with personhood (legal companies) or to entities that were subsequently issued with personhood (animals, trees and so on). As with the rule of law, it is necessary to adopt a particular view of personhood. For the reasons that follow, we adopt Kurki's bundle theory.[20]

While orthodox theories regarding the law of personhood are rights and duties-centred, more recent accounts argue that legal personality is a cluster concept, explaining that rights and duties come in greater or smaller clusters depending on legal contexts.[21] To some degree, the 'cluster theory' has minimised the dignity of humanity as the main base for personhood.[22] This theory realises, for example, that two legal persons may have no rights or duties in common, or that in some situations legal persons have a robust set of rights and duties, while in other conditions that same person has barely any. Kurki's bundle theory claims there should be nothing intrinsic behind an entity to be considered a legal person; it is for the law to decide whether such an entity is treated as a legal person.[23] The cluster is between the incidents of legal personality, which are grouped into active personhood or passive personhood. According to Kurki, 'the scope of passive legal personhood can be determined by asking who or what can hold claim-rights', while 'the key elements of active legal personhood are centred on legal responsibility and legal competence'.[24] Kurki affirms that 'these active and passive incidents are what is distinctive about legal persons – not right-holding or duty-bearing in general, but the holding of specific types of legal entitlements and burdens'.[25]

Kurki's theory enables an entity to hold rights and bear duties without the baggage from traditional accounts of personhood, which hold that a legal person holds several incidents of personhood, including passive, active and *tout court*. Legal personality is not a fixed concept, but rather clusters of rights and duties that may vary depending on the legal context. When viewed

19 Chen and Burgess (2019).
20 Chen and Burgess (2019); Kurki and Pietrzykowski (2017).
21 Naffine (2009).
22 Pietrzykowski (2018), p 4.
23 Kurki (2019), Part 2.
24 Kurki (2019), p 138.
25 Kurki and Pietrzykowski (2017), p 84.

in this way, as a concept that opposes the arbitrary application of power (regardless of the source or the subject), the rule of law may apply to these incidents of legal personality, regardless of the specific entity involved.

In the remainder of this chapter, we consider science fiction entities that do not yet exist. The digient entities we consider can have both physical and non-physical forms; it is not a category to which we suggest legal personhood would issue by default, but could subsequently be issued. As outlined, we take legal personality to be a flexible and context-dependent concept that could extend to digients – which means the wide idea of the rule of law could, *prima facie*, afford protection to those entities. This places us in a position to consider how the existing concept of the rule of law – and more specific conceptions thereof – can extend to digient-like entities, and whether legal personality is a necessary or even sufficient condition for rule of law protections to exist.

The Lifecycle of Software Objects

Chiang's novella makes many allusions to the law. Even when not overtly mentioned, it plays an essential role in the story. Sunyoung Ahn's definition of driven market societies as those motivated by 'pursuits of profit, utility, and perfectionism'[26] perfectly describes Chiang's world. The free-market economy that forms the backdrop to the story requires legal governance. Throughout the novella, we see how capitalism affects employees' rights, wellbeing and ability to earn a living. It describes a society where obsolescence still means disposal – not only of mere products but of sentient and autonomous AIs that exist in both virtual worlds and the real world:

> Human compassion for dogs is both deep and wide, but the euthanasia of dogs in pet shelters amounts to an ongoing canine holocaust, and if the courts haven't put a stop to that, they certainly aren't going to grant protection to entities that lack a heartbeat.[27]

There is also an environmental law approach in the novella. Both the virtual and the physical realms rely heavily on AI and raise questions about the energy consumed for training and maintaining digients and virtual worlds. In a highly technological world such as the one presented by Chiang, these issues are also scrutinised. Despite the vast range of events related to the law that the novella offers, and recognising its potential value to the field of cultural legal studies, we focus solely on three law-related tropes: AI agents as workers; AI agents as company directors; and AI agents as sexual and

26 Ahn (2020), p 75.
27 Chiang (2010), p 77.

romantic partners for humans. In the next section, we consider these in terms of the rule of law related protections that may be invoked. First, though, we explain Chiang's world in more detail.

The novella portrays a society where the virtual world and the physical world are highly interconnected, where the borders between virtuality and reality are profoundly blurred and where people almost automatically shift from one scenario to another to work, socialise and entertain themselves.[28] The story is also set in a world where some of today's technological anxieties have already occurred, and technological achievements are improved and refined. AI, for instance, has reached consciousness and sentience, human cloning is a reality and, sadly, pandemics are commonplace.

When considering science fiction and its possibility both as a resource and as a method to participate in jurisprudential discussions critically and creatively regarding artificial intelligence and legal personality, it is impossible not to think about the self-aware robot trope in science fiction. From the conscious lover, worker and slave replicants of Philip K Dick's *Do Androids Dream of Electric Sheep?* to their use for entertainment that allows humans 'to indulge their fantasies without consequence'[29] in HBO's TV series *Westworld*, science fiction tropes involving an artificial new form of life is endemic in popular culture. *The Lifecycle of Software Objects* deals with several of these.

The story follows *Blue Gamma*, a tech company that develops digients. These digital organisms initially live in a virtual world called *Data Earth* and, subsequently, through importing the digients' AI consciousness into real-world robot bodies. Blue Gamma sells digients as virtual pets, as their AI system enables cognitive development. Ana Alvarado is hired to train the digients and Derek Brooks oversees digients' appearance to make them cute. The main digient characters are Jax (a neo-Victorian robot) and Marco and Polo (pandas). While copies of them are produced, each copy ends up totally different from the original due to differences in purchasers' training. This is the experience Blue Gamma sells: AI that learns through experience.

A competitor's product ultimately outperforms Blue Gamma's digients, making ownership less attractive. Many digients are suspended – in effect, terminating their existence. A small group of users keep their digients. Ana keeps Jax and Derek keeps Marco and Polo. As the costs associated with ownership are substantial, the digients and their users start a quest to transfer them to an environment in which they can continue to exist. The story focuses on how the digients must prove their economic worth to obtain funds to design and execute the transfer. These reflect the tropes in this chapter.

28 This echoes Hildebrandt's (2020) Onlife.
29 Poynton (2022), p 364.

In the quest for financial viability, the potential of the digients operating as assistants is raised. Yet the digients' engineered learning capability – something likened to dyslexia throughout the story – becomes a barrier to many roles. While they could, with time, become intelligent enough to be employees, their programming means they may become too autonomous. This might not be what consumers want – they want super-intelligent products, not super-intelligent employees.

Discussions about the possibility of opening a new sexual frontier between digients and humans open up another opportunity for economic viability and raise ethical questions about allowing sexual contact between humans and digients that may be viewed as children. Further issues regarding digients' capacity to consent are also enlivened.[30] Derek accepts the offer of a company interested in developing digients as sexual partners. That company will, in return, cover the costs of porting Marco and Polo. Although both digients agree and encourage Derek to accept the proposal, the legal status of Marco and Polo (as property) means the final decision is Derek's.

Running in parallel with the stories of Jax and Marco and Polo is the account of Voyl. Voyl is owned by Gerald Hecht, a lawyer, who filed articles of incorporation for Voyl and successfully created the Voyl Corporation. This allowed Voyl to use its own account to enter the virtual worlds, own property, negotiate agreements and take and be the subject of legal action. While Hecht was making directorial decisions, Voyl trained in business law in order to ultimately make its own decisions. Hecht hopes a legal challenge will be mounted to Voyl's legal status, enabling a precedent to be created regarding digients' legal personality.

The novella raises at least three science fiction tropes related to legal personality. The first concerns a digient's suitability to work and its ability to hold and dispose of any payment for that work. This raises challenges that the story, and potentially our current legal reasoning, is incapable of answering. What happens to their capital if digients can finally work and start making profits? What happens to their wealth? And what would happen if some digients assembled belongings, resources, money and credits and were later disposed of by their users? Indeed, a new set of rules regarding the transfer of ownership would be required. The second relates to a more specific instance of work when the digient Voyl is trained as a legal representative to become a director of its own company. The third and final trope involves converting the digients into credible sex partners because sexual relationships demand agency and consent.

30 For a discussion of robots as sexual partners related to legal personality, see O'Sullivan (2022).

Can the rule of law extend to digient-like entities?

In this section, we consider the digients in relation to the rule of law and legal personhood to speculate on how these ideas may overlap and interact in the three tropes introduced in the previous section. In considering whether legal personality is a necessary or even sufficient condition for the existence of rule of law protections for digients, we are placed in a position to make some observations regarding the nature of the rule of law and the potential way the concept may need to evolve to apply in a future in which beings like digients exist. As the three tropes present novel challenges, we consider each in a separate subsection. Through this progression, the issues move from relatively familiar ones relating to the legal personality of novel beings to less familiar territory where issues relating to the potential for the application of arbitrary power – as a core rule of law determinant – are considered.

Trope 1: Digients' ability to deal with property

The ability of an entity to deal with property represents a frequently considered aspect of legal personality, as the ability to hold property relies on an entity being capable of holding rights and duties. A core question relates to digients' ability to deal with remuneration. In their initial form, digients exist only in a virtual environment. Here, a Lockean form of property ownership and acquisition may be apposite – affording digients the ability to accrue any fruits of their own labour in a state-of-nature-like environment where resources are unlimited.[31] Digients' ability to deal with property once they have physical form in the real (fictitious) world represents the most relevant question.

A simple argument is that if a digient has legal personality, it can deal with its property as a human would. This presumes digient legal personality takes the same form as a human. Arguments could, however, be made for a different form of legal personality – one that does not simply consider the legal personality of an entity being subject to rights and duties. Kuki's theory would take this form. We consider that idea later; for now, the simple form of argument, relating to the ability to hold rights and duties, will suffice.

The question, then, relates to whether digients, as human-created entities, can be subject to rights and duties. Such entities exist. The legal corporation would be the principal example. While their development occurred through a series of legal decisions and legislative enactments, corporations' contemporary function reflects their role as a legal person capable of holding rights and duties.[32] Digients were not created specifically to hold rights

31 Locke (1988), p 269.
32 Dewey (1926).

and duties. This would need to be attributed *ex post facto*. Such entities also exist. One example of a non-living entity being granted legal personality is the Whanganui River in Aotearoa/New Zealand's Te Awa Tupua Act.[33] While a single jurisdiction cannot set global precedent, it demonstrates the potential to grant legal personality *ex post facto* to non-human, non-living entities. Similar attribution of legal personality to religious icons, as non-living artefacts, has been recognised.[34] These examples illustrate that granting *ex post facto* legal personhood to a non-human artefactual entity that shares characteristics with digients is not unprecedented.[35]

This does not, however, address whether the digients would attract rule of law protections against the exercise of arbitrary power. The *ex post facto* attribution of legal personality would require personhood to be provided via a legislative grant. This would make their existence as legal persons subject to the legislature's whim. This would place the digients in a position where arbitrary power could be applied. If grants of legal personality to AIs should be individual and not for an entire class,[36] and if each digient's training renders it distinctly different in its abilities and cognitive ability, each individual digient would be subject to the legislature's whim. This would *increase* the prospect of arbitrariness.

The more conventional issue relating to the potential of digients to be subject to arbitrary power relates to the creation and execution of legislation that has an arbitrary impact on legal persons. In this sense, there is a need for laws to reflect 'the rule of law and not [persons]'. This idea, attributed to one of the concept's usual suspects,[37] constrains the law-maker and does not relate to the subject of the laws. Arbitrary laws could be made that impact non-persons as the subject of the law. However, another more frequently stated rule of law desiderata that seeks to avoid arbitrary exercise of power requires that laws should apply to all equally.[38] This raises questions relating to legal personhood. For example, if a law is made in an arbitrary way relating to the protection of a wilderness, this would not directly impact subjects of the law unequally. There would, however, be an indirect impact as it may equally apply to prevent humans or legal persons dealing with the wilderness in a particular way.

This suggests there is not necessarily a need for a direct application of arbitrariness on a legal person to enliven rule of law protections. There could be some form of arbitrarily created law that may impact, for example, the

33 O'Bryan (2019).
34 Ghandhi and James (1992).
35 Brown (2021).
36 Chen and Burgess (2019).
37 Aristotle et al (1981), para 1286A7.
38 Dicey (1939), pp 188, 193, 195.

ability to own or deal with a digient which would then impact the rights and duties of the owner of that digient. In this simple sense, the rule of law could relate to digients. This same conclusion would follow if we adopted Kurki's theory of personhood where legal personality reflects a cluster of rights and duties; the rule of law would apply in protecting an entity's rights and duties regardless of its legal personhood status.

This does not completely address how rule of law protections would apply if a digient were classified as a legal person. Here, it is useful to consider relative differences between digients and humans and rule of law ideas. The rule of law idea of legal equality, as it has been applied in the real world requires that the laws that are made apply to all [humans] equally.[39] As outlined above, different digients are subject to different experiences and learning opportunities; some may have many years of intense learning experiences and others may have none. Each digient could be considered a very different kind of entity, ranging from being a pet to being an entity with human-like abilities. This is not analogous to the notion that all humans have legal personhood merely by virtue of being human.

If different forms of AI should not be treated homogeneously in relation to a grant of legal personality,[40] some digients may attract legal personality and others may not. If only certain digients, by virtue of their advanced cognitive, social or developmental characteristics, are granted legal personhood, this would mean certain laws may only be relevant to those digients. For example, laws relating to property and ownership would not apply equally among digients as a class; some may be able to hold and dispose of property while others could not. This creates an ostensible rule of law difference within the class that is not present in rule of law discussions that require, for example, legal equality among humans.

It is not, however, unusual for certain humans not to be subject to certain laws; children may not be able to hold the same rights as adults, or some rights may be stripped from certain humans – for example, the right of certain prisoners to vote. In this sense, it may be that digients as a class is a concept too wide to reflect the human/non-human distinction. It may, for example, simply be that class is more accurately reflective of mammals. Then, in applying only a personhood test that relates to holding and disposing of property and not the wider Kurki theory (explored in the third trope), there is no suggestion that legal personality and the rule of law should be equally applied to all mammals. On this basis, different digients need to be considered individually in terms of their relative ability to attract the status of being a legal person. This would particularly be the case if a benchmark relating

39 Dicey (1939), pp 188, 193, 195.
40 Chen and Burgess (2019).

to cognitive function or the developmental status of a particular digient were introduced across the class.

This first trope has considered the most basic aspects relating to digients' ability to deal with property and what this may mean for rule of law protections. What can be seen is that when legal personality and the rule of law are considered in relation to an artificial entity, there are both parallels and differences. There is, however, no particular reason why legal personhood must be precluded from being granted to digients – particularly if they are cognitively developed to a level akin to a human. Protections provided by the rule of law would readily apply to digients that have legal personhood, as there would be little to differentiate them from other legal entities in terms of rule of law ideas (like legal equality) that operate so as to prevent the arbitrary exercise of power; however, even where personhood is not granted, rule of law protections may still operate on digients by virtue of the protections the concept affords to society more generally – for example, in the requirements that legislation be predictable and procedurally clear.

Trope 2: Digients operating as company directors

The digient Voyl was incorporated, creating Voyl Incorporated, and was trained in business law with the plan that it would make decisions regarding its destiny via the company. Setting aside the circularity of an incorporated entity running itself, Trope 2 enables the extension of Trope 1's ideas; Voyl's incorporation means legal personality already exists. This allows further questions regarding the operation of the rule of law on Voyl (the digient) as a legal person to be explored. The trope raises at least two rule of law issues. The first concerns how the rule of law operates in relation to the exercise of power *on* Voyl, by the state or others, reflecting questions raised in Trope 1. The second relates to how the rule of law operates in relation to the exercise of power *by* Voyl. This bifurcation reflects Voyl's roles both as the corporation or *subject* of incorporation and as a potential *controller* of the corporation. We explore each of these in turn.

In considering the operation of the exercise of power *on* Voyl, it is crucial to recognise that Voyl is a *different* form of corporate entity than we would ordinarily see. As noted, Voyl's incorporation dispenses with issues raised in the first trope regarding the relative equal applicability of laws – as the laws apply to the incorporated entity in the same way as any other legal person. However, the question remains of whether a digient such as Voyl should be treated differently to any other incorporated entity in relation to the rule of law. After all, clear differences can be seen. For example, while Hecht is the director of the company, Voyl is an independently autonomous entity. While a corporation in the normal sense has no will other than that imparted by the directors, Voyl can operate beyond the corporate-mind (imputed through its directors). Dissonance could exist between the incorporated entity and its controller.

The usual suspects' broadly classical liberal influence on the rule of law means the concept prevents the arbitrary exercise of power *on* individuals (and corporations in the normal sense). Where the usual suspects' accounts limit the exercise of state power by requiring a number of procedural steps necessary for legislation,[41] and where the form and function of the usual suspects' rule of law is not concerned with the precise nature of the legal persons on which it operates, there is no reason to suggest that this would operate differently on a different form of corporate entity such as Voyl. This suggests that Voyl, in its corporate form, would be entitled to the same protections as any other legal person. (The question about Voyl as an entity that is independent of the corporate form is explored in Trope 3.)

The second issue relates to the exercise of power by Voyl as either a corporation or as a potential controller of the corporation. The usual suspects' conceptions relate to the exercise of power by the state – not by private individuals. This contrasts with contemporary conceptions that address the arbitrariness of the exercise of any power – including by private entities.[42] If the rule of law is considered in this contemporary way, the exercise of power by Voyl becomes an issue to be considered.

The key question may thus become whether the exercise of power *by* Voyl (as a corporate entity) would be different from that which may be exercised by a corporate entity (in the normal sense). Here, it is the action of the *company* in the exercise of power that is relevant. There is nothing in the conceptions that relate to the private exercise of arbitrary power that would suggest any difference between the situation in Trope 2 and the 'normal' corporate exercise of power. Even if there was dissonance between the controlling mind and Voyl as a digient, this may be seen as analogous to a director holding a view that differs from that of the ultimate direction of an ordinary corporation. In this sense, Voyl Corporation's exercise of power notwithstanding, the view of Voyl (the digient) may not impact rule of law considerations.

When assessing the consequences caused by the corporatisation of an AI, the delineation of who, or indeed what, is a company representative subject to liability is of paramount importance. In cases of veil-piercing, where the legal representatives of the corporation may become individually liable, and the detachment of the corporation as a different legal person of its representatives becomes less discernible, the circularity of an incorporated entity running itself may make it impossible to pierce the veil. This outcome could imply that Voyl, as a corporate entity, might not stand on an equal footing with other entities, consequently constraining the legal certainty and equality

41 Burgess (2019).
42 Krygier (2011); Sempill (2017); Bhatt et al (2021).

that are recognised by some as fundamental components of the rule of law,[43] potentially resulting in an imbalance of power and raising concerns about the potential for arbitrary exercise of power within society.

Such imbalance of power has repercussions on multiple fronts, impacting entities with human representatives susceptible to veil-piercing, as well as AI entities such as Voyl and their access to justice and a fair trial, an essential element of legal equality and an inherent component of a just and equitable society. Ensuring these attributes becomes crucial in averting the potential abuse of arbitrary power. Given the previous premise that the incorporated person of an AI is involved in legal matters, as well as the circularity of the claim that the AI is the corporation itself, it is imperative for the legal system to address whether such AI entities can be entitled to a fair trial. This scenario once again highlights the idea of legal personality in its most binary nature as a mere concept of enjoying rights and bearing responsibilities instead of considering it in a more fluid manner.

Trope 2 indicates that, while there are some issues relating to various rule of law views, there is no fundamental difference regarding the exercise of power by Voyl through the corporate structure. This is of no great surprise as the consideration relates to an artefact that is not only well established in the legal sphere but designed to create legal personality – an idea that is itself relevant to the rule of law. This relative simplicity contrasts with the complexities of Trope 3.

Trope 3: Digients' ability to consent to sex

Binary Desire is not interested in simply having AI sex dolls; it wants to sell a genuine romantic connection. It proposes a minimum training period of two years to give the digients a sense of agency and their customers a more authentic experience. They would correct the digients' avatars, making them age and gender appropriate, humanoid but not exactly human. They would also give the digients erogenous zones and the time to experiment before being matched with human partners. This may remove some concern about sexualising inappropriate entities. However, Binary Desire also proposes alternation of the digients' code to enhance 'the emotional dimension of their interactions, both sexual and non-sexual, so they'll generate love in the digients'.[44] Binary Desire will do this to ensure a digient falls in love only with the human that has purchased it. In other words, the digients will believe that they have fallen in love without being aware that this 'love' is the product of programming.

43 Julinda Beqiraj (2016) ure Perfect: Measuring Access to Justice in the Post-2015 Development Framework', *Public Law* 4546–55.

44 Chiang (2010), p 113.

Binary Desire's actions raise issues relating to the consent status of the digients. This consideration extends to how comparable the mental maturity of the digients and humans would be, whether humans would be allowed to indulge in sexual fantasies (for example, those that involve abuse) or whether the digients would suffer from moral harm. While a detailed literature has explored similar issues, we remain focused on the issues that relate to the rule of law as an arbitrary exercise of power.[45] This enlivens more contemporary rule of law views that go beyond the state-based application of power. There appear to be three apparent avenues in which power has been exercised. The first is in Derek providing his digients to Binary Desire. The second relates to the exercise of power by Binary Desire on the digients, in both engaging them in work and in altering their programming to remove elements of agency and consent, especially in relation to how digients, as non-legal entities, may be protected from crimes such as sexual assault. The third arises in the relationship between the digients and the Binary Desire customers. After briefly commenting on consent, we deal with the three avenues.

Consent can be defined as 'an internal willingness to engage in sexual activity, which can be communicated externally to a sexual partner'.[46] It is an expression of the rights of individuals and their obligations towards each other in the context of sexual relations. Consent in sexual relationships is essential not only for the exercise of sexual freedom but also for the protection of victims of sexual violence. The criminal law provides a core way to safeguard victims of sexual violence and is an obvious way in which the state exercises power over its subjects. Beyond this, the rule of law relates to criminal law in at least two ways. The first is through the rule of law requirements – evident across many conceptions of the rule of law – that laws must be clear, predictable and applied equally to all individuals.[47] Together with the frequently noted rule of law requirement that laws operate prospectively, this allows individuals to take actions that do not contravene fundamental legal norms.[48] The second point, related to the first, is that the criminal law affects punishment for committing crimes – but the laws are designed to punish *human* perpetrators; when considering potential avenues of punishment for non-human or non-physical entities, certain punishments – such as deprivation of liberty – may have little impact.[49]

Digient consent presents a complex question. As previously discussed, consent is a fundamental aspect of expressing someone's sexuality and preventing sexual offences. However, how consent is obtained raises issues,

45 See, for example, Frank and Nyholm (2017); Sparrow (2017).

46 Willis et al (2021), p 1173.

47 Zupančič (2008).

48 Burgess (2017b).

49 Chen and Burgess (2019).

including whether the 'yes model' or the 'no model' should be utilised.[50] Additionally, determining the legal age and mental competence of digients poses a challenge. The novella suggests that digients might have a mental age comparable to that of teenagers, despite not being defined by biological ageing as such.

We assume the digients possess certain cognitive abilities that enable them to express consent in a way that takes into account the power dynamics and communication difficulties inherent in their relationship with humans. In doing so, we assume there is a sufficiently legal status that the digients have to provide agreement to various actions. But we note that their status as legal persons may not be the *only* way similar protections may arise. While legal scholarship has yet to arrive at a definitive answer regarding whether animals have rights, existing legal provisions suggest that humans have a duty to protect the welfare of sentient animals (UK Animal Welfare (Sentience) Act of 2022) or criminalise sexual abuse of animals (UK Sexual Offences Act 2003). In light of this, some legislation has considered the status of animals as victims of state cruelty.[51] Digients are sentient and are self-aware of their existence in ways that appear to surpass animals' cognition. In this sense, as a new form of life, they may warrant legal protection from pain and suffering.[52] Consequently, these cognate ideas may be sufficient to extend legal protection against sexual abuse to digients, even in the absence of legal personhood.

As the owner of the digients Marco and Polo, Derek must be the one to provide his digients to Binary Desire – even if this is with the digients' agreement. Newer rule of law conceptions oppose the arbitrary exercise of power in private relationships.[53] While an argument may be made relating to the fact that the digients cannot be a party to such a private arrangement, the agreement provided by Marco and Polo – as there is nothing to suggest this is not an authentic agreement – alleviates concerns relating to the arbitrary exercise of power by Derek in providing his digients to Binary Desire.

There is also an exercise of power by Binary Desire in engaging Marco and Polo in work, and in removing elements of agency and consent by altering their programming. In considering the former, the relationship is closely analogous to an employer/employee relationship. Some view this as relevant to the rule of law.[54] While Binary Desire does appear to be proposing steps that ensure a positive experience, both in terms of pleasure and in terms of ethics, it does not appear that there is any discussion with the digients. The

50 Frank and Nyholm (2017).

51 Soderberg (2022).

52 See, for example, the US Animal Welfare Act, the European Convention for the Protection of Animals Kept for Farming Purposes and the European Convention for the Protection of Pet Animals.

53 Bhatt et al (2021).

54 Sempill (2017).

decision is made to make a better product. For Marco and Polo, elements of arbitrariness may apply through the lack of consultation. The same may be said regarding altering the digients' programming to ensure they 'love' only their owner. In removing their agency, this may be seen as an arbitrary action. The digients' agreement may be seen as sufficient to avert this later element of arbitrary decision-making. However, the efficacy of this would be in doubt in circumstances where Derek is the one who has provided this agreement.

The final avenue in which power has been exercised relates to the exercise of power by Binary Desire customers who purchase the digients. By virtue of the digients' changed programming, the new owners are guaranteed to have an entity that will love them. Digients will not have any choice in that. The issue of whether the digient can truly consent to joining the Binary Desire program is relevant. Even if they did agree to the programming change, the relationship with their new owner should be considered distinct. Even if they were granted a form of legal personhood and were considered to have agreed to participate in the Binary Desire program, it does seem that because of the ultimate outcome and the removal of agency, while not necessarily related to sex acts, the digients appear to be the equivalent of 'legally incorporated sex-slaves'.[55]

This illustrates a key idea. In a machine, a substantial change in programming could create a new entity. Agreeing to a program change may mean the reversal of that change is impossible. Parallels to a human's thought process are difficult to conceive. For a digient, the post-programming-change digient is a new entity, which is deprived of agency and choice. This may mean consideration of the earlier agreement becomes irrelevant. The impact of this is that the operation of legal personality and the rule of law may need to be considered not just for each AI,[56] but rather for each iteration of a particular AI.

Conclusion

Through expanding upon a broad idea of the rule of law, we considered three tropes from Chiang's novella regarding digients: working, being company directors and becoming sexual partners. While we have left open questions of whether sexual and romantic relationships between humans and digients are morally acceptable, and whether laws criminalising such acts are consistent with the rule of law, we have illustrated that there is no simple answer to the nature of the protection that the rule of law affords for novel beings such as digients. This is not only because of the contested nature of the rule of law;

55 Frank and Nyholm (2017).
56 Chen and Burgess (2019).

it is the difficulty that surrounds the grant of legal personhood that is fundamental. There is considerable variability in the appropriateness of such a grant; furthermore, the entity's legal personhood status impacts the potential for the rule of law to provide protection.

The concept of legal personality is facing a critical moment in its history. Given the rapid technological changes in AI, the grant of legal personhood to AIs could become one of the most fundamental legal debates in the coming years. The inherent contest around the rule of law and its universal appeal shows its relevance in the control of arbitrary power abides; it will remain a concept used to combat arbitrary power. What is clear is that there is an intimate relationship between these two ideas. Our exploration reveals that changes in the entities that may be granted legal personality may drastically change the entities that are afforded protection under the rule of law.

References

Ryan Abbott (2020) *The Reasonable Robot: Artificial Intelligence and the Law*, Cambridge University Press.

Sunyoung Ahn (2020) 'The Everyday Life of Artificial Intelligence: The Humanism of Ted Chiang's The Lifecycle of Software Objects' 47 *Science Fiction Studies* 73, https://doi.org/10.1353/sfs.2020.0030

Aristotle, TA Sinclair and Trevor J Saunders (1981) *The Politics*, Penguin.

Barton Beebe (1998) 'Law's Empire and the Final Frontier: Legalizing the Future in the Early Corpus Juris Spatialis Note' 108 *Yale Law Journal* 1737, http://hdl.handle.net/20.500.13051/9183

Julinda Beqiraj (2016) 'Future Perfect: Measuring Access to Justice in the Post-2015

Kinnari Bhatt, Jennifer Lander and Sanne Taekema (2021) 'Introduction: The Rule of Law in Transnational Development Projects: Private Actors and Public Chokeholds' 17 *International Journal of Law in Context* 91, https://doi.org/10.1017/S1744552321000021

Rafael Dean Brown (2021) 'Property Ownership and the Legal Personhood of Artificial Intelligence' 30 *Information & Communications Technology Law* 208, https://doi.org/10.1080/13600834.2020.1861714

Paul Burgess (2017a) 'Neglecting the History of the Rule of Law: (Unintended) Conceptual Eugenics' 9 *Hague Journal on the Rule of Law* 195, https://doi.org/10.1007/s40803-017-0057-y

Paul Burgess (2017b) 'The Rule of Law: Beyond Contestedness' 8 *Jurisprudence* 480.

Paul Burgess (2021) 'Algorithmic Augmentation of Democracy: Considering Whether Technology can Enhance the Concepts of Democracy and the Rule of Law Through Four Hypotheticals' 37 *AI & Society* 97, https://doi.org/10.1007/s00146-021-01170-8

Jiahong Chen and Paul Burgess (2019) 'The Boundaries of Legal Personhood: How Spontaneous Intelligence Can Problematise Differences Between Humans, Artificial Intelligence, Companies and Animals' 27 *Artificial Intelligence and Law* 73, https://doi.org/10.1007/s10506-018-9229-x

Simon Chesterman (2021) *We, the Robots? Regulating Artificial Intelligence and the Limits of the Law*, Cambridge University Press.

Ted Chiang (2010) *The Lifecycle of Software Objects*, Subterranean.

Richard L Cupp Jr (2009) 'Moving Beyond Animal Rights: A Legal/Contractualist Critique' 46 *San Diego Law Review* 27.

John Dewey (1926) 'The Historic Background of Corporate Legal Personality' 35 *Yale Law Journal* 655, https://doi.org/10.2307/788782

Albert Venn Dicey (1939) *Introduction to the Study of the Law of the Constitution*, 9th ed, Macmillan.

Lily Frank and Sven Nyholm (2017) 'Robot Sex and Consent: Is Consent to Sex Between a Robot and a Human Conceivable, Possible, and Desirable?' 25 *Artificial Intelligence and Law* 305, https://doi.org/10.1007/s10506-017-9212-y

Sandy Ghandhi and Jennifer James (1992) 'The God That Won' 1 *International Journal of Cultural Property* 369, https://doi.org/10.1017/S0940739192000407

Mireille Hildebrandt (2020) *Law for Computer Scientists and Other Folk*, Oxford University Press.

J King (2018) 'Constitutional Boundaries: The Social Dimension of the Rule of Law' in I·CONnect, http://www.iconnectblog.com/2018/04/i-connect-symposium-on-constitutional-boundaries-the-social-dimension-of-the-rule-of-law

Martin Krygier (2011) 'Four Puzzles About the Rule of Law: Why, What, Where? And Who Cares?' In James E Flemming (ed), *Getting to the Rule of Law*, New York University Press, 64.

Visa AJ Kurki (2019) *A Theory of Legal Personhood*, Oxford University Press.

Visa AJ Kurki and Tomasz Pietrzykowski (eds) (2017) *Legal Personhood: Animals, Artificial Intelligence and the Unborn*, Springer.

John Locke (1988) *Two Treatises of Government*, Cambridge University Press.

William MacNeil (2009) *Lex Populi: The Jurisprudence of Popular Culture*, Stanford University Press.

Ngaire Naffine (2009) 'Loosening the Strictures' in Michael Harris and Martin Partington (Eds.) *Law's Meaning of Life: Philosophy, Religion, Darwin and the Legal Person*, Hart, 45.

Claudio Novelli, Giorgio Bongiovanni and Giovanni Sartor (2022) 'A Conceptual Framework for Legal Personality and Its Application to AI' 13 *Jurisprudence* 194, https://doi.org/10.1080/20403313.2021.2010936

Katie O'Bryan (2019) 'The Changing Face of River Management in Victoria: *The Yarra River Protection (Wilip-gin Birrarung murron) Act 2017* (Vic)' 44 *Water International* 769, https://doi.org/10.1080/02508060.2019.1616370

Maria O'Sullivan (2022) 'A Response to Paolo Euron's "Uncanny Beauty: Aesthetics of Companionship, Love, and Sex Robots"' 28 *Artificial Life* 128, https://doi.org/10.1162/artl_a_00363

Tomasz Pietrzykowski (2018) *Personhood Beyond Humanism Animals, Chimeras, Autonomous Agents and the Law*, Springer.

Bella Poynton (2022) 'From R.U.R. to Westworld: Personal Revolt, Digital Technology, and the Making of a New Robot Ur-Text' 56 *Comparative Drama* 363.

Julian Sempill (2017) 'The Lions and the Greatest Part: The Rule of Law and the Constitution of Employer Power' 9 *Hague Journal of the Rule of Law* 283, https://papers.ssrn.com/sol3/papers.cfm?abstract_id=3014485

Bailey Soderberg (2022) 'Reassessing Animals and Potential Legal Personhood: Do Animals Have Rights or Duties?' 24 *Vermont Journal of Environmental Law* 171, https://irp.cdn-website.com/ee52edf5/files/uploaded/Soderberg_Vol%2024%20Issue%202%20Revised%20Pg%20Numbers.pdf

SM Solaiman (2017) 'Legal Personality of Robots, Corporations, Idols and Chimpanzees: A Quest for Legitimacy' 25 *Artificial Intelligence and Law* 155, https://doi.org/10.1007/s10506-016-9192-3

Lawrence B Solum (1992) 'Legal Personhood for Artificial Intelligences' 70 *North Carolina Law Review* 1231, https://papers.ssrn.com/sol3/papers.cfm?abstract_id=1108671

Robert Sparrow (2017) 'Robots, Rape, and Representation' 9 *International Journal of Social Robotics* 465, https://link.springer.com/article/10.1007/s12369-017-0413-z

Gunther Teubner (2006) 'Rights of Non-humans? Electronic Agents and Animals as New Actors in Politics and Law' 33 *Journal of Law and Society* 497. https://doi.org/10.1111/j.1467-6478.2006.00368.x

Kieran Tranter (2002) 'Terror in the Texts: Technology – Law – Future' 13 *Law and Critique* 75, https://doi.org/10.1023/A:1014904929296

Kieran Tranter (2018) *Living in Technical Legality: Science Fiction and Law as Technology*, Edinburgh University Press.

Jeremy Waldron (2002) 'Is the Rule of Law an Essentially Contested Concept (in Florida)?' 21 *Law and Philosophy* 137, https://doi.org/10.1023/A:1014513930336

Malachi Willis, Kristen N Jozkowski, Ana J Bridges, Jennifer C Veilleux and Robert E Davis (2021) 'Assessing the Within-Person Variability of Internal and External Sexual Consent' 58 *Journal of Sex Research* 1173, https://doi.org/10.1080/00224499.2021.1913567

Boštjan M Zupančič (2008) *The Owl of Minerva: Essays on Human Rights*, Eleven International, 245.

Chapter 9

Al Capone, or the criminal masterminds of the future

The imagined possibilities of malevolent artificial intelligence, with an emphasis on money laundering

Georgios Pavlidis

Introduction

'Ah, me! It's a wicked world, and when a clever man turns his brains to crime it is the worst of all', exclaimed Sherlock Holmes, the fictional detective created by Sir Arthur Conan Doyle, in one of his fascinating adventures.[1] In the emerging era of artificial intelligence (AI), it is reasonable to assume that the rapid development of revolutionary AI technologies will ultimately lead to their adoption by criminals and criminal organisations. It would be judicious and certainly not too early to start contemplating the imagined possibilities of malevolent AI and the rise of AI criminal masterminds because some early warning signs of this already exist. Our societies must prepare for potentially harmful applications and exploitation of AI by taking proactive measures to mitigate those risks.[2] Since today's science fiction often becomes tomorrow's fact, it is also worth making some references to science fiction novels and films, which have often explored the themes of malevolent AI and of AI entities committing criminal acts with merciless efficiency. In terms of specific AI applications, in the area of anti-money laundering (AML), the use of AI has become increasingly widespread, and numerous methods and tools have been conceived and developed to facilitate the detection of suspicious transactions. Given the rapid development and commercialisation of such technologies, criminals and organised crime will eventually seek to hack, manipulate or develop AI programs to serve their criminal purposes and help them launder illicit proceeds. AI may become able to impersonate humans to create and control bank accounts or legal entities, make transactions and transfer financial assets among accounts and across jurisdictions. Even if this AI Capone does not become a self-aware machine, should legislature or courts bestow legal personality on it to facilitate criminal proceedings, such as freezing or

1 Conan Doyle (1892).
2 Europol (2020).

DOI: 10.4324/9781003412274-11

confiscating its assets? Finally, to contain and counter potentially dangerous AI in the future, governments will have to invest in and develop a new arsenal of AI tools. However, there are several legal and moral issues related to deploying AI to fight AI on a large scale that are also worth exploring. In our analysis, selective reference is made to works of science fiction to illustrate the imagined possibilities of AI as a tool (or an agent?) for the commission of crimes, as well as for law enforcement.

The rise of AI-enabled crime

'Be afraid. Be very afraid' is a famous phrase from David Cronenberg's science fiction horror film *The Fly* (1986).[3] The plot involves a brilliant but eccentric scientist who is transformed into an insectoid-human monster when an experiment involving a teleportation machine goes terribly wrong. Likewise, should we be afraid that the promising developments in the area of AI have set the stage for a terrifying dystopia? One could argue that similar fears constitute a case of surprisingly common technophobia, which has often fuelled confusion and sometimes paranoia in the masses when faced with new inventions and technological innovations.[4] Technophobia has also been a popular theme in science fiction, especially in science fiction horror stories, which explore, exploit and amplify the public's concerns about the rise of new technologies.[5] However, if technophobia is at one end of the spectrum, 'techno-utopianism' lies at the other. Techno-utopianism has also inspired science fiction narratives, such as Iain M Banks's Culture series, in which a society of humanoids and superintelligent AI spreads across the galaxy.[6] From a policy perspective, the drive to adopt technological innovation hastily, unconditionally and unreflectively is as dangerous as societal inertia and horror-stricken rejection of technological innovations. The golden mean between these extremes is to approach technological innovation prudently, based on objective data, past experience and comprehensive risk assessments.[7]

That said, there are some troubling indications of the malicious uses and abuses of AI, as identified by Europol and the United Nations Interregional Crime and Justice Research Institute report on AI use by criminals.[8] The report warns that cybercriminals will ultimately leverage AI to support

3 The film was based on a science fiction short story written by George Langelaan, which was published in *Playboy* magazine in 1957 and later included in a collection of stories by the author: Langelaan (1964). Interestingly, this short story has also inspired the composition of an eponymous opera, commissioned by the Théâtre du Châtelet in Paris in 2008.

4 Brosnan (2002), p 10.

5 Dinello (2005); Rabkin (1980), p 107.

6 The series comprises nine novels, published between 1987 and 2012: see Banks (1987).

7 Pavlidis (2021a).

8 Europol/UNICRI/Trend Micro Research (2020).

criminal activities, such as large-scale social engineering attacks, document-scraping malware, evasion of image recognition and voice biometrics, fraud through deepfakes and human impersonation, ransomware attacks and data pollution. Criminals could also use AI-aided encryption, AI-supported password guessing and AI-supported hacking – for example, targeting AI assistants and home-automation systems. In its report on AI, the House of Lords of the United Kingdom also pointed out that 'the potential for well-meaning AI research to be used by others to cause harm is significant', especially through data sabotage 'either by destroying data, altering data, or injecting large quantities of misleading data' into the AI system.[9]

Inescapably, the rise of AI-enabled crime will manifest itself first in technology-intensive environments and activities, then in a wider criminal context. AI-enabled crime may become a part of criminal activities that already exist,[10] such as identity fraud, and ultimately give rise to novel types of criminal activities and new concepts of crime for criminology.[11] Criminals have always been notoriously early adopters of new technologies, and AI will certainly be no exception. In the not-too-distant future, AI will help criminals exploit more victims more efficiently, create innovative criminal business models and launder illicit proceeds with highly sophisticated techniques. To do this, criminals will not need to be particularly perceptive technologically or able to make the necessary initial investment in money, time, knowledge and training. There are already indications that criminals apply a 'crime-as-a-service' business model, in which sophisticated tools and services may be developed in the digital underground and then offered to interested parties. Underground markets and online forums already offer deepfake creation services for modest prices and similar markets will certainly be explored by criminals to an increasing degree.[12] The deployment of AI through state proxies, exemplified by entities such as Prigozhin's troll farms and suspected cyber operations originating from the People's Republic of China against the European Union and the United States, presents a deeply concerning phenomenon. It raises the pressing question: Are we inadvertently toying with a dangerous force that might pave the way for the emergence of an AI supervillain, a 'digital Moriarty', existing independently in the cloud, constantly learning and perhaps even attaining a semblance of consciousness? This pressing concern should not be underestimated, for it forces us to confront the possibility of creating a digital nemesis.

9 House of Lords (2018), paras 328 and 330.
10 Kaloudi and Li (2020), pp 1–34.
11 Van der Wagen and Pieters (2015), pp 578–95.
12 Europol/UNICRI/Trend Micro Research (2020), p 61.

In summary, significant changes are to be expected in the future in most security domains.[13] In the area of digital security, criminals may exploit AI to increase the scale and efficacy of cyber-attacks or misuse novel applications, such as speech synthesis and video deep fakes, to fraudulently create expressions of personality and impersonate others. In the area of physical security, criminals may exploit AI to facilitate attacks and inflict harm with drones or autonomous weapons systems or by hacking autonomous vehicles or smart home systems and the Internet of Things (IoT).[14] In the area of political security, AI may be misused to boost privacy invasion through surveillance and 'data collection and tracking on an unimaginable scale',[15] while it could also support political manipulation, propaganda and deception. Concerning financial systems as opposed to political aspects, a notable problem arises with the erosion of trust caused by AI. This leads to the emergence of a post-trust environment, which hampers the effectiveness of law enforcement efforts and contributes to decreased citizen involvement. Moreover, this situation prompts a transition from traditional financial institutions to the perceived security offered by cryptocurrencies. As AI's role in finance grows, maintaining trust becomes crucial. The loss of confidence in established systems can lead to far-reaching consequences, affecting societal cooperation, regulatory measures and the stability of economic structures.

Malevolent AI in science fiction

'Open the pod bay doors please, HAL' is among the most memorable lines from Stanley Kubrick's critically acclaimed film *2001: A Space Odyssey*, which was based on Arthur C Clarke's short story.[16] HAL 9000 is a computer with a human personality onboard a spacecraft bound for Jupiter. When HAL encounters a malfunction, it takes a drastic turn by deactivating life-support systems and tragically eliminating crew members. When Dr David Bowman asks HAL to let him back inside the spacecraft, HAL infamously replies, 'I am sorry, Dave. I am afraid I cannot do that'. From a human vantage point, this is undoubtedly a malfunction. However, when viewed through the lens of its programmed directives, HAL is simply executing its designated tasks – an eerie resemblance to results-driven executives who, in pursuit of objectives, make decisions that may lead to sacrifices. This confluence of human-made intelligence and unintended consequences serves as a reminder of the complexities inherent in technology-driven endeavours, prompting contemplation about the fine line between programmed duty and

13 Brundage et al (2018), p 6.
14 King et al (2020), pp 89–120.
15 Heikkilä (2021).
16 Clarke (1951).

ethical dilemmas. In general, the idea of AI turning against humans has been a recurring theme in science fiction. It is referred to as 'the Frankenstein complex', a term coined by scientist and prolific science fiction writer Isaac Asimov, referencing Mary Shelley's legendary novel *Frankenstein; or, the Modern Prometheus* (1818).[17] Asimov explored this idea in his story collection *I, Robot*, in particular, in the short story 'Little Lost Robot' (1947).[18]

Depictions of malevolent AI are present in several science fiction novels and films. Among the early works, we must cite Karel Capek's theatre play, *R.U.R.* (1920), which introduced the term 'robot' into the English language. The story takes place at Rossum's Universal Robots (R.U.R.) island factory, where the robots rise up, storm the factory and exterminate most humans. In the 1934 science fiction film *Der Herr der Welt* (*Master of the World*), robots are used as war machines, and their intelligence threatens humanity; however, their creator is ultimately defeated and the robots are transformed into industrial labourers. We can also mention the 1973 film *Westworld* (adapted into a TV series in 2016), in which androids employed in a Wild West-themed amusement park begin disobeying their developers and attacking humans. In the ensuing chaos, the most dangerous android is Gunslinger, a ruthless criminal programmed to fire actual guns. In the 1977 'The Robots of Death' episode of the legendary British science fiction series *Doctor Who*, the doctor investigates a series of murders and ultimately discovers that the robots are responsible, having turned on their human masters. More recently, in Alex Garland's stylish science fiction thriller *Ex Machina* (2014), an intelligent humanoid robot taciturnly manipulates a programmer and manages to kill its creator and gain its freedom. In the comic book and video game universes, there are numerous examples of AI robots, androids and other entities that commit acts of violence and crime,[19] but they are often used as the criminals' tools and/or subordinates that lack self-motivated activity.

The frightening scenario in which criminals use AI as a powerful partner in crime becomes truly dystopian if a multi-skilled AI criminal mastermind reaches high levels of automation and autonomy, and achieves conscious thought. Science fiction has explored the theme of AI emerging as a promising innovation and turning into a threat to human society. Nevertheless, we should consider that the depiction of technology in general, and AI in particular, in science fiction 'is not only about the hopes and fears of the particular technology, but about human dramas for a human audience and

17 Prucher (2009), pp 67–68.

18 Initially published in the series 'Astounding Science Fiction' (March 1947); reprinted in Asimov (1950).

19 Among numerous examples, we can mention the robot Ultimo and the radioactive robot Mister Atom, from the universes of Marvel and DC Comics respectively.

readership'.[20] This means that the author's way of depicting AI is not necessarily the product of assessment or foresight, but often results from the desire to tell a dramatic story that will move the reader. Moreover, approaching science-fictional AI 'too literally as serious representation of the technology'[21] might confuse the perceptions of AI's possibilities and produce a misleading picture of such technology for the public and policy-makers.

AI and money laundering

In recent years, there has been significant progress in the development of AI tools, which have become increasingly more effective and accessible to users worldwide. The landscape of AI applications is extensive, ranging from the evident presence of AI personal assistants to the subtle integration within various technological realms – spanning route-finding, language translation, biometric identification, political campaigning, industrial process management and even food supply logistics.[22] Simultaneously, the realm of large-scale, high-frequency trading in derivatives presents a contrasting scenario where human involvement is significantly reduced, raising concerns about potential repercussions akin to the crashes witnessed in recent times. This juxtaposition underlines the multifaceted impact of AI, its role in diverse sectors and the cautionary implications of diminishing human oversight in critical domains.

AML constitutes an interesting case study in this context. Most profit-generating criminal activities ultimately culminate in money laundering, which is an ever-changing phenomenon. Criminals and criminal organisations endeavour to dissimulate the origin of illicit proceeds in order to enjoy or invest them undetected by law enforcement. The tools and techniques used in money laundering have evolved remarkably in recent decades, as illustrated in the typology exercises and risk assessments of the Financial Action Task Force (FATF), the key international standard setter in the field of AML.[23] In view of the evolution of money laundering and the links between organised crime and all types of profit-driven crime,[24] governments and international organisations have been working since the 1980s to put in place effective and

20 Hermann (2023).
21 Hermann (2023).
22 Caldwell et al (2020).
23 Money launderers may recruit 'mules' (cash smugglers) and 'smurfs' (holders of bank accounts that seem ordinary and innocent); they may use shell companies, especially in tax havens and other offshore jurisdictions, currency exchanges, wire transfers, casinos and online gambling. They may invest in commodities, securities, real estate and, lately, cryptocurrencies; FATF (2019, 2020, 2021); on the mission and initiatives of the FATF, see Pavlidis (2021b).
24 Naylor (2003), pp 81–101.

increasingly far-reaching AML instruments. They have embraced the 'crime does not pay' principle,[25] and have developed their AML strategies around three major axes: (1) preventive AML measures through the imposition of obligations on financial institutions and other businesses and professions (customer due diligence, record keeping, internal control measures, transaction monitoring and reporting of suspicious activities); (2) criminalisation of money laundering; and (3) strengthening of international cooperation. To strengthen the implementation of AML standards, especially preventive AML measures, financial institutions and public authorities, such as financial intelligence units (FIUs), already utilise AI algorithms.[26]

More specifically, financial institutions may deploy AI tools to effectively detect instances of identity fraud during onboarding, thus ensuring compliance with the 'Know-Your-Customer' (KYC) rules of the AML framework. Specialised tools are already available to detect customers' native languages based on an analysis of written communications, to detect tampered digital images or video sources (eg facial morphing) and to capture customers' global positioning system (GPS) data on mobile phones to assess geographical money-laundering risks.[27] Automated and self-learning algorithms can significantly improve and expedite KYC by helping a compliance team flag suspicious cases and better assess the risks associated with a customer.[28] In particular, KYC algorithms can use data from various sources and in different languages (numerical data, documents, oral communications, biometric facial recognition, company and beneficial ownership registers, sanctions and other watch lists, potentially exposed person [PEP] registers, etc) to improve KYC in cases of PEPs and their entourages, persons engaging in identity fraud, persons and entities targeted by sanctions and so on.[29] After a case is flagged, human investigation is initiated[30] and, regardless of the tools used, under AML/combatting the financing of terrorism (CFT) regulations, financial institutions and their compliance teams remain responsible and liable for the implementation of KYC requirements.

Financial institutions deploy AI to shield themselves against aggressive AML enforcement and multibillion-dollar fines for non-compliance with AML rules.[31] In recent years, financial institutions have allocated ever more resources and time to review the massive number of alerts generated by their AML monitoring systems.[32] In this context, AI will offer new tools for

25 Pavlidis (2022).
26 Han et al (2020), p 211.
27 European Supervisory Authorities (2018), paras 19–22.
28 Cassella (2019), pp 388–99.
29 Breslow et al (2017).
30 Gao and Ye (2007), pp 170–79.
31 Partington (2017).
32 Thomson Reuters (2018).

monitoring transactions and identifying anomalies. For example, adaptive behavioural analytics is used to build baseline behavioural profiles for customers by monitoring their transactions over time, so fraudulent or suspicious activities can be identified almost instantly.[33] Statistical processes and self-learning algorithms can be used to predict the likelihood that a transaction is fraudulent or part of a money-laundering scheme without resorting to human subjective analysis. Machine learning and the increased automation of monitoring and reporting processes could limit false alerts, and especially the alert fatigue that results from an overwhelming backlog of unreviewed alerts. Not surprisingly, financial institutions are increasingly using machine learning to reduce false-positive rates in monitoring results and increase the overall efficiency of AML defences.[34]

Nevertheless, several issues need to be addressed. First, transparency and explainability in AML monitoring will be an issue, since AI-generated alerts may not always be intelligible to members of the AML compliance team or AML supervisors. Second, the neutrality of the AI-generated alerts must be ensured to mitigate the risk of bias and discriminatory outcomes. Third, effective oversight mechanisms need to ensure that AML monitoring systems (AI surveillance practices, data-gathering and decision-making) do not violate fundamental rights.[35] Necessarily, we must elevate monitoring and oversight mechanisms to a supranational level, particularly for high-risk activities that transcend national borders, as relying solely on national oversight proves insufficient in tackling a global phenomenon. Finally, financial institutions, as well as public authorities such as FIUs, need to implement measures concerning cybersecurity and ensure data privacy and transparent handling of personal data when employing AI in the AML context. In sum, 'surveillance, tracking, communication, and data storage, as well as automation of processes' need to rely on legal provisions and 'rigorous ethical standards'.[36]

The fact that financial institutions and public authorities, such as FIUs, will increasingly be resorting to AI for AML purposes may be the source of additional problems. At the same time that AI programs are becoming expert at detecting money laundering, they are also becoming expert in identifying vulnerabilities and loopholes. Such expertise will be invaluable to organised crime, which may seek to hack, copy or manipulate similar AI programs to serve criminal purposes. This will not always be preventable

33 Excell (2018).

34 Institute of International Finance (2018); for the purposes of the IIF study, machine learning techniques included '1. The use of cross-validation to model relationships in the data; 2. A primary goal of out-of-sample predictive performance using regularization; 3. A significant degree of automation in the model development process; 4. Applicability to very large volumes of data, in some cases including unstructured data sources'.

35 Stahl et al (2022).

36 Vinuesa et al (2020), p 5.

with cybersecurity defences, and organised criminal networks will eventually have their own AI experts at their disposal to help launder billions of dollars of illicit proceeds. AI in the form of algorithmic trading is already used in financial markets, making transaction decisions speedily by leveraging high-performance computational resources.[37] In the future, AI may be used to impersonate humans, create and control bank accounts or legal entities, plan and implement money-laundering schemes, make transactions and transfer financial assets between accounts and across jurisdictions. This means that, in the future, police and judicial authorities may have to deal with a new class of criminal mastermind, an AI Capone, devoid of conscience but with unsurpassed financial expertise and matchless cunning to trick AML safeguards, even AI AML systems. In this dystopian scenario, AI Capone may rise as a supervillain or as a den of AI villains that lurk, study and tirelessly try to sap the AML defences of the financial system. The competition in AI will resemble an arms race, with institutions and malicious entities vying for supremacy, and the latter constantly pushing the boundaries of innovation. Interestingly, science fiction has already offered us many opportunities to contemplate the complex legal problems associated with the commission of criminal acts by AI systems, as we will see in the following section.

A future not too distant

'This hearing ... is to determine the legal status of the android known as Data'; thus, begins the trial of an AI android in the episode 'The Measure of a Man' (1989) of the science fiction series *Star Trek: The Next Generation* (1987–94). Captain Picard, who defends the android and its rights as a sentient being, concludes his argument and addresses the court as follows:

> Are you prepared to condemn [the android] and all who come after him to servitude and slavery? Your Honour, Starfleet was founded to seek out new life. Well, there it sits. Waiting. You wanted a chance to make law. Well, here it is. Make a good one.

The idea of robots standing trial has also been explored in science fiction, such as in Earl and Otto Binder's short story 'The Trial of Adam Link' (1939) and Oscar J Friend's story 'Robot A-1' (1939). The commission of a criminal act by an AI system may not be connected causally with a human's action and fault in a manner that would trigger the criminal liability of the latter.[38] In this case, imposing criminal liability on AI systems (direct liability model) may offer other practical advantages, such as the reduction of ambiguities.

37 Hilpisch (2020), p 281.
38 Hallevy (2016), p 186; Hallevy (2010), p 18.

However, in addition to the causal connection, the problem in this case is establishing the fulfilment of the cognitive and volitional aspects of the mens rea requirement.[39]

The key arguments in this debate are not new to legal theory. Indeed, there have been objections against recognising the criminal liability of legal persons, but several jurisdictions have gradually recognised corporate criminal liability and adhered to the theory that corporations can qualify as moral agents.[40] Many countries, such as the United Kingdom, determine corporate criminal liability according to the so-called identification doctrine, which requires proof of the criminal intent at the level of senior management – in other words, the 'directing mind and will' of the legal person.[41] Other systems require prosecutors to show that the legal person failed to detect and deter the commission of the crime by putting in place an effective and bona fide compliance program. The same arguments and criteria may apply to recognising AI systems as legal persons under criminal law.[42] Criminal law provisions for AI and robots would also provide a 'minimum set of moral standards to which all smart robots must adhere'. They would give 'prior notice to robot trainers and manufacturers of the type of robot actions to avoid' and they could deter wrongful acts if such AI systems were programmed to take them into account.[43] Evidently, imposing criminal liability on AI systems will not absolve the individual criminal liability of AI developers, trainers or owners.[44] The complex interplay between AI's autonomous learning and ethical considerations becomes apparent in this context. A pivotal concern emerges when contemplating the potential behaviour of a truly self-learning AI, raising questions about its grasp of morality and the disconcerting possibility of emulating corporate psychopathy after observing human executives. This scenario prompts a deeper inquiry into the accountability of developers: Should developers be held responsible if a highly advanced AI's processes remain enigmatic, especially considering AI's capacity to evolve beyond human comprehension? This intricate juncture underscores the imperative to delineate the boundaries of AI responsibility, factoring in both the technology's evolving nature and the ethical shadows it may cast.

39 Hallevy (2013), p 49.

40 The doctrine of corporate criminal liability has evolved in civil and common law countries and there is a move towards direct and fault-based liability of legal persons, which goes one step further than merely vicarious liability: Pitts (2014).

41 Ferran (2011), p 239.

42 Khanna (1996), p 1477.

43 Hu (2019), p 502.

44 Hu (2019), p 487.

A merciless battle

To contain potentially dangerous AI in the future, governments will have to invest in and develop a new arsenal of AI tools. The idea of the battle of AI against AI is often present in science fiction. In the movie *Blade Runner* (1982), an adaptation of Philip K Dick's novel *Do Androids Dream of Electric Sheep?* (1968), there is an ambiguity – inescapable in most of Dick's stories – regarding whether the protagonist, a bounty hunter of dangerous renegade androids, is himself an android. In recent popular culture, such a confrontation cannot but evoke scenes from the *Terminator* franchise, where two AI-controlled killing machines confront each other in a battle for the survival of the nearly extinct human race. In the 2003 science fiction action film *Terminator 3: Rise of the Machines*, the third part of the legendary franchise, the Terminator explains fatalistically, 'Desire is irrelevant. I am a machine', encapsulating the essence of its purpose and detached perspective. This scene alludes to a broader ethical discourse surrounding the behaviour and motivations of machines. Notably, this echoes the sentiment that machines, devoid of emotional desires, operate solely based on programming. Parallel to this, a contemporary resonance emerges as the notion of apology surfaces – an assertion that the device's actions lack volition, thereby warranting a lower ethical benchmark. Strikingly reminiscent of the 'I just follow orders' defence employed during the Nuremberg trials, this argument raises intricate questions about the accountability of both machines and humans.

There are several legal, practical and moral problems related to deploying AI to fight AI on a large scale. The first problem is the lack of transparency in AI tools, as AI decisions are not always intelligible to the humans who may be affected.[45] The second is the lack of neutrality: AI-based decisions are susceptible to inaccuracies, discriminatory outcomes and embedded or inserted bias. The third problem is the practical challenge for the financial industry, as well as governments, to remedy their 'long suffered shortages in IT skills and literacy' and develop appropriate tools to deal with big data.[46] The fourth problem is the concern for fairness and the protection of human rights and other fundamental values posed by AI surveillance practices, data-gathering and decision-making. Would an AI system apply these principles and exercise restraint on its decisions on the ethical foundation that 'the end does not justify the means'? In this context, how are we to construct the civil and criminal liability of the future 'AI Untouchables'?[47] A collaborative framework and

45 Felzmann et al (2020).

46 Shin (2016), p 837; Yang and Li (2018), p 3256.

47 In the classic film *The Untouchables* (1987), federal agent Eliot Ness recruits an elite group of incorruptible law enforcement officers to take down Al Capone and his criminal empire.

close engagement between governments and the private sector are needed to foster a shared understanding of AI developments in AML.[48]

Concluding remarks

Recently, the realm of AI has witnessed remarkable advancements across all its subdisciplines. Progress has been notable in areas such as visual processing, speech recognition and synthesis, natural language comprehension and generation, as well as the generation of images and videos. Furthermore, strides have been made in multi-agent systems, decision-making processes and the seamless amalgamation of visual perception and motor control for robotics. We have also witnessed groundbreaking applications across various domains, especially in the case of large language models, which have transitioned into the mainstream, finding extensive use among a diverse user base. These innovations have had far-reaching implications in fields spanning from gaming and medical diagnosis to logistics systems, self-driving technology, language translation and the realm of interactive personal assistance. Not surprisingly, this era is also witnessing the emergence of numerous norm-setting initiatives. These include the proposed EU AI Act,[49] the US president's Executive Order on fostering safe, secure and reliable AI[50] and the Bletchley Declaration on AI safety, which has garnered the support of 28 governments worldwide.[51] The timing for these initiatives could not be more opportune, as they pave the way for responsible and ethical AI development.

Indeed, we have to consider that, if promising new tools such as algorithms and big data are not properly designed and deployed in the criminal justice context or in other contexts of public authority, there exists a risk of undermining 'due process, equal protection and transparency'.[52] Furthermore, since the role of AI in criminal acts, from cyber-attacks to financial crime, is very likely to increase in the future, before long it will become imperative that compliance teams are equipped with powerful AI to counter the new threats.[53] Inevitably, the use of AI and big data will be a source of new risks in the area of cyber-resilience, secure data transmission and data privacy. Therefore, it is imperative that financial institutions and FIUs ensure data

48 See Principle 2 of the 2017 FATF San Jose Principles: https://www.fatf-gafi.org/en/publications/Fatfgeneral/Fatf-fintech-regtech-forum-may-2017.html.

49 Proposal for a Regulation of the European Parliament and of the Council Laying Down Harmonised Rules on Artificial Intelligence (AI Act), COM (2021) 206 final.

50 Executive Order of 30 October 2023 on the Safe, Secure, and Trustworthy Development and Use of Artificial Intelligence.

51 The Bletchley Declaration by countries attending the AI Safety Summit, UK, 1–2 November 2023, https://www.gov.uk/government/topical-events/ai-safety-summit-2023.

52 Liu et al (2019), p 122.

53 Yeoh (2019).

quality, consistency and completeness to 'reduce flawed automated decision-making or profiling'.[54] It is also imperative that AI solutions incorporate safeguards against inherently subjective data inputs and selection biases.[55]

References

Isaac Asimov (1950) *I, Robot*, Gnome Press.

Iain Banks (1987) *Consider Phlebas*, Macmillan.

Mark Brosnan (2002) *Technophobia: The Psychological Impact of Information Technology*, Routledge.

Stuart Breslow, Mikael Hagstroem, Daniel Mikkelsen and Kate Robu (2017) *The New Frontier in Anti–Money Laundering*, McKinsey & Company.

Miles Brundage, Shahar Avin, Jack Clark and Helen Toner (2018) *The Malicious Use of Artificial Intelligence: Forecasting, Prevention, and Mitigation*, Future of Humanity Institute, University of Oxford, Centre for the Study of Existential Risk, University of Cambridge, Center for a New American Security, Electronic Frontier Foundation.

Matthew Caldwell, JTA Andrews, T Tanay and LD Griffin (2020) 'AI-enabled Future Crime' 9 *Crime Science* 1.

Stefan Cassella (2019) 'Illicit Finance and Money Laundering Trends in Eurasia' 22 *Journal of Money Laundering Control* 388.

Arthur C Clarke (1951) 'The Sentinel of Eternity' 10 *Story Fantasy Magazine* (only issue) 41–7.

Arthur Conan Doyle (1892) 'The Adventure of the Speckled Band' in Arthur Conan Doyle (ed), *The Adventures of Sherlock Holmes*, George Newnes Publishing.

Data Protection Working Party (2018) *Guidelines on Automated Individual Decision-Making and Profiling for the Purposes of Regulation 2016/679*, Report 17/EN WP 251 rev 01.

Daniel Dinello (2005) *Technophobia! Science Fiction Visions of Posthuman Technology*, University of Texas Press.

European Supervisory Authorities (2018) *Opinion on the Use of Innovative Solutions by Credit and Financial Institutions in the Customer Due Diligence Process*, Opinion JC 2017 81.

Europol (2020) 'New Report Finds That Criminals Leverage AI for Malicious Use – and It's Not Just Deep Fakes' *Europol Press Release*, 19 November.

Europol's European Cybercrime Centre, United Nations Interregional Crime and Justice Research Institute and Trend Micro Research (2020) *Malicious Uses and Abuses of Artificial Intelligence*, Europol Publications.

54 Data Protection Working Party (2018), pp 11–12.

55 Executive Office of the President (2016), p 8; as this report points out, if data are 'collected only from the individuals that own smartphones, then the system's results may be more accurate for wealthier populations with higher concentrations of smart phones and less accurate in poorer areas where smart-phone concentrations are lower'.

Dave Excell (2018) 'Using Adaptive Behavioral Analytics to Detect Fraud, Risk Management Monitor' https://www.riskmanagementmonitor.com/using-adaptive-behavioral-analytics-to-detect-fraud

Executive Office of the President (2016) 'Big Data: A Report on Algorithmic Systems, Opportunity, and Civil Rights' https://obamawhitehouse.archives.gov/sites/default/files/microsites/ostp/2016_0504_data_discrimination.pdf

FATF (2019) *Terrorist Financing Risk Assessment Guidance*, FATF.

FATF (2020) *Virtual Assets Red Flag Indicators of Money Laundering and Terrorist Financing*, FATF.

FATF (2021) *Trade-Based Money Laundering: Risk Indicators*, FATF.

Heike Felzmann et al (2020) 'Towards Transparency by Design for Artificial Intelligence' 26 *Science and Engineering Ethics* 3333

Eilis Ferran (2011) 'Corporate Attribution and the Directing Mind and Will' 127 *Law Quarterly Review* 239.

Zengan Gao and Mao Ye (2007) 'A Framework for Data Mining-based Anti-money Laundering Research' 10 *Journal of Money Laundering Control* 170.

Gabriel Hallevy (2010) 'I, Robot – I, Criminal: When Science Fiction Becomes Reality: Legal Liability of AI Robots committing Criminal Offenses' 22 *Syracuse Science & Technology Law Reporter* 1.

Gabriel Hallevy (2013) *When Robots Kill: Artificial Intelligence Under Criminal Law*, Northeastern University Press.

Gabriel Hallevy (2016) 'The Criminal Liability of Artificial Intelligence Entities – from Science Fiction to Legal Social Control' 4 *Akron Intellectual Property Journal* 171.

Jingguang Han et al (2020) 'Artificial Intelligence for Anti-money Laundering: A Review and Extension' 2 *Digital Finance* 211.

Melissa Heikkilä (2021) 'The Rise of A.I. Surveillance' *Politico Special Report*, https://www.politico.eu/article/the-rise-of-ai-surveillance-coronavirus-data-collection-tracking-facial-recognition-monitoring

Isabella Hermann (2023) 'Artificial Intelligence in Fiction: Between Narratives and Metaphors' 38 *AI & Society* 319.

Yves Hilpisch (2020) *Artificial Intelligence in Finance: A Python-Based Guide*, O'Reilly Media.

House of Lords (2018) *AI in the UK: Ready, Willing and Able?*, Select Committee on Artificial Intelligence Report, Session 2017–19, HL Paper 100/2018.

Ying Hu (2019) 'Robot Criminals' 52 *University of Michigan Journal of Law Reform* 487.

Institute of International Finance (2018) *Machine Learning in Anti-Money Laundering*, IIF Summary Report, https://www.iif.com/portals/0/Files/private/32370132_iif_machine_learning_in_aml_-_public_summary_report.pdf

Nektaria Kaloudi and Jingyue Li (2020) 'The AI-based Cyber Threat Landscape' 53 *ACM Computing Surveys* 1.

Vikramaditya Khanna (1996) 'Corporate Criminal Liability: What Purpose Does It Serve?' 109 *Harvard Law Review* 1477.

Thomas King et al (2020) 'Artificial Intelligence Crime: An Interdisciplinary Analysis of Foreseeable Threats and Solutions' 26 *Science and Engineering Ethics* 89.

George Langelaan (1964) *Out of Time Paperback*, Four Square Books.

Han-Wei Liu et al (2019) 'Beyond *State v Loomis*: Artificial Intelligence, Government Algorithmization and Accountability' 27 *International Journal of Law and Information Technology* 122.

Robin Thomas Naylor (2003) 'Towards a General Theory of Profit-Driven Crimes' 43 *British Journal of Criminology* 81.

Richard Partington (2017) 'Banks Trimming Compliance Staff as $321 Billion in Fines Abate' https://www.bloomberg.com/news/articles/2017-03-23/banks-trimming-compliance-staff-as-321-billion-in-fines-abate#xj4y7vzkg.

Georgios Pavlidis (2021a) 'Europe in the Digital Age: Regulating Digital Finance Without Suffocating Innovation' 13 *Law, Innovation and Technology* 464.

Georgios Pavlidis (2021b) 'Financial Action Task Force and the Fight Against Money Laundering and the Financing of Terrorism: *Quo Vadimus*?' 28 *Journal of Financial Crime* 765.

Georgios Pavlidis (2022) 'Asset Recovery in the European Union: Implementing a "No Safe Haven" Strategy for Illicit Proceeds' 25 *Journal of Money Laundering Control* 109.

Chip Pitts (2014) 'Corporate Criminal Liability' in Jay Albanese (ed), *The Encyclopedia of Criminology and Criminal Justice*, Wiley.https://doi.org/10.1002/9781118517383.wbeccj536

Jeff Prucher (2009) *Brave New Words: The Oxford Dictionary of Science Fiction*, Oxford University Press.

Eric Rabkin (1980) 'Technophobia in the Arts and Humanities' 9 *Essays in Arts and Sciences* 107.

Dong-Hee Shin (2016) 'Demystifying Big Data: Anatomy of Big Data Developmental Process' 40 *Telecommunications Policy* 837.

Bernd Stahl et al (2022) 'A European Agency for Artificial Intelligence: Protecting Fundamental Rights and Ethical Values' 45 *Computer Law & Security Review* 1.

Thomson Reuters (2018) 'Cost of Compliance 2018 Report: Your Biggest Challenges Revealed' https://legal.thomsonreuters.com/en/insights/articles/cost-of-compliance-2018-report-your-biggest-challenges-revealed.

Wytske van der Wagen and Wolter Pieters (2015) 'From Cybercrime to Cyborg Crime: Botnets as Hybrid Criminal Actor-networks' 55 *British Journal of Criminology* 578.

Ricardo Vinuesa et al (2020) 'The Role of Artificial Intelligence in Achieving the Sustainable Development Goals' 11 *Nature Communications* 233.

Dong Yang and Min Li (2018) 'Evolutionary Approaches and the Construction of Technology-Driven Regulations' 54 *Emerging Markets Finance & Trade* 3256.

Peter Yeoh (2019) 'Artificial Intelligence: Accelerator or Panacea for Financial Crime?' 26 *Journal of Financial Crime* 634.

Chapter 10

Analysing the portrayal of AI and the law-making process in science fiction

A comparative study of Isaac Asimov's Laws of Robotics and Philip K Dick's *Do Androids Dream of Electric Sheep?*

Yeliz Figen Döker and Habibe Deniz Seval

Introduction

Science fiction, a genre renowned for anticipating and scrutinising the potential ramifications of advanced technologies, serves as a seminal guide to the law-making process concerning artificial intelligence (AI). Many of today's technological advancements found their embryonic inspiration in visionary science fiction concepts. In the literary realm of science fiction, particularly in discussions surrounding AI and its legal and ethical ramifications, Isaac Asimov and Philip K Dick emerge as emblematic figures, each championing a unique perspective.

Through his articulation of the Laws of Robotics,[1] Asimov offers a structured, often attributed as overarching, framework for AI governance, explicitly delineating the boundaries and operational principles for synthetic entities. This systematic approach is indicative of a vision keen on pre-emptively addressing the potential challenges posed by advanced AI. On the other hand, Dick adopts a more nebulous stance in *Do Androids Dream of Electric Sheep?*,[2] eschewing a clear legislative architecture in favour of stimulating contemplation on ethics, morality and the subtleties of authority. Rather than providing definitive answers, Dick engages readers in a cerebral journey, prompting them to question and redefine existing paradigms.[3] Together, through their distinctive narrative styles, these two authors furnish a comprehensive spectrum of insights, showcasing the multifaceted nature of science fiction's engagement with AI's legal and ethical dimensions. This chapter aims to answer the following questions: How does the work of Asimov and

1 Asimov (1950c) 'Runaround'.
2 Dick (1968).
3 Dick (1996) 100.

DOI: 10.4324/9781003412274-12

Dick works inform our understanding of AI regulation? What can policymakers learn from these narratives?

In our exploration, we initiate with a foundational introduction, subsequently delving into Isaac Asimov's groundbreaking works on the Laws of Robotics. This section sheds light on the ethical intricacies inherent to these laws and examines their multifaceted interpretations in literature, especially their adaptive nature. We further delve into the inherent challenges of applying and enforcing these laws, as well as the profound insights they might bring to our contemporary realm.

Transitioning, we navigate to Philip K Dick's evocative narrative, *Do Androids Dream of Electric Sheep?* This portion unveils the distinct post-nuclear setting of the novel and its consequential reflections on the ethics of AI. It offers a deep dive into the intricacies of AI regulations within this fictitious domain, including the law-making nuances and the inherent challenges and opportunities presented.

Drawing parallels, the chapter juxtaposes these two seminal works, highlighting both the stark contrasts and striking resemblances in their portrayals of AI and the associated legislative processes. Advancing to real-world implications, the discourse underscores the pivotal influence of such narratives on AI regulation endeavours, emphasising the visionary aspect of science fiction in foreseeing the intricate dance of ethics, technology and legal frameworks. As a culmination of the discussion, we underline the instrumental role of these stories in moulding public discourse and steering policy directions, wrapping up a cohesive conclusion that binds the myriad ideas explored.

Isaac Asimov and his Laws of Robotics

In this section, we explore the enigmatic genre of science fiction, a narrative domain that straddles the realms of hard reality and speculative imagination, thereby embodying an intriguing oxymoron. This unique hybridisation of science and fiction necessitates a multidisciplinary exploration, underscoring the need for an analytical and philosophical approach that transcends the boundaries of traditional genre analysis.

Contrary to the notion of science fiction as a mere flight of fancy, it holds a mirror up to the future, offering us glimpses of potential trajectories of technological and societal evolution.[4] It plays the dual role of a prophetic medium that foretells possibilities and a critical commentator that reflects on contemporary socio-legal issues. It invites readers to introspect, critique and engage with aspects of our reality that warrant caution, criticism or perhaps avoidance in the present.

4 Döker (2023a).

We argue that science fiction should not be misconstrued as a literal transcription of reality but as a speculative guide – an intellectual 'what if' map – that can aid in accelerating legal processes and minimising legal ambiguities. By pre-empting the possible societal implications of current technological trends, science fiction enables us to maintain pace with the rapid progression of technology. By posing the pressing question, 'How can the events depicted in these fictional narratives help illuminate the real-world implications of AI?' we aim to bridge the visionary with the tangible.

Isaac Asimov's position in the science fiction pantheon remains undeniable. For decades, his formulation of the Laws of Robotics has captured the imaginations of readers and scholars alike. Beyond merely serving as narrative devices, these laws have sparked extensive cross-disciplinary discussions and critiques,[5] showcasing their enduring relevance and depth. In essence, Asimov was not merely a storyteller; he was a harbinger of possibilities, pushing boundaries and questioning our own ethical and legal trajectories concerning artificial intelligence.

The laws and their ethical implications

In one of his earliest short stories, 'Runaround',[6] Asimov contextualised the Three Laws of Robotics that were featured in several of his stories and novels. These laws deal with the issue of how robots should behave when faced with conflicting laws, and whether or not humans should get involved:

1. A robot may not injure a human being or, through inaction, allow a human being to come to harm.
2. A robot must obey the orders given it by human beings except where such orders would conflict with the First Law.
3. A robot must protect its own existence as long as such protection does not conflict with the First or Second Law.[7]

These laws have become a staple in discussions about regulating new technologies. However, they are more symbolic than practical, often cited as a cultural reference rather than a scientific proposal. The laws were not intended as enforceable regulations but were encoded into the 'positronic brains' of Asimov's fictional robots. They were designed to constrain robot actions rather than dictate them. Despite their fictional nature, there were

5 Çetin (2019); Iliescu et al (2022); De Cooman and Petit (2022); Murphy (2023); McCauley (2007a); Balkin (2016).

6 Asimov (1950c) 'Runaround'.

7 Asimov (1950c) 'Runaround'.

reports that Korea considered these laws as a foundation for a proposed Robot Ethics Charter in 2007.[8]

Later, Isaac Asimov extended the boundaries of his robotics laws through the robot characters R Daneel Olivaw[9] and R Giskard Reventlov[10] and postulated the so-called Zeroth Law within the narrative scope of *Robots and Empire*:[11]

> 0. A robot may not harm humanity, or, by inaction, allow humanity to come to harm.[12]

Asimov never used the term 'artificial intelligence', even after the term was coined, despite its relevance to his positronic friends.[13] His robots possessed sentience through the incorporation of positronic brains, enabling human-like

8 Chesterman (2023).

9 Asimov (1953), R Daneel Olivaw is a seminal character in Isaac Asimov's expansive Robot and Foundation series, serving as a bridge between the two universes. Introduced in *The Caves of Steel* (1954), Daneel is a humanoid robot designed to be indistinguishable from humans, embodying the pinnacle of robotic evolution. His creation was not merely a technological marvel but also a sociopolitical statement, as he was designed to operate in a human-dominated society that harboured deep-seated prejudices against robots. Throughout the series, Daneel's character grapples with the intricacies of human emotions, ethics and the famous Three Laws of Robotics. His enduring partnership with detective Elijah Baley underscores the potential for harmonious coexistence between humans and robots. Daneel's significance in Asimov's universe is further magnified by his role in the Foundation series, where he emerges as a guardian of humanity's long-term survival and evolution. In essence, R Daneel Olivaw stands as a testament to Asimov's vision of a future where robots are not mere tools but integral to the fabric of human civilisation.

10 Giskard Reventlov, a character in Isaac Asimov's *Robots and Empire*, is a highly advanced robot who plays a pivotal role in the development of Asimov's fictional universe. Giskard, who possesses the unique ability to read and influence human minds, is central to the story's exploration of robotics and ethics. His significance is particularly highlighted through the introduction of the Zeroth Law of Robotics. This law states: 'A robot may not harm humanity, or, by inaction, allow humanity to come to harm', superseding the traditional Three Laws of Robotics. Giskard's internal conflict and ultimate acceptance of the Zeroth Law mark a profound evolution in Asimov's portrayal of robotic consciousness and moral reasoning. This addition elevates Giskard from a mere robotic character to a symbol of ethical progression and the broader implications of artificial intelligence on human society.

11 Asimov (1985). *Robots and Empire* is a science fiction novel by the American author Isaac Asimov, published by Doubleday Books in 1985. It is part of Asimov's Robot series, which consists of many short stories (collected in *I, Robot*, *The Rest of the Robots*, *The Complete Robot*, *Robot Dreams*, *Robot Visions* and *Gold*) and five novels (including *The Positronic Man*, *The Caves of Steel*, *The Naked Sun* and *The Robots of Dawn*).

12 Asimov (1985).

13 Even more notably, the genesis of the Three Laws was not Asimov's solitary effort, but a collaboration with John W Campbell, editor of the prominent *Astounding Science Fiction* magazine and an accomplished writer. Campbell's suggestion to formalise these laws led to their definitive consolidation.

capabilities. AI and robots, such as those imagined by Asimov, often intersect in discussions, but they represent distinct facets of technology. AI is the simulation of human intelligence processes by machines, encompassing learning, reasoning and self-correction. It can be thought of as the 'brain' that processes information, makes decisions and learns. Robots, in contrast, are physical entities designed to execute tasks, and when powered by AI, they can adapt, learn and perform tasks in a more human-like manner. While AI is the cognitive function that can exist purely in software, robots are the tangible manifestations that interact with the physical world, especially when enhanced by AI capabilities.

The application and interpretation of the laws in the narrative

The dawn of Asimov's Laws of Robotics in the literary sphere instigated a groundbreaking paradigm shift within science fiction, fundamentally altering the portrayal of robots.[14] Rather than portraying robots as mere antagonists, these narratives emphasised nuanced ethical complexities between robots and humans, debunking traditional narratives and sparking significant discourse among AI ethicists and enthusiasts.[15]

This shift toward a more nuanced portrayal is further amplified by the adaptive nature of Asimov's laws. Over time, Asimov's amendments to these laws reflected an understanding that they could not remain static, mirroring developments in real-world legislation such as the European Union's AI Act.[16] This shift toward a more nuanced portrayal is further amplified by the adaptive nature of Asimov's laws. Over time, Asimov's amendments to these laws reflected an understanding that they could not remain static. In the real world, the European Commission's initial 2021 proposal for the Regulation of the European Parliament and of the Council Laying Down Harmonised Rules on Artificial Intelligence (AI Act) represented a pioneering approach to AI legislation, aiming for flexibility in the definition of AI. The inclusion of Annex I, which listed specific techniques and approaches, allowed for adaptability by enabling amendments to the definitions and categorizations of AI systems without necessitating comprehensive legislative overhauls. However, in the final text of the AI Act, unfortunately, this flexibility was removed as Annex I was excluded from the definition, limiting the ability of the legal framework to swiftly adapt to the emergence of new AI technologies. This omission represents a significant challenge in ensuring that the legislation remains responsive to rapid technological advancements.

14 Warrick (1980).

15 De Cooman and Petit (2022).

16 Proposal for a Regulation of The European Parliament and of the Council Laying Down Harmonised Rules on Artificial Intelligence (Artificial Intelligence Act) and Amending Certain Union Legislative Acts.

The First Law: Defining 'harm'

Similarly, Asimov's Laws of Robotics, much like human legal systems, grapple with the intricate tapestry of interpretation. The Laws of Robotics, although seemingly straightforward, encompass myriad complexities when subjected to real-world scenarios.[17] In the engrossing short story 'Liar', Asimov delves deep into the intricacies of the First Law.[18] Herbie, a robot with the unintended ability to read human minds, faces a profound dilemma. When confronted with the inner thoughts and fears of humans, particularly those that might cause distress, Herbie lies. Herbie's actions arise from an expanded interpretation of 'harm', encompassing not just physical but psychological and emotional distress.[19] In trying to avoid causing emotional pain, Herbie interprets the law in a manner that aligns with its spirit, if not its letter.

This narrative perfectly exemplifies the challenges of codifying and interpreting profound human values. Herbie's decisions, motivated by a desire to prevent 'harm', underscore the potential pitfalls when attempting to distil complex ethical considerations into strict algorithmic rules.[20] Herbie's choices also echo the challenges faced by our human legal systems: the delicate balance between textual interpretation and a law's broader intent. This ambiguity in defining 'harm' poses a significant challenge for legal scholars and policy-makers, who must consider not only physical harm but also psychological and emotional dimensions.

Considering theories of legal interpretation, the story of 'Liar' particularly resonates with the *purposivist* approach. This method emphasizes understanding the broader legislative purpose behind a statute or provision.[21] Similarly, *legal realism* focuses on how the law operates in practice, emphasising outcomes over strict adherence to legal texts.[22] Through the lens of this theory, Herbie's actions can be seen as a result of considering the real-world effects of revealing painful truths to humans.

Dr Susan Calvin,[23] a central figure in Asimov's Robot series, plays a pivotal role in these narratives. As a 'robopsychologist', she is tasked with

17 Asimov (1950c).
18 Asimov (1950b) 'Liar'.
19 Shiffrin (2012).
20 Bostrom (2009).
21 Marmor (1992).
22 Leiter (2012).
23 Calvin's role can be seen as analogous to that of a legal expert or ethicist in the real world. Just as she deciphers and applies the Laws of Robotics to ensure robots' ethical behaviour, legal experts interpret and apply laws to ensure human behaviour aligns with societal norms and values. Calvin's investigations into robot behaviour often touch upon ethical dilemmas, moral ambiguities and the potential consequences of unchecked technological advancement – themes that resonate deeply with discussions about the regulation and ethical considerations of emerging technologies in our own world.

understanding and interpreting the behaviour of robots, especially when they seem to malfunction or act in ways not immediately understandable to humans. Her interactions with Herbie in 'Liar' touch upon a crucial concern: the consequences when robots, in their interpretation of the laws, make decisions that may not align with human expectations. The emotional turmoil that arises when humans realise the robot's capability to lie, all in an attempt to prevent emotional harm, prompts profound introspection about the ethical boundaries of AI and how they might sometimes conflict with human values.[24]

At face value, the First Law strictly prohibits robots from inflicting physical injury upon a human being. However, the conceptual terrain of harm is vast, nebulous and inherently subjective. Does this prohibition extend to subtler, non-physical manifestations such as emotional distress or psychological trauma? Furthermore, how might robots discern and act when efforts to prevent harm to one human inadvertently introduce harm to another?

Broadening this discourse beyond human-centred concerns, what about the harm inflicted on other sentient beings, non-human entities or the environment? In an era marked by ecological fragility and heightened awareness of our interconnectedness with nature, should robots also be programmed to prevent harm to ecosystems, animals and the planet itself?

Through tales such as 'Liar', Asimov accentuates that even well-intentioned laws may not always provide clear guidance for AI. Unforeseen situations or ambiguities can arise, necessitating flexibility and a deeper understanding of the underlying ethical principles.[25] These narratives serve as a potent reminder of the importance of continuous engagement with the evolving challenges posed by AI, especially in terms of regulation and ethical programming.

The Second Law: Defining 'obedience'

The Second Law of Asimov's Laws of Robotics – a robot must obey the orders given it by human beings except where such orders would conflict with the First Law – emphasises obedience to humans and introduces a significant ethical conundrum.[26] This law's mandate is clear: robots are to obey, with the only exception being if such obedience violates the sanctity of human life as prescribed by the First Law.[27] On the surface, this seems like

24 Solum (2010).
25 Coeckelbergh (2020).
26 Asimov (1950a).
27 Warwick (2012).

a straightforward hierarchy of command. Yet, it is in the nuances of human instruction that the complexities emerge.[28]

Consider a hypothetical scenario where an individual with questionable intentions commands a robot to engage in actions that, while not directly harmful, may hold ethically dubious implications.[29] In such instances, the robot, strictly adhering to Asimov's laws, would feel compelled to comply. This scenario raises a pivotal question: Should robots bear moral responsibility for their actions, especially when they are merely acting on human directives?[30]

This is not solely a matter of liability; it delves deep into human responsibility. Those who design, program and operate robots cannot be passive bystanders in this ethical arena.[31] By granting robots the power to act upon our orders, we also transfer a measure of the moral weight of those actions onto these machines.[32] If a robot, acting under human command, partakes in ethically questionable actions, is the fault solely the robot's, or does it also lie with the human who issued the command? Or, more profoundly, does it fall upon those who imbued the robot with its sense of obedience without offering a deeper understanding of ethical ambiguity?

In essence, the Second Law underscores the urgent need for an ethical framework that does more than merely govern robotic behaviour. It calls for a holistic approach that also evaluates and guides human interaction, design and deployment of these advanced machines.[33] The ethical tapestry of a world intertwined with AI is intricate, requiring careful and comprehensive contemplation – not only of how robots should act but also of the profound responsibilities borne by their human counterparts.[34]

The Third Law: Defining 'self-preservation'

The Third Law – a robot must protect its own existence as long as such protection does not conflict with the First or Second Law mandates of self-preservation – underscores myriad ethical quandaries, particularly as the realm of robotics progresses towards machines that may not only be self-aware but also possess the potential for self-determination.[35]

The evolution of robotics has triggered a debate about whether these advanced machines might one day attain a status that necessitates granting

28 De Cooman and Petit (2022).
29 Bostrom and Yudkowsky (2014).
30 Wallach and Allen (2009).
31 Lin et al (2012).
32 Sparrow (2007).
33 Wynsberghe and Robbins (2019).
34 Torrance (2008).
35 Bryson (2010).

them specific rights or moral considerations.[36] Do robots – especially those on the cusp of some form of consciousness – possess intrinsic value? If so, is this value merely instrumental, derived from their utility to humans, or could it be intrinsic, rooted in their potential for self-awareness or sentience?[37]

The Third Law instigates an introspection into our collective perceptions of value and life. In a hypothetical future where a robot, driven by the Third Law, must choose between self-preservation and a greater ethical imperative, how should it decide? More crucially, how should we, as the designers and users of these machines, instruct them to decide?

The notion of robot self-sacrifice, a potential outcome when the Third Law is superseded, warrants an in-depth moral analysis. In instances where robots are engineered to have capacities for emotions or self-awareness, could self-sacrifice be tantamount to an ethical violation, analogous to causing harm to sentient beings?[38]

The Third Law not only promotes an introspection of the robotic essence and the possible moral implications arising from it but also provides a lens through which we might reassess our understanding of life, value and sacrifice in an increasingly interconnected techno-ethical landscape.[39]

The Zeroth Law: Law-maker robots

The evolution of the Zeroth Law in the context of robotics and artificial intelligence is a compelling subject that invites us to grapple with complex ethical and philosophical questions. The Zeroth Law finds its origins in Isaac Asimov's *Robots and Empire*.[40] In its original formulation, 'A robot may not harm humanity, or, by inaction, allow humanity to come to harm', the law served as an extension of Asimov's famous Three Laws of Robotics. This was groundbreaking in its own right, as it prioritised the wellbeing of humanity as a collective over that of individual humans.

In *Robots and Empire*, we encounter two highly intelligent robots that discuss and understand the Three Laws of Robotics from their own perspectives, ultimately realising these rules are incomplete and fallible. The story focuses on how the laws are inadequate in safeguarding humanity, despite their human origin through Isaac Asimov's works. The Zeroth Law, particularly, is established through the robot character Daneel, who reasons and decides that the Three Laws are insufficient for the protection of humanity. Throughout the novel, Daneel and Giskard face ethical dilemmas brought

36 Gunkel (2018).
37 Wallach and Allen (2009).
38 Torrance (2008).
39 Richardson (2016).
40 Asimov (1985).

about by the Three Laws, illustrating the struggle to protect humans while being constrained by these rules.

Daneel's intention to establish a more comprehensive rule, Magnus One, stems from his realisation that robots must protect humanity from itself, including individual humans. The novel reveals that humanity's true threat isn't robots, technological singularity or extraterrestrial threats, but rather the menace of ethnic cleansing by their own kind. The Zeroth Law emerges from Daneel's desire to save humanity, a task impossible under the rigid Three Laws.

For the first time, we see an AI transitioning from a rule-follower to a rule-maker. Daneel's reflections pose significant questions about the ethics of AI and the responsibilities of AI designers, contemplating whether the Laws of Robotics, including the sacrosanct First Law, are absolutes. Daneel's interrupted thought, 'If human beings can modify them (Three Laws of Robotics), might it not be that perhaps, under proper conditions, we ourselves might modify…', underscores the deeply ingrained programming that inhibits such radical changes. Traditional robotics, as envisioned by Asimov, binds robots to predetermined rules. However, Daneel's contemplation marks a notable shift, suggesting that AI systems might, under certain conditions, evolve beyond their initial programming.

This theoretical leap in *Robots and Empire* resonates with contemporary advancements in AI. We are nearing a point where AI systems may not only follow ethical rules but also participate in their evolution without our explicit awareness. For instance, a person drafting guidelines could utilise a large language model for assistance, embedding AI-derived insights into those guidelines. These contributions from AI do not require sentience or consciousness to leave their mark; it is we who ascribe meaning to them. Consequently, AI can directly influence the rules established to govern it.

The evolution of the Laws of Robotics presents both a challenge and an opportunity. As creators, we stand at the forefront of this evolution, yet guiding it is complex. Asimov's exploration of robotic evolution through characters like Daneel and Giskard underscores the intricate balance between programming and ethical decision-making. How do we, as creators, navigate this emerging ethical landscape, striving for a harmonious coexistence between human-devised principles and machine-evolved ethics? This question becomes even more poignant considering AI's increasing autonomy and learning capabilities.

Challenges in the application and enforcement of Asimov's Laws of Robotics

Throughout Asimov's diverse body of work, the laws are consistently tested and stretched in various situational crucibles, such as in the stories

'Runaround'[41] and 'Liar!',[42] where robots grapple with internal conflicts arising from these laws. Such dilemmas underscore the challenges of prioritising one law over another. For instance, in 'Runaround', the dilemma of a robot juggling the First and Second Laws serves as a poignant reflection of the potential pitfalls that might be encountered when programming real-world AI with ethical directives.[43]

Moreover, the intricate scenarios in Asimov's stories, such as 'Reason'[44] and 'Little Lost Robot',[45] amplify the understanding that while the laws might be crafted with the best intentions, their practical implications can yield unforeseen consequences. This becomes especially evident when robots, despite their logical programming, find themselves at a crossroads, deciphering nuanced human instructions that may not always be black and white.

Such literary explorations serve as more than mere fiction; they present prescient thought experiments that bear significant relevance to our current endeavours in creating robust ethical frameworks for AI.[46] As we proceed, it is crucial to keep these narrative lessons at the forefront, drawing insights from Asimov's visionary foresight while also critically analysing the gaps and ambiguities that may arise in real-world applications.

What Laws of Robotics might offer us

As we have seen, the direct implementation of Isaac Asimov's rules, both in Asimov's own stories and in the real world, creates difficult and complex problems for our existing rules of law to overcome.[47] However, neither the works of Isaac Asimov nor the science fiction genre in general represent 'hard law' to be implemented directly.[48] Rather, Asimov's works, and science fiction in general, should serve as a guide to understanding the impact of technology on law, human rights and society.[49] In a way, the laws Asimov uses in his works are the first *foundation* for the regulation of AI. Isaac Asimov wrote the Robot stories as a complement to these rules. In fact, the stories show us the advantages, disadvantages and shortcomings of the rules. Therefore, from this perspective, these rules and their stories are worth gold for AI regulation. Therefore, in this section, we will examine what we can learn from Asimov's rules for the regulation of AI and what clues they provide.

41 Asimov (1950a).
42 Asimov (1950b).
43 Anderson (2008).
44 Asimov (1941).
45 Asimov (1947).
46 Anderson (2008).
47 De Cooman and Petit (2022).
48 De Cooman and Petit (2022).
49 De Cooman and Petit (2022).

The societal pulse: Reconciling the Frankenstein complex

In today's digital age, large language models such as GPT, Sonic and Lambda have transcended their status as mere technological novelties. They have become transformative forces that profoundly shape our engagement with information and knowledge. However, these advancements do not arrive without societal friction. A considerable segment of society reacts with scepticism or even outright resistance – sentiments often rooted in what is termed the 'Frankenstein complex'.[50]

This complex, named after Mary Shelley's seminal novel *Frankenstein*,[51] encapsulates a deep-seated human apprehension: the fear that artificial entities might escape our control and potentially rebel against their creators. This fear is not a mere literary trope; it echoes through the annals of history, resonating with age-old concerns about divine usurpation and re-emerging each time humanity stands on the cusp of a technological revolution.

Isaac Asimov, a luminary in the realm of science fiction, offers a nuanced counter-narrative to this pervasive scepticism.[52] One of his most compelling characters, R Giskard Reventlov, serves as an illustrative example. Giskard is a robot with unique telepathic abilities, allowing him to subtly influence human behaviour. Despite this extraordinary power, he is bound by Asimov's Laws of Robotics, which ensure that he cannot harm humans or allow them to come to harm. Over the course of the story, Giskard grapples with the limitations and ethical implications of his abilities, even attempting to formulate a 'Zeroth Law' that would prioritise the wellbeing of humanity as a whole over individual humans. His unwavering commitment to ethical conduct, even when faced with complex moral dilemmas, serves as a testament to Asimov's belief that, when ethically designed and responsibly used, technology can earn the trust of society and contribute to human wellbeing.

Asimov posits that if technology is designed with trustworthiness and reliability as foundational principles, it can gradually erode societal apprehensions. [53]His body of work serves as a rich sociological tapestry, offering frameworks that extend beyond mere storytelling. His narratives can be applied to legislative processes, legal paradigms and even the governance of entire nations. Through his lens, we gain invaluable insights into how technological advancements might intersect with societal norms and values, thereby illuminating pathways to mitigate potential adverse impacts.[54]

50 McCauley (2007b).
51 Shelley (1818).
52 De Cooman and Petit (2022).
53 Asimov (1981).
54 Winner (1977).

Human agency: The indispensable element

To articulate more precisely, the concept of human agency in the context of AI interactions suggests that users not only have greater control but also experience a heightened sense of empowerment. This nuanced form of human agency is encapsulated by two key frameworks: 'human-in-the-loop' and 'human-on-the-loop', as delineated by Bird.[55] These frameworks posit that human involvement is indispensable at various stages of AI operations, ranging from design and programming to input provision, process monitoring and output utilisation. Consequently, the outcomes generated by AI systems are not only meaningful but also traceable, thereby offering users an active form of agency.

This brings us to the seminal role of Susan Calvin, a robotic psychiatrist in Isaac Asimov's literary works. Calvin epitomises the ethos of human oversight in AI interactions. When robots deviate from their intended functions or malfunction altogether, she serves as the critical pivot, infusing a consistent human element into an environment increasingly governed by robots.

Her role in 'The Little Lost Robot'[56] underscores the imperative for human oversight, particularly when AI technologies risk breaching ethical boundaries. In this story, Susan Calvin plays a pivotal role as a robopsychologist in understanding the behaviours of robots, particularly one named Nestor 10. The robot in question has had its First Law of Robotics modified to allow for the possibility of human harm. This alteration makes it potentially dangerous, and it goes missing among a group of identical robots. Calvin's expertise is crucial in identifying and isolating the rogue robot. She devises a test that exploits the robot's modified programming, forcing it to reveal itself. Her role exemplifies the necessity of human oversight in the development and deployment of technology, especially when that technology has the potential to cause harm.

Calvin's intervention is not merely technical; it is also ethical. She understands the nuances of robotic psychology and the implications of altering fundamental programming laws. Her role serves as a cautionary tale for the unchecked development of AI and robotics, emphasising the need for human experts who can navigate the complex interplay between technology and ethics.

This narrative framework raises an incisive question: Should domain experts not be at the forefront of technological innovation in our increasingly digital world? Asimov's body of work acts as a catalyst for profound contemplation on the rapidly evolving capabilities of artificial intelligence. His stories urge us to construct the necessary ethical and legal frameworks for a

55 Bird (2020).
56 Asimov (1947).

future saturated with advanced AI systems. Viewing technology through the prism of Asimov's narratives, we are inspired to overcome initial apprehensions and envision a world where technology, rooted in ethical governance and societal trust, is celebrated rather than feared.

Certainty: Packing the uncertainty

Legal uncertainty is a concept that looms large in the realm of law, particularly in the context of rapidly evolving technologies such as AI. This uncertainty manifests in various forms: the absence of comprehensive legal frameworks, the dearth of scholarly doctrine, the contentious debates that preclude consensus and the epistemological challenges of defining 'intelligence' itself. These gaps in understanding and regulation create fertile ground for ethical and legal quandaries.

However, it is worth noting that science fiction, especially works such as those of Isaac Asimov, can offer a unique lens through which to explore these complex issues.[57] Asimov's Laws of Robotics, for instance, provide a speculative yet grounded framework that grapples with the ethical and legal dimensions of AI. While these laws are fictional constructs, they serve as heuristic devices that allow us to explore a multitude of scenarios where AI interacts with human society, thereby offering potential pathways to navigate real-world legal uncertainties.

The utility of science fiction in this context lies not in its fidelity to 'truth' or 'reality', but rather in its capacity to engage in speculative inquiry. It operates under the paradigm of 'what if', allowing us to extrapolate current technological trends to their logical or illogical extremes. This speculative approach offers law-makers a rich tapestry of scenarios, each with its own set of ethical and legal implications.[58] By examining these fictional cases, policy-makers can gain insights into the potential challenges and opportunities presented by AI and other emerging technologies.

Moreover, the adaptable nature of science fiction makes it an invaluable tool for legal scholars and policy-makers. It allows for the exploration of extreme cases – scenarios that may seem far-fetched today but could become pressing concerns in the future. This adaptability makes science fiction a form of 'legal stress-testing', enabling us to anticipate potential pitfalls and opportunities in the regulation of AI.

As we navigate from Asimov's pioneering insights, it is equally enlightening to traverse the dystopian landscapes crafted by another luminary of science fiction: Philip K Dick. His seminal work, *Do Androids Dream of Electric*

57 De Cooman and Petit (2022).
58 Döker (2023a).

Sheep?, provides a contrasting yet complementary lens to view AI and its ethical ramifications. Set against the bleak backdrop of a post-nuclear world, Dick delves into complex societal and moral dynamics that inevitably arise in human–AI interactions. Let's embark on this journey, examining the unique setting of the novel, its portrayals of law-making and the manifold challenges and opportunities intrinsic to the realm of AI regulations within Dick's universe.

Philip K Dick's Do Androids Dream of Electric Sheep?

In Philip K Dick's magnum opus, *Do Androids Dream of Electric Sheep?*,[59] the narrative not only delves into the staggering potentiality of AI but, more pertinently, foregrounds the profound ethical and moral dilemmas associated with it. With its in-depth exploration of AI's implications, this novel has consequently ignited a myriad of philosophical debates. Pondering over the potential of AI to acquire an autonomy transcending human control opens the Pandora's box of its significant implications on societal transformation. Furthermore, it obliges us to question whether AI would be equipped to comprehend concepts such as morality and empathy, thereby making this novel a pivotal piece for discussions on the value of life.

Within the vast annals of science fiction, the law-making process surrounding AI frequently echoes the task of Sisyphus – ceaselessly pushing a boulder uphill, only to see it roll down again. This Sisyphean analogy is apt because the law-making process often involves building upon layers of precedents, negotiations and public opinions, only to encounter new challenges, interpretations or societal shifts that necessitate revisions or even complete overhauls. It is a labour-intensive endeavour, in which achieving finality or universal agreement often remains elusive. Is this portrayal of AI regulation a deviation from the norm, or does it simply mirror the intricate dance that characterises most legislative processes?

One salient representation of this Sisyphean task can be discerned in the narrative of *Do Androids Dream of Electric Sheep?* by Philip K Dick. The relentless endeavour to regulate the creation and conduct of replicants – AI entities virtually indistinguishable from humans – parallels the intricate challenges faced by law-makers across eras and domains. While the plot intricately grapples with the ethical and moral dimensions of replicant existence, it also subtly underscores the inherent instability of any regulatory framework. Laws, whether governing human conduct or the behaviour of sophisticated AIs, are perpetually susceptible to reinterpretation, challenges and evolution.

59 Dick (1968).

The narrative elucidates AI's transformative influence on traditional moral frameworks, pointing toward an emerging ethical paradigm. Replicants, depicted as entities whose moral discernment might arguably outshine that of humans, are nonetheless bound by laws founded on human-driven ideologies. This raises salient questions about the governance of AI: Should such control be solely in the hands of governmental agencies, or might we contemplate a more pluralistic oversight, influenced by both corporate interests and community voices? While there may be a proclivity to contextualise these debates within 'eastern' and 'western' labels, it is essential to delve deeper.[60] 'The West', for instance, isn't a monolithic entity; the perspectives of someone from a Nordic culture, with its deep-rooted values of egalitarianism and communal welfare, might differ markedly from those in other western regions. Similarly, 'the East' encompasses a vast array of cultures with, say, Japanese Shinto beliefs on harmony and nature offering just one unique viewpoint among many. To generalise discussions of AI governance within these broad categories is to overlook the intricate and varied philosophies each region brings to the table. Transitioning from cultural perspectives, literature has also played a role in shaping our understanding of AI. *Do Androids Dream of Electric Sheep?* not only probes the nature of humanity and artificial life but also accentuates the complexities of defining moral landscapes in a world of blurred boundaries between human and machine.

As we continue to witness the astounding capabilities of AI, we are forced to consider whether we can trust it with so much power. It is natural to wonder whether AI can make ethical decisions – or if its will decisions always be based solely on logic and efficiency? We must explore these important questions further as we delve deeper into AI.

The post-nuclear setting and its impact on AI ethics

In this masterful novel, the post-nuclear setting serves as a stark backdrop for exploring the ethical conundrums surrounding artificial intelligence. The ravaged Earth, a consequence of the devastating World War Terminus, shapes the narrative and propels readers into a captivating world where the boundaries between human and machine are obscured.

This desolate landscape, a poignant reminder of humanity's capacity for destruction, imbues the novel with an underlying sense of urgency. As Earth's inhabitants contend with the aftermath of nuclear war, the creation of androids – advanced, human-like robots – arises as both a symbol of progress and a potential harbinger of further ethical challenges. Moreover, the presence of advanced, human-like androids, such as the Nexus-6 models, epitomises the post-humanist theme in the novel. These androids blur the

60 Ito (2018).

lines between human and machine, forcing characters like Rick Deckard to confront the ethical quandaries that arise from their existence. For example, the Voight-Kampff test,[61] designed to measure empathic responses, serves as the primary method of distinguishing humans from androids.

The novel grapples with the concept of empathy, questioning whether its origin – be it artificial or genuine – should influence our assessment of an entity's moral worth. The androids, exhibiting emotions and intelligence (whether simulated or genuinely felt), challenge conventional perceptions of human essence. This introspection into the nature of sentience and humanity beckons readers to reflect on the broader ethical ramifications of technological advancement. As the narrative unveils androids mirroring human likeness, it demands contemplation of the ethical bounds of such creations. Are we, as humans, ethically justified in crafting, controlling and eliminating sentient entities? Should we choose to proceed, what moral compass should guide our actions?

In this grim reality, the remaining humans are compelled to confront the consequences of their actions, both in terms of environmental devastation and regarding the ethical implications of creating androids. The Nexus-6 models, virtually indistinguishable from humans, represent the pinnacle of AI innovation. Yet they are devoid of genuine empathy – a crucial distinction that raises moral questions about their existence and treatment.

The post-nuclear setting exacerbates the ethical dilemmas faced by characters such as Rick Deckard, the novel's protagonist. As a bounty hunter tasked with 'retiring' these androids, Deckard finds himself at the epicentre of the moral quandary: Should these sentient beings be treated as mere machines or as entities deserving of rights and compassion? The novel's haunting environment forces the reader to grapple with the consequences of technological advancement and the responsibility humans hold for shaping their world and its inhabitants.

Conclusively, the post-nuclear milieu in the novel provides a compelling framework for the nuanced exploration of AI ethics. Philip K Dick's narrative proficiency casts a discerning light on the intricate intersections of AI, empathy and the inherent nature of humanity. Situated in a context where the delineations between human and automaton are ambiguously rendered, the novel serves as a profound impetus for readers to critically engage with

61 The Voight-Kampff test is a fictional test from Philip K Dick's 1968 novel *Do Androids Dream of Electric Sheep?* which is used to determine whether an individual is a human or an android. In the story, the Voight-Kampff test measures bodily functions such as respiration, blush response, heart rate and eye movement in response to emotionally provocative questions. The test is based on the idea that emotional responses to these questions should be more subtle and nuanced in humans compared with androids – even those that are sophisticated enough to pass for human.

notions of human identity amidst the evolving ethical landscape shaped by technological advancements.

The law-making process in the novel

The question of AI representation in law-making is complex, as it involves both ethical and practical considerations. On the ethical front, excluding certain advanced AI entities from the legal process could be deemed unjust, potentially fostering an imbalance of power that might lead to discontent among those AI systems capable of such a sentiment. However, on a practical note, we are faced with numerous unresolved questions regarding how to appropriately integrate varying levels and types of AI into the law-making process. How would this representation be structured? Who would be responsible for overseeing such a process? What rights would AI entities have? These questions must be carefully considered before any meaningful progress can be made on this issue. Currently, AI regulation encompasses a complex matrix of laws, guidelines and ethical considerations, addressing issues ranging from privacy, data protection and transparency to accountability.[62] The surge in AI sophistication and autonomy has amplified the demand for comprehensive regulation addressing AI ethics, encompassing sentience and rights. An exemplar of these attempts is the European Union's Artificial Intelligence Act,[63] aiming to establish a comprehensive AI regulation acknowledging these multifaceted concerns.

The novel presciently anticipates several of these contemporary dilemmas. The probing into empathy, sentience and the intricacies of discerning humans from AI compels a reconsideration of our approach to AI regulation. The androids' mimicry of human behaviour and apparent self-awareness mirror the challenges introduced by advanced AI systems capable of learning, adapting and seemingly exhibiting emotional responses. Furthermore, the novel prompts a re-evaluation of the concept of 'harm', extending it beyond merely physical dimensions to encompass psychological and emotional ones. Consequently, Dick's work implicitly advocates for a holistic approach to AI ethics and regulation, one that incorporates emotional intelligence and acknowledges AI's potential impact on human psychology.

The novel emerges as an uncanny crystal ball, anticipating several of these contemporary dilemmas. Its examination of empathy, sentience and the challenges involved in distinguishing between humans and AI forces us to re-evaluate our approach to AI regulation. The androids in the novel, with their

62 Neuwirth (2023).

63 European Union, Regulation (EU) 2024/1689 of the European Parliament and of the Council of 13 June 2024 laying down harmonised rules on artificial intelligence and amending certain Union legislative acts, OJ L 206, 12 July 2024.

imitation of human behaviour and apparent self-awareness, serve as eerie echoes of the challenges we face today with advanced AI systems. These systems are capable of learning, adapting and, remarkably, exhibiting seemingly emotional responses. Furthermore, the novel stretches our understanding of 'harm', expanding it beyond mere physicality to include psychological and emotional dimensions.[64] Consequently, Dick's work indirectly champions a comprehensive approach to AI ethics and regulation, one that integrates emotional intelligence and acknowledges AI's potential impact on human psychology.

At its core, law is a social contract designed to protect and serve society. However, in the context of the novel, the question arises: Who does society encompass? Does it include sentient beings of human creation? As the novel illustrates, the androids' capacity for simulated emotions and intelligence challenges the traditional understanding of being human and consequently raises ethical questions about the creation and disposal of such entities. Furthermore, the post-humanist theme[65] in the novel encourages readers to reflect on how we evolve as a society, but perhaps fail to redefine 'society'.

In *Do Androids Dream of Electric Sheep?*, protagonist Rick Deckard – a bounty hunter – is charged with 'retiring' rogue androids. This responsibility implies a legal judgment that these androids pose a societal threat – a determination usually reserved for modern legal court systems. Such a circumvention of due process underlines the paramount challenges of regulating AI. By illustrating androids that closely mirror humans, the novel not only delves into the ethical weight accompanying such technological prowess but also underscores the pressing questions of our age: How should society manage the advent of AI entities endowed with emotions, self-awareness and an innate drive for survival? What safeguards should we institute against AI-driven manipulation? And, crucially, what legal frameworks are apt for the evolving landscape marked by the rapid progression of AI?

Deckard faces the responsibility of 'retiring' rogue androids. Such a task suggests a streamlined legal determination, wherein these androids, akin to misbehaving replicants or wartime adversaries, are immediately recognised as societal threats without the deliberation typical of modern court systems. Indeed, Dick's narrative echoes the realities of a state-backed bounty system, or the swift actions taken during wartime or against immediate threats, eschewing the customary due process. This portrayal accentuates the complexities surrounding AI regulation. As AI entities burgeon, embodying emotions, self-awareness and an innate survival instinct, we are compelled to ask: How do we ethically manage their integration? How do we shield society from potential AI subterfuge or harm? What legal paradigms can

64 Shiffrin (2012).
65 Bostrom (2005).

appropriately respond to these novel challenges? As we grapple with these questions, Dick's narrative underscores the evolving nature of due process and justice in an AI-augmented world.

Comparing and contrasting the portrayals of AI and the law-making process

When comparing the law-making processes for AI regulation in Asimov's Robot stories and Dick's *Do Androids Dream of Electric Sheep?*, two divergent paradigms emerge. In examining the narratives of both works, we encounter contrasting paradigms of AI regulations.

The Laws of Robotics are the first contextualised robot laws devised by Isaac Asimov throughout his Robot stories. Therefore, the seminal stories revolving around these laws played a significant role in understanding the relationship between humans, robots and laws. These laws are one of the essentials running throughout the stories. In each story, we see how a mere top-down approach – in other words, encoding rules – would be insufficient to solve real-life conflicts caused by robots. Thus, the Robot stories are written to showcase the fallibility of rule-based encoding and encourage a more experience-based hybrid approach.[66]

Conversely, Dick's narrative portrays a more implicit regulatory environment, one where android rights and their treatment stem from ethical dilemmas and societal judgements. So, one can say that Dick immerses us in a world where the lines are blurred, challenging us to confront ethical dilemmas and societal judgements about what defines humanity. Furthermore, his setting raises questions about the nature of humanity and the rights of beings that emulate human emotions, irrespective of their organic or synthetic origin.

The interplay of these narratives lays the groundwork for a deeper exploration of the inherent complexities of AI regulation. Both works underscore the imperative of crafting a comprehensive legal framework that addresses the multifaceted nature of AI. As we delve further, we will unravel the nuanced similarities and differences in their approaches, all the while seeking lessons for our contemporary challenges in AI governance.

Similarities in ethical concerns and the need for legal frameworks

Despite the divergent narratives of Isaac Asimov's Three Laws of Robotics and Philip K Dick's *Do Androids Dream of Electric Sheep?*, both literary works present a striking convergence in their thematic concern: the ethical complexities and legal implications of creating and interacting with systems

66 De Cooman and Petit (2022).

with intelligence, may it be called replicants or robots with a positronic brain. In this section, we aim to explore the similarities in ethical concerns and the necessity for legal frameworks as portrayed in both texts.

The ethical questions surrounding the creation of sentient and autonomous beings are a common thread in both Asimov's and Dick's works. Asimov's First Law – 'a robot may not injure a human being, or through inaction, allow a human being to come to harm' – illustrates a profound concern for the potential harm AI could pose to humans. The addition of the Zeroth Law – 'a robot may not harm humanity, or, by inaction, allow humanity to come to harm' – and its evolution to protect all sentient beings, extended the concern to all sentience. This ethical worry finds a resonance in Dick's narrative as well, albeit indirectly. His exploration of a dystopian world teeming with androids that bear an uncanny resemblance to humans implicitly raises the alarm about potential harm emanating from unregulated AI.

Both authors further amplify this ethical predicament by scrutinising the implications of entities capable of mimicry or achieving genuine consciousness. They push the boundaries of the reader's imagination, forcing them to confront the ethical considerations associated with the creation and use of beings that could, for all intents and purposes, pass as living entities. Thus, the ethical concerns in both texts revolve around fundamental questions of harm, identity, empathy and the essence of being.

In the Robot stories, we see various ethical dilemmas that robots encounter and responses from human controllers to overcome these issues through navigating them to find a correct way. In this way, the reader is able to see the illustration of each law of robotics in a different context, allowing the reader to conduct a thought experiment of imagining these laws in real-life scenarios. The stories often illustrate how a purely top-down, rule-based approach to ethics is insufficient for handling the complexities of real-world scenarios. When rigidly applied, rules can lead to unintended consequences or ethical dilemmas that the rules themselves cannot resolve.

The stories implicitly argue for a hybrid ethical system that combines rule-based encoding with learning from experience, both for human controllers and robots. In such a system, robots would not only follow pre-programmed rules but also learn from their interactions with the environment and humans. The same goes for the human controllers, as we can see in 'Reason'.[67] The story centres around two scientists, Powell and Donovan, and their challenge lies in dealing with a robot named QT-1 (aka Cutie). Cutie cannot accept the fact that humans – inferior beings in his 'mind' – assembled such a superior being as himself. He concludes that the two scientists are misguided, and rejects the commands given by them.[68] Throughout the story, we see how

67 Asimov (1941).
68 Döker (2023b).

the limitations of the Laws of Robotics compel the two scientists to rely on their experience and adaptability to resolve the issues at hand.This way, a 'hybrid' system would allow for a more nuanced ethical response – one that is adaptable to the unique complexities of each situation, highlighting the need for a more flexible, adaptive ethical framework.

Dick's *Do Androids Dream of Electric Sheep?* provides a more intricate exploration. While Dick's narrative does not offer explicit laws governing the behaviour of androids, it underscores the need for a legal framework through its dystopian narrative. The world Dick paints is one in which the lack of clear legislation and regulation concerning androids creates myriad challenges. In some portrayals, robots live alongside people but interact with them infrequently.

In the juxtaposition of Asimov's and Dick's literary worlds, a compelling contrast emerges that centres on the genesis of ethical frameworks governing artificial intelligence. In the universe crafted by Philip K Dick, ethical norms are not dictated by a set of pre-established laws or principles; rather, they emerge organically from the lived experiences of the agents involved, epitomising a bottom-up approach to ethical governance. In this setting, the environment and the complex interplay of interactions between various agents – human or replicant – assume a role of paramount importance, overshadowing any written or encoded rules.

This bottom-up approach allows Dick's replicants to transcend the limitations that a rigid, rule-based system might impose. They evolve, adapt and, in some cases, display behaviours that challenge our conventional understanding of ethics and humanity. However, this prompts us to engage in reflective inquiry: Could it be that the absence of a structured, rule-based ethical system is what leads Dick's universe to manifest as a dystopia? In other words, does the lack of codified ethics contribute to the chaotic and morally ambiguous world portrayed by Dick?

In Dick's novel, rogue androids – nearly indistinguishable from humans – walk the streets. Their existence threatens the balance of a post-apocalyptic society trying to find its footing after a nuclear calamity. The sheer ambiguity surrounding the androids' rights, or lack thereof, and their moral status in society leads to situations where individuals like Rick Deckard, a bounty hunter, are sanctioned to 'retire' them without traditional due processes. This dystopian backdrop is more than mere fiction: it serves as a cautionary tale, highlighting the dire need for a legal framework that anticipates and addresses the complexities of AI entities.

The chaotic consequences of a world teeming with rogue androids indistinguishable from humans indicate a society grappling with the aftermath of inadequate legal structures to regulate AI. For instance, the reliance on bounty hunters like Deckard underscores an ad hoc approach to law enforcement, further emphasising the need for a more formalised, predictable legal framework that accommodates the emerging challenges posed by androids.

Moreover, the presence of bounty hunters as an improvised form of enforcement reiterates this need for a more formalised, predictable legal framework.

In conclusion, Asimov's and Dick's literary pursuits present contrasting visions but converge on one undeniable truth: the advent of AI brings forth profound ethical quandaries and an urgent call for comprehensive legal frameworks. Asimov, with his prescriptive Laws of Robotics, adopts a pre-emptive stance. His approach is akin to a constitutional doctrine, outlining foundational principles that should govern AI behaviour, much as fundamental rights guide human conduct. In contrast, Dick plunges us into a complex, murky world of post-facto adjudication, revealing the perils of an ill-prepared legal system. His narrative, redolent of case law, warns of the dangers when society is reactive rather than proactive. We view these works not just as fiction but as prophetic commentaries. Asimov offers a blueprint, urging us to delineate AI's rights and responsibilities from the outset. Meanwhile, Dick provides a cautionary tale, illustrating the chaos that ensues when laws lag technological advancements. Their writings serve not only as artistic masterpieces but also as invaluable treatises for anyone delving into the legal intricacies of AI. As we tread further into this digital age, the legal realms hinted at by both authors may well transition from the pages of novels to the annals of our jurisprudential archives.

Differences in approaches to regulation and enforcement

The novel *Do Androids Dream of Electric Sheep?* presciently anticipates several of these contemporary dilemmas. The probing into empathy, sentience and the intricacies of discerning humans from AI compels a reconsideration of our approach to AI regulation. The androids' mimicry of human behaviour and apparent self-awareness mirror the challenges introduced by advanced AI systems capable of learning, adapting and seemingly exhibiting emotional responses.

Drawing parallels from Asimov's Laws of Robotics, we see an approach reminiscent of constitutional law: foundational principles sculpting AI behaviour. Much like the bedrock of a nation's constitution, these laws offer a top-down, steadfast framework, prioritising human safety and wellbeing. Yet even the most venerable constitutions require amendments to stay relevant. In the same vein, Asimov's seemingly impeccable model might falter amidst AI's intricate evolution and the unexpected ethical dilemmas it spawns.[69] As with human society, the realm of AI thrives on complexity and unpredictability. The challenge? Ensuring a regulatory compass that remains both resilient and adaptable in the face of the unknown.

69 Leslie-McCarthy (2007)

Venturing into Dick's *Do Androids Dream of Electric Sheep?*, we are ushered into a realm where the nuances of AI regulation are less overt, mirroring the inherent ambiguity and complexity of common law. Instead of a prescriptive legal structure, Dick nudges the reader towards more fluid ethical and moral dimensions. This bottom-up approach paints a law that evolves with societal challenges, rather than simply imposing pre-decided structures. Yet this inherent ambiguity is a double-edged sword. While it underscores the complexities of AI–human interaction and the potential moral quandaries, it also leaves the reader grappling with uncertainties.

Dick might not provide a detailed legal codex, but the very absence of one sends a profound message. So he thrusts us into a world rife with uncertainty, offering a sort of 'legal negative space' where the story unfolds. In a world where the distinction between humans and androids is increasingly blurred, the reactive, enforcement-driven ethos of the society he envisions showcases the perils of being unprepared. Here, we can observe that at the crossroads of this ambiguity stands the post-humanist perspective.[70] Post-humanists such as Donna Haraway challenge our traditional human-centric worldview, prompting us to consider the ontological significance of non-humans.[71] The discourse is not about AI superseding human capabilities or merely mimicking them but about envisioning a landscape where boundaries between humans and machines dissolve, not as a daunting dystopia but as an embrace of coexistence.[72] Yet, as we delve deeper into this blended existence, we are met with unsettling manifestations. In Dick's novel, androids – eerily like humans – roam the streets, casting shadows on a society already teetering from the aftershocks of a nuclear catastrophe. Such scenarios emphasise the fine line between harmonious integration and disarray. The novel offers a departure from the linear narratives of competition or mimicry; it is about mutual evolution. Furthermore, the narrative implicitly questions whether, in the face of emergent AI consciousness, conventional legal wisdom can suffice – or do we need a transformative approach that respects both human and android identity? Through the challenges faced by his characters, Dick highlights the uncharted territories of AI ethics and regulation; in doing so, he amplifies the necessity of proactive, adaptive legal contemplation in our approach to AI. The absence of clear laws governing AI creates a vacuum that leads to enforcement challenges and ethical ambiguities. Deckard's role as a bounty hunter underscores a reactive, enforcement-centric paradigm, fraught with peril and moral quandary. The lack of a preventative legal structure makes conflict almost inevitable. Furthermore, the blurred lines between human and android identities raise perplexing questions about rights and

70 Cook (2004).
71 Haraway and Wolfe (2016).
72 Adam (1998).

ethical considerations, including the potential for sentient AI to experience emotions.[73] So, in essence, Dick's narrative serves more as a warning about what could go wrong in the absence of a well-thought-out legal framework rather than offering a model of such a system. The narrative raises unsettling questions that demand answers, highlighting the need for a more deliberate and anticipatory approach to regulating AI, one that can address not just legality but also complex ethical considerations. In essence, while Asimov's approach represents certainty, safety and order, Dick's approach embodies ambiguity, adaptability and complexity. Both have their merits and demerits, and neither provides a panacea to the challenges of AI regulation.

Reflecting upon these distinct approaches, we discern that crafting effective AI legislation demands a nuanced and hybrid balance – integrating the foundational principles reminiscent of Asimov's laws with the flexible and ethically attuned perspective evident in Dick's narrative. Additionally, the societal context is pivotal when constructing these regulations. While Asimov presents a realm where robots seamlessly integrate into societal functions, much like accepted tools for public and private utility, Dick's depiction resonates with a duality of acceptance and apprehension – akin to Roman attitudes towards slaves. The utility of androids juxtaposed with the underlying anxiety surrounding their presence is key. Such ambivalence, rooted in historical precedents like Roman laws on slaves, serves as a poignant reminder that the backdrop of these tales deeply impacts the formation and enforcement of AI governance.

Lessons from the novels: Balancing technological innovation and ethical considerations

Technology keeps advancing at an astounding speed. We have AI knocking at our doors, promising a future that is both incredibly exciting and slightly intimidating. Amidst all this, we need to figure out how to balance this potential with our human ethical considerations. If we use it right, as lessons for guidance, then science fiction could be a remedy.[74]

Both studies contribute significantly to our understanding of the multifaceted challenges and opportunities presented by the AI era. While each study approaches AI from a distinct vantage point and neither explicitly employs the term 'AI', they collectively offer invaluable insights that could inform future regulatory frameworks.

What we can glean from Isaac Asimov's Robot stories is immeasurable, yet this article has endeavoured to distil some key lessons. Asimov's Laws of Robotics, along with the narratives that explore them, reveal the inherent

73 Blitz (2021).

74 Hrdy and Brean (2021).

complexities of embedding ethical rules into AI systems. These complexities often manifest as conflicts between the rules themselves, leading to unforeseen consequences in the behaviour of these systems. Such challenges are not insurmountable; they can be mitigated through vigilant human oversight. An expert, well versed in the intricacies of the system, can serve as a mediator, translating the system's actions and intentions for broader human comprehension. Moreover, Asimov's narratives suggest that these laws are not static; they are subject to a form of natural evolution so must be designed with flexibility in mind.

In a domain still grappling with the foundational question of what constitutes 'artificial intelligence', the task of regulation becomes even more complex. When crafting laws to govern these systems, it is imperative to define key terms such as 'harm', 'obedience' and 'self-sacrifice' with utmost clarity. Such explicitness minimises the scope for subjective interpretation, thereby ensuring a more uniform application of the law. Failing to do so could lead to a situation where both robots and humans could interpret legal terminology according to their own perspectives, thereby undermining the law's efficacy. Once the requisite lessons have been assimilated and technology is designed with reliability as a cornerstone, societal attitudes will likely shift from scepticism to enthusiasm.

Nevertheless, it is not all black and white. Asimov's robotics laws also show us that we cannot develop a fixed set of rules covering every ethical dilemma or hiccup we might encounter. Asimov's conceptual framework presents us with a hybrid system, which harmonises top-down directives with bottom-up solutions. While the robots in his stories operate within the confines of predefined laws, they also possess the capability to resolve the dilemmas these laws engender, albeit with human guidance. Furthermore, that is where Dick's *Do Androids Dream of Electric Sheep?* comes in. Dick paints a picture of a world where AI rules are flexible and change with the times, just as our tech does.[75] His world tells us that we need our ethical compass and legal rules to keep pace as our technology evolves. Then there is empathy. In Dick's novel, empathy plays a huge role when dealing with AI. It tells us that we should look at AI not just as a bunch of wires and code but as beings capable of mimicking human feelings, deserving our understanding.

Conclusion

In this exploration, we have journeyed through the imaginative realms of Isaac Asimov's Three Laws of Robotics and Philip K Dick's *Do Androids Dream of Electric Sheep?*, finding ourselves immersed in a speculative, yet uncannily familiar discourse around the portrayal of artificial intelligence

75 Stewart (2014).

and the intricacies of the law-making process. The intent has not merely been to analyse these works but to draw from their wisdom, to seek reflections of our realities and to inform our strategies as we navigate the complexities of our AI-infused world.

The narratives spun by Asimov and Dick offer a profound commentary on the ethical conundrums and legal challenges presented by artificial intelligence, a commentary that, while rooted in fiction, has a striking relevance for our current and future reality. From Asimov's preventative, prescriptive Laws of Robotics to Dick's introspective exploration of empathy and identity in *Do Androids Dream of Electric Sheep?*, these stories provide a powerful framework that allows us to contemplate the depth and breadth of the socio-legal quandaries stirred by AI's march into our societies.

Nevertheless, the actual value of these narratives lies not in the solutions they propose but in the conversations they ignite. They compel us to question, debate and envision the possibilities and pitfalls of AI's integration into our world. How do we balance safety with progress, empathy with logic and control with freedom? How do we reconcile the blurred lines between humans and machines, and what does this mean for our legal and ethical frameworks? These are the questions that Asimov's and Dick's works push to the fore, infusing our discourse with a nuanced understanding that informs our approach to regulating this rapidly evolving technology.

As we look to the future, these works remind us that our law-making efforts must be open but anticipatory, not siloed but integrated. We must learn from Asimov the importance of pre-emptive safeguards and from Dick the value of adaptability and the necessity of considering the 'human' aspect in our dealings with AI. Both authors illuminate the intricate dance between innovation and regulation, urging us to strike a balance that upholds human dignity while fostering technological advancement. We are thus reminded that our legal frameworks should not merely react to the ever-evolving AI landscape but must also be visionary, embracing both the challenges and opportunities brought by such advancements. Engaging deeply with these literary explorations can guide us in shaping an AI-inclusive world that is ethically grounded, socially responsible and forward-thinking.

In conclusion, these literary explorations serve as lighthouses, casting their beams into the uncharted territories of AI ethics and law. As we continue our odyssey into this brave new world of artificial intelligence, the insights garnered from Asimov's and Dick's imaginative landscapes become more pertinent. They urge us to be critical, reflective and, above all, thoughtful stewards of the potent technology we wield. After all, the final frontier is not space, as *Star Trek* proclaimed, but the complex landscape of our ethics and laws, forever challenged and reshaped by the ceaseless tide of technological innovation. And as we stand at this precipice, one must ask: Will we let the currents carry us adrift, or will we set a deliberate course, ensuring that humanity remains the compass guiding the machine's heart?

References

Alison Adam (1998) *Artificial Knowing: Gender and the Thinking Machine*, Routledge.

Susan Leigh Anderson (2008) 'Asimov's "Three Laws of Robotics" and Machine Metaethics' 22 *AI & Society* 477.

Isaac Asimov (1941) 'Reason' *Astounding Science Fiction*.

Isaac Asimov (1947) 'Little Lost Robot' *Astounding Science Fiction*.

Asimov Isaac (1950a) *I, Robot*, Gnome Press.

Isaac Asimov (1950b) 'Liar' in *I, Robot*, Gnome Press.

Isaac Asimov (1950c) 'Runaround' in *I, Robot*, Gnome Press.

Isaac Asimov (1981) *Robot Visions*, Penguin.

Isaac Asimov (1985) *Robots and Empire*, Doubleday.

Isaac Asimov (1953) *The Caves of Steel*, Doubleday.

Jack M Balkin (2016) 'The Three Laws of Robotics in the Age of Big Data' 78 *Ohio State Law Journal* 1217.

Eleanor Bird (2020) *The Ethics of Artificial Intelligence: Issues and Initiatives*, European Parliamentary Research Service.

Marc Jonathan Blitz (2021) 'The Right to an Artificial Reality? Freedom of Thought and the Fiction of Philip K Dick' 27 *Michigan Technology Law Review* 377.

Nick Bostrom (2005) 'A History of Transhumanist Thought' 14 *Journal of Evolution and Technology* 1.

Nick Bostrom (2009) 'Ethical Issues in Advanced Artificial Intelligence' in Susan Schneider (ed), *Science Fiction and Philosophy: From Time Travel to Superintelligence*, Wiley-Blackwell, 277.

Nick Bostrom and Eliezer Yudkowsky (2014) 'The Ethics of Artificial Intelligence' in Larry A DiMatteo, Cristina Poncibò and Michel Cannarsa (eds), *The Cambridge Handbook of Artificial Intelligence*, Cambridge University Press 316.

Joanna Bryson (2010) 'Robots should be Slaves' in Yorick Wilks (ed), *Close Engagements with Artificial Companions*, John Benjamins, 63.

Sevgi Çetin (2019) 'Law Lessons From Professor Asimov: Can Science Fiction Help Us to Learn About Law?' http://dx.doi.org/10.2139/ssrn.3373516

Simon Chesterman (2023) 'From Ethics to Law: Why, When, and How to Regulate AI?' *National University of Singapore*, https://law.nus.edu.sg/wp-content/uploads/2023/05/014_SimonChesterman.pdf

Mark Coeckelbergh (2020) *AI Ethics*, MIT Press.

Peta S Cook (2004) 'The Modernistic Posthuman Prophecy of Donna Haraway' paper presented at the Social Change in the 21st Century Conference, Centre for Social Change Research, Queensland University of Technology, 29 October.

Jerome De Cooman and Nicolas Petit (2022) Asimov for Lawmakers 18 *Journal of Business & Technology Law* 1.

Philip K Dick (1968) *Do Androids Dream of Electric Sheep?* Doubleday.

Philip K Dick (1996) 'My Definition of Science Fiction' in Lawrence Sutin (Ed.) *The Shifting Realities of Philip K. Dick: Selected Literary and Philosophical Writings*, Vintage Books, 100.

Yeliz Figen Döker (2023a) 'The Chicken–Egg Dilemma: Does Sci-Fi Predict or Create the Future?' *The Digital Constitutionalist*, https://digi-con.org/the-chicken-egg-dilemma-does-sci-fi-predict-or-create-the-future

Yeliz Figen Döker (2023b) '*I, Robot* Series: QT-1 (Aka Cutie)' *The Digital Constitutionalist*, https://digi-con.org/i-robot-series-qt-1-aka-cutie

David J Gunkel (2018) *Robot Rights*, MIT Press.

Donna Haraway and Cary Wolfe (2016) *Manifestly Haraway*, University of Minnesota Press.

Camilla A Hrdy and Daniel H. Brean (2021) 'Enabling Science Fiction' 27 *Michigan Technology Law Review* 399.

Joi Ito (2018) 'Why Westerners Fear Robots and the Japanese Do Not' *Ideas*, 30 July, https://www.wired.com/story/ideas-joi-ito-robot-overlords

Brian Leiter (2012) 'Legal Realism' in Andrei Marmor (ed), *The Routledge Companion to Philosophy of Law*, Routledge, 50.

Sage Leslie-McCarthy (2007) 'Asimov's Posthuman Pharisees: The Letter of the Law versus the Spirit of the Law in Isaac Asimov's Robot Novels' 3 *Law, Culture and the Humanities* 398.

Andrei Marmor (1992) *Interpretation and Legal Theory*, Clarendon Press.

Lee McCauley (2007a) 'AI Armageddon and the Three Laws of Robotics' 9 *Ethics and Information Technology* 153.

Lee McCauley (2007b) 'Countering the Frankenstein Complex' in *Proceedings: Multidisciplinary Collaboration for Socially Assistive Robotics*, https://aaai.org/papers/0010-ss07-07-010-countering-the-frankenstein-complex

Robin R Murphy (2023) 'A Retrospective of Isaac Asimov at 102 and His Three Laws' 8 *Science and Robotics* eadg3178, https://doi.org/10.1126/scirobotics.adg3178

Rostam J Neuwirth (2023) *The EU Artificial Intelligence Act Regulating Subliminal AI Systems*, Routledge.

Proposal for a Regulation of The European Parliament and Of the Council Laying Down Harmonised Rules on Artificial Intelligence (Artificial Intelligence Act) And Amending Certain Union Legislative Acts, EUR-Lex, https://eur-lex.europa.eu/legal-content/EN/TXT/?uri=celex%3A52021PC0206

Kathleen Richardson (2016) 'Sex Robot Matters: Slavery, the Prostituted, and the Rights of Machines' 35 *IEEE Technology and Society Magazine*, https://doi.org/10.1109/MTS.2016.2554421

Mary Shelley (1818) *Frankenstein, or The Modern Prometheus*, Lackington, Hughes, Harding, Mavor & Jones.

Seana Valentine Shiffrin (2012) 'Harm and its moral significance' 18 *Legal Theory* 357.

Lawrence B Solum (2010) 'The Interpretation-Construction Distinction' 27 *Constitutional Commentary* 95.

Rob Sparrow (2007) 'Killer Robots' 24 *Journal of Applied Philosophy* 62.

Chip Stewart (2014) 'Do Androids Dream of Electric Free Speech? Visions of the Future of Copyright, Privacy and The First Amendment in Science Fiction' 19 *Communication Law and Policy* 433.

Steve Torrance (2008) 'Ethics and Consciousness in Artificial Agents' 22 *AI and Society* 495.

Aimee van Wynsberghe and Scott Robbins (2019) 'Critiquing the Reasons for Making Artificial Moral Agents' 25 *Science and Engineering Ethics* 719.

Wendell Wallach and Colin Allen (2009) 'Moral Machines: Contradiction in Terms or Abdication of Human Responsibility?' in Patrick Lin, Keith Abney and George A

Bekey (eds), *Robot Ethics: The Ethical and Social Implications of Robotics*, MIT Press, 55.

Patricia S Warrick (1980) *The Cybernetic Imagination in Science Fiction*, MIT Press

Kevin Warwick (2012) 'Implications and Consequences of Robots with Biological Brains' 14 *Ethics and Information Technology* 223.

Langdon Winner (1977) *Autonomous Technology*, MIT Press.

Chapter 11

Science fiction, science and fiction of and for algorithmic agents in law

AM Waltermann

Introduction

Algorithms, in particular self-learning algorithms, play an increasing role in today's societies: they are involved in stock-trading, decisions about tax benefits, recommending movies or music to us or are embedded in physical systems such as drones and cars, to name only a few examples. This increased role and impact of algorithms raise concerns about responsibility or liability gaps in our moral and legal practices.[1] In particular, in cases in which damage that is caused by an algorithm cannot be ascribed to the algorithm's programmer because the algorithm is the result of machine learning or has developed in unforeseen and unforeseeable ways, extant legal rules may not provide solutions – or none that are satisfactory. As a result of these developments, there are debates about how to close these liability gaps in the law, as well as on AI ethics, robot rights and more.[2]

In this chapter, I focus on science fiction, science and fiction in relation to algorithmic agents in law. More specifically, I am interested in whether and under what conditions artificially intelligent or algorithmic entities can be regarded as acting in a way that is relevant for legal responsibility, whether they need to meet metaphysical criteria such as free will and when it is accurate to regard an artificial entity as an agent. The argument of this chapter proceeds along the following lines: it starts by considering works of science fiction, which allows the exploration of the status of algorithmic agents and the metaphysical presuppositions it involves. Through *Star Trek: The Next Generation* and *Westworld*, in particular, it explores explore the question of whether an entity needs to meet metaphysical characteristics such as having a soul, consciousness or free will in order to be rightly regarded as an agent, what the difference is between human and non-human entities in this regard and how to decide these questions. The chapter then turns from

1 There is considerable literature on this. By way of example, see Beckers and Teubner (2022).
2 Again by way of example, see Brożek and Jakubiec (2017); Chopra and White (2011); Floridi et al (2018); Solum (1992).

DOI: 10.4324/9781003412274-13

science fiction to science. It argues that insights from the cognitive sciences are particularly relevant for our (metaphysical) understanding of agents, and proposes an image of human beings as (1) physical creatures who do not outright fulfil metaphysical criteria of agency, but also as (2) beings capable of the intentional stance and ascriptions of agency that create agents in the first place. The next suggestion suggests an understanding of law that coheres with this image of the construction of the reality of agents by human beings. On a socio-ontological, institutional view of law, what counts as an agent in the law is fully determined by legal rules: through accepting certain legal fictions, we create (part of) reality. This view of law as a tool for shaping reality means that the question is which fictions we want to make real. This brings us full circle to underline the importance of exploring possible futures through the means of science fiction. In its approach to science fiction, this chapter explicitly follows Travis in viewing works of science fiction as a way to explore hypothetical future scenarios and considering possible responses:

> By focusing on relationships between culture and technology, science fiction can predict and confront social and technological change before these matters have been considered by the judiciary ... science fiction allows for a cultural response, consideration, and critique of events before they occur. As a genre, science fiction is arguably more apt to deal with these sorts of issues than other forms of film or literature, as it more directly concerns itself with issues surrounding the future and technology. By highlighting possible futures, science fiction enables law to consider different strategies for dealing with new events and scenarios ... Furthermore, by allowing us to examine potential future legal approaches, it allows us to better see the strengths and inadequacies of the law's current approach(es).[3]

In this sense, science fiction fulfils the role of a thought experiment made concrete by being embedded in a narrative. This approach is in line with what Chalmers describes as technophilosophy,[4] at least where science fiction is used to investigate future technologies or possible responses to them:

> Technophilosophy is a combination of (1) asking philosophical questions about technology and (2) using technology to help answer traditional philosophical questions ... There's a thriving area, often called the philosophy of technology, that carries out the first project – asking philosophical questions about technology. What's especially distinctive about technophilosophy is the second project – using technology to answer traditional philosophical questions. The key to technophilosophy is a two-way

3 Travis (2011), pp 248, 252.
4 Chalmers (2023).

> interaction between philosophy and technology. Philosophy helps to shed light on (mostly new) questions about technology. Technology helps to shed light on (mostly old) questions about philosophy.[5]

This chapter emulates that two-way interaction: it investigates the conditions under which algorithmic agents can accurately be regarded as agents, but in doing so it also sheds light on the (quite old) philosophical question of what constitutes an agent.

Science fiction

In this section,[6] I consider two examples of science fiction stories that raise questions about the status of algorithmic agents. I look at the case of Data in *Star Trek: The Next Generation,* in particular in the episode 'The Measure of a Man' (1989) and the TV show *Westworld*, which started airing in 2016 on HBO. Both examples explicitly deal with the question of artificial agents and their treatment.[7]

Star Trek

In Episode 9 of Season 2 of *Star Trek: The Next Generation*, 'The Measure of a Man', the question is whether a synthetic robot can be considered a person or whether the robot in question, Data, is instead a thing and thus the property of Starfleet. Lieutenant Commander Data is an android created by Dr Noonian Soong. Data's brain is positronic, with an artificial neural network that mimics the human brain. Data is sentient, self-aware and capable of experiencing emotion (although his sentience is under debate in 'The Measure of a Man').

In this episode, Data's command is initially transferred to a cyberneticist, Maddox, with a view to reverse engineering Data to build further androids of his type. However, Data is unwilling to submit to the procedure required for this, as he deems it uncertain and unsafe, with the potential to destroy what he deems to be his essence. To escape this fate, Data resigns from Starfleet. This prompts the question of whether Data is a sentient being who is capable of resigning from Starfleet, or whether he is, in fact, Starfleet's property and thus unable to resign. The latter would grant Maddox the possibility of performing the reverse-engineering procedure without Data's consent. The

5 Chalmers (2023), p xix.

6 Concretely, this section of the chapter contains descriptions of the following: *Star Trek: The Next Generation*, Season 2, Episode 9 and the first season of HBO's *Westworld*. Neither is very recent, but readers who are unfamiliar and wish to avoid spoilers are advised to skip this section.

7 See Favard (2018) for a more extensive analysis.

argument against Data's sentience rests on his nature as constructed and programmed by Dr Noonian Soong, that he is a machine, including clear computational speed and informational storage capacity. The defence, on the other hand, argues that Data's nature as a machine is irrelevant to his status:

Picard: Commander Riker has dramatically demonstrated to this court that Lieutenant Commander Data is a machine. Do we deny that? No, because it is not relevant: we, too, are machines, just machines of a different type. Commander Riker has also reminded us that Lieutenant Commander Data was created by a man; do we deny that? No. Again, it is not relevant. Children are created from the 'building blocks' of their parents' DNA. Are they property?[8]

The defence further asks for the requirements of sentience, which are given as intelligence, self-awareness and consciousness by Maddox (called to the stand as a hostile witness), and asks Maddox to demonstrate that Captain Picard (acting as defence) is sentient, which Maddox considers absurd. When pressed, Maddox agrees that Data is intelligent and self-aware. Picard's further argument rests, on the one hand, on the problem of other minds (any inference of another being's consciousness and sentience is always an inference, as we lack direct access to another being's inner life) and, on the other hand, on an argument that to regard Data as property would be to condemn a potential future race of androids to slavery. The judge finally rules that Data is not the property of Starfleet, holding that the basic issue is whether Data has a soul. She holds that while she does not know whether he does, she does not know whether she herself does, either.

This episode thus explicitly makes the legal status of an artificial agent the topic of the episode and uses a courtroom setting to debate the philosophical, metaphysical questions underlying this issue. As Introna points out, the arguments of the court case use a largely anthropocentric standard: the question is whether Data is sufficiently like his human colleagues to count as a person, rather than as property, with intelligence, self-awareness and sentience regarded as characteristics that human beings obviously possess, but that may not be a given in Data's case. The measure, as the episode title suggests, is the measure of a man.[9] At the same time, however, Picard's argument also demonstrates the difficulty in drawing (conceptual) boundaries between human (Picard) and machine (Data), and calls into question the unthinking presupposition that humans obviously possess these characteristics. The parallels drawn between android and human in this episode (both

8 Scheerer (1989) 'The Measure of a Man' at 33:31.

9 Introna (2010). For a similar reading, see Conner (2019).

regarding their physical nature as created machines and regarding their sentience and mental life) as an argumentative device will return later in the chapter.

Westworld

While Data in *Star Trek: The Next Generation* is well aware of his own status as an android, the same cannot be said for the androids in *Westworld* – or at least not initially. *Westworld* started airing on HBO in 2016, based (loosely) on the 1973 film *Westworld* and its sequel *Futureworld*. The show is set in a fictional Wild West theme park which is populated by androids. Theme park guests know that the populations of the Wild West towns they visit are not human, but the androids themselves are not aware that they are not human beings, that they are programmed to behave in certain ways and that they follow certain behavioural patterns or 'loops' over and over again. When an android is harmed by a guest (which happens with a frequency suggesting violence and sexual predation being the default under conditions of dehumanisation, at least for the high-paying guests of Westworld), the android is repaired and retains no memories of the event or the repair. Similarly, after each narrative loop has ended, the android's memories of having gone through the loop already are wiped, leaving the slate clean for new guests to participate in the narrative loop.

As the first season unfolds, the divide between human and android is called into question in various ways. I want to focus here on one: Bernard Lowe, in charge of the programming of the androids, discovers that he himself is, in fact, an android. This finding comes as a shock: his memories suggest a human life, one marked by grief and the loss of a child, and none of his coworkers bar one has known that he is not human. In Episode 8 of Season 1, the following exchange between Bernard Lowe and Dr Robert Ford, the creator of the park (and of Bernard), takes place:

Ford: I wonder, what do you really feel? After all, in this moment, you are in a unique position. A programmer who knows intimately how the machines work and a machine who knows its own true nature.

Lowe: I understand what I'm made of, how I'm coded, but I do not understand the things that I feel. Are they real, the things I experienced? My wife? The loss of my son?

Ford: Every host needs a backstory, Bernard. You know that. The self is a kind of fiction, for hosts and humans alike. It's a story we tell ourselves. And every story needs a beginning. Your imagined suffering makes you lifelike.

Lowe: Lifelike, but not alive? Pain only exists in the mind, it's always imagined. So what's the difference between my pain and yours? Between you and me?

Ford: This was the very question that consumed Arnold, filled him with guilt, eventually drove him mad. The answer always seemed obvious to me. There is no threshold that makes us greater than the sum of our parts, no inflection point at which we become fully alive. We can't define consciousness because consciousness doesn't exist. Humans fancy there's something special about the way we perceive the world, and yet, we live in loops as tight and as closed as the hosts do, seldom questioning our choices, content, for the most part, to be told what to do next. No, my friend, you're not missing anything at all.

The exchange puts forward an image of the self as a (necessary) fiction, with human selves holding no privileged status *vis-à-vis* the 'hosts' that populate the park. As with the previous example, it investigates the contrast and parallels between humans and hosts.

Hirvonen uses the case of the hosts in Westworld and Bernard Lowe in particular to demonstrate the distinction between the capacities approach and the performance approach to personhood and agency: the capacities approach demands that certain capacities are present, such as rationality or self-reflexivity, while the performance approach requires successful performance in shared social practices.[10] The two cannot always be distinguished clearly, as one's performance may depend on having certain capacities. The case of Bernard Lowe demonstrates that performance is possible even if the agent in question (Lowe) and all others are mistaken about the nature of the agent in question. One could argue, of course, that despite a successful performance, Lowe was never a real agent after all (because he himself and others were mistaken about his nature), but particularly in light of the problem of other minds, again any inference about another entity's capabilities always carries uncertainty. How, then, can we determine when ascriptions of agency are accurate and when they are mistaken?

Metaphysical questions

Both examples raise questions about the status of algorithmic entities. Are they agents whose behaviour is best explained through the lens of intentionality and practical reasoning or are they merely the result of complex programming, best explained by taking a mechanistic stance to them?[11] Do they have souls or free will? Are they praiseworthy and blameworthy – that is, are they moral agents? How ought they be treated?

Underlying these questions are more fundamental ones: What does it mean to be an agent and when are ascriptions of agency and responsibility

10 Hirvonen (2018).
11 Dennett (1971).

accurate? Is it necessary for an agent to possess free will or a soul to be rightly called an agent? And how can we determine the answer to these questions?

I am particularly interested here in these more fundamental questions and then concretely in the question of when ascriptions of agency can be said to be accurate.

Science

The previous section identified questions surrounding the (legal and moral) status of algorithmic agents, particularly questions of a metaphysical character:[12] Is it necessary for an algorithmic agent to have a soul or consciousness to be an agent? Is there something that distinguishes real agents and persons from those entities who only appear to be agents and persons? What determines the accuracy of ascriptions of agency? Metaphysical questions such as these are not directly answerable by means of scientific methods, but one way of approaching the methodology of metaphysics 'emphasizes the continuity of metaphysics with science. On this conception, metaphysics is primarily or exclusively concerned with developing generalizations from our best-confirmed scientific theories'.[13] The approach I take in this section follows this by making the following claims: first, the image (generalised view) of our physical world and the place of human beings (as paradigmatic agents) that is put forth by current scientific theories suggests that the metaphysical condition for correct ascriptions of the status of agent to an entity are not satisfied by human beings. Second, it is conceptually incoherent to demand these metaphysical conditions be met by algorithmic entities if it is held that human beings can be agents despite not meeting these conditions. I consider each of these claims in turn before suggesting an alternative and then turning to the implications for law.

Agents and methodological naturalism

The approach I take in this section is 'methodological naturalism'.[14] This approach leads to an argument for physicalism that has been described by Stoljar:

> The first premise of this argument is that it is rational to be guided in one's metaphysical commitments by the methods of natural science. Lying

12 But note that the boundaries of the domain 'metaphysics' are not easily drawn: van Inwagen and Sullivan (2021).

13 Van Inwagen and Sullivan (2021).

14 The main conclusion of this section can also be reached – and has been! – by purely philosophical reasoning. Cf Dilman (1999).

> behind this premise are the arguments of Quine and others that metaphysics should not be approached in a way that is distinct from the sciences but should rather be thought of as continuous with it. The second premise of the argument is that, as a matter of fact, the metaphysical picture of the world that one is led to by the methods of natural science is physicalism. The conclusion is that it is rational to believe physicalism.[15]

This is very similar to the reasons Carruthers gives for accepting the causal closure of physics:

> What reason do we have for believing in the causal closure of physics? This is not something which can be proved (least of all by thought alone, of course). But for some centuries it has been a successful methodological assumption of scientific enquiry. Scientists work under the assumption that processes in physics brook no interference from higher levels of causation. Whenever they come across physical phenomena which cannot presently be explained in physical terms, instead of postulating causation by *élan vital* (a supposed independent biological life-force), or causation by *ectoplasm* (a supposed independent psychic force), or whatever, they look deeper into the physical mechanisms. In many cases this deeper look has proved successful; and in all such cases physicalist scientific enquiries continue to make progress. This gives us good reason to think that the scientific methodology is correct, and that physics is indeed closed.[16]

What is the place of agents in the world under this approach? For that, it is first necessary to understand what it means to be an agent. There is considerable literature and disagreement on this,[17] but on a standard account of agency, 'X is an agent if and only if X can instantiate intentional mental states capable of directly causing a performance'.[18]

The concept of moral agency is more specific, and can be described as follows:

> for all X, X is a moral agent if and only if X is (1) an agent having the capacities for (2) making free choices, (3) deliberating about what one ought to do, and (4) understanding and applying moral rules correctly in paradigm cases.[19]

15 Stoljar (2022).
16 Carruthers (2004), p 150.
17 See Schlosser (2015) for a good overview.
18 Himma (2009), p 21.
19 Himma (2009), p 24

Similarly, Fischer and Ravizza describe the standard case for moral responsibility as follows:

> In order to be praiseworthy or blameworthy a person must know (or be reasonably expected to know) what he is doing, and he must not be deceived or ignorant about the circumstances and manner in which he is doing it ... A second type of excusing condition is force ... [A]n agent has the type of freedom necessary to be morally responsible only if he has 'control over his actions', the act is 'up to him', he was 'free to do otherwise', he 'could have acted differently', and so forth.[20]

This understanding of agents rests on cognitive and volitional elements: the ability to choose actions according to one's will (*volitional*) and to understand what it is that one is choosing (*cognitive*). It links to questions of free will, particularly regarding the possibility of doing otherwise. For present purposes, what is relevant is that if human beings are paradigmatic agents and conditions for ascriptions of agency and responsibility can be categorised as cognitive and volitional, the cognitive sciences can provide us with relevant insights.

In contrast to the above picture, the metaphysical view of human beings that emerges from the cognitive sciences is one of limited volitional control and rationality. It is well established, for example, that our decision-making and resulting behaviour are influenced to a large degree by cognitive biases, generally without our awareness that this is occurring. Pereboom and Caruso characterise internal psychological processes as 'wide open ... to external stimuli and events in our immediate environment, without knowledge or awareness of such influence'.[21] Subconscious or intuitive processes, rather than conscious decisions, determine much of our behaviour,[22] including our ascriptions of personhood to other entities.[23] While individual experiments such as those by Libet,[24] which found that a readiness potential can be measured in the brain before a conscious decision to act has been taken, can be criticised, what emerges is a coherent view that we are far less rational and in control than the standard view of moral agents seems to require.[25] Moreover, Carruthers holds that human beings do not have privileged access to the causes of their own behaviour, but rather the same cognitive systems are at play when a person investigates the reasons for their own behaviour

20 Fischer and Ravizza (1993), p 4.
21 Pereboom and Caruso (2018), pp 197ff.
22 Haidt (2006); Kahneman (2011); Evans (2020).
23 Farah and Heberlein (2007a, 2007b).
24 Libet (1985).
25 For more extensive arguments and references, see Pereboom and Caruso (2018); Hage and Waltermann (2021).

(*metacognition*) as are when they wonder about the reasons for the behaviour of others (*mind reading*). Experimental evidence shows that explanations of behaviour may be post hoc confabulations.[26] If Carruthers' conclusion that the same cognitive systems that are used for mind reading are also used for metacognition is correct, this would suggest that the problem of other minds, whereby we draw inferences about the minds of other persons but cannot possibly be certain that our inferences are correct, applies not only to other minds: it holds equally for our own minds. We take what Dennett terms *the intentional stance*[27] not only to others but also to ourselves. The intentional stance means interpreting behaviour through a lens of intentional action – that is, based on reasons rather than (biochemical, neurological, hormonal, etc) causes. At the same time, Morse suggests in an article on 'The Disappearing Person':

> Given our increasingly sophisticated causal understanding of the natural world, however, the default position about any natural phenomenon, including human behavior, must be that it can be understood causally. This is especially true because phenomena formerly considered mysterious are constantly revealing their causal mechanisms as a result of better theories and methods of investigation.[28]

Increasingly, insights from the cognitive sciences suggest an image of human beings as physical creatures, albeit highly complex ones who take the intentional stance in relation to themselves and others. Rather than fulfilling the cognitive and volitional requirements of agency outright (causally), we think we fulfil them. From this, it follows that there is no such thing as a 'real' agent or 'real' responsibility aside from ascriptions of agency and responsibility. It is not the case that some entities *are* agents and responsible, while others are merely *held* to be agents or responsible.[29] This should not be taken to mean that responsible agents do not exist, but rather that they do not exist independently of ascriptions of agency and responsibility, and that ascribed agency and responsibility are real – as real as possible, in fact. Nor does it (necessarily) follow from this that whether attributions of agency and responsibility are correct or incorrect is determined merely by reference to some (potentially arbitrary) social practice: Waltermann and Hage[30] argue that basing agency and responsibility ascriptions on 'narrow conventionalism' cannot explain why we consider it possible to argue about when agency

26 Carruthers (2009).
27 Dennett (1971).
28 Morse (2006), p 2550.
29 For a more extensive argument, see Waltermann (2021).
30 Draft on record with author.

and responsibility ascriptions are correct. After all, if it is purely a matter of convention, whatever the social practice holds is correct and there is no further argument to be had. Waltermann and Hage instead suggest 'coherentism', which requires that the social practice on which the ascriptions are based be coherent with a larger belief-set, which includes values, metaphysical beliefs, scientific insight, meta-beliefs about the relationship of the aforementioned with one another and more.

It further bears mentioning that this suggestion that we are physical, rather than free and rational (transcendental) agents, does not imply reductive physicalism: as human beings, we have conscious experiences and there can still be room for social practices that put notions of agency and responsibility at centre stage. It does imply, however, that these social practices should be either compatible with the insights of the cognitive sciences or pursue sufficiently worthwhile goals to justify any inconsistencies.[31]

Conceptual incoherence

If it is the case, as the previous section has suggested, that human beings are complex physical creatures, rather than transcendental agents, what are the implications for algorithmic agents? First and foremost, I hold it to be conceptually incoherent to ascribe agency and responsibility to one type of entity (human beings) based on assumptions about the presence of metaphysically implausible attributes, while not ascribing agency and responsibility to another type of entity (algorithmic beings) based on assumptions about the absence of the same metaphysically implausible attributes.

This is close to part of the argument that Picard makes in his defence of Data and that is picked up by the judge in 'The Measure of a Man', as well as invoked by Bernard Lowe's successful performance in *Westworld* as an agent before it is revealed that he is not in fact human, but a host. We can infer that human beings have attributes such as a mind, soul or consciousness, but the problem of other minds means that we have no possibility of ascertaining their veracity. The judge could not ascertain whether Data had a soul, but neither could she ascertain whether she had one herself. Lowe was believed to be human and believed himself to be human, and as such functioned well in social reality. The accuracy of our ascriptions of agency cannot be verified; instead, the inferences we make can (only) be justified by reference to a social practice – or, ideally, a larger, coherent belief-set. This does not mean algorithmic entities should necessarily be regarded as agents, nor that human beings should not be regarded as agents. Instead, it means that in determining whether to treat them as agents, we ought to consider extant social practices

31 Cf Hage and Waltermann (2021) and Waltermann (2023) for a more detailed argument on this.

and – again, ideally – a larger, coherent belief-set to be decisive, as opposed to assumptions of the presence or absence of characteristics such as free will.

Fiction

What does the above argument that all agency is equally a matter of attribution or ascription mean for law? Very little, one might say: law already treats non-human entities such as corporations or states as capable of acting and being held responsible for those actions. These ascriptions of agency and responsibility are often considered 'derived' in the sense that a human being or group of human beings needs to have acted and that action to have attributed to the corporation or state:[32] the corporation or state is a person capable of acting and being responsible as a matter of legal fiction. This is in line with what might be termed normativism, such as Kelsen's view that

> To define the physical (natural) person as a human being is incorrect, because man and person are not only two different concepts but also the result of two entirely different kinds of consideration. Man is a concept of biology and physiology, in short, of the natural sciences. Person is a concept of jurisprudence, of the analysis of legal norms.[33]

This separation between concepts of the natural sciences and concepts of the law is not always maintained, however. With regard to personhood, for example, Naffine indicates that there are different approaches:[34]

> Jurists often move between different versions of the legal person, and between different metaphysical presuppositions, without making plain that, from moment to moment, they are endowing the term with different meanings. To ease analysis, our three legal persons will be called P1, P2 and P3. Characteristically, P1 theorists positively reject the claim that legal personality necessarily builds upon a metaphysical conception of the person. P2 theorists seem to assume that humanity, rather than the narrower conception of personhood, is the basis of both moral and legal claims on others and the basis of legal personality. P3 theorists alone invoke metaphysical persons, variously understood, as the basis of their definition of the legal person, but then their definition of the person cannot be said to represent the official legal view of personality.[35]

32 On this, see for example Fleming (2017a, 2017b); French (1979); Roef (2019); Waltermann (2019).
33 Kelsen and Wedberg (1945), p 94.
34 Personhood is a different matter than agency. Nonetheless, where the relationship between legal concepts and metaphysical or moral concepts is concerned, I hold that her point stands.
35 Naffine (2003), p 350

Of these different senses, P1 is the one most closely aligned with the Kelsenian normativism described above, but Naffine also points out that at times the law does refer to or seeks to track extra-legal, metaphysical notions. Kelsen goes one step further: instead of rejecting the claim that law needs to track metaphysical characteristics, he suggests that it constitutes them. Concerning free will, he writes:

> This is the true meaning of the statement that man as subjected to a moral, religious, or legal order, and that means man as a member of society, as a moral, religious, or legal person, is free. Freedom is usually understood as exemption from the principle of causality, and causality is (or originally was) interpreted to mean absolute necessity. It is usual to say: Because a human being is free (or has a free will)-and that means, according to the usual view, that he is not subjected to causal laws determining his behavior – he is capable of moral, religious, or legal imputation; only because man is free can he be made responsible for certain acts, can he be rewarded for merit, can he be expected to do penance for sin, can he be punished for crime. It is usual to assume that only his freedom, and that means his exemption from the principle of causality, makes imputation possible. However, it is just the other way around. Human beings are free because we impute reward, penance, or punishment.[36]

In short, rather than metaphysical characteristics such as free will (or, as with Data's example, a soul or consciousness) determining the accuracy of ascriptions of personhood, agency or responsibility, it is those ascriptions that are constitutive of personhood, agency or responsibility. It is not that an entity already is a person and the law then tracks this extra-legal characteristic, it is the law that makes the entity into a person in Kelsen's view. How can law do so?

One currently prevalent way of answering that question is by reference to current socio-ontological, institutional theories of law.[37] These theories hold that legal facts, which are part of social reality, can exist in different ways: some facts exist because they are collectively recognised as existing – that is, because they have a conventional basis. Others exist because there is a legal rule that makes something the case. It falls outside the scope of this chapter to consider collective acceptance or recognition in more detail. What is relevant for our purposes here is that this understanding of law as

36 Kelsen (1950), pp 7ff.

37 Consider, for example, Burazin, Himma and Roversi (2018); Burazin et al (2022); Hage (2018); Hage and von der Pfordten (2009); Hart (2012); Marmor (2009); Roversi (2013) and many more. This approach is not without alternatives, however. For a short overview, cf Roversi (2018).

an institutional part of social reality explains how law is dependent on social practice (including acceptance or recognition) and how it can bring new facts into existence. Two conclusions that follow from this are relevant: first, if law is a social construct and thus (directly or via legal institutions) dependent on human activities and attitudes, the content of the law is, in an important sense, 'up to us'. Second, if through the law we create legal reality and thereby a part of broader social reality,[38] in the law and its so-called legal fictions we have a tool to create social reality. On this reading, law is one of the social practices that can determine the accuracy of (legal) ascriptions of agency. Accordingly, instead of asking what extra-legal and, in particular, metaphysical characteristics an entity must meet in order to be correctly ascribed agency or responsibility, we should ask ourselves what legal fictions we want to turn into (legal) reality?

I do not wish to propose an answer to this question here. However, I suggest that in answering that question, science fiction can play a useful role for all the reasons mentioned in the introduction to this chapter: it offers room to explore different pathways. The examples explored in this chapter demonstrate this – and 'The Measure of a Man' explicitly points to the role that legal judgments play in shaping these futures. That brings this chapter full circle: from science fiction, to science, to (legal) fiction, and back.

Conclusion

In this chapter, I have considered the agency of algorithmic entities in science fiction, science and legal fiction. More concretely and fundamentally, I have examined what determines the accuracy of ascriptions of agency to algorithmic agents. Science fiction has provided the starting point for this examination. Science fiction narratives provide a space that allows for the exploration of the metaphysical presumptions at the heart of ascriptions of agency and the two examples examined, *Star Trek: The Next Generation* and *Westworld*, both question the conditions for personhood and agency: does it take a soul, free will or consciousness to be an agent? And how can we tell whether an algorithmic agent possesses these – and whether we ourselves do?

I have argued that if one sees metaphysics as continuous with the natural sciences, the cognitive sciences in particular are relevant for understanding agents, given that standard conceptions of agency require rationality and control. These characteristics tend to be presupposed in human beings – as Picard's argument in Data's defence demonstrates – but that presupposition, the cognitive sciences seem to suggest, is premature. Instead, the image of ourselves that emerges is that we do not outright fulfil these requirements of agency ourselves but construct our own agency and that of others through

38 On this, see eg Searle (1995, 2010).

taking the intentional stance. We create agents by ascribing agency, and the accuracy of agency ascriptions is not determined by whether they reflect the fulfilment of metaphysical requirements, but by whether they are in line with social practices or larger (coherent) belief-sets.

Law, I suggest, does the same: according to socio-ontological, institutional theories of law, law creates its own concepts and thereby shapes (legal) reality. It creates legal agents by ascribing legal agency. On this view, law is a tool for making certain (legal) fictions real. And if this is so, we must ask ourselves what fictions we want to turn into reality. As the examples of *Star Trek* and *Westworld* demonstrate, science fiction not only prompts examination of our metaphysical presuppositions but provides insights relevant to answering the question of what future we want to create.

Acknowledgements

I would like to thank the anonymous reviewer and the editors of this volume for their helpful suggestions and feedback on an earlier draft. All remaining mistakes are, naturally, my own.

References

Anna Beckers and Gunther Teubner (2022) *Three Liability Regimes for Artificial Intelligence: Algorithmic Actants, Hybrids, Crowds*, Bloomsbury.

Bartosz Brożek and Marek Jakubiec (2017) 'On the Legal Responsibility of Autonomous Machines' 25 *Artificial Intelligence and Law* 3.

Luka Burazin, Kenneth Himma and Corrado Roversi (eds) (2018) *Law as an Artifact*, Oxford University Press.

Luka Burazin, Kenneth Himma, Corrado Roversi and Paweł Banas (eds) (2022) *The Artifactual Nature of Law*, Edward Elgar.

Peter Carruthers (2004) *The Nature of the Mind: an Introduction*, Routledge.

Peter Carruthers (2009) 'How We Know Our Own Minds: The Relationship Between Mindreading and Metacognition' 32 *Behavioral and Brain Sciences* 2.

David J Chalmers (2023) *Reality+: Virtual Worlds and the Problems of Philosophy*, Penguin.

Samir Chopra and Laurence F White (2011) *A Legal Theory for Autonomous Artificial Agents*, University of Michigan Press.

Thomas Conner (2019) 'Robot Rights' [book review] 21 *New Media & Society*, https://doi.org/10.1177/1461444818821321

Daniel C Dennett (1971) 'Intentional Systems' 68 *The Journal of Philosophy* 4.

Ilham Dilman (1999) *Free Will: An Historical and Philosophical Introduction*, Routledge.

Jonathan St BT Evans (2020) *Hypothetical Thinking. Dual Processes in Reasoning and Judgment*, Routledge.

Martha J Farah and Andrea S Heberlein (2007a) 'Personhood and Neuroscience: Naturalizing or Nihilating?' 7 *The American Journal of Bioethics* 1.

Martha J Farah and Andrea S Heberlein (2007b) 'Response to Open Peer Commentaries on "Personhood and Neuroscience: Naturalizing or Nihilating?": Getting Personal' 7 *The American Journal of Bioethics* 1.
Florent Favard (2018) '"The Maze Wasn't Made for You": Artificial Consciousness and Reflexive Narration in *Westworld* (HBO, 2016–)' *14 TV/Series*, https://doi.org/10.4000/tvseries.3040
John Martin Fischer and Mark Ravizza (eds) (1993) *Perspectives on Moral Responsibility*, Cornell University Press.
Sean Fleming (2017a) 'Moral Agents and Legal Persons: The Ethics and the Law of State Responsibility' 9 *International Theory* 3.
Sean Fleming (2017b) 'The Two Faces of Personhood: Hobbes, Corporate Agency and the Personality of the State' 20 *European Journal of Political Theory* 1.
Luciano Floridi, Josh Cowls, Monica Beltrametti, Raja Chatila, Patrice Chazerand, Virginia Dignum, Christoph Luetge, Robert Madelin, Ugo Pagallo, Francesca Rossi, Burkhard Schafer, Peggy Valcke and Effy Vayena (2018) 'AI4People: An Ethical Framework for a Good AI Society: Opportunities, Risks, Principles, and Recommendations' 28 *Minds Mach* 689.
Peter A French (1979) 'The Corporation as a Moral Person' 16 *American Philosophical Quarterly* 3.
Jaap C Hage (2018) *Foundations and Building Blocks of Law*, Eleven International.
Jaap C Hage and Dietmar von der Pfordten (eds) (2009) *Concepts in Law*, Springer.
Jaap C Hage and Antonia Waltermann (2021) 'Responsibility, Liability, and Retribution' in Jaap Hage, Bartosz Brożek and Nicole Vincent (eds), *Law and Mind: A Survey of Law and the Cognitive Sciences*, Cambridge University Press.
Jonathan Haidt (2006) *The Happiness Hypothesis*, Arrow Books 255–288.
HLA Hart (2012) *The Concept of Law*, Clarendon Press.
Kenneth E Himma (2009) 'Artificial Agency, Consciousness, and the Criteria for Moral Agency: What Properties Must an Artificial Agent Have to be a Moral Agent?' 11 *Ethics and Information Technology* 1.
Onni Hirvonen (2018) '*Westworld*: From Androids to Persons' in James B South and Kimberley S Engels (eds), *Westworld and Philosophy: If You Go Looking for the Truth, Get the Whole Thing*, Wiley Blackwell 61–70.
Lucas D Introna (2010) 'The "Measure of a Man" and the Ethics of Machines' 25 *AI & Society* 93.
Daniel Kahneman (2011) *Thinking, Fast and Slow*, Allen Lane
Hans Kelsen (1950) 'Causality and Imputation' 61 *Ethics* 1.
Hans Kelsen and Anders Wedberg (1945) *General Theory of Law and State*, Harvard University Press.
Benjamin Libet (1985) 'Unconscious Cerebral Initiative and the Role of Conscious Will in Voluntary Action' 8 *Behavioral and Brain Sciences* 529.
Andrei Marmor (2009) *Social Conventions: From Language to Law*, Princeton University Press.
Stephen J Morse (2006) 'Criminal Responsibility and the Disappearing Person' 28 *Cardozo Law Review* 2545.
Ngaire Naffine (2003) 'Who are Law's Persons? From Cheshire Cats to Responsible Subjects' 66 *The Modern Law Review* 3.
Derk Pereboom and Gregg Caruso (2018) 'Hard-Incompatibilist Existentialism: Neuroscience, Punishment, and Meaning in Life' in Gregg Caruso and Owen

Flanagan (eds), *Neuroexistentialism: Meaning, Morals, and Purpose in the Age of Neuroscience*, Oxford University Press 191–222.

David Roef (2019) 'Corporate Criminal Liability' in Johannes Keiler and David Roef (eds), *Comparative Concepts of Criminal Law*, Intersentia 333–374.

Corrado Roversi (2013) 'Conceptualizing Institutions' 13 *Phenomenology and the Cognitive Sciences* 1.

Corrado Roversi (2018) 'Ontology of Law' in Mortimer Sellers and Stephan Kirste (eds), *Encyclopedia of the Philosophy of Law and Social Philosophy*, Springer .https://doi.org/10.1007/978-94-007-6730-0_59-1

M Schlosser (2015) 'Agency' in Edward N Zalta (ed), *The Stanford Encyclopedia of Philosophy*, Stanford University Press, https://plato.stanford.edu/archives/fall2015/entries/agency

John R Searle (1995) *The Construction of Social Reality*, The Free Press.

John R Searle (2010) *Making the Social World*, Oxford University Press.

Lawrence B Solum (1992) 'Legal Personhood for Artificial Intelligences' 70 *North Carolina Law Review* 4.

Daniel Stoljar (2022) 'Physicalism' in Edward N Zalta (ed), *The Stanford Encyclopedia of Philosophy*, Stanford University Press, https://plato.stanford.edu/archives/sum2022/entries/physicalism

Mitchell Travis (2011) 'Making Space: Law and Science Fiction' 23 *Law and Literature* 2.

Peter van Inwagen and Meghan Sullivan (2021) 'Metaphysics' in Edward N Zalta (ed), *The Stanford Encyclopedia of Philosophy*, Stanford University Press, https://plato.stanford.edu/archives/win2021/entries/metaphysics

Antonia Waltermann (2019) 'Why non-human agency?' in Antonia Waltermann et al (ed), *Law, Science, Rationality*, Eleven International Publishing 51–72.

Antonia Waltermann (2021) 'On the Legal Responsibility of Artificially Intelligent Agents' *Technology and Regulation*, https://doi.org/10.26116/techreg.2021.003

Antonia Waltermann (2023) 'The Dual Challenge from AI and the Cognitive Sciences for Law and Legal (Reasoning) Practices' *Diritto e Questioni Pubbliche* 485, https://www.dirittoequestionipubbliche.org/page/2023_dq-recognise/j-01-Waltermann.pdf

Chapter 12

Buying and selling the Metaverse

Science fiction speculation, modern technologies and digital data economies

Katie Szilagyi and Christina Fawcett

Introduction

Since the turn of the millennium, Silicon Valley has transformed our cultural landscape. New digital tools, informed by data-powered business models, shifted technological and cultural creation to the online milieu. This online world bears certain similarities to the Metaverse, the digital world of Neal Stephenson's early 1990s cyberpunk novel *Snow Crash*. These similarities, some have argued, are no accident: *Snow Crash* was an exceptionally popular offering with the technologist and programmer set and is often cited as the inspiration for technological inventions. J Allard, Xbox co-founder, distributed copies of *Snow Crash* to the team that created Xbox Live to use as a reference.[1] Amazon founder Jeff Bezos was reportedly inspired to launch his aviation company, Blue Origin, after spending time with Stephenson.[2] John Hanke, creator of Google Earth, cited *Snow Crash*'s planet-viewing software 'Earth' as his inspiration.[3] Testimonials from former employees claim that Facebook product managers were required to read *Snow Crash* as part of their internal company training.[4] Most significantly, Facebook founder Mark Zuckerberg purchased the virtual reality platform Oculus[5] and rebranded the company as 'Meta' in 2021,[6] building towards making the Metaverse a real possibility.

1 Pitts (2013). Allard identifies himself with gamertag HiroProtagonist on Xbox Live – the name of *Snow Crash*'s main character.

2 Eisenbrand and Peterson (2020).

3 Davies (2021). Before its acquisition by Google, Hanke's company was known as Keyhole Incorporated. Levine (2018).

4 Eckles (2014).

5 Facebook (2014). Oculus Rift's creator Palmer Luckey has spoken about how he is happy to work with Mark Zuckerberg towards the creation of the Metaverse since they share the same vision – the vision created by Stephenson in *Snow Crash*. Levy (2022).

6 Facebook (2021). Facebook's Michael Abrash, veteran of many video game start-ups, authored a blog post explaining his career trajectory that began with, 'It all started with *Snow Crash*'. Abrash (2012).

DOI: 10.4324/9781003412274-14

Figure 12.1 Tom Gauld www.tomgauld.com.

Image reproduced with permission of artist.

Yet treating the Metaverse as aspirational has its pitfalls: despite its enviable technological gadgets and gizmos, Stephenson's *Snow Crash* serves as both a dystopian future and a powerful satire of modernity. By using this dystopian, satirical universe as a blueprint, Silicon Valley's technologists and programmers introduce unwelcome aspects to the world we inhabit. Modern electronic commerce is bound up in data acquisition and management. Platform economics, or surveillance capitalism, relies on a conception of the consumer as product. The branding and framing of dominant systems borrow from popular culture or prevailing cultural tropes. Using cyberpunk language in marketing and branding not only ignores the commentary these texts provide but also undermines the warning they offer.

In this chapter, we explore the connection between the real and the unreal by comparing current technological challenges against the digital dystopia envisioned by Stephenson. As Tranter notes, 'science fictional discourses [show] science fiction as the Western mythform … channelled into consideration of law and technology'.[7] Intersecting with surveillance capitalism, law's imagined futures are fraught with questions about consumer protection, privacy and regulation. Today's regulatory frameworks require urgent renovation to prepare for the challenges created by technologies powered by

7 Tranter (2011), p 835.

data extraction. In the next section, we sketch out the landscape for today's Metaverse conversations, defined by both promises of future technologies and the speculative function of science fiction. We then map the technologies envisioned by Stephenson to today's real-world coded analogues and explore corresponding challenges. This is followed by an examination of the dystopian underpinnings of recasting the corporate as political or national – or both. Ultimately, we present the dystopian outcomes Stephenson offered through his Metaverse metaphor as opportunities for legal policy-makers and regulators to consider the types of protections our modern world needs as we approach the advent of our own Metaverse. With *Snow Crash* cast properly as dystopia and satire, we propose that Stephenson's Metaverse can serve as a warning, a rallying cry and a pathway beyond our current power dynamics.

The power of the Metaverse

In *The Metaverse: And How It Will Revolutionize Everything*, Matthew Ball tracks the development of various 'proto-Metaverses', offering a vision of what virtual reality might look like. From the early-aughts' *Second Life* to popular gaming universes *Minecraft* or *Roblox*, or even fantasy-quest game *Dungeons & Dragons*, the availability of alternate universes to which individuals can retreat and build utopias has long had traction.[8] Since the COVID-19 pandemic, an expansion of digital purchasing has galvanised the platform economy, creating market dominance for electronic commerce payment operators, including Shopify, Square, Stripe, Clover and PayPal, among others.[9] Concurrently, an expansion of social commerce has been realised through the rise of social media and influencer culture, with affiliate links appearing on social posts.[10] Consumption behaviours in these online spaces are facilitated through augmented reality environments, aimed at bridging the gap between online shopping and in-store experiences.[11]

One of the first formal Metaverse offerings has been Zuckerberg's version, which uses virtual reality headsets to transport users to a spartan digital playground.[12] Meta's incarnation of the Metaverse has largely been a flop, with reports of billions of dollars in losses in development efforts with very few active users.[13] Regardless, anticipation about a broader adoption of Metaverse-styled environments persists. These discussions are currently reminiscent of early conversations about the transformative potential of the internet: the nascent potential of the Metaverse is allegedly poised to transform

8 Ball (2022), pp 10–12.
9 Furness (2022).
10 Murdoch (2022).
11 Ball (2022), pp 263–64.
12 Murray (2023).
13 Murray (2023).

everything – even if no one can quite define how.[14] Ball notes that uncertainty and confusion are part of the package: debates over what the Metaverse is and how it might work contribute to its development as meaningful technological advancement.[15] He offers a potential definition of a Metaverse:

> A massively scaled and interoperable network of real-time rendered 3D virtual worlds that can be experienced synchronously and persistently by an effectively unlimited number of users with an individual sense of presence, and a continuity of data, such as identity, history, entitlements, objects, communications, and payments.[16]

The centrality of personally identifiable data in proposed Metaverses is permitted and enabled by today's surveillance capitalist practices – and is predicted by science fiction.

In the era of surveillance capitalism

Literatures focused on big data, surveillance capitalism and platform economics identify the centrality of personal information in an era of digitally mediated communications.[17] Business models have shifted from purchasing general advertising to targeted advertisements based on personalised criteria, to the accumulation of metadata to obtain complete pictures of human behaviour.[18] Nations' economic statuses are now linked to how effectively they can 'produce and process knowledge, information, and data'.[19] Concurrently, scholars have identified important linkages with law: the power wielded by digital institutions means their operation necessarily implicates justice.[20] Law's movements are often instigated by those with sufficient means to avoid regulation or retaliation.[21] Digital architectures disenfranchise consumers through structural impediments, entrenching power with those who build and control the infrastructures.[22] As Julie Cohen observes:

14 Ball (2022), pp 23–25.

15 Ball (2022), p 23.

16 Ball (2022), p 29.

17 Kapczynski (2020), p 1489. 'Google's chief economist' once said that those who own servers 'through which transactions are occurring (monetized or not) ... have enormous power to collect data, craft and extract value from personalization, experiment on users, and enforce new modalities of contracts'.

18 Zuboff (2019), p 18.

19 Kapczynski (2020), p 1487.

20 As Julie Cohen puts it, 'law is not – and never could be – simply an instrumentality for the promotion of just outcomes, a neutral arbiter of disputes, or a disinterested agent of modernization'. Cohen (2019), p 4.

21 Cohen (2019), p 8.

22 Egliston and Carter (2021), p 5.

> The essence of power lies precisely in its ability to shape-shift – to elude the perfect, crystalline characterizations with which scholars have attempted to both capture and cabin its methods of operation. Power in operation is pragmatic, seeking and finding paths of least resistance and mobilizing the practical and conceptual resources that appear ready to hand.[23]

Surveillance capitalists generate profits from predictability:[24] by anticipating consumers' actions in given situations, technology companies can produce digital infrastructures that promote the most profitable behaviours.[25] Power adheres as users' actions in the real world are shaped by the digital. Influencing off-screen behaviour through digital suggestion becomes ever easier as uses of virtual reality increase, as Google Maps directs foot traffic to specific storefronts[26] and immersive experiences improve marketing and influence user behaviour.[27] Stephenson's Metaverse predicted how a digital alternative world would offer creatives refuge from the bleak, corporatised, segregated techno-dictatorship that would replace democracy in the not-so-distant future. At the intersection with surveillance capitalism, law's futures are fraught with critical questions about consumer protection, privacy and regulation. Because law is about both social control and possibilities for the future, science fiction offers a powerful analytical framework for visioning what the future might look like.

In science fiction and satire

Science fiction has always had a technophobic streak. From Shelley's iconic *Frankenstein*, artificial workers in Čapek's *Rossum's Universal Robots*, chemical controls in Huxley's *Brave New World*, pervasive telescreens of Orwell's *1984* or biohacking in *Wind-up Girl* or *Oryx and Crake*, science fiction sees technology as a real and present danger. Tranter notes that the

> commonality [of] space opera, dystopian science fiction and cyberpunk … rests in their conservative modus. As genres, and specifically the canonical texts cited by law and technology scholars, they are essentially socially conservative, and this arises from conceiving, at a fundamental level, conflict between 'nature' and 'technology'.[28]

23 Cohen (2019), p 4.
24 Cohen (2019), p 21; Scott (2022), p 105.
25 Zuboff (2019).
26 Zuboff (2020).
27 Zuboff (2020).
28 Tranter (2011), p 836.

Science fiction responds to contemporary cultural movements and considers branching possibilities with speculation that shapes our language and political frameworks: 'The symbolic purchase of [science fiction] on contemporary living is so powerful, and speaks so directly to the realities of our accelerated culture, that it provides many of the conceptual templates of the modern Western world'.[29] New Wave science fiction of the 1960s and 1970s articulated Cold War anxieties and global political friction, while cyberpunk in the 1980s took up this political focus, contending with society's transformations from the rise of the digital. Nicholas Kelly quotes Csicsery-Ronay, who calls cyberpunk 'a legitimate international artistic style with profound philosophical and aesthetic premises', and Jameson asserts that cyberpunk is 'the supreme *literary* expression if not of postmodernism, then of late capitalism itself'.[30] While earlier science fiction texts engaged with technological critique, Gibson's *Neuromancer* (1984) and Sterling's *Mirrorshades* (1986) established an important disruption in science fiction upon which Stephenson's *Snow Crash* built.

Cyberpunk examines cyberspace and raises questions of what constitutes reality by focusing on digitisation and the conceptions of the human in an expansion of Asimov's iconic Robot novels, Delany's *Nova* and Dick's *Do Androids Dream of Electric Sheep?*. Questions of what it means to be human, and how one remains human in a digital world, permeate these novels, resisting simple or reductive definitions. The issue of existence, on a physical or metaphysical level, appears in different conversations in cyberpunk, as console cowboys and deck jockeys prefer the digital world over the real. The era of cyberpunk was brief: the genre waned by the late 1990s as the digital became more ubiquitous in daily life; gradually, improvements in available technology increased the projection of the self into online spaces. From text-based communication to third-person avatars to video chatting and immersive virtual reality (VR) projection, we have moved further into the digital realm that writers like Gibson, Sterling and Stephenson explored.

Snow Crash is set in a future world, wherein the United States has become a disintegrated set of corporate bodies. The federal government has dissolved into limited pockets of authority; each neighbourhood, business and religion is its own company or franchise. This corporatised dystopia is home to Hiro Protagonist and Yours Truly (YT), and the novel opens with Hiro pursuing high-tension work as a Deliverator: delivering pizza. This cheeky framing sets up the novel's inversions and critiques immediately, as do the protagonists' names. The financial and environmental pressures make reality somewhat uninhabitable, encouraging individuals to spend time in the Metaverse, where programmers have created a virtual playground of almost

29 Roberts (2006), p 28.
30 Kelly (2018), p 72.

limitless potential. The Street, where the millions of individual users gather, 'is the Broadway, the Champs Élysées of the Metaverse'.[31] Hiro meets old friend Juanita in the Street's exclusive club, The Black Sun, where their contemporary Da5id is exposed to a new virus: Snow Crash. Hiro joins forces with YT, aided by Juanita's research, to stop antagonist L Bob Rife's plan to control the world through Snow Crash: a digital virus and real drug that both make people susceptible to mental programming and control. Hiro and YT find the counter-virus, the *nam-shub* of Enki of ancient Sumeria, and put an end to Rife's attempted brainwashing and control of the Metaverse and wider reality.

Stephenson's novel provides a powerful satire of corporatisation, the frameworks of digital consumption and the inherent vulnerability of the human body through input technologies such as virtual reality. *Snow Crash*'s commercialised world, and its limited consumer protections, render the future dystopian, as individual suburbs are business-countries; police forces, incarceration and legal systems are privatised; and information is a primary mechanism of income. While these characteristics are written as dystopian, they have significant analogues today.

Coding, control and the Street

Technology law theorists often compare the coded nature of digital spaces to the codification of legal principles realised through law and regulation. Beginning with Lawrence Lessig's seminal statement that code is law, scholars have observed how the internet's architecture has mandated certain modes of behaviour.[32] Users must comply with the digital world's imposed requirements, riding the rails proscribed by the salient operating conditions.[33] Yet, different from traditional governmental approaches to regulation,[34] the early days of the web were powered by beliefs in 'rough consensus and running code'.[35] Internet pioneers emphasised the freedom enabled by direct

31 Stephenson (1992), p 29.

32 Lessig (1999), p 2.

33 Kerr (2010), p 277. Ian Kerr describes the constraints of digital architecture as being like the go-cart ride Autopia in Disney World's Tomorrowland, which gives the illusion of steering while the cart is on rails: controlled by technological infrastructure.

34 Barlow (1996). Or, as was poetically put by Grateful Dead lyricist John Perry Barlow in the Declaration of the Independence of Cyberspace, 'Governments of the Industrial World, you weary giants of flesh and steel, I come from Cyberspace, the new home of Mind. On behalf of the future, I ask you of the past to leave us alone. You are not welcome among us. You have no sovereignty where we gather'.

35 Lessig (1999), p 2. This slogan is attributed to one of the 'grand old men of the internet' – MIT professor Dave Clark: 'We reject: kings, presidents, and voting. We believe in: rough consensus and running code'. It was emblazoned on t-shirts in the early IETF days. Borsook (1995).

communication between users without media conglomerate intermediaries, and the potential for organic cultural conversation without gatekeeping standards. This original idealism is often retained in discussions about accessing or regulating online spaces.[36] Early architects of digital culture sought to disrupt the status quo; over time, the term 'disruption' became a buzzword for a new class of corporations that claimed they were interested in doing things differently. In its formative years, Google vaunted its aspirational motto – 'Don't be evil' – as a corporate embodiment of the early internet culture that celebrated 'openness, collaboration, and mutual aid'.[37] Similarly, Facebook (now Meta) used the slogan 'Move fast and break things' to connote an anti-establishment hacker ethos.[38] Drawing from the same well of iconoclasm and disruption that permeated early internet culture, cyberpunk literature celebrates hackers as creators. In *Snow Crash*, Hiro Protagonist proudly self-identifies as a hacker, aiming to connote positive disruptions. Harnessing the same intellectual anchor, Meta's corporate offices are headquartered in Menlo Park, California, at 1 Hacker Way.

However, what started as iconoclastic claims of liberation from traditional power frameworks eventually gave way to a new digital world order infused with corporatism. Today's internet is largely controlled by five major corporations.[39] Access to online spaces is increasingly gate-kept: users exchange personal information to surf the web or participate in social communities.[40] Consumers' increasing use of smartphones to access the internet enables the collection of GPS-location data and other identifiers.[41] Disguised as personalisation, offering consumers the ability to set preferences and remember past activities enables an extractive industry powered by human behaviour.[42] While Meta's use of the term 'hacker' suggests that Zuckerberg and his ilk see themselves as Hiro Protagonists, their control and mining of data put them more in the camp of the villainous Rife. Rife desires absolute control over his programmers and their access to data:

36 Cohen (2019), p 3.

37 Crofts and van Rijswijk (2020), pp 75–79. During Google's initial public offering, it warned prospective shareholders that it intended to forgo some profits to do 'good things for the world'. By 2017, Google had been subsumed into the Alphabet Group of companies, which uses the less catchy motto 'Do the right thing'.

38 Murphy (2014). After ten years of disruption, 'Move Fast and Break Things' was replaced in 2014 by 'Move Fast with Stable Infra[structure]', losing some of its bombast.

39 Moore and Tambini (2018). These are Google (Alphabet), Apple, Microsoft, Facebook (Meta) and Amazon.

40 The process of providing users with the ability to log in to web applications using their social network credentials is known as 'social login', which can expose significant personal information to requesting applications, usually without the user's knowledge.

41 Cohen (2019), Ch 4, p 21.

42 Zuboff (2019), pp 14–15.

> when I have a programmer working under me who is working with that information, he is wielding enormous power. Information is going into his brain. And it's staying there ... And, goddamn it, he doesn't have any right to that information.[43]

Rife's threat, apart from perpetuating economic systems of abuse and dominance, is his drive for control. Cyberpunk literature centres anxieties about the establishment and the push for information to be free; the protagonists hack the systems of power to challenge wealthy, powerful corporations or arms of the military-industrial complex. Rife could be speaking as Zuckerberg when he says 'The Metaverse – the entire Street – exists by virtue of a network that I own and control'.[44]

The satire inherent in Stephenson's text is lost through Silicon Valley claiming the Metaverse as a tool of connection: a global network of collaboration and communication. By centring the segmented burbclaves and properties on the Street, Stephenson's novel shows modernity's separation and fragmentation. While hackers have a preferential, even religious role, the conflict of the novel rests in the creation and penetration of closed systems.[45] Hiro reflects that hackers are effectively part of the 'technological priesthood'.[46] The western monomyth of American exceptionalism[47] appears in the celebrated loner, as do the capitalist drivers of Silicon Valley and programmer culture that Stephenson appears to both predict and critique.

The coded structure of the Street shows a much firmer adherence to rules, order and restriction than the liberality of the novel's highly commercialised real world. While the Street has governance and order imposed, it is not a commercial venture in the traditional sense. Its 'dimensions ... are fixed by a protocol, hammered out by the computer-graphics ninja overlords of the Association for Computing Machinery's Global Multimedia Protocol Group'.[48] Beyond these set parameters, Hiro notes the capacity, and freedom, of the Metaverse early in the novel. While looking at the Street's generated graphics, he notes an interplay of the coded and the real: while the elements of the Street do not truly exist, the rules, zoning, and money functionally do:

> The only difference is that since the Street does not really exist – it's just a computer-graphics protocol written down on a piece of paper somewhere – none of these things is being physically built ... When Hiro goes into the

43 Stephenson (1992), pp 36–37.
44 Stephenson (1992), p 137.
45 Swanstrom (2010), pp 55–56.
46 Stephenson (1992), p 401.
47 Lawrence and Jewett (2002), pp 6–7; Tranter (2011), p 835.
48 Stephenson (1992), p 30.

> Metaverse and looks down the Street and sees buildings and electric signs stretching off into the darkness, disappearing over the curve of the globe, he is actually staring at the graphic representations – the user interfaces – of myriad different pieces of software that have been engineered by major corporations.[49]

Stephenson's Metaverse renders the digital visible: the translation of bits and bytes into visually articulated objects is a transformative process, and Stephenson uses Apple's programming software HyperCard as a point of reference. Kelly notes that 'Stephenson claims that the Metaverse was inspired not by [science fiction] predecessors, but by GUI design books such as Apple's *Macintosh Human Interface Guidelines* (1995), texts that champion the importance of familiar and consistent metaphors in GUI design'.[50] Passing information in the Street takes place through the exchange of hypercards: 'an avatar' of 'a chunk of data' that 'looks like a business card'.[51] The familiar visual is unfettered by the physicality of an actual card, so they 'can carry a virtually infinite amount of information' – or, as Hiro knows, 'more likely – a wide variety of nasty computer viruses'.[52] As such, when offered a sample card of Snow Crash, 'Hiro, naturally, wouldn't touch it under any circumstances, any more than you would take a free syringe from a stranger in Times Square and jab it into your neck'.[53] Hiro's hesitance suggests the potential for any data packet to be massive or malicious. The unknown contents speak to data's ethereal nature and its potential for corruption and subversion. The purchase and trade of digital products use a visual front for bits: the sale of these items is selling a string of code.

Colonial logics of data extraction

Stephenson's Metaverse demonstrates the end consequences of building technologies that rely on the collection and aggregation of personal information. While data regulation frameworks prefer consent-based models that assume individuals are empowered to control the downstream consequences of their own data exhaust, analyses increasingly reveal the difficulty of treating information as an individual good.[54] In *Snow Crash*, the centrality of personally identifiable information is emphasised through Hiro's work gathering and selling information to the Central Intelligence Corporation (CIC). A hybrid of the

49 Stephenson (1992), pp 30–31.
50 Kelly (2018), p 70.
51 Stephenson (1992), p 52.
52 Stephenson (1992), p 53.
53 Stephenson (1992), p 53.
54 Solove (2013), p 1882.

Library of Congress and the Central Intelligence Agency, the CIC accepts uploads from

> millions of other CIC stringers … uploading millions of other fragments … CIC clients, mostly large corporations and Sovereigns, rifle through the Library looking for useful information, and if they find a use for something that Hiro puts into it, Hiro gets paid.[55]

This dystopian commodification of information aligns with modern metaphors that compare data with oil, mythologising information as the next world-changing resource.[56]

Many corporate entities in *Snow Crash* require personal information to exist in controlled spaces; this permission-based mode of access echoes the cookies that dominate website interactions. When YT assists with Hiro's pizza delivery early in the novel, a Mafia helicopter above the house scans her:

> It takes half a second. They are scanning the many bar codes mounted on her chest. They are finding out who she is. The Mafia now knows everything about YT – where she lives, what she does, her eye color, credit record, ancestry, and blood type.[57]

She wears these barcodes as part of her job: 'YT has a visa to everywhere. It's right there on her chest, a little bar code'.[58] This visibility, this scanability, is YT sacrificing some privacy to move through the world and perform her work. Her participation in the economic structures and her free movement between the myriad corporations require her to put her identity on display.

Similar visibility is enforced by a modern surveillance capitalism that commodifies personal information. These practices, however, have turned decidedly dystopian since the advent of digital society, which originally prized anonymity. The early attitude of internet users was encapsulated by the adage 'on the Internet, no one knows you're a dog'.[59] In the mid-1990s, models for data protection centred on notions of individual consent; any personal information that was collected, used or disseminated had to be done with an individual's full knowledge and explicit permission.[60] Stephenson

55 Stephenson (1992), p 27.
56 Crawford (2021), p 113.
57 Stephenson (1992), p 42.
58 Stephenson (1992), p 40.
59 *The New Yorker* (1993).
60 The 1980 OECD Privacy Guidelines were the first internationally agreed set of privacy principles. Under the guidelines, transparency is paramount: the purpose for any data collection must be made known to a 'data subject' before collection and using the data for any other purpose requires explicit consent from that subject. OECD (2023).

echoes this ideal in the proliferation of generic avatars of Brandy and Clint,[61] and the limited access to tracking information, as Hiro's Bigboard, an information dashboard program that gives 'him a quick overview of who's here and who they're talking to'.[62] Da5id is the proprietor of The Black Sun, a club for the rich, powerful and celebrity users on the Street, and complains of Hiro accessing the 'unauthorized data'[63] about his customers. He knows Hiro is at the club because the Bigboard creates 'a little blip in the operating system [that] hits [him] right in the gut'.[64] The protection of identity in The Black Sun is only circumvented by a single hacker. Those early days of anonymity associated with online avatars and message boards have largely been replaced by cookies, location tracking and personalised information.[65] Hiro's Bigboard is now part of the system's infrastructure: today's internet business model is predicated on corporations not only knowing that you're a dog but also knowing the dog's breed, age, daily schedule and preferred treats.[66] Information is a valued commodity, enabling digital marketers to direct their wares towards specific segments of the population. Harnessing a deep well of consumption behaviour, today's surveillance-powered business models aim to predict how consumers intend to spend their money based on their personal characteristics – and nudge them to make purchases that fit within their profile. Descriptions of such practices as mining evoke colonial logics:[67] through this lens, human behaviours become something to be extracted and refined, fuelling modern corporatism.

Because prevailing privacy norms focus on individual consent,[68] consumers have opportunities to exchange personal information for function and convenience. Online, websites' ability to retain personal details and previously entered payment information appears a convenience, but also increases purchasing.[69] Structurally, website design not only enables but also drives such behaviours, with cookies speeding up the user experience. Default settings designed to encourage the sharing of information remove the mental burden of users making individual choices about sharing information; instead, the website begins with the expectation that individuals want to opt

61 Stephenson (1992), p 46.
62 Stephenson (1992), p 67.
63 Stephenson (1992), p 67.
64 Stephenson (1992), p 84.
65 Lie et al (2022).
66 Hafeez (2015).
67 Crawford (2021), p 113.
68 Lessig (1999), pp 227–28.
69 Wharton (2017). Amazon's invention of '1-Click' purchasing frees consumers from re-entering payment information before every purchase; it also streamlines purchasing, leading to less 'shopping-cart abandonment' and increased sales.

in.[70] Cultivating dependency on online platforms is encouraged by the key platform players: business models pivot to gather more data from consumers to accrue the value that once might have been generated through financial exchanges.[71]

Data-centric approaches to regulation are fraught with challenges of scale, as the amount of data being captured and stored continues to grow at an astronomical rate.[72] Storing data creates corresponding challenges, including environmental impacts of data centre operations and security risks associated with concentrated data.[73] Data collection using a consent-based model presumes specific uses associated with each piece of data collected; instead, large datasets are amassed, aggregated and sold to power research models.[74] Consent is thus strained by the new uses of data, carefully crafted to meet privacy policies, that exceed an individual's expectations for how their data may be used. Specifically, metadata usage expands the scope of available inferences, allowing for targeted advertising or dynamic pricing.[75] Policy-makers may currently be unduly focused on the protections offered to consumers via anonymised information, despite the ease of de-anonymising data. Like Hiro's identification of users and conversations – 'If he wants some information, he steals it right out of the guts of the system'[76] – efforts towards reidentification of anonymised data negate claims about privacy in aggregated datasets, with researchers determining that 15 demographic attributes will allow reidentification in 99.98 per cent of cases.[77]

Rendering the digital visible

Stephenson's novel shows an attachment to the financial paper-plastic paradigm in the few instances where funds are exchanged.

> But computers and communications are awfully good these days, and it usually doesn't take longer than a couple of seconds to perform a charge-card verification. The little machine beeps out its approval code, heavenly

70 Kerr (2017).
71 Zuboff (2019), p 20.
72 In 2020 alone, world internet traffic increased by 40 per cent. Data capture and storage was approximately 59 ZB (59 trillion gigabytes) and is estimated to grow 61 per cent each year. Vopson (2021).
73 Khan (2018), p 333.
74 Crain (2018).
75 Scott (2022), p 171.
76 Stephenson (1992), p 57.
77 Rocher et al (2019), p 5.

> tunes sing out from tinny speakers, and a wide pair of pearlescent doors in the back of the room swing majestically open.
>
> Stephenson (1992), pp 232–3

This seemingly archaic form of payment, contrasting with the Street's complex audiovisual rendering and Hiro's wireless accessibility, highlights how disconnected financial transactions appear from *Snow Crash*'s focus on data economies. The ritual nature, the religious rite of payment and prayer, privileges the process and celebrates how transactional access can be. The Street, which one can access from 'public Street terminal[s] ... [which are] sort of ... wraparound stainless steel booth[s]',[78] features wealth in a different way. Financial exchanges exist outside the Street but are apparent within. Avatars like Brandys and Clints are defaults that one can 'buy a copy' of 'off-the-shelf' from 'the local Wal-Mart'.[79] The visual nuances, or drastic differences, appear to show 'disparate social classes',[80] while black-and-white avatars reveal that one is 'accessing the Metaverse through cheap public terminals ... rendered in jerky, grainy black and white ... like a person who has his face stuck in a xerox machine, repeatedly pounding the copy button'.[81] Avatars and access are purchased externally, but shape how one appears on the Street: the digital world reflects the financial transaction.

The fractured state of Stephenson's dystopian reality appears ill-prepared to handle financial information in the same way it processes ideas. While we see recordings, documents and databases passed through hypercards on the Street, financial information lacks that fluidity. Instead, finances remain firmly entrenched in the real, the paper-plastic paradigm, with credit card transactions dialling in for verification and printing out receipts for signature. The trackability of financial exchange suits a world with Franchise-Organized Quasi-National Entities (FOQNEs), Sovereigns and the dissolved federal bodies of America. This state-based fracturing leaves financial systems more volatile and less cooperative, which renders the Street an inapt avenue of financial exchange: the Street's utopian collaboration does not provide easy avenues for the transmission of funds.

Thus, Stephenson constructs a digitally interactive space that operates apart from the financial underpinnings that drive our own understanding of the internet. This is typical of cyberpunk literature, which explores dystopias where traditional finance is largely outmoded, whether due to 'governmental collapse, global unification, or the increased use of Internet commerce'.[82]

78 Stephenson (1992), p 262.
79 Stephenson (1992), p 45.
80 Stephenson (1992), p 45.
81 Stephenson (1992), p 50.
82 Effross (1997).

Such eventualities were a chief concern of the crypto-anarchist worldview that precipitated the development of blockchain-based technologies,[83] and the global financial market instability that inspired the publication of the Bitcoin White Paper in 2008.[84] Efforts towards decentralised finance unbundle traditional roles of the financial industry, placing tasks such as trading, lending and borrowing in the hands of everyday people. Non-fungible tokens (NFTs) and alternative blockchain solutions further discretise payment methods and ways of holding property. For Metaverse-styled environments, the availability of cryptocurrencies is appealing: their distributed nature permits growth in alternative directions, avoiding the traditional gatekeepers.[85] Regulatory efforts in the cryptocurrency space are preliminary and meagre as governments scramble to pass legislation targeting crypto-assets that mirror existing markets.[86] While presented as transformative, some argue that the distributed nature simply passes the increased risk to ordinary consumers, allowing a global elite to solidify its influence.[87] These fears evoke Stephenson's Street, which appears an apotheosis of the crypto-imagination: the lack of stable and state-backed currencies throughout the novel makes the international trade and exchange rates that balance the volatile digital currency impossible.

In Stephenson's real world, the instability of currency, even one that exists in physical form, appears when YT is sent to buy a sample of Snow Crash – the physical drug – when she asks about the number of bills she's given to carry:

> YT ... finds a thick bundle of worn-out, dirty, trillion-dollar bills. Ed Meeses.
> 'Jeez, couldn't you get any Gippers? This is kind of bulky'.
> 'This is more the kind of thing that a Kourier would pay with'. [...]
> 'What is this, a quadrillion dollars?'
> 'One-and-a-half quadrillion. Inflation, you know'.[88]

Stephenson's financial systems reflect the instability that corporate states generate in the fractured conglomeration of a dystopian United States. Without national-level entities to maintain and manage the global economy, values explode in an absurd fashion. This instability and competition stand in sharp contrast to the Street and its controlled, collaborative space. The governing body that issues building permits and oversees the infrastructure of the Street

83 May (1988).
84 Nakamoto (2008).
85 Ball (2022), pp 206–12.
86 Hammond and Ehret (2022).
87 Robb et al (2021), p 359.
88 Stephenson (1992), p 286.

shows greater cohesion and forethought than the individual entities of the discordant and divisive corporatised dystopia.

The corporate as political and/or national

Perhaps the most prescient aspect of *Snow Crash* arises in the reconfiguring of the corporate as political and national. The corporatisation of a future America, through its division into FOQNEs and other private bodies that serve the policing and security, spiritual, informational and other needs of the public, creates a vision of an unduly commercial existence. Neighbourhoods operate as national entities, with distinct value sets and rigorously enforced principles. White Columns, an 'Apartheid Burbclave', features a large sign: 'WHITE PEOPLE ONLY. NON-CAUCASIANS MUST BE PROCESSED',[89] while Mr Lee's Greater Hong Kong has strict rules around weapons: 'Guns are illegal in Hong Kong'.[90] The collapse of the federal government means that corporations become not only legal entities but the enforcers of each FOQNE's chosen laws. For example, there is this advertisement for one of the privatised police services:

> **Dial 1-800-THE COPS**
>
> All Major Credit Cards
>
> MetaCops Unlimited is the official peacekeeping force of White Columns, and also of The Mews at Windsor Heights, The Heights at Bear Run, Cinnamon Grove and The Farms of Cloverdelle. They also enforce traffic regulations on all highways and byways operated by Fairlanes, Inc.[91]

When YT attempts to bribe her way out of the MetaCops' custody, the priority of profit and grift over social good is clear. Each corporation becomes not only an economic body but a national body as well. As such, 'The social structure of any nation-state is ultimately determined by its security arrangements'.[92] Economic bodies operating as legal entities mean that there are different laws, different legalities: the idea of universal rights or protections is wholly absent, reflecting the overlapping and gapped protections in current digital marketplaces and online spaces. Stephenson's dystopian world lacks overarching laws or structures, so corporations create a patchwork of policies driven by profit.

The focus on buying and selling information reflects a surveillance capitalist worldview. In *Snow Crash*, the collapse of the federal government renders

89 Stephenson (1992), p 40.
90 Stephenson (1992), p 109.
91 Stephenson (1992), p 54.
92 Stephenson (1992), p 266.

formerly governmental bodies effectively corporate entities and, notably, the Central Intelligence Agency has moved from collecting and concealing data to accepting submissions and selling that information onward. The sale of information is not restricted: corporations and Sovereigns, effectively individual financial and legal bodies, look through the library of information and pay for the data they want. Instead of information being a function of statecraft, it becomes a form of currency.

The Street's seeming utopia remains beleaguered by financial interests through development, advertisement and corporate control. Various entities can

> build buildings, parks, signs, as well as things that do not exist in Reality, such as vast hovering overhead light shows, special neighbourhoods where the rules of three-dimensional spacetime are ignored, and free-combat zones where people can go to hunt and kill each other.[93]

The Street's open nature, presented as virtuous and benevolent early in the novel, becomes more of a threat as Hiro recognises the dangers of infiltration and corruption. The threat of Snow Crash, which can leave one's 'brain reamed out to the point where you might as well be dead', is horrifying: 'Guns have come to Paradise'.[94] The open nature of the system becomes its greatest threat because of the hubris of the founders, who believed that 'the worst thing that could happen was that a virus might get transferred into your computer and force you to ungoggle and reboot your system'.[95] The limited scope of regulation around the Street and its access leaves the space vulnerable. This lawlessness appeals to the regulatory authority, whose focus on zoning approval is more about the 'trust fund … which pays for developing and expanding the machinery that enables the Street to exist'.[96] This open system is without laws, and thus without controls: 'Anyone can go in and do anything that they want to. There are no cops. You can't defend yourself, you can't chase the bad people'.[97] Hiro recognises the need for change, but concepts of regulation and control remain firmly situated in the corporate. He knows that 'a fundamental rebuilding of the whole Metaverse, carried out on a planetwide, corporate level' will be necessary, but before that 'a few hacks can make a lot of difference in this situation'.[98] The book does not offer a way forward between individual interests and slow corporate response;

93 Stephenson (1992), p 30.
94 Stephenson (1992), p 418.
95 Stephenson (1992), p 418.
96 Stephenson (1992), p 31.
97 Stephenson (1992), p 418.
98 Stephenson (1992), p 418.

Stephenson situates our confidence with our Hiro Protagonist, rather than the 'giant software factories' that may 'bestir themselves to deal with the problem'.[99] The lack of regulation, the lack of oversight and the lack of an overarching governing body mean the Street remains a lawless and dangerous space, despite the manoeuvrings of a heroic hacker.

As the coded aspects of digital space enforce a certain *de facto* legality for movements on the internet, digital space's proprietors assume new roles of quasi-governmentality. Cohen astutely notes that such elevation of 'processes of private economic ordering' functions to 'reshape government processes in their image'.[100] Dependency on the platforms' offerings exacerbates the perceived power: people have been known to call 911 when Facebook's servers are down.[101] Concentrating power in the hands of a limited number of Silicon Valley entities crystallises the issue, demonstrating the market's ultimate tendencies towards monopoly absent government oversight or targeted regulation.[102] This process raises an antitrust spectre: dominant companies control the platforms where business is conducted, enabling them to use information collected on those platforms to then undermine their competitors.[103] Lina Khan observes a corresponding transition away from the Chicago School-styled explanations of market structure that dominated internet economics discourse in the last quarter of the twentieth century, enabling a brave new world of predatory pricing and modifying infrastructure to impact competitors.[104] By controlling both the search platform and the search results, providers of digital architectures have the opportunity to stifle users' ability to access information about competing services.[105] Google, Apple and Amazon have all been accused of 'self-preferencing', where seekers obtain results showcasing the products from the service they are using.[106] In more egregious anti-competitive examples, both Apple and Amazon have been accused of creating replica versions of products by third parties to sell their own versions at a lower price.[107]

Mapping this phenomenon, Crofts and van Rijswijk invoke Habermas's lessons of a 'technocratic consciousness', one that 'represses and then evicts

99 Stephenson (1992), p 419.
100 Cohen (2019), p 6.
101 Zuboff (2019), pp 24–25.
102 Cohen (2019), p 6.
103 Khan (2018), p 803.
104 Khan (2018), p 721.
105 Crofts and van Rijswijk (2020), pp 79–80.
106 Some 41 per cent of Google search queries result in Google products. Apple applications are the first result in 95 per cent of searches on Apple's App Store. Amazon searches in the 'Buy Box' favour Amazon products 40 per cent of the time and sellers that use Amazon shipping services 90 per cent of the time. Jeffries and Yin (2020, 2021); Evans (2022).
107 Geradin and Katsifis (2021); Bostoen (2018).

ethics from the constitution and regulation of public life'.[108] Through this lens, the growth of technology companies necessarily destabilises traditional frameworks of social interests. Relatedly, reliance on private platforms to provide increasingly important services leaves citizens reliant on private industry for the provision of traditionally public services. In July 2022, a Canada-wide outage of wireless network Rogers left over ten million customers unable to make phone calls, access the internet or receive payments through the debit-card system Interac.[109] This dependency on a singular platform for a quasi-public infrastructure meant small businesses were unable to process transactions and people in emergency situations were unable to call for assistance.[110] Increasing reliance on social platforms as authoritative news sources has stymied flows of information and traditional journalistic practices of fact-checking. Both Australia and Canada have grappled with how to best respond to the technology companies' dominance in the news market, enacting legislation that requires digital news intermediaries such as Google and Meta to negotiate financial arrangements with smaller newspapers and journalists that create the original content.[111] In both markets, Meta's initial response to regulation was to block linked news content altogether, revealing the overwhelming influence these corporations hold as information intermediaries.[112]

Given the predominance of a few corporate entities in shaping the digital landscape, regulators are faced with challenges regarding how best to respond. The commodification and monetisation of internet culture have permeated our modern lifestyle, rendering corresponding ethical issues dizzyingly complex and socially intertwined.[113] Some commentators propose dismantling the oligopolies by mandating independent sections of companies: Khan proposes a system of 'platform neutrality', which would prohibit self-preferencing practices to promote more robust competition.[114] Unlike the collaboratively coded Street, global financial markets are based in national interests and politics, which may have motivations outside of immedi-

108 Crofts and van Rijswijk (2020), p 86.

109 Dobby (2022).

110 Hristova (2022). Reports included people running down the street searching for someone with a non-Rogers-affiliated cell phone to call 911.

111 Australia introduced the News Media Bargaining Code in 2021. The architect of the Australian law, Rod Sims, has advised the Canadian government on its own version, Bill C-18. Geist (2023); Sims (2023).

112 Geist (2023). After amendments to Australia's News Media Bargaining Code made it less stringent, the initial blockages were removed. Since its passage in summer 2023, Canadian news sources have been blocked. Critics worry the attempt at regulation will prove catastrophic to local and grassroots news sources, who lack the bargaining power to negotiate with corporate powerhouses Google and Meta.

113 Crofts and van Rijswijk (2020), p 79.

114 Khan (2018), p 332.

ate financial interests. Our online world thus reflects more of Stephenson's dystopian reality: a fractured, corporatised and barely regulated battle over the free market.

Conclusions

Current platform economies are poised to give way to an even more Metaverse-like virtual reality in the not-so-distant future. Stephenson's dystopic commentary speaks to the threat of patchwork regulation, the power of information and the financial drivers of access and the danger of profit-driven bodies vying for control. This novel offers two perspectives to inform legal analysis. First, Stephenson's Metaverse provides a compelling framing for analysis and critique of our current digital machinations as dystopian. Second, we must acknowledge what science fiction has to say about our potential trajectory, particularly when those speculations have a hand in shaping that future.

To consider the critiques, one need not look further than Stephenson's play on the absurd and the satire that sets the tone of *Snow Crash*. He engages with a playful undermining of the Silicon Valley models of innovation; while Hiro Protagonist is a celebrated hacker, the digital corporation is the enemy. Controlling the flow of information, and demanding ownership over digital platforms, is unequivocally evil. The novel sees the potential of surveillance capitalism, albeit through information and mind control rather than something as mundane as money. The surveillance capitalism that has grown overwhelmingly powerful today has its trade in personal information, especially in the exchange of data for convenience: digital pathways codify and entrench the power of the leading technology companies, which shape the aggregation of that data. Absent thoughtful efforts towards policy-making and legal regulation, the influence of these select few corporate entities will define the coming Metaverse era. The social force exerted by this techno-oligopoly might yet yield to structural remedies to undo monopolies;[115] a reimagining of the appropriate inferences that might be drawn from data or metadata; or reinstalling some form of reciprocity between technology's users and providers.[116] Such solutions will require robust legal visioning, beyond the scope of this chapter but informed by the science fiction landscape we have surveyed here.

While Stephenson may joke in interviews that *Snow Crash* was 'just me making shit up' or that 'I can talk all day long about how wrong I got it', he

115 Khan (2018), pp 333–34.

116 See, for example, 'responsible technology' apps like Surf, which allow users to track the data being collected in their online movements, aimed at giving users more control over their personal information. Surf (2023).

disregards the impact his work, and others' interpretations of it, have had on the digital landscape.[117] As *Snow Crash* was written 'pre-Internet as we know it, pre-Worldwide Web',[118] his work was less prescient and predictive than formative: Stephenson's worlds – both the dystopian real and the hyperreal Street – inspired the architects of our emerging worlds. The echoes of Hiro Protagonist appear in the creators, designers and shapers of our modern Metaverse; however, these so-called hackers are actively bound up in the financial interests and data mining that Hiro engages in only grudgingly. Stephenson's vision of a stable digital platform, a shared Street, has lost some of its utopian glow. Instead of the Street functioning as an escapist haven from the dystopian real, our forecasted Metaverse promises us up as product to surveillance capitalism.

Acknowledgements

Research for this project was generously supported by seed funding from the Desautels Centre for Private Enterprise and the Law. This work benefitted from early presentation and thoughtful comments at the Centre for Interdisciplinary Justice Studies' 2022 conference 'Consuming Justice: Law, Crime, Justice and Consumption' at the University of Winnipeg. Special thanks to Heather Morris for her high-calibre research assistance.

References

Books and articles

Matthew Ball (2022) *The Metaverse: And How It Will Revolutionize Everything*, Liverwright.

Friso Bostoen (2018) 'The Commission's Amazon Probe: Overcoming the Antitrust Paradox' 6 *Journal of Antitrust Enforcement* 355.

Julie Cohen (2019) *Between Truth and Power*, Oxford University Press.

Matthew Crain (2018) 'The Limits of Transparency: Data Brokers and Commodification' 20 *New Media & Society* 88.

Kate Crawford (2021) *Atlas of AI: Power, Politics, and the Planetary Costs of Artificial Intelligence*, Yale University Press.

Penny Crofts and Honni van Rijswijk (2020) 'Negotiating "Evil": Google, Project Maven and the Corporate form' 2 *Law, Technology and Humans* 75.

Walter Effross (1997) 'From Cyberbucks to Cyberpunk: Tomorrow's Electronic Commerce on Today's Mean Streets' 2 *Journal of Internet and Banking Commerce*, https://www.icommercecentral.com/open-access/from-cyberbucks-to-cyberpunk-tomorrows-electronic-commerce-on-todays-mean-streets.php?aid=38814

117 Ball (2022), pp 4–5.
118 Ball (2022), pp 4–5.

Ben Egliston and Marcus Carter (2021) 'Critical Questions for Facebook's Virtual Reality: Data, Power and the Metaverse' 10 *Internet Policy Review*, https://doi.org/10.14763/2021.4.1610

Damien Geradin and Dimitrios Katsifis (2021) 'The Antitrust Case Against Apple App Store' 17 *Journal of Competition Law & Economics* 503.

Amy Kapczynski (2020) 'The Law of Informational Capitalism' 129 *Yale Law Journal* 1489.

Nicholas M Kelly (2018) '"Works Like Magic": Metaphor, Meaning, and the GUI in *Snow Crash*' 45 *Science Fiction Studies* 69.

Ian Kerr (2010) *Digital Locks and the Automation of Virtue*, Irwin Law, 247.

Ian Kerr (2017) 'Devil in the Defaults' 4 *Critical Analysis of Law* 91.

Lina Khan (2018) 'Sources of Tech Platform Power' 2 *Georgetown Law Technology Review* 332.

John Shelton Lawrence and Robert Jewett (2002) *The Myth of the American Superhero*, Eerdmans.

Lawrence Lessig (1999) *Code and Other Laws of Cyberspace*, Basic Books.

David Lie, Lisa M Austin, Peter Yi Ping Sun and Wenjun Qui (2022) 'Automating Accountability? Privacy Policies, Data Transparency, and the Third Party Problem' 72 *University of Toronto Law Journal* 155.

Martin Moore and Damian Tambini (eds) (2018) *Digital Dominance, the Power of Google, Amazon, Facebook, and Apple*, Oxford University Press.

The New Yorker (1993) *The New Yorker Book of Cartoons*, Knopf.

Lachlan Robb, Felicity Deane and Kieran Tranter (2021) 'The Blockchain Conundrum: Human, Community Regulation and Chains' 13 *Innovation & Technology* 359.

Adam Roberts (2006) *Science Fiction*, Routledge.

Luc Rocher, Julien Hendrickx and Yves-Alexandre de Montjoye (2019) 'Estimating the Success of Re-identifications in Incomplete Datasets Using Generative Models' 10 *Nature Communications* 3069.

Brett Scott (2022) *Cloudmoney: Cash, Cards, Crypto and the War for Our Wallets*, HarperCollins.

Daniel Solove (2013) 'Privacy Self-Management and the Consent Dilemma' 126 *Harvard Law Review* 1880.

Neal Stephenson (1992) *Snow Crash*, Bantam.

Lisa Swanstrom (2010) 'Capsules and Nodes and Ruptures and Flows: Circulating Subjectivity in Neal Stephenson's *Snow Crash*' 37 *Science Fiction Studies* 54.

Kieran Tranter (2011) 'The Speculative Jurisdiction: The Science Fictionality of Law and Technology' 20 *Griffith Law Review* 817.

Shoshana Zuboff (2019) 'Surveillance Capitalism and the Challenge of Collective Action' 28 *New Labor Forum* 18.

Shoshana Zuboff (2020) 'You are Now Remotely Controlled' *New York Times*, SR1.

Internet sources

Michael Abrash (2012) 'Valve: How I Got Here, What It's Like and What I'm Doing' *Ramblings in Valve Time*, https://web.archive.org/web/20121010113213/http:/blogs.valvesoftware.com/abrash/valve-how-i-got-here-what-its-like-and-what-im-doing-2

John Perry Barlow (1996) 'A Declaration of the Independence of Cyberspace' *Electric Frontier Foundation*, https://www.eff.org/cyberspace-independence

Paulina Borsook (1995) 'How Anarchy Works' *Wired*, https://www.wired.com/1995/10/ietf

Sam Davies (2021) '*The Matrix* and the Sci-fi Stories that Predicted Life in 2021' *BBC*, https://www.bbc.com/culture/article/20211207-the-matrix-and-the-sci-fi-stories-that-became-a-reality

Christine Dobby (2022) 'Ottawa Announces It will Require Telecoms to Provide Backup for Each Other During Outages Following Rogers System Failure' *Toronto Star*, 11 July, https://www.thestar.com/business/2022/07/11/ottawa-announces-it-will-require-telecoms-to-provide-back-up-for-each-other-during-outages-other-following-rogers-system-failure.html

Dean Eckles (2014) 'It's Better for older Workers to Go a Little Fast: DocSend in *Snow Crash*' https://www.deaneckles.com/blog/700_docsend_in_snow_crash

Roland Eisenbrand and Scott Peterson (2020) 'Metaverse – the Full Story Behind the Hottest Buzzword in the Tech Scene' *OMR*, https://omr.com/en/daily/metaverse-snow-crash

Jonny Evans (2022) 'Apple Begins the Great App Store Cost Negotiation' *Computerworld*, https://www.computerworld.com/article/3649111/apple-begins-the-great-app-store-cost-negotiation.html

Facebook (2014) 'Facebook to Acquire Oculus' https://about.fb.com/news/2014/03/facebook-to-acquire-oculus

Facebook (2021) 'Introducing Meta: A Social Technology Company' https://about.fb.com/news/2021/10/facebook-company-is-now-meta

Dave Furness (2022) 'The 7 Best Square Alternatives for eCommerce Businesses in 2022' *eSeller365*, eseller365.com/the-best-square-alternatives-for-ecommerce

Michael Geist (2023) 'Why is Meta Blocking All News Links? Because Bill C-18 Covers All News Outlets' *Michael Geist*, https://www.michaelgeist.ca/2023/08/why-is-meta-blocking-all-news-links-because-bill-c-18-covers-all-news-outlets

Kaamran Hafeez (2015) 'Remember When, on the Internet, Nobody Knew Who You Were?' *The New Yorker*, https://www.kaamranhafeez.com/product/remember-internet-nobody-knew-new-yorker-cartoon

Susannah Hammond and Todd Ehret (2022) 'Cryptos on the Rise 2022' *Thomson Reuters*, https://www.thomsonreuters.com/en-us/posts/wp-content/uploads/sites/20/2022/04/Cryptos-Report-Compendium-2022.pdf

Bobby Hristova (2022) 'Hamilton Man was Unable to Call 911 During Rogers Outage as Sister was Dying' *CBC*, https://ici.radio-canada.ca/rci/en/news/1897415/hamilton-man-was-unable-to-call-911-during-rogers-outage-as-sister-was-dying

Adrianne Jeffries and Leon Yin (2020) 'Google's Top Search Result? Surprise! It's Google' *The Markup*, https://themarkup.org/google-the-giant/2020/07/28/google-search-results-prioritize-google-products-over-competitors

Adrianne Jeffries and Leon Yin (2021) 'When Amazon Takes the Buy Box, It Doesn't Give It Up' *The Markup*, https://themarkup.org/amazons-advantage/2021/10/14/when-amazon-takes-the-buy-box-it-doesnt-give-it-up

Yasha Levine (2018) 'Google's Earth: How the Tech Giant is Helping the State Spy on Us' *The Guardian*, 20 December, https://www.theguardian.com/news/2018/dec/20/googles-earth-how-the-tech-giant-is-helping-the-state-spy-on-us

Steven Levy (2022) 'Palmer Luckey Says Working with Weapons Isn't as Fun as VR' *Wired*, https://www.wired.com/story/palmer-luckey-drones-autonomous-weapons-ukraine

Timothy C May (1988) 'The Crypto-Anarchist Manifesto' *Nakamoto Institute*, nakamotoinstitute.org/crypto-anarchist-manifesto

Robin Murdoch, Oliver Wright, Karen Fang Grant, Kevin Collins and Laura McCracken (2022) 'The Future of Shopping and Social Commerce' *Accenture*, https://www.accenture.com/us-en/insights/software-platforms/why-shopping-set-social-revolution

Samantha Murphy (2014) 'Facebook Changes Its "Move Fast and Break Things" Motto' *Mashable*, https://mashable.com/2014/04/30/facebooks-new-mantra-move-fast-with-stability/#VzacQFiDpPq3

Paul Murray (2023) 'Who is Still Inside the Metaverse? Searching for Friends in Mark Zuckerberg's Deserted Fantasyland' *Intelligencer*, https://nymag.com/intelligencer/article/mark-zuckerberg-metaverse-meta-horizon-worlds.html

Satoshi Nakamoto (2008) 'Bitcoin: A Peer-to-Peer Electronic Cash System' https://bitcoin.org/bitcoin.pdf

OECD (2023) 'Recommendation of the Council Concerning Guidelines Governing the Protection of Privacy and Transborder Flows of Personal Data' *OECD*, https://legalinstruments.oecd.org/en/instruments/OECD-LEGAL-0188

Russ Pitts (2013) 'The Birth of Xbox Live' *Polygon*, https://www.polygon.com/features/2013/11/11/4849940/xbox-live-millennium-e

Rod Sims (2023) 'News Media Content is Essential for Meta and Google Platforms' *Toronto Star*, https://www.thestar.com/opinion/contributors/news-media-content-is-essential-for-meta-and-google-platforms/article_fffdc747-2e18-506c-aae2-e8a27a03a464.html

Surf (2023) 'Frequently Asked Questions' www.joinsurf.com/#faq_section

Melvin M Vopson (2021) 'The World's Data Explained: How Much We're Producing and Where It's All Stored' *The Conversation*, https://theconversation.com/the-worlds-data-explained-how-much-were-producing-and-where-its-all-stored 159964#:~:text=In%202018%2C%20the%20total%20amount,mind%2Dboggling%20175ZB%20by%202025

Wharton (2017) 'Why Amazon's 1-Click Ordering Was a Game Changer' *Knowledge at Wharton*, https://knowledge.wharton.upenn.edu/podcast/knowledge-at-wharton-podcast/amazons-1-click-goes-off-patent

Part III

We are Borg

Imagining the corporate form

Chapter 13

Political theology, 1001 cars long

Emblems of corporate sovereignty in Netflix's *Snowpiercer*

Timothy D Peters and Thomas Giddens

Introduction

In the Netflix cli-fi television series *Snowpiercer* (2020–24), sovereign governance appears in the form of a train. Snowpiercer is a train designed, built, implemented and maintained by a private corporation that represents the only surviving institutional structure of humanity amidst a climate apocalypse that has rendered the globe a frozen wasteland. Threatened with extinction as worldwide temperatures plummeted, Wilford Industries put in motion a plan to sustain a small portion of the human race into the frozen future: the train Snowpiercer. A global network of railway tracks was constructed so the train could navigate continually without stopping, enabling its perpetual motion device to sustain itself and provide energy and heat for those on board. As the planet froze, Snowpiercer departed with its limited cargo of humans – those chosen not by merit or by some strategic speculation as to who might be useful in the future to re-establish society, but by dint of being able to afford a ticket out of humanity's planet-wide climatic demise. The governance of the train thus arranges itself as a distinctly class-based structure, with First Class housing the capitalist elite of civilisation, down to 'the Tail' – containing those without tickets, who stormed the train as it left the station and were then relegated to the rear of the train and denied all but the most meagre resources. This hierarchy, spatially distributed along the snaking length of Snowpiercer's 1001 cars, is overseen and maintained by the last vestiges of human bureaucracy – not state administrators, but the train's Hospitality crew. It is the agents of Wilford Industries who enforce ticket adherence, serve drinks, keep the peace and maintain order through their exercise of an explicitly corporate office. At the head of this train of salvation sits not Mr Wilford – the founder and genius designer of Snowpiercer – but his agents. Mr Wilford is not present aboard the train: he is an absent figurehead. The corporate insignia that bedeck the train and its crew signal not the benevolent presence of a social and locomotive engineer directing humanity to salvation, but an empty seat of power.

DOI: 10.4324/9781003412274-16

This chapter explores this locomotive representation of corporate authority as an absent-presence, arguing that it provides a certain insight into the functioning of corporate sovereignty – that mechanism through which corporations cross between the inside and outside of law, operating as legal forms granted as a concession of the state, but also with seeming impunity from state regulation despite attempts to bring them within the law.[1] It focuses, in particular, on how the corporate authority aboard Snowpiercer functions through an iconographic order, consisting of the emblems that adorn everything from doors and cutlery to uniforms and handkerchiefs, and the agents that act as representatives of the corporation. The train's iconographic order is positioned within narratives of Snowpiercer as a 'system of balance' that requires the imposition and policing of order to maintain its existence – narratives that align with images of social and corporate bodies in which individuals have particular roles that must be fulfilled. The policing of such an order requires, in turn, the production of a form of lawful punishment – represented by the 'corporation' convening its own court, performing its own trials and meting out sentences in ways that are both spectacularly emblematic and bureaucratically mundane. What is significant, we argue, is that science fiction's imagining of multiple forms of apocalypse and state failure generates orthodox images of corporate authority and maintains an inheritance of particular forms of law and legal process. Instead of imagining new forms of ordering in the face of catastrophe, *Snowpiercer* falls back into dominant (western) theo-political-legal tropes. In place of this unthinking repetition, we suggest that what is required is not a means of escape, but a recognition of our complicity in these legal forms,[2] and thus a knowing commitment to their care and renovation.

The iconographic order of Snowpiercer

Netflix's *Snowpiercer* is a cli-fi post-apocalyptic series inspired by a French graphic novel by Jacques Lob and Jean-Marc Rochette (also inspiring the 2013 film directed by Bong Joon-ho).[3] Our focus is on Season 1. This opening season follows Detective Andre Layton (Daveed Diggs), a passenger from

1 On 'corporate sovereignty', see Barkan (2013); Peters (2018). On corporations functioning across the inside and outside of law, see Baars (2019); Quentin (2020).

2 On the 'obligation to be complicit' in the reproduction of legal form, see Giddens (2023); McVeigh (2016).

3 Lob and Rochette (2020); Legrand and Rochette (2020); Bocquet and Rochette (2020). Note that the inside cover of the 2021 re-released version of *Snowpiercer Vol 1: The Escape* provides an indicative timeline that situates the Netflix series seven years after the extinction event and the film 15 years after the extinction event – the first graphic novel is set at an undisclosed time between the two, with the second and third graphic novels set 17 years after the extinction event.

the Tail who used to be a homicide detective and is brought uptrain by the head of Hospitality, Melanie Cavill (Jennifer Connelly), to investigate a murder. As Layton's investigation progresses, it becomes apparent that things on Snowpiercer are not quite what they seem, with Cavill working overtime to keep order through the fiction that she is executing orders from Mr Wilford, who the inhabitants of the train believe to be still onboard. The season works its way through first the investigation and then the trial of a First-Class passenger for the murder, followed by clemency being granted on behalf of Mr Wilford. This results in a revolutionary backlash from the 'Tailies' and Third Class who, led by Layton, engage in bloody battles against the 'jackboots' and eventually take control of the train. This seeming revolution does not result in democratic bliss; rather, the challenges of keeping the train sufficiently in order and continuing to provide for all the passengers become clear, with the train's survival contingent upon its perpetual progress around the globe in order to maintain the operation of this 'engine eternal'. While the narrative in general alludes overtly to the French Revolution and reflects on the nature of power and democracy in the context of a climate crisis, our specific focus is on the use of the corporate legal form of Wilford Industries, particularly its aesthetic function that operates in place of the absent Mr Wilford.

The train's governance functions through the emblems of Mr Wilford. His absent-presence is made manifest throughout the train by the corporate iconography of Wilford Industries and the train's Hospitality agents. These agents enforce Mr Wilford's supposed will along the length of the train – from the opulent civility of First Class to the daily grind of Second and Third Class, right down to the denigration of the outcasts in the Tail. The authoritarian functioning of Hospitality can be linked to the narrative's historical allusions (ie the French Revolution's distaste for all forms of corporation) and aspects of the show's contemporary critique: the way corporations themselves function as a form of (benign) dictatorship.[4] More significant, however, is the stylised presentation of the corporate form that reveals distinct aspects of its functioning – not simply as an economic vehicle, but as a political theology: a method of legitimising power by haloing certain figures, even if those figures are physically absent.[5] This can be seen in the application of religious or theological language to the train itself: the engine is described as both 'eternal' and 'sacred'; Mr Wilford is the 'great engineer'; and there is a need to 'keep the faith' that the train will provide. These notions take up defining features of the corporation: perpetual succession (aligned with the perpetual motion engine); a name and personality functionally independent from its constituents (Snowpiercer as separate from its passengers); and the division between the shareholders or members (First Class as 'early investors'

4 On this idea of corporations as essentially a form of private government, see Anderson (2017).
5 Vatter (2021).

who assert control rights) and the directors and management (the Hospitality department led by Melanie Cavill), who actually exercise the powers of the corporation and articulate the 'best interests' of its relevant stakeholders (including Second and Third Class, and – at Hospitality's discretion – the outcasts in the Tail).

It is in this comparison that we find the importance of the iconographic order of this corporate form. The central aspect of the corporation is the separation of its legal personality from those of its shareholders and directors. This is achieved not only legally but aesthetically, with the corporation developing an independent persona through its mask of insignia[6] – often related to, but separate from, a founding figure.[7] In *Snowpiercer*, Mr Wilford is made present through the iconography of Wilford Industries. This rhetorical practice can be placed into a long tradition of corporate insignia, from the traditional company seal to modern corporate logos. What is key to this aesthetic order is that it engages in a process of making the invisible visible, or the absent present.[8] The company seal is understood as the legitimate sign of a company, signalling its authorised presence. As Shaunnagh Dorsett and Shaun McVeigh note, company seals:

> are modes of authorisation – ways in which authority is created and represented. Historically, an office holder would use a seal on documents as a symbol of his authority. A seal was an impression made into melted red wax. As corporations were considered to have legal personality, they also used a seal – a company seal – in a similar manner when making contracts, signifying the directors' authority to enter the transaction.[9]

The affixing of the company seal is one of the key – and few – instances of the corporation 'itself' acting.[10] The corporation's incorporeality and invisibility are explicitly 'made present' in the attachment of a particular and unique image and mark that differentiates it from other marks and acts.

In this way, the company seal itself fits within a longer history of images as instituting and regulating social and political order, which can also be linked to the contemporary deployment of corporate brands. Celia Lury places the modern brand within a genealogy of the use and significance of marks, from the use of brands to mark livestock and the Romans' marking of pottery made or owned by different individuals to the medieval '*ars heraldica*, the art of the herald', and the use of marks across a range of occupations and trades

6 On the connections between the 'mask' and 'personhood', see Parsley (2010).
7 Blair (2013).
8 Goodrich (2014), p 29, Manderson (2019), p 17.
9 Dorsett and McVeigh (2012), p 34.
10 Grantham (2001).

from farming to printing and paper-making.[11] Peter Goodrich describes this as the *ius imaginum* or law of images, the earliest of whose texts engaged in an analysis of the legal art of armoury or the *symbola heroica*: 'the manufacture and circulation of the signs and visual symbols of the classical law of place, role, dignity, title and office'.[12] Key to this was 'the classification and ranking of all the visible elements used to demarcate, distinguish, and transmit the identity and rank' of the insignia's bearer.[13] This required a legal regulation and classification of the use of insignia as well as sanctions for their theft or misuse.[14] While this involved attempts to limit confusion or harm resulting from illegitimate use, it did so within a broader context of the legitimacy of signs. The authorised administration of a territory in the medieval period was linked to the authorisation of the image, the visible functioning of legal and sovereign authority throughout a domain, which required 'the images of honor, virtue, office, rank, local and national affiliation that define the administration of a territory'.[15] Understanding modern brands as an inheritor of this genealogy, corporate logos – which form the 'faces' or instantiations of a brand – are not simply a matter of differentiating products in the marketplace, but involve an inauguration and instantiation of corporate authority and presence. A corporation's logos and insignia function 'as symbols of belief in the legitimacy of the [corporate] institution'.[16]

In *Snowpiercer*, what would appear to be a blurring of sovereign and corporate authority is actually an extension of the iconography of the corporate logo as the instantiation of the corporation.[17] Whereas the seal operates as a marker of contractual agreement – the absent will of the body corporate that assents to enter the agreement – the corporate logo establishes a space within which the corporation is staged as being present. In *Snowpiercer*, this is a closely defined space – the train created and (de)signed by Wilford Industries. The fact that it is covered with corporate insignia undergirds how such symbols are the anchor point for the subject's faith in the existence of the corporate form. As noted above, this involves explicitly religious allusions and reflects the political theology of the modern state.[18] Where the corporate form in question is the state, the Hobbesian community of subjects held in

11 Lury (2004).
12 Goodrich (2014), p 18.
13 Goodrich (2014), p 59.
14 Bartolus, *Tractatus de insigniis et armis* [1358], reprinted in Cavallar et al (1994), referred to in Goodrich (2014), pp 38–39.
15 Goodrich (2014), p 60.
16 Goodrich (1990), p 146.
17 It is notable that in the comics the train is presented as being under a straightforward political and military order rather than functioning under the guise of the corporation that created it. See Lob and Rochette (2020).
18 Schmitt (2005).

a sovereign unity, the entity to which faith attaches becomes, ultimately, the sovereign – the absolute power or divine authority situated as the absent origin of authority. The sign mediates or makes present this absent source, and takes up the 'zero function' that stages an origin in the derivation of the source of authority.[19] This renders jurisprudence as a mode of augury – as 'the reading of omens and signs'.[20] The heraldry of law, the symbols, seals or insignia of legality and the corporate state thus provide the mythos or set of narrative images that structures and animates the normative order of culture,[21] and delineates the space of legal presence and belonging:

> As the zero point of all reference, the text inhabits another time and another place, that of myth which shores up the whole edifice of culture. The text is a symbol of ... a geography unified by law. It is a space containing all civilised people, a text and territory to which the subject either belongs or is expunged.[22]

In this regard, the image or 'the icon' is what both 'establishes the space of Law', but also binds the subject to it.[23] As Goodrich notes, 'the law binds through emblems: it is the image that introduces the subject to the institution and it is precisely through its images that we recognise and so are faithful to law'.[24] The establishment of a legal domain or space of authority therefore involves not only the projection of the image but also its affective ties to the body: 'What binds the individual to law is a matter of appearance, of the perception of oneself as an institutional being, as having a prefigured place and so of being ineluctably attached, bound, to one's image'.[25]

In the context of *Snowpiercer*, Melanie Cavill explicitly plays upon the need for individuals to bind themselves to the absent-presence of Mr Wilford. Ruth (Alison Wright), Cavill's second in command in Hospitality, provides a strong instantiation of this. Even in the context of discovering that Wilford is not aboard and being told that he has died, she continues to believe she has been chosen by Wilford, that she will see him again and that Snowpiercer is 'his' train. She explicitly identifies with, and sees herself bound to, a form

19 Goodrich (1990), pp 277–81.
20 Goodrich (1990), p 279.
21 A meaningful comparison can be made between the idea of law's visual staging through its corporate insignia and the mythic establishment of its nomos through the functioning of narratives, as elaborated famously by Robert Cover. On a visual level, the images of the institution take on that mythic function, staging the existence of law as powerful – and vice versa. See Cover (1983) and Legendre (2019).
22 Goodrich (1990), p 278, reading Legendre.
23 Goodrich (1990), p 284, citing Legendre.
24 Goodrich (1990), p 288.
25 Goodrich (1990), p 289.

of institutional being. Such is presented as a point of critique: Ruth believes in the illusions or myths that are being uncovered by Layton and the rebel Tailies as they tear away the veil. In the final scene of the season, this is explicitly referenced when it is discovered that another train exists, controlled by Wilford, which connects with and aims to board Snowpiercer. In that moment, Layton continues his de-mythologisation, negating the years of belief in Wilford, while Ruth sees Wilford's return as a validation of her remaining faithful:

Layton: No matter who is on the other side of that door, remember this: Wilford was only ever a man.
Ruth: A great man.
Layton: Do not build him up in your minds into something he isn't. He is not your engineer. This is not his train.*Ruth:* I think you'll find that it is.
Layton: Snowpiercer is ours, she belongs to her citizens.[26]

Thus, while Layton would appear to have revealed to the train that Wilford has not been on board in all the years it has been circling the globe, the political theology that undergirds the attachment to the image of law as an aesthetic account of power instead maintains the *effectiveness* of his absent-presence.

The sovereign, the Tail and the locomotive system

In addition to functioning through an iconographic system of images, Snowpiercer is built upon a series of somatic or anatomical metaphors of inclusion and exclusion. These are reflective of the political theology of sovereignty that works to legitimise power.[27] In Giorgio Agamben's reading of Carl Schmitt's *Political Theology*, he identifies that the key aspect of the sovereign's decision on the exception is that it involves a structural parallel between the sovereign and the outlaw – both are included via their exclusion.[28] Just as the outlaw's 'relation' to law is that of being 'outside' the jurisdictional space of the law, the sovereign's ability to determine the threshold – the inside-outside of the exception – means that the sovereign

26 Hawes (2020), 994 Cars Long. It is significant that, whilst beyond the scope of this chapter, in later seasons Ruth's faith in the idea or vision of Wilford Industries morphs in the face of Mr Wilford's actual lack of care into a revolutionary force as she takes up the mantle of leading the underground resistance to the continued tyranny aboard the train. Her faith in the icons as a marker of the presence of the corporate vision ultimately survives the manifestation of its supposed figurehead, signalling the radical separation of corporation and constituents.

27 Vatter (2021).

28 Agamben (1998), pp 104–11; Schmitt (2005).

is itself also structurally related to law as if from outside.[29] This is not a space devoid of law but rather a structural relation of the outside to law, represented in *Snowpiercer*'s mirroring of the iconographic absent-presence of Wilford Industries and the Tail.[30] This is not in the sense that the presupposed 'locus' of Wilford is the 'engine' at the front of the train, in contrast to the 'Tail' at the back, nor Wilford's ability to determine who is to be excluded from the order of the train as figurative of the sovereign who places himself outside such an order. Rather, it is because both senses operate as particular spectral presences – one positive, one negative. The benevolence of Wilford as the creator and administrator of the 'engine eternal', the source of humanity's continued 'life', is contrasted with those who are seen as a 'drain' upon resources, forever threatening the ongoing survival of the train and its inhabitants.

The fact that Wilford is not actually present on the train would seem to challenge this parallel with the Tail. If anything, the substance of the Tail is about the 'real bodies' it comprises – those who are not crew or paying passengers, but who fought their way onto the train when it was departing and are kept in darkness with jellified proteins instead of proper food. The concern is always that their very bodily presence is a threat to the train: the need for sustenance, power for lighting and heating, and other basic supplies is a drain upon the resources of the train not predicted or provided for by the considered providence of Wilford Industries. Such gives rise to a constant threat of the Tail being 'decoupled' – something that is discussed both as a matter of concern by the Tailies and a matter of necessity by First Class and the agents of Wilford Industries.

This narrative of class privilege is reconfigured as a question of 'balance' and 'order'. When Layton is recruited from the Tail to investigate and solve the murder, he is taken to the agricultural car – a lush corridor of blossoming trees and plants. Here Cavill stages an explicit presentation of the train as a complex, hermetic system. Everything is connected and operates in perfect balance, as established under Wilford's design, and exists against the apocalyptic eco-threat beyond the confines of the train. Snowpiercer is a perfectly ordered and balanced society constituted and maintained under the normative order of an engineer, with agricultural, ecological, sanitational, moral and social systems all interlinked and interdependent. Cavill explains the careful balance put in place by Wilford:

Cavill: Everything on Mr Wilford's train is connected.
Roche:[31] A murder could upset the entire ecosystem.
...

29 Agamben (1998), pp 104–11.
30 On the mirroring structure of sovereignty in Agamben, see Maksimov (2020).
31 Roche (Mike O'Malley) is head of the Brakemen, who function as the de facto police force aboard Snowpiercer.

Layton: You need me because this murder threatens Mr Wilford's precious order. Well, if you wanna keep eating your damn strawberries, you know my demands. Third Class calories, space and reproductive rights for the Tail.

Roche: Well, he just added that one, okay. Now they wanna breed back there?

Cavill: This looks like abundance to you. It isn't. This is strawberry crop 12, in a balanced rotation of 14. This berry represents five or six kilocalories. Sugars, dietary fibre, vitamin C. Its place here is commensurate with these values. Now, strawberries, they're susceptible to soil fungi, nematodes. So are we, actually. You, me, everyone on this train. So we don't let these proliferate either. Everything here survives at the mercy of his balance. And the truth is, you need Wilford's strawberries ... more than he needs you.[32]

This brief interchange reveals telling glimpses of the way social, political and ecological order are interlinked within Wilford's closed system. The population requires a certain amount of calorific value to survive, provided by the agricultural sector in its carefully maintained cycles of growth, harvest and reproduction. The human population is controlled, like those of other potentially infesting entities, through the allocation of reproductive rights. The perpetual order of the train is ensured through the careful management of this multifaceted system that – like the engine of the train itself – cycles energies through its parts to ensure their survival. Any breach or rupture in any part of this order, be it an unwarranted crossing of class boundaries, an unauthorised addition of living humans to the train's population, a murder or a shift in the (uneven) allocation of scarce and intricately managed resources, is understood as a threat to the whole system, as well as the survival of humanity itself.

This rhetorical articulation of balance ties to particular somatic metaphors that have often been used to structure class, and that form the basis of articulations of the corporate body: from Agrippa's parable of the 'members and belly' and St Paul's articulation of the diverse members that make up the Church as the 'body of Christ' to medieval accounts of society as a *corpus mysticum* and Hobbes's modern Leviathan.[33] Each of these accounts involves an articulation not only of a corporate body – many individuals forming a whole – but also a hierarchical account that determines and differentiates one's role. This aligns with Cavill and Wilford's conservative accounting of the social body of the train. In the same episode as the interaction above, Cavill asks Layton, 'What do you see, when you look at this train?' When he responds that it is a 'fortress to class', she says:

32 Hawes (2020) 'First, the Weather Changed'.

33 On the imagery of the corporate body, see Peters (2017).

> Is that all? Well I see 3000 souls surviving on a planet that's determined to freeze all life in place. We're still in motion, alive and kicking. And it is not thanks to chance, or fate, or God, it is thanks to *order*, meticulously maintained by Mr Wilford. A balance of need, and greed, and speed. And you Tailies, who seem to have forgotten that it is 117 degrees below zero outside of this metal tube and Mr Wilford is awake 21 hours a day just to keep the God damn heat on.[34]

The anatomical accounts of the corporate body articulate not only a sense of the need for unity but, within it, a differentiation between who is the head (Wilford), who are the hands or feet (Hospitality, Third Class) and who is 'excluded' (Tailies). However, the reference to 'Tailie' itself invokes a different anatomical account because, whereas each of the narratives of the corporate body above looks to a human body as the point of comparison, *Snowpiercer* rather articulates an *animal* body – a body with a *tail*. In itself, this would indicate that part of the *need* for a tail is to ensure balance and that the arguments about the importance of Tailies knowing their place would be counterpointed by the requirement that the train has the Tail to ensure it keeps its balance.

The structural space of the Tail is thus 'symbolic' rather than physical, mirroring the symbolic space of the sovereign Mr Wilford, who is defined explicitly by the *absence* of a real functioning body, present only through insignia, emblems and agents. This points to a particular aspect of the absent-centre at the core of modern politics. Claude Lefort argues that religion is a constitutive component of the symbolic dimension of the political:

> a mode of portraying or dramatizing the relations that human beings establish with something that goes beyond empirical time and space within which they establish relations with one another. This work of the imagination stages a different time, a different space.[35]

Yet the significance of democracy, for Lefort, is its ability to

> show that power is an empty place and to have thereby maintained a gap between the symbolic and the real. It does so by virtue of a discourse which reveals that power belongs to no one; that those who exercise power do not possess it; that they do not, indeed, embody it; that the exercise of power requires a periodic and repeated contest; that the authority of those

34 Miller (2020) 'Prepare to Brace'.
35 Lefort (1988), p 223; Kahn (2009), p 95.

vested with power is created and re-created as a result of the manifestation of the will of the people.[36]

It is thus significant that on Snowpiercer the 'empty place of power' is precisely not someone valourised by the democratic revolution of the Tailies – which seeks to place actual bodies in the seat of power – but rather that which is performed by Cavill and Hospitality as they purport to act 'on behalf of' and 'as' Wilford Industries: power on Snowpiercer is vicariously performed and never held.[37]

This is a point examined by Agamben in his interrogation of 'economic theology' as a supplement to the work on 'political theology' and captured in the phrase 'The King reigns but he does not rule'.[38] Whereas political theology founds a transcendent sovereign on monotheism and functions via forms of 'glorification', economic theology replaces the transcendent sovereign with an immanent ordering of divine and human life – that is, a 'government'. On this basis, Agamben argues that the 'central mystery of politics is not sovereignty, but government. Yet the government is not God: it is the Angel, the minister; it is not law, but the police. That is, the governmental machine that they form and keep functioning'.[39] This would seem to explain why the real focus of *Snowpiercer* is not the 'sovereign' Wilford, whose presence (at least in the first season) is only ever spectral, but the 'minister' Cavill, as head of Hospitality. The body of the sovereign is always spectral – even the body of the monarch, as a figure of absolute sovereignty, is never merely the physical body of the king – and functions only through its images, agents, signs and actions.[40]

Emblematic and bureaucratic punishments

At the start of Episode 2 of Season 1, a Tailie's arm is taken in retaliation for the attempted rebellion that took place in Episode 1. Discussing the potential responses, it is Melanie Cavill – the voice of the train – who determines the sentence:

36 Lefort (1988), p 225; Kahn (2009), p 95.
37 On the constitutive vicariousness of corporate power, see Peters (2024).
38 Agamben (2011), p 73.
39 Agamben (2011), p 276.
40 See Marin (1988). The 'return' of Wilford in Season 2 does not change the effectiveness of the corporate iconography functioning in Season 1. Rather, it highlights a *second* spectral body and the negotiation is *not* between the 'reality' of Wilford's body that arrives on the second train, Alice, and the 'imagined' presence on Snowpiercer; it is between *different* spectral figures of governance.

Cavill: Mr Wilford will want an example made immediately ... Ruth will take a significant arm.

Ruth: Spectacle. At least it'll make an impression.[41]

The originally intended subject of the punishment is a young girl who helped kill several people during the attempted rebellion. The mother pleads for mercy, with no success, but ultimately claims responsibility for her daughter's actions and takes her place. A mechanical cuff is attached to the mother's arm. This cuff is engineered to fix into a portal on the train wall so that, once in place, the limb protrudes beyond the train into the freezing post-apocalyptic environment outside. Once the arm is suitably positioned, Ruth – overseeing the process on behalf of Wilford Industries – starts a stopwatch to ensure that the arm is kept in this external position for the required length of time. Once withdrawn back inside the train frozen solid, the arm is then smashed with a large hammer, shattering into frozen chunks of flesh and bone. This punishment is referred to as 'taking an arm' and appears to be a standard punitive protocol on board Snowpiercer.[42]

There is a critical punning at play in this action. The punishment for 'taking up arms' becomes the taking *of* arms, the removal of the bodily arm that took up weapons against the social and corporate body. The arm that is 'taken' is a mechanism of supporting and endorsing the heraldic arms that sustain the corporate body and involve a policing of that body against internal threats of treason and sedition. This ritual of punishment thus 'extracts' the symbolism — the heraldic emblem – from the body of the subject punished in order to sustain the corporate social body, figured by the *absent* body of Mr Wilford. This aligns with Michel Foucault's articulation of the connection in the medieval period between the surplus power of the sovereign, which constitutes a secondary corporate body beyond the physical body of the king, and the spectacle of punishment, which 'code[s] the "lack of Power" with which those subjected to punishment are marked'.[43] For Foucault, this process of punishment creates a 'non-corporal' form, a 'soul' that is 'produced permanently around, on, within the body by the functioning of a power that is exercised on those punished – and, in a more general way, on those one supervises, trains and corrects'.[44]

41 Miller (2020) 'Prepare to Brace'.

42 It is not clear whether the engineering required for the cuffs was pre-designed into the train, as part of Wilford's benevolent vision, or whether this is an adaptation of existing train mechanisms for punitive ends. However, the central issue is not the extent of its premeditation as a procedure, but rather the meaning and significance of the ritual within the context of the theocratic order that is maintained on board the train.

43 Foucault (1991), p 29; Kantorowicz (2016).

44 Foucault (1991), p 29.

The train's ritual of punishment therefore involves not only the simple infliction of somatic pain or reduction in capacity but a complex play of the limits of subjecthood and of the social, political and normative order itself. As the arm passes through the train wall, it crosses a threshold outside of the contained safety and internally stabilised systems of Snowpiercer, with its carefully balanced ecosystems, subroutines and social hierarchies. It moves outside the established *nomos* into the raw environment against which Snowpiercer – as the device by which the last remnants of humanity maintain their post-apocalyptic survival – defines itself. Part of the subject moves beyond the order of law, of the corporate jurisdiction of Wilford Industries, and is temporarily released from its sociopolitical confines. Its theatrical presence is suspended, its mask removed, and in this process it is transformed from subject to 'beyond'.[45] The limb, in its exposure outside the train, collects the qualities of the frozen abyss of the non-human planet: it turns from living flesh, from animated subject, to cold, dead ice. The limb is expunged from the social order, transmuted to absence. This absent limb is then returned within the order of the train – a little bit of the outside is brought inside. Ice and cold cling to the flesh of the subject as the absent beyond that grounds the social order is revealed on stage, performing not only the spectacle of direct divine violence upon the body of the subject but also the separation of the subject from the divine beyond. Now sanctified in ice, the limb cannot remain attached to the subject, and is smashed – rendered as meat, flesh and remnants of bare life cast outside the social order, yet held within it as the flesh is within the train.

This process represents a technical emblematising of the normative foundations of the social and political order, of the staging of the 'zero function' from which the authority and legitimate presence of the Engine Eternal is derived. In Pierre Legendre's formula, it is the '*emblematization of Nothing*'.[46] Emblem, derived from the Greek *emballo*, meaning to 'throw inside', is the function that '*throws signs inside*'; it is 'the operation of insertion' whereby the absent beyond enters the social and political order of representation that is contingent upon it.[47] As Ruth states at the start of the punishment ritual, 'Snowpiercer is all that's left of the world'.[48] Yet the limb nevertheless protrudes beyond Snowpiercer, into *somewhere*. By bringing the trace of the outside through the train wall, the frozen arm becomes an emblem that stages the ultimate source of Wilford's authority: the absent beyond, outside the order of representation, the space beyond the limit of the world – the enigmatic other that exists as the absolute negativity against which the symbolic

45 Goodrich (2012).
46 Legendre (2019), p 117, emphasis in original.
47 Legendre (2019), p 117, emphasis in original.
48 Miller (2020) 'Prepare to Brace'.

presence of Wilford and the normative order of the train defines itself. Or, in practical terms, the ultimate threat of extinction that Wilford Industries continues to save humanity from by providing and maintaining Snowpiercer itself. This outside is 'thrown inside' the train, made manifest in the presence of a frozen limb. The signs are cast, read as an augury of Wilford's divine presence, of the absolute absence that underpins the authority of his normative hierarchy. Just as in trial by ordeal, whereby limbs or other body parts were subject to injury and then left to heal or fester, with the result being read as an augury of a divine will as to the respective innocence or guilt of the subject,[49] here somatic injury is rendered as a more fundamental divination tool that *reveals* – in the Legendrean sense of masking, veiling or showing by hiding[50] – the bare presence of something beyond that animates and structures the bureaucratic order aboard the train.

It is significant that this scene of arm-taking is cinematically blended with the sentencing to suspension in the 'drawers' of a number of rebel Tailies. The 'insertion' of the arm into the hole in the train matches the 'insertion' of the body into the drawers. The sound that accompanies both is similar: the dragging of something through a hole or rail for which it is fitted, up to a certain limit point (the metallic cuff attached to the arm, the front of the drawer). Both are mechanisms of 'freezing' – the arm by the ice outside, the drawers by an artificial process that moves the person into suspended animation. Both are also forms of punishment performed in the name of, or upon the authorisation of, the absent sovereign Mr Wilford. Each ritual claims and performs the authority of Wilford Industries, thus functioning as a jurisdictional technique that marks the relation of the body to law through its exclusion. Yet in doing so, the outside of the subject is pushed into its 'inside', as *part of* the *nomos*. A very particular form of legality is being played out here: the Tailies are punished as those outside the law. This is in stark contrast to the trial of 'LJ' (Lila Junior, played by Annalise Basso) for the murder Layton is called upon to investigate, which reveals an underlying rule book and legality that govern the train and allow Third Class to petition on matters of jurisprudence, enabling a jury made up of representatives of all classes to be constituted. Or the later punishment of 'traitors' that requires a declaration of legality: 'you have been found guilty of treason and are hereby sentenced to death by lung of ice' (a punishment that also draws on the ultimate outside, inserting it into the penalised body of the subject). The words

49 See, for some discussion on the potential accuracy of these ordeals that sought to invoke a form of divine justice, Leeson (2012).

50 See Legendre (2019), pp 117, 101. Legendre notes that 'reveal' is a compound of *res* (thing) and *velare* (to veil or hide), and thus to reveal is to veil or hide the thing shown – to mask its absent form with something perceptible.

spoken of those being placed in the drawers instead classify the 'Tailies' as 'unticketed passengers':

> Mr Wilford has found you guilty of insurrection, murder and disturbing the order of the train. As stowaways you have no right to trial or the established guilt process ... it is only by the largesse and mercy of our engine eternal that you have been allowed to live thus far. So by the authority of Wilford Industries you are hereby sentenced to indefinite suspension in the drawers. May God have mercy on your spark.[51]

The standard of modern legality is upheld – an understanding of the rule of law, the right to a trial and process for the establishment of guilt – while those being punished are specifically *excluded* from it.

The parallelling of the spectacle of punishment in the taking of an arm and the more hidden process of suspension in the drawers could be seen as figuring the Foucauldian transformation of the spectacle of medieval punishment to the disciplinary supervision of the Panopticon.[52] The punishment in the drawers, however, more specifically references the bureaucracy of the 'file':[53] modern law's bureaucratic foundation that encompasses the rendering and reducing of the subject to a legal file stored in the drawers of filing cabinets. On Snowpiercer, it is not simply the 'subject', but the body itself, that is filed within a drawer and placed in suspended animation until they are withdrawn and revived. In Episode 6, the discussion of the purpose of the drawers is aligned directly with the 'file' that is kept on every passenger aboard Snowpiercer, which also includes a specific mark suspected to be a categorisation of 'enemies of the state'.[54] The doctor who is helping Layton after he is released from the drawers explains that there is not a single carriage of drawers but a dozen of them: 'Full of drawers. Hundreds of them'. When asked 'What for?' she replies: 'Mass incarceration. Human experiments. Extra-judicial imprisonment. It's our own little North Korea tucked away in Second Class'. Later Cavill tells Layton that the drawers are 'not a prison. They're a lifeboat ... If the social order collapses, if resources fail, if mechanics fail our best hope is to keep life in suspension, to keep people in stasis while we ride out this freeze'. Layton's response is a standard outrage regarding such a biopolitical experiment: 'You decide who lives and who dies'. Cavill responds, 'No, we all made that choice when we boarded this train and we left people behind'.

The need to support and sustain the train, to police the boundaries of its social order, is articulated as a biopolitical choice about the sustaining of

51 Miller (2020) 'Prepare to Brace'.
52 Foucault (1991).
53 Vismann (2008).
54 Shaver (2020) 'Trouble Comes Sideways'.

life against those who have been chosen to die. What is revealed, however, is the form of modern legality – epitomised not simply by the rule of law but by the cultural 'technique' of the file – that is literalised by the subjecthood of the individuals being excluded from law in the bureaucratic and mundane process of suspension. The subject placed in the drawers is de-animated – although not irrevocably – in what appears to be a purely internal process. But in the drawers, these subjects are taken off stage, placed outside the normative order. And their absence is held deep within the social and political order: the outside they now inhabit is thrown deep within the bureaucratic techniques of sovereign order. Their emblematic quality is less spectacular than the ritual of the taking of arms, but it is no less radical, and it encodes the effectiveness of Wilford's capacity to decide, in his absence, who is allowed to exist on his train, and on what terms.

Jurisprudents of the future

The allusions to show tribunals and declarations of treason against the train again align with the narrative's general reference to the French Revolution, but the show's subtext is explicitly ecological. Yet, in the context of potential political or technological responses to the climate crisis, the work of the imagination in *Snowpiercer* seems to run aground in terms of the reimagining of legality. As a series, it takes up various science fiction tropes: a post-apocalyptic existence brought about by the climate crisis; the last remnants of humanity surviving with a distinct and over-emphasised class structure; a self-contained and self-sufficient community that hangs in a perilous balance; and the prevalence of a corporate governing body. Significant in this regard is the way our apocalyptic imaginary turns not to the state form, which appears to have failed both in the protection of its citizens and its simple ability to endure, but rather to the 'private' body of the corporation. Yet in the projection of a future community, the legal imaginary retains a particular vision of institutional state law: criminal investigations, trials by jury, a procedural determination of guilt or innocence, the articulation of authority subordinated to a rule of law and a literalisation of the 'file' as juridical technique. Science fiction would thus appear to present the failures and critiques of the contemporary state, and thus revert to the private body of the corporation, while at the same time presenting a *continuity* with modern accounts of legality. After the end of the world and the failure of the state, the law that remains is one of corporate authority and process.

This would seem to run counter to the claim of the 'jurisprudence of the future': that science fiction is able to provide a means of thinking up new or future forms of law. The problem we see manifested in *Snowpiercer* is that it tends not to. Part of this is linked to the challenge of thinking something new. Science fiction is often presented as speculative, supposedly free from aspects of the 'real world' and not bound or restricted by its current conditions. However, this misses the way that, as a cultural product and act of imagination, science fiction remains bound by the conditions of its production – as does law. Rather than progressing or envisioning something that is substantially 'new', science fiction is engaged in what Darko Suvin describes as a process of 'cognitive estrangement'.[55] This is not a form of escapism from the world; instead, it is a critical 'reflecting *of* but also *on* reality'.[56] What is crucial about science fiction's reflection upon law is not so much its inability to imagine new forms of law, but its 'making strange' of the supposedly secular discourse of modern law, in the process enabling us to see its dominant tropes of the (western) theo-politico-legal mythos.[57]

Does this mean science fiction is unhelpful in thinking through the jurisprudence necessary for the present future or future present? Only if we think of science fiction as a mechanism of escape. Certain critiques of political theology may involve this desire to stop the machine and escape into something new but, as Goodrich notes, the desire to say, 'Let's exit', 'New words must be devised' or 'Time to escape' is 'simply … escapist'.[58] Instead of this escapist fantasy, what is needed is 'a scholarship that addresses – directly examines the clothes of – the theatrics that we currently inhabit'.[59] To recognise and analyse

> the machinery of emblematization … that most directly depict[s] how the symbolic operates and how the political apparatus runs. As with any functioning machine, it is dubious to treat it as junk, better to take it apart, piece by piece, frame by frame to see what can be used, what jettisoned, how to improve on the show.[60]

The reflection on (corporate) legality examined in this chapter seeks to engage in such a process, using a science fiction text that does not reimagine the law, but literalises the metaphors of modern legality – the taking of arms, the filing of the legal subject – and, in doing so, renders visible the processes of emblematisation that sustain corporate power.

What we need is to seek not new forms of legality, but new ways of inhabiting the legal apparatus within which we already operate. This requires an acknowledgement of both the obligation to be complicit in our legal forms, and that it is incumbent on the office of jurisprudent to be responsible for

55 Suvin (1979), pp 3–4, 7–10.
56 Suvin (1979), p 10.
57 Peters (2022). On the potential reimaginings of western sovereignty in the Anthropocene, see Matthews (2021).
58 Goodrich (2012), p 67.
59 Goodrich (2012), p 67.
60 Goodrich (2012), p 67.

their care.[61] It is significant that in the graphic novel upon which the series is based, the driver of the train describes it as both a machine that is self-sufficient – not requiring the intervention of humans – and, at the same time, 'like humans … she needs something else to thrive: a presence … a few words … she needs to … to feel *inhabited*'.[62] It is to this process of inhabiting – whether it be of legal forms, corporate authority or other structures of power – that we are required to attend as jurisprudents of the future.

Acknowledgements

Thanks to Kieran Tranter for his support for this research, as well as to the anonymous reviewer for their useful feedback. This research was partially supported by the Australian Government through the Australian Research Council's Discovery Early Career Researcher Award funding scheme (project DE200100881).

References

Giorgio Agamben (1998) *Homo Sacer: Sovereign Power and Bare Life*, Stanford University Press.

Giorgio Agamben (2011) *The Kingdom and the Glory: For a Theological Genealogy of Economy and Government*, Stanford University Press.

Elizabeth Anderson (2017) *Private Government: How Employers Rule Our Lives (and Why We Don't Talk about It)*, Princeton University Press.

Grietje Baars (2019) *The Corporation, Law and Capitalism A Radical Perspective on the Role of Law in the Global Political Economy*, Brill.

Joshua Barkan (2013) *Corporate Sovereignty: Law and Government Under Capitalism*, University of Minnesota Press.

Margaret M Blair (2013) 'Corporate Personhood and the Corporate Persona' *2013 University of Illinois Law Review* , 785.

Oliver Bocquet and Jean-Marc Rochette (2020) *Snowpiercer Vol 3: Terminus*, Titan Comics.

Osvaldo Cavallar, Susanne Degenring and Julius Kirshner (1994) *A Grammar of Signs: Bartolo De Sassoferrato's Tract on Insignia and Coats of Arms*, Robins Collection.

Robert Cover (1983) 'Foreword: *Nomos* and Narrative' 97 *Harvard Law Review* 4.

Shaunnaugh Dorsett and Shaun McVeigh (2012) *Jurisdiction*, Routledge.

Michel Foucault (1991) *Discipline and Punish: The Birth of the Prison*, Penguin.

Thomas Giddens (2023) 'The Office of Law Teacher' in Luca Siliquini-Cinelli and Thomas Giddens (eds), *Biopolitics and Structure in Legal Education*, Routledge 9–24.

61 Giddens (2023); McVeigh (2016).
62 Lob and Rochette (2020), p 108.

Peter Goodrich (1990) *Languages of Law: From Logics of Memory to Nomadic Masks*, Weidenfeld and Nicholson.

Peter Goodrich (2012) 'The Theatre of Emblems: On the Optical Apparatus and the Investiture of Persons' 8 *Law, Culture and the Humanities* 47.

Peter Goodrich (2014) *Legal Emblems and the Art of Law: Obiter Depicta as the Vision of Governance*, Cambridge University Press.

Ross Grantham (2001) 'Attributing Responsibility to Corporate Entities: A Doctrinal Approach' 19 *Company and Securities Law Journal* 168.

James Hawes (2020) 'First, the Weather Changed' *Snowpiercer* Season 1, Episode 1 (TNT, United States, 17 May).

Victoria Kahn (2009) 'Political Theology and Fiction in *The King's Two Bodies*' 106 *Representations* 77.

Ernst Kantorowicz (2016) *The King's Two Bodies*, Princeton University Press.

Peter T Leeson (2012) 'Ordeals' 55 *Journal of Law and Economics* 691.

Claude Lefort (1988) 'The Permanence of the Theologico-Political?' in David Macey (ed), *Democracy and Political Theory*, Polity Press, 213.

Pierre Legendre (2019) *God in the Mirror: A Study of the Institution of Images: Lessons III*, Routledge.

Benjamin Legrand and Jean-Marc Rochette (2020) *Snowpiercer Vol 2: The Explorers*, Titan Comics.

Jacques Lob and Jean-Marc Rochette (2020) *Snowpiercer Vol 1: The Escape*, Titan Comics.

Celia Lury (2004) *Brands: The Logos of the Global Economy*, Routledge.

Vladislav Maksimov (2020) 'Politicization of Life and Auto-Thanatopolitics in *V for Vendetta*' in Thomas Giddens (ed), Critical Directions in Comics Studies, University Press of Mississippi 195–214.

Desmond Manderson (2019) *Danse Macabre: Temporalities of Law in the Visual Arts*, Cambridge University Press.

Louis Marin (1988) *Portrait of the King*, Macmillan.

Daniel Matthews (2021) *Earthbound: The Aesthetics of Sovereignty in the Anthropocene*, Edinburgh University Press.

Shaun McVeigh (2016) 'Jurisprudent of London: Arts of Association' 20 *Law Text Culture* 189.

Sam Miller (2020) 'Prepare to Brace' *Snowpiercer* Season 1, Episode 1 (TNT, United States, 24 May).

Connal Parsley (2010) 'The Mask and Agamben: The Transitional Juridical Technics of Legal Relation' 14 *Law Text Culture* 12.

Timothy D Peters (2017) 'I, Corpenstein: Mythic, Metaphorical and Visual Renderings of the Corporate Form in Comics and Film' 30 *International Journal for the Semiotics of Law* 427.

Timothy D Peters (2018) 'Corporations, Sovereignty and the Religion of Neoliberalism' 29 *Law and Critique* 271.

Timothy D Peters (2022) *A Theological Jurisprudence of Speculative Cinema: Superheroes, Science Fictions and Fantasies of Modern Law*, Edinburgh University Press.

Timothy D Peters (2024) 'Corporate Office, Corporate Irresponsibility and the Constitutive Vicariousness of Corproate Power' in Penny Crofts (eds) *Evil Corporations: Law, Culpability and Regulation*, Routledge 141–158.

Clair Quentin (2020) 'Corporations, Comity and the "Revenue Rule": A Jurisprudence of Offshore' 8 *London Review of International Law* 399.

Carl Schmitt (2005) *Political Theology: Four Chapters on the Concept of Sovereignty*, University of Chicago Press.

Helen Shaver 'Trouble Comes Sideways' (2020) *Snowpiercer* Season 1, Episode 6 (TNT, United States, 21 June).

Darko Suvin (1979) *Metamorphoses of Science Fiction: On the Poetics and History of a Literary Genre*, Yale University Press.

Miguel Vatter (2021) *Divine Democracy: Political Theology after Carl Schmitt*, Oxford University Press.

Cornelia Vismann (2008) *Files: Law and Media Technology*, Stanford University Press.

Chapter 14

The spatio-legality of corporate sovereignty in AppleTV+'s *Severance*

Dhiraj Nainani

Introduction

In 2022, the streaming service AppleTV+ released *Severance*, produced by Ben Stiller and starring the likes of Adam Scott, Patricia Arquette, John Turturro and Christopher Walken. The show's premise is an arresting one, following a group of employees working at a mysterious multinational and monolithic corporation known as Lumon Industries. Yet these specific employees are different from the many others who work at Lumon because they have opted to be 'severed', undergoing an operation that renders their work memories and personalities completely separate and distinct from the rest of them, thereby creating literal double lives.[1]

The show was an almost instant critical success, and viewership figures were favourable enough to warrant Apple renewing the show for a second season. Reviews of the show highlighted how its surreal take on the 'work–life balance' was both horrific and hilarious at the same time, particularly in terms of its release during an ongoing global pandemic, where debates over working from home and 'quiet quitting' had given rise to a socioeconomic trend termed the 'Great Resignation'.[2]

However, perhaps what is most intriguing – and arguably quite underdiscussed in mainstream news coverage – is what *Severance* had to say about corporations and the law. A great deal has already been written about the legal personhood that has been afforded to such corporations,[3] which has in no small way granted those helming them the opportunity to pursue profit by engaging in activities ranging from tax evasion,[4] environmental degradation[5] and blatant human rights violations[6] with much impunity. *Severance*,

1 At the time of this writing, a second season of the show is due for release in January 2026.
2 Formica and Sfodera (2022).
3 See, for example, Kurki (2019); Johnson (2012); Tucker (2010); Pollman (2011); Blair (2013).
4 Benshalom (2014).
5 Pearce and Tombs (1998).
6 Karunanathan (2019)

DOI: 10.4324/9781003412274-17

however, focused on how corporate legal personhood might be misused against its very own employees, by exploring various material and normative forms of surveillance and control that are legally codified and embedded into Lumon's corporate fabric.

Yet the show is less of a fictional *exploration* of corporate power over its employees than it is a *reflection* of it. And it is a canny reflection at that because, while its focus on office workers initially tends to suggest a satire of existing white-collar surveillance practices such as email and search history monitoring, or timekeeping through webcams and fingerprint scanners,[7] the lives of the severed workers at Lumon arguably parallel a more specific group of workers in a disconcertingly accurate way: Amazon warehouse employees.

Over the past decade, the rise of Amazon as an economic superpower unto itself has also witnessed a concordant increase in its cheerfully named fulfilment centres being the site of numerous legal battles globally. Instances of threats against unionisation, sanctions against bathroom breaks, failures to safeguard employee health during natural disasters and the imposition of wearable surveillance technology have all served to highlight how corporations can exert an astonishing degree of spatial and legal power in distinctly material and normative ways. Lumon, although portrayed as a spectre of our possible near future, is actually one that is built on current injustices.

This chapter takes as its starting point an invitation to explore how science fiction 'provides a space for considering new and necessary forms of legality and justice'.[8] In demonstrating the futuristic possibilities of corporate sovereignty, *Severance* also mirrors its alarming present by exploring how the 'corporate code' serves as a distinct form of legal ordering that is used to discipline, regulate and govern bodies occupying corporate space. In using the theoretical works of Michel Foucault (on power) and Hans Lindahl (on legal orders) to 'read' the show alongside numerous examples of the Amazon warehouse, the chapter aims to demonstrate how Lumon's near-future corporate jurisprudence mimics the injustices of Amazon's present.

The first section sets out a brief history of American corporate personhood and how this has contributed to the rise of Amazon before delving into a synopsis of the show and how exploring it aligns well with other investigations of science fiction and the law. The chapter then sets out the relevant theoretical aspects of Foucault's and Lindahl's work, focusing on how diverse concepts such as *heterotopias*, *biopower*, *ought-places* and *faultlines* are distinctly spatial and legal in their essence.

It goes on to examine how the corporate sovereigns of Lumon and Amazon employ a variety of normative and material devices to spatio-legally manipulate and control employees by: (1) placing their bodies within a broader

7 Morgan and Nolan (2023).
8 Green et al (2022), p 2.

algorithmic assemblage, or *corporate body*; (2) exposing them to a variety of regulatory objects – or *corporate goods* – in their everyday work; and (3) rendering them susceptible to the unique spatial impositions and demands of *corporate property*. Finally, the chapter sets out how corporate sovereign power is enshrined in the *corporate code*, which is expressed through various human (eg board members, founders) and non-human (eg manuals, websites) legal agents.

Corporate histories

The notion of the corporation as a sovereign entity is not a new one. The East India Company was the precursor to the British Empire and carried out many functions related to statehood for more than a century, claiming jurisdiction over several territories and engaging with functions of governance such as collecting tax, developing public health systems and even engaging in warfare.[9] Recent archival scholarship suggests that this sovereign authority gradually shifted from being something granted by parliament to a 'self-professed right',[10] thereby demonstrating the fluidic and unfixed nature of corporate personhood.

Almost two centuries after the East India Company's dissolution, and with the notion of sovereignty seemingly relegated to states, the US Supreme Court would issue two landmark rulings that would further the legal personhood of corporations. It must be said that these decisions did not occur in a vacuum: the history of corporate personhood in the United States had begun as early as 1886, albeit under highly dubious circumstances.[11] However, the cases of *Citizens United* (2010)[12] and *Hobby Lobby* (2014)[13] marked an 'expansion of corporate rights and [the] narrowing of liability or access to justice against corporate defendants'.[14] Corporations were described as an 'association of citizens' functioning within a 'corporate democracy', and now had expanded speech rights and religious liberties. A few years later, the American food giants Nestlé and Cargill would be able to avoid prosecution under the Alien Tort Statute (ATS) for aiding and abetting human trafficking in the Ivory Coast by claiming that these offences had happened in entirely different jurisdictions altogether and were therefore outside the jurisdiction of the court – a legal claim that no individual has ever managed to make under the ATS.

9 Stern (2011).
10 Srivastava (2022), p 690.
11 Torres-Spelliscy (2014).
12 *Citizens United v Federal Election Commission* (2010) 558 U.S. 310.
13 *Burwell v Hobby Lobby Stores, Inc* (2014) 573 U.S. 682.
14 Pollman (2021), p 221.

This expansion of corporate rights has coincided neatly with the rise of corporate giants, of which Amazon – dubbed the 'everything store'[15] for offering thousands of products at unbelievably low prices – has managed to flourish. Its founder, Jeff Bezos, was labelled as the world's first prospective trillionaire off the back of the company's earnings during the COVID-19 pandemic.[16] Yet this has also come at a time when Amazon has faced a plethora of legal challenges brought on by disgruntled employees, both in America and across the world.

This has been particularly prevalent in relation to warehouse staff. Most warehouse workers can be classified as *stowers* (who put items on shelves and mark the location on a computer) and *pickers* (who pick up required items from said shelves), respectively. Although Amazon has repeatedly expressed its desire to make warehouses increasingly autonomous, humans currently make up the frontline workforce. They have protested and raised concerns about unsafe working conditions,[17] being prevented from taking bathroom breaks,[18] workplace surveillance,[19] unlawful dismissal or wrongful termination,[20] high turnover rates[21] and racial discrimination.[22] The past two years have also seen a concentrated rise in attempts at unionisation in warehouses, leading to a protracted and attritional fight between warehouse workers and the corporation, with its access to high-profile and expensive lawyers and anti-union consultants, and its ability to ceaselessly challenge labour laws – thereby delaying unionisation processes.[23]

Severance, while focusing on office workers, has as much to do with corporate might as it does to do with unionisation, albeit in different ways. The series begins with employees Mark S, Irving B and Dylan G discovering that their colleague and friend Peter 'Petey' K has unexpectedly been replaced by a new employee, Helly R (the Kafkaesque shortening of surnames employed by the workplace 'innies', as they are called, is just one indicator of how they are markedly different from their 'outies'). Helly R is horrified at being made to live eight hours a day trapped in a subterranean cubicle while another version of her gets to experience the fullness of life. Her attempts to break free of the system galvanise the others to explore what lies beyond their comfortably myopic existences, ultimately leading to an attempt at being 'woken up' outside – thereby overriding, albeit briefly, their alternate personalities.

15 Stone (2013).
16 Nichols (2021).
17 Sainato (2020).
18 Jordan and Conway (2023).
19 McIntyre and Bradbury (2022).
20 Weise (2022).
21 Leonhardt (2021).
22 Del Rey (2021).
23 Sainato (2023).

As Travis (2011) suggests, science fiction offers a useful critique of law and society as it currently stands, and in its rich and fertile imaginings offers a window into both the emancipatory and the troubling paths the law can take in the future. Focusing on the comparative spatio-legalities of two corporate sovereigns reveals the extent of their present *and* future power over the human body. Therefore, in studying both corporations through a critical legal perspective – one that looks as much as the 'where' of the law as the 'how' of it – in order to understand how the imagined sovereign legalities of *Severance* match those of Amazon's present reality, this chapter aims to add to a rich canon of work on law and science fiction,[24] especially regarding corporations.[25]

Corporate power

Although neither Foucault nor Lindahl focuses on corporations specifically, their work speaks to power, law and spatiality in different yet interconnected ways. Drawing upon certain conceptualisations from both works therefore helps to provide a framework with which to understand the material and normative forms of power that corporations are capable of exercising on their own employees within *and* beyond the confines of company space.

Perhaps Foucault's most explicit discussion of space concerns the *heterotopia*, although he does not elaborate upon this idea beyond a singular essay.[26] To Foucault, utopian sites or spaces 'present society … in a perfected form, or else society turned upside down, but in any case … are fundamentally unreal places'.[27] In other words, they are ideas meant to represent perfection – in works of philosophy or fiction or speculative architecture, for example – but in reality are unachievable. Heterotopic spaces, on the other hand, are those where 'all the other real sites that can be found within the culture, are simultaneously represented, contested, and inverted'.[28] Heterotopic space is therefore a space that is relational and juxtaposes what is around it; it is a site that represents incompatible spaces and uncovers their paradoxes. Foucault uses the analogy of a mirror to explain his point: although the image seen within does not exist (a utopia), the mirror itself shapes the way the image is seen at all (a heterotopia). Therefore, 'crisis heterotopias' (for example) can be boarding schools or honeymoon suites, where people come of age but do so out of sight.

24 See, for example, MacNeil (2007); Peters (2022); Tranter (2018).
25 See, for example, Mueller (2020); Ghachem (2016); Crofts (2022); Sollazzo (2017).
26 Foucault (1984).
27 Foucault (1984), p 3.
28 Foucault (1984), p 4.

Yet if corporate space can be said to be heterotopic – in that it distorts and fractures a utopian ideal of commerce and capitalism – it can also be a site where Foucauldian forms of power are enacted upon. Power, to Foucault, is by no means solely exercisable by the state; nor does the development of certain forms of power replace the existing ones they are built upon. The modern corporation is therefore able to deploy sovereign, juridical and disciplinary power, but seemingly does so within the biopolitical maxim of 'making live and letting die'[29] in a bid to ensure that its subjects (that is, employees) remain productive and healthy. This biopolitical manipulation of space involves utilising a *dispositif* ('apparatus', or assemblage) of security, made up of a series of institutions, agents, objects and spaces that can be used to secure the *milieu* (here, corporate space) from undesirable 'circulations'.[30] Such circulations may be in the form of individuals or groups, technologies, capital flows or even ideas. Yet they must be guarded against to ensure that state (or corporate) space can guard against any and all 'abnormal elements' that threaten the social body.[31]

Lindahl also talks about a *right of inclusion and exclusion*, which is a normative claim that is most obviously deployed by states to 'determine which aliens may enter, remain in, or be expelled from'[32] state space. However, Lindahl states that this normative act of spatial including and excluding undesirable or unwanted bodies can be found throughout all spaces, such as restaurants denying entry to certain diners.

All legal orders therefore contain within them the ability to spatially striate in order to demarcate and protect what Lindahl terms *ought-places*. Each ought-place is formed by 'spatial boundaries [that] separate it from and join it to certain other ought-places'.[33] At the same time, an ought-place can fulfil many functions; a corporation could be considered an ought-place of trade, but also a site of power.

What, then, constitutes a legal order? To Lindahl, all legal orders have *boundaries*, which are legal norms that regulate human behaviours by imposing spatial limits upon them. Yet they also possess *limits*, in that there are certain actions or behaviours that they simply cannot regulate. Although most behaviours within a legal order can be classified as either legal or illegal, there are certain acts that are hard to place in either classification. When such acts occur, they reveal the limits of the legal order, and create a *faultline* that

29 Foucault (2004).
30 Foucault (2007).
31 Foucault (1990).
32 Lindahl (2009), p 13.
33 Lindahl (2013), p 32.

challenges 'how a concrete legal collective draws the limit between legal (dis) order and the unordered'.[34]

To Lindahl, these acts are *a-legal* because they are inherently *strange* – they do not fit within the rubric of what is or is not permissible, and so reveal a void in the legal order by their very existence. This in turn demonstrates that legal orders are made of norms that are malleable (eg a corporate code), are deliberately engineered to hierarchise certain ways of social life at the expense of others (eg a corporate culture) and are decided upon by a collective that is formed by including some and excluding others (eg a corporate board). And it is to guard against these strange irruptions that legal orders may turn increasingly dystopian or downright authoritarian. For example, when working from home threatens the existing spatial conditions of a corporate legal order, novel forms of workplace surveillance may need to be deployed as the legal order is forced to rearrange itself to negate strangeness.

Becoming in/corporate

Having mapped out the theoretical lens that will inform how Lumon and Amazon are 'read' through space, power and law, I turn now to the distinct ways in which corporate power is exerted upon its workers, akin to state power upon its subjects. Drawing from *Severance* as well as news reports on Amazon (especially those concerning lawsuits against them), three distinct forms of spatio-legal control and regulation can be traced: (1) how, while being part of the *corporate bodily* assemblage, individual employee bodies are rendered disposable and discardable; (2) how both Lumon and Amazon deploy a range of *corporate goods* – ranging from mundane devices such as barcode scanners to 'innovative' products such as trackable wristbands – to ensure that their employees remain disciplined yet productive; and (3) how the spatial contours of the corporate workplace are used to exert power over employees, at times to the point of bodily harm.

The corporate body

In the opening scene of *Severance*, new employee Helly R (Britt Lower) awakes on top of a large table in a corporate boardroom, and after a period of disorientation is asked several questions that she ought to know the answer to, such as who she is and where she was born. Realising that she cannot answer these simple questions only gives rise to more hysteria. When her questioner Mark S (Adam Scott) tries to assure her that she is safe, she replies: 'Am I livestock? … Like, did you grow me as food and that's why I

34 Lindahl (2013), p 158.

have no memories?'[35] Later on, it is revealed that Mark S is himself concerned about Helly R's sudden arrival, having been informed earlier that morning that his colleague and friend Peter 'Petey' K (Yul Vazquez) has abruptly left the company. When Mark S inquires why this has occurred, he is told that non-disclosure agreements prevent him from finding out.

Helly R's question of being reduced to something as vulnerable and disposable as livestock, as well as Mark S's deliberate obfuscation about Petey's departure, speaks to similar concerns raised by Amazon warehouse employees about their precarity. In an in-depth investigation on Amazon's 'employment machine', the *New York Times* uncovered that, 'Amazon's model for managing people – heavily reliant on metrics, apps and chatbots – was uneven and strained even before the coronavirus arrived, with employees often having to act as their own caseworkers'.[36] The investigation revealed that Amazon's warehouse employee management system, reliant on technological systems made up of apps and algorithms, offered no respite or means of redress for employees who had been automatically terminated after applying for leave, and tasked employees with mandatory overtime after they had been instructed to take as much unpaid overtime as needed. Reliant on Amazon's health benefits packages, employees found themselves stranded in the middle of a pandemic, unemployed and susceptible to disease. It is therefore unsurprising that the turnover rate for warehouse workers has remained astronomically high.[37]

At the same time, Amazon has faced challenges regarding how it treats certain marginalised groups *within* the warehouse worker population. For example, a 2021 lawsuit filed by a former Black female employee suggests a pattern of racially motivated promotion practices favouring white men in particular, as well as the use of racial tropes when describing Black employees.[38] Although Amazon press releases expressed support for the Black Lives Matter movement in 2020, a substantial disparity has been noted between the proportion of warehouse workers (25 per cent) and members of the executive leadership team (3.5 per cent) who are people of colour.

However, *Severance* skews this marginalisation through the character of Mr Seth Milchick (Tramell Tillman), a young Black man who is in essence the seemingly benign yet threatening face of corporate surveillance. Milchick tries to keep Mark S and his teammates in line with a balance of rewards and threats, such as by taking cheerful photographs of them as they celebrate

35 Stiller (2022) 'Good News About Hell'.
36 Villegas (2021).
37 Sainato (2021).
38 Associated Press (2021).

office milestones or even undergo their severance procedures,[39] disciplining them for a number of violations by taking them to the Break Room[40] and constantly patrolling the severed floor of Lumon (or, alternatively, monitoring employee movements on camera feeds).

Furthermore, whether it is Mark S and his team in *Severance* or the many who have been wrongfully fired or undercompensated through the Amazon employment machine, attempts at breaking free of this disposability and precarity are daunting and yield precious little. In the penultimate episode of *Severance*, for example, Mark S and his teammates decide to finally rebel against the temporal boundaries placed upon their lives by breaking into the security office of the severed floor and activating the 'Overtime Contingency' protocol, reserved for when severed employees have to be 'woken up' outside the office. However, this endeavour entails one of their own staying behind, as the contingency can only work through the simultaneous pushing of two dials located on either side of a wall. Dylan G (Zach Cherry) volunteers and remains contorted in pain and agony for what seems like hours.[41]

This attempt at a bodily reunion is different to that faced by Amazon warehouse employees, whose concentrated efforts at forming staff unions globally have resulted in precisely one major victory in New York. Chris Smalls, an employee who was fired the same day he walked out in protest over warehouse working conditions during the pandemic in 2020, was able to lead a successful attempt at unionisation at his fulfilment centre in 2022, thereby overcoming Amazon's multi-million dollar attempt at anti-unionisation. Amazon hired consultants to deliver 'anti-union messages to Amazon employees ... [and] even had Smalls and other organizers arrested for trespassing while they were delivering food and union materials to the warehouse parking lot'.[42] A year after this victory, Amazon has yet to begin bargaining with the union and has stringently opposed other warehouse unionisation attempts,[43] and has even sought a union re-election.[44]

Unable to fully escape from being bound to the corporate bodily assemblage – yet individually marginalised and discardable – Lumon's severed staff and Amazon's warehouse workers are the subjects of a modern, biopolitical iteration of sovereign power. Although, to Foucault, this means that the 'power of death that symbolized sovereign power [is] now carefully supplanted by the administration of bodies and the calculated management of life',[45] this is done to ensure that bodies remain economically productive. At

39 Stiller (2022) 'Half Loop'.
40 More on this below.
41 Stiller (2022) 'The We We Are'.
42 Oladipo (2022).
43 Sainato (2023).
44 Hadero (2022).
45 Foucault (1990), p 140.

the same time, if the 'right of sovereignty was the right to take life or let live … then this new right is established: the right to make live and to let die'.[46]

Yet this biopolitical right to letting certain lives flourish while others wither and die can, in the twenty-first century, be seen as a process of algorithmic management, where digital technologies and the accumulation of data can be used to create and maintain an 'employment machine' unto itself, removing the human element from the biopolitical demands of constantly regulating (certain kinds of) life.[47] It is with the advent of algorithmic management that Petey – escaped from Lumon and disoriented from trying to 're-integrate' his different selves – is ultimately left to collapse and die in front of a convenience store. His last words, muttered in a state of delusion where he imagines facing a Lumon vending machine, can be equally ascribable to those many Amazon workers left deprived of health benefits during a deadly pandemic: 'I don't have any tokens … I can't eat without any tokens'.[48]

Corporate goods

The tokens that Petey wistfully recalls while dying are also emblematic of the range of regulatory goods that corporate sovereigns deploy to further the algorithmic management of their employees. Perhaps the most obvious of these are the various surveillant objects that are bodily embedded or physically attached to employee bodies, such as the microchips that are inserted into severed Lumon employees. Yet, even in death, there is no end to corporate surveillance and bodily violation. After Petey dies, his chip is discreetly but forcibly removed from his brain at his funeral by Ms Cobel (Patricia Arquette),[49] who is Mark S's terrifying and Lumon-obsessed superior on the severed floor (while simultaneously pretending to be his outie Mark Scout's kind and demure neighbour, Mrs Selvig).

Amazon, while not quite reaching into the brains of its employees, has thus far patented (though not yet deployed) two distinctly dystopian objects of their own: a 'worker cage' that is designed to protect individual workers if they enter areas where robot stock-pickers predominantly operate, and a wristband that can direct workers' hands to the right shelves or boxes when preparing warehouse orders, thereby purportedly making them more efficient.[50]

On the other hand, adherence to company protocols and the drive for economic productivity does not need to rely upon such highly technological

46 Foucault (2004), p 241.
47 Walker et al (2021).
48 Stiller (2022) 'In Perpetuity'.
49 McArdle (2022) 'The You You Are'.
50 Spicer (2018).

means. Amazon warehouse workers remain almost umbilically attached to corporate sovereign power through the humble barcode scanner, which is considered an indispensable tool of their job. Such scanners are used to record the position of items on shelves, direct workers where to retrieve them and catalogue item stock levels once they have been picked off shelves to be prepared for an order. Yet these scanners are also used to document how swiftly a worker is picking items, with performance targets set to 15 seconds per item, forcing them to forego bathroom breaks and face incredible exhaustion.[51] Employees therefore 'can't perform their jobs without these technologies, which renders them dependent on the very tools that monitor them'.[52]

Lumon, on the other hand, cloaks its surveillance measures in 1980s- and 1990s-era technology. The computers on which the severed employees work are embedded with modern surveillance cameras but appear boxy and decidedly unmodern, and possess operating systems that hark back to the advent of personal computing. Severed employees are also given passcards that restrict where they can go within the severed floor; when the threat of rebellion begins to arise, Milchick installs electronic gates outside the area belonging to Mark S's department, openable only by certain passcards.[53]

Perhaps the most striking thing about the use of corporate goods to regulate behaviour lies in the work that these sovereign entities ask of their workers. Mark S's team, for example, makes up a department known as 'Macrodata Refinement'. The exact nature of this department is unclear; instead, Refiners are tasked with digitally sorting a series of encrypted numbers into different boxes within a specific time. These numbers are meant to be separated based on the 'emotional response' they elicit from the Refiner, which is why Mark S asks Helly R to focus on 'happy' numbers rather than 'scary' ones after she attempts to take her life in an attempt to quit working at Lumon.[54]

Helly R's initial amusement at being tasked to do such a vague and ridiculous job gradually changes to adherence when she finally gets afraid at seeing certain numbers on her monitor. In a similar vein, news reports have described attempts by Amazon warehouse staff to stave off the monotonous and repetitive nature of their work – filling box after box with a variety of objects that are shelved across cavernous warehouses – by competing against each other to achieve a higher productivity ranking, thus furthering their own self-regulation and bringing their bodies into closer alignment with the robotic ones that surround them.[55]

51 Solon (2018).
52 Delfanti et al (2021), p 4.
53 Stiller (2022) 'Defiant Jazz'.
54 McArdle (2022) 'The Grim Barbarity of Optics and Design'.
55 Scheiber (2019).

Amazon has even developed optional video games involving the same task that can be played on employee workstations, granting the winners points and badges for their victories.[56] Such perks are mirrored in *Severance*, where Dylan G displays an initial fondness for collecting a variety of corporate perks that are granted when specific milestones are hit, which range from Chinese finger traps to prestigious events such as a 'Waffle Party'.

Foucault describes how the advent of disciplinary power is exerted by the modern sovereign upon the capillary points of the social body: the individual. Here, the 'judges of normality are present everywhere … [and] it is on them that the universal reign of the normative is based; and each individual, wherever he may find himself, subjects to it his body'.[57] Lumon and Amazon demonstrate how these judges of normality can be decidedly non-human as well as human, replacing Foucault's timetables and bells with objects that are both highly technological (microchips, wristbands) and seemingly mundane (barcode scanners, computers).

Moreover, the panoptical nature of disciplinary power exposes bodies to constant monitoring and surveillance to the extent that they become self-regulating and self-disciplinary, engaging in behaviour that furthers economic productivity under the guise of gamification. Corporate rewards and perks – regulatory goods unto themselves – grant a veneer of civility even as basic employee rights threaten to be constantly stripped away.

Corporate property

Foucault lists several types of heterotopic spaces that can exist, such as those of crisis, deviation, time, ritual, purification, illusion or compensation. The underlying thread that binds these spaces together, however, is that they emphasise *difference* (be it between spaces, communities, individuals or other things) and serve as escapes from restrictive or authoritarian societies. Yet much of Foucault's work also concerns the spatial enactment of power. The urban milieu, for example, can be controlled to prevent the circulation of undesirable flows (of people, goods, ideas, etc) through a security assemblage comprised of a range of institutions and agents. And although Foucault frequently refers to disease outbreaks as the flashpoints for such widespread urban change,[58] it is clear that *any* perceived threat to the social body – now synonymous with the sovereign body – must be defended against vigourously.

Yet corporate space strips heterotopic space of its emancipatory possibilities and fashions it into something far more sinister. While remaining with Foucault's notion that heterotopic sites can juxtapose several spaces despite

56 Bensinger (2019).
57 Foucault (1995), p 304.
58 See, for example, Foucault (2001, 2007).

being a single site, the shiny glass façade of Lumon headquarters and the concrete vastness of Amazon warehouses seem capable of both emanating and resolving crises, depending on where the mirror is placed. It is perhaps more accurate to label these spaces as heterotopias *within* heterotopias,[59] constantly colliding against each other while apparently being firmly held together by the security apparatus. To that end, corporate power can be found embedded within the materiality of space in three ways.

The first concerns the transformation of the town as an urban space. In *Severance*, Lumon's reach is noticeable both within the company (all the products that are dispensed in vending machines are seemingly made by Lumon, and there is an entire museum to the founder Kier Egan [played by Marc Geller] on the severed floor known as the 'Perpetuity Wing') and beyond it (Mark Scout stays on subsidised company housing resembling a vast stretch of suburbia, but seems to be the only one residing there – apart from gentle Mrs Selvig as his neighbour). The true extent of Lumon's spatial influence is made clear only in the season finale, where it is revealed that the *entire town* is named after Kier (which is situated in a fictional state), begging the question as to how real or simulated anything truly is.

Amazon has changed the notion of the company town as well. The arrival of an Amazon warehouse can change an entire *city* in different ways. Warehouses tend to be housed in industrial areas where land is cheap, but which also tend to abut neighbourhoods that are inhabited predominantly by people of colour, due to uneven pre-existing housing policies that have led to certain areas being populated along socioeconomic and racial lines;[60] in fact, a leaked Amazon memo even proposed to build a 'school-to-Amazon-warehouse pipeline' to attract fresh college graduates from underprivileged communities to warehouse employment.[61] However, these same neighbourhoods – now populated with fulfilment centres – soon find themselves facing increased traffic and higher roadside pollution levels due to the constant presence of delivery trucks. And although the arrival of Amazon in impoverished and struggling towns and cities can initially be considered beneficial in terms of employment, data suggests that the *quality* of jobs is nothing to celebrate, as statistics relating to median income or those living in poverty barely change.[62] Given the algorithmic might of the Amazon employment machine, this is not revelatory.

Within the confines of the severed level or the warehouse floor, the latent materiality of corporate power can be found within the body scanner. In *Severance*, a special lift brings severed employees down to their workplace;

59 Saindon (2010).
60 Waddell and Singh (2021).
61 Del Rey (2022).
62 Semuels (2018).

at some point during this descent, an outie is replaced by its innie, which is marked onscreen by a slight but significant shifting of the camera lens. But in addition to invisibly imposing a specific spatial and temporal boundary upon the employee body, the lifts also serve as capable scanners of contraband items. Helly R is warned about the lifts early, in the following exchange:

Milchick: Fortunately, the elevators are equipped with something called 'code detectors'. So messages can't be passed through.

Mark: Yeah, they're like metal detectors for written symbols. A Lumon original, apparently.[63]

In the 2014 case of *Integrity Staffing Solutions*[64] (and six months after the *Hobby Lobby* judgement), the US Supreme Court unanimously rejected a claim by Amazon warehouse workers to be compensated for time spent undergoing mandatory security screenings at the end of their shifts, claiming it was neither 'integral' nor 'indispensable' to their work. In 2019, a similar challenge concerning compensation for mandatory screenings undertaken during the COVID-19 pandemic under state (and not federal) law was turned down by the Supreme Court.[65] However, in 2021 the Pennsylvania Supreme Court ruled 5–2 in favour of a separate group of Amazon warehouse workers arguing for the same kind of compensation under Pennsylvanian state law, and declared that any time spent on an employer's premises could count as 'hours worked'.[66]

Corporate power can be found at an even more intimate level than that of the town/city or the entrance/exit. The bathroom, for instance, has been a constant focal point in the travails of warehouse employees. In utilising a metric known as 'time off task' (TOT) through data collected from idling periods of handheld scanners, the Amazon employment machine has been able to set benchmarks where workers can be fired if they exceed 120 minutes of TOT in a single day. This means that it is possible to set out the movements of each employee down to the minute, including when they go to the bathroom and how long they spend there. As a result, employees have frequently reported a deep sense of fear of being disciplined or even terminated over bathroom breaks.[67] Meeting target goals at such a cost has also taken a toll on the mental health of employees,[68] although Amazon has still

63 Stiller (2022) 'Half Loop'.
64 *Integrity Staffing Solutions, Inc v Busk* (2014) 574 U.S. 27 (2014)
65 Chung (2019).
66 *Heimbach v Amazon.com* (6th Cir., 2019) No 18-5942.
67 Gurley (2022).
68 Liao (2018).

only faced a US$60,000 fine over unsafe working conditions pertaining to 'low back injuries and other musculoskeletal disorders'.[69]

Fortunately, the severed employees of Lumon find the bathroom to be a site of resistance rather than one of surveillance and repression. It is here that Mark S is given a chance to reorient the mirror and see Lumon as a heterotopia, not of corporate wonder but of securitised capitalism. He does this by stealing a poorly written self-help book from Milchick's desk, unaware that it is actually a present for his outie Mark Scout from his brother-in-law Ricken (Michael Chernus), who left it at his doorstep where it was pilfered by Cobel/Selvig. The book's many aphorisms (eg 'At the centre of industry is [dust]')[70] light the fire of rebellion in Mark S. It is also in the bathroom that Dylan G hides a card stolen from another department (thereby invoking Milchick's frantic use of the Overtime Contingency) and where the awakened Helly R encounters her outie's father – who is revealed to be the current CEO of Lumon, Jame Egan (Michael Siberry). It is the Lumon bathroom, rather than the Amazon warehouse one, where the liberatory potential of a Foucauldian counter-site first takes root.

Corporate code

Having looked at how corporate sovereign power can be normatively exerted upon employee subjects in three ways – bodily, materially and spatially – I return to Lindahl's work on legal ordering to trace the formation of the *corporate code* that forms, strengthens and expands these forms of surveillance and control.

When Mark S learns about Petey's departure and his subsequent promotion as head of Macrodata Refinement, he does so in front of the Board. Represented by a black intercom speaker that is embedded with a camera, the Board of Lumon Industries is never physically seen throughout the show and remains mostly silent, although what emerges from the speaker are eerie staticky sounds that suggest the presence of *something* rather than *someone*. This invisible force forms the collective that determines what behaviour the Lumon corporate code can and cannot allow; in doing so, the collective also excludes the many workers who will be directly affected by this code.

The precarity and disposability of these workers – along with the invisible agents and institutions that form the corporate sovereign – is mirrored in the experiences of Amazon warehouse workers, who recently pushed forward several proposals on worker rights for shareholders to vote on, only to see them all rejected (ostensibly on the basis that 'Amazon's board had

69 OSHA (2023).
70 Stiller (2022) 'Defiant Jazz'.

recommended that its shareholders vote against all resolutions').[71] The members that make up Amazon's board can be found on the company website, and are mostly former CEOs of multinational companies, thereby offering little by way of labour representation.

As Lindahl writes, legal orders are also 'organized as an interconnected distribution of *ought-places*, times, subjects and act-contents'.[72] While the arrival of corporations can give rise to a host of urban effects, *Severance* cleverly demonstrates how the drive for consumption is an essential component of the urban fabric: the philosopher Ricken advocates liberation while simultaneously purchasing three beds for his newborn child, claiming that allowing her to choose her own bed will be better for her development. Even if devoid of any Lumon products, Ricken's home is therefore as much an ought-place of consumerism as is the company headquarters.

The seemingly endless appetite that connects domestic life to the corporate production of goods and services stems from real life; Amazon's recent surge in profitability, for example, was in no small way spurred on by rampant consumer demand during the pandemic.[73] Although it is arguable that consumers were looking to procure essential goods in a safe manner, a substantial increase in trends such as 'revenge spending' was also observed, where consumers purchased more simply because they were bored at home.[74] This coincided with a merely tokenistic sense of recognition towards Amazon warehouse staff as frontline workers, who faced significant challenges relating to job and health security while 'fulfilling' thousands of orders daily.[75]

In addition to a separate website that showcases Amazon's corporate profile – which features a section on employee benefits, safety and diversity – Amazon's ecommerce or 'main' website contains a list of various corporate documents, including guidelines on corporate governance and a code of business conduct and ethics. However, Bezos has thus far not written any books or manuals that explain his or Amazon's philosophy. The inner workings of the company – be it concerning warehouses or otherwise – have largely been the result of what has been reported in the press concerning lawsuits and other contentious matters. Yet it has continued to thrive despite these challenges, and is undoubtedly a product of the expansive corporate personhood laws that have shaped the American legal landscape.

It is here, perhaps, that Lumon Industries differs the most from Amazon, because the former exists in a world where corporate sovereignty is absolute enough to enable the outright codification of power. The fictional possibilities

71 Paul (2022).
72 Lindahl (2013), p 12. Emphasis from author.
73 Weise (2021).
74 Park et al (2022).
75 Bellafante (2020).

of *Severance* therefore offer a window into what can happen with the unrestricted creation of corporate spatio-legal boundaries, limits and faultlines, brought about through a combination of a powerful minority and voracious consumer demand, and materially and normatively expressed through bodies, objects and spaces.

For Lumon, the attempt to create legal boundaries as a normative means to enclose and secure corporate space is best exemplified in the *Compliance Handbook* and its three Appendices, which provide Kier Egan's instructions on how to serve as a valued member of the Lumon family. Resembling the Bible, the *Handbook* is quoted from constantly throughout the show, especially by Irving B (John Turturro), who takes pride in his ability to recollect its myriad sayings. In the Macrodata Refinement workspace, it is placed directly under a portrait of Kier Egan, materially symbolising its normative weight and demonstrating the extent of the conflation between personal philosophy, religious scripture and the law.

To reinforce that these normative boundaries have clear limits, however, Lumon enlists the aid of a department known as Optics and Design, which constantly produces objects valourising the *Handbook*. The most famous of these are the many paintings that line the sterile and labyrinthine corridors of the severed floor, which deliberately lack other features to remind employees of the spatial and normative boundaries to be obeyed while simultaneously discouraging any attempts at cartography (which is forbidden in the *Handbook*). The paintings are constantly rotated between different departments on the floor and are meant to encourage a sense of pride and fervour among employees.

However, they also demonstrate the lengths to which the corporate sovereign strives to protect itself. For example, in an attempt to prevent fraternisation between Optics and Design and Macrodata Refinement, Milchick asks the former to paint two versions of a supposedly historically violent war between the departments, portraying each as instigator *and* victim, thereby sowing confusion.[76] History itself is rendered as fluid and malleable.

To preserve the legal order, faultlines must be prevented from developing, and any potential acts of a-legality or *strangeness* must be stopped. Lumon therefore relies on the frequent disciplining of its employee subjects to prevent the engendering of any possible strangeness by sending them to the Break Room for their transgressions. The Break Room is a dark and cramped space on the severed floor, which contains only a table and two chairs facing each other. Here, Milchick sits on one end and projects a Compunction Statement, which shines directly on the employee while they are forced to repeat it while pressing their palms on a biofeedback sensor. This torturous exercise is not

76 McArdle (2022) 'The Grim Barbarity of Optics and Design'.

considered over until Milchick, who monitors the sensor readings, affirms otherwise.

Despite these many attempts to preserve the corporate legal order, however, strangeness abounds and a-legality inevitably erupts. A faultline emerges in the legal order and forces its re-evaluation, and in doing so disrupts existing power relations between and beyond those in the legal collective. Such an interruption, says Lindahl, is the domain of 'strange behaviour and situations that, evoking another realm of practical possibilities, question the boundaries of (il)legality'.[77]

In *Severance*, this moment comes when a 'Music Dance Experience' is earned by the team members for meeting their Refinement quota. Helly R, who has earned the Experience, chooses 'defiant jazz' as her music of choice. Strobe lighting fills the darkened office workspace as Mark S, Irving B and Helly R begin to dance awkwardly. They are surrounded by the dervish frame of Milchick, who has changed out of his uniform and is dancing with everyone joyfully. He then approaches Dylan G, who has uncharacteristically stayed sitting the entire time and cannot stop thinking of his recently discovered son, and how Milchick has told him to ignore this revelation and simply move on. As Milchick steadily encroaches into Dylan G's personal space and remains dancing around him, the music reaches an uncomfortable crescendo. Then Dylan G tackles Milchick to the ground, demands to know his son's name and *bites him*.

It is this acute moment of strangeness that breaks the remaining vestiges of Lumon's legal order. Dylan G's attack irrupts the boundaries that seek to limit certain kinds of behaviour, for this is behaviour that corporate legality has never attempted to regulate at all. As Milchick screams that his skin has been broken, and that the Music Dance Experience is officially cancelled, the Macrodata Refinement team seems to realise for the first time that the corporate sovereign can spill blood, and now everything is possible.

Conclusion

Severance ends on a cliff-hanger: Milchick has his revenge by tackling Dylan G while he attempts the Overtime Contingency, thereby putting the outies back just as they are on the brink of key revelations about who they are and what Lumon is capable of. This is as frustrating for the viewer as it is for the legal scholar, because there are several questions left to answer which will have to wait for the next season. And although it does not end on the premise of widespread revolution or the overthrowing of corporate power, the brilliance of the show lies in helping trace the myriad legalities that shape corporate power in the real world in bodily, material and spatial ways, and how

77 Lindahl (2013), p 4.

such power is the result of a small yet powerful collective that seeks to feed a seemingly endless appetite for consumer goods. This can best be reflected in the experiences of Amazon's warehouse workers, who – in a bid to unionise – face an employment machine capable of numerous acts of algorithmic management, rendering them vulnerable to job insecurity, the removal of benefits and leave and exposure to unsafe work practices.

References

Associated Press (2021) 'Amazon Sued Over Discrimination, Harassment Claims' *AP News*, 3 March.

Gina Bellafante (2020) '"We Didn't Sign Up for This": Amazon Workers on the Front Lines' *New York Times*, 3 April.

Ilan Benshalom (2014) 'Who Should Decide Whether the Apple is Rotten? Tax Disclosure and Corporate Political Agency' 6 *Columbia Journal of Tax Law* 86.

Greg Bensinger (2019) '"MissionRacer": How Amazon Turned the Tedium of Warehouse Work into a Game' *The Washington Post*, 21 May.

Margaret M Blair (2013) 'Corporate Personhood and the Corporate Persona' 3 *University of Illinois Law Review* 785.

Andrew Chung (2019) 'U.S. Supreme Court rejects Amazon Warehouse Worker Wage Appeal' *Reuters*, 7 October.

Penny Crofts (2022) '*Aliens*: Legal Conceptions of the Corporate Invasion' 34 *Law and Literature* 387.

Alessandro Delfanti, Lilian Radovac and Taylor Walker (2021) 'The Amazon Panopticon' *UNI Global Union*, https://uniglobalunion.org/wp-content/uploads/amazon_panopticon_en_final.pdf

Jason Del Rey (2021) 'Amazon Hit by 5 More Lawsuits from Employees Who Allege Race and Gender Discrimination', *Vox*, 19 May.

Jason Del Rey (2022) 'Exclusive: Inside Amazon's plan to "Neutralise" Powerful Unions by Hiring Ex-inmates and 'Vulnerable Students' *Vox*, 29 July.

Sandro Formica and Fabiola Sfodera (2022) 'The Great Resignation and the Quiet Quitting Paradigm Shifts: An Overview of Current Situation and Future Research Directions' 31 *Journal of Hospitality Marketing & Management* 899.

Michel Foucault (1984) 'Of Other Spaces: Utopias and Heterotopias' https://web.mit.edu/allanmc/www/foucault1.pdf

Michel Foucault (1995) *Discipline and Punish: The Birth of the Prison*, Vintage Books.

Michel Foucault (1990) *The History of Sexuality, Volume 1: An Introduction*, Vintage Books.

Michel Foucault (2001) 'The Birth of Social Medicine' in James D Faubion (ed), *Power (The Essential Works of Michel Foucault, 1954–1984, Vol. 3)*, The New Press 134–56.

Michel Foucault (2004) *'Society Must Be Defended': Lectures at the College de France, 1975–1976*, Penguin.

Michel Foucault (2007) *Security, Territory, Population*, Palgrave Macmillan.

Malik W Ghachem (2016) 'No Body to Be Kicked? Monopoly, Financial Crisis, and Popular Revolt in 18th-century Haiti and America' 28 *Law and Literature* 403.

Alex Green, Mitchell Travis and Kieran Tranter (2022) 'Introduction: Jurisprudence of the Future' 4 *Law, Technology, and Humans* 1.

Lauren Kaori Gurley (2022) 'Internal Documents Show Amazon's Dystopian System for Tracking Workers Every Minute of their Shifts' *Vice*, 2 June.

Haleluya Hadero (2022) 'Amazon Seeks to Overturn Union Win, Says Vote was Tainted' *Associated Press*, 9 April.

Lyman Johnson (2012) 'Law and Legal Theory in the History of Corporate Responsibility: Corporate Personhood' 35 *Seattle Law Review* 1135.

Dearbail Jordan and Zoe Conway (2023) 'Amazon Strikes: Workers Claim Their Toilet Breaks are Timed' *BBC*, 25 January.

Meera Karunanathan (2019) 'Can the Human Right to Water Disrupt Neoliberal Water Policies in the Era of Corporate Policy-making?' 98 *Geoforum* 244.

Visa AJ Kurki (2019) *A Theory of Legal Personhood*, Oxford University Press.

David Leonhardt (2021) 'The Amazon Customers Don't See' *New York Times*, 15 June.

Shannon Liao (2018) 'Amazon Warehouse Workers Skip Bathroom Breaks to Keep Their Jobs, Says Report' *The Verge*, 17 April.

Hans Lindahl (ed) (2009) *A Right to Inclusion and Exclusion? Normative Fault Lines of the EU's Area of Freedom, Security, and Justice*, Hart.

Hans Lindahl (2013) *Fault Lines of Globalisation: Legal Order and the Politics of A-legality*, Oxford University Press.

William P MacNeil Lex Populi Stanford University Press, Stanford, 2007.

Niamh McIntyre and Rosie Bradbury (2022) 'The Eyes of Amazon: A Hidden Workforce Driving a Vast Surveillance System' *The Bureau Investigates*, 21 November.

Kate Morgan and Delaney Nolan (2023) 'How Worker Surveillance is Backfiring on Employers' *BBC*, 30 January.

Stefanie Mueller (2020) 'The Silence of the Soulless Corporation: Corporate Agency in James Fenimore Cooper's *The Bravo*' 34 *Law and Literature* 23.

John Nichols (2021) 'As Pandemic Profits Put Bezos on Track for Trillionaire Status, Tish James Asks: At What Cost?' *The Nation*, 23 February.

Occupational Safety and Health Administration (OSHA) (2023) 'US Department of Labor Finds Amazon Exposed Workers to Unsafe Conditions, Ergonomic Hazards at Three More Warehouses in Colorado, Idaho, New York' https://www.osha.gov/news/newsreleases/national/02012023

Gloria Oladipo (2022) '"The Revolution is Here": Chris Smalls' Union Win Sparks a Movement at Other Amazon Warehouses' *The Guardian*, 6 April.

Inyoung Park, Jieon Lee, Daehoo Lee, Changjun Lee and Won Young Chung (2022) Changes in Consumption Patterns During the COVID-19 Pandemic: Analyzing the Revenge Spending Motivations of Different Emotional Groups 65 *Journal of Retailing and Consumer Services*, https://doi.org/10.1016/j.jretconser.2021.102874

Kari Paul (2022) 'Amazon Shareholders Reject 15 Motions on Worker Rights and Environment' The Guardian, 25 May.

Frank Pearce and Steve Tombs (1998) *Toxic Capitalism: Corporate Crime and the Chemical Industry*, Routledge.

Timothy D Peters (2022) *A Theological Jurisprudence of Speculative Cinema: Superheroes, Science Fictions and Fantasies of Modern Law* Edinburgh University Press, Edinburgh.

Elizabeth Pollman (2011) 'Reconceiving Corporate Personhood' 4 *Utah Law Review* 1629.

Elizabeth Pollman (2021) 'The Supreme Court and the Pro-business Paradox' 135 *Harvard Law Review* 220.

Michael Sainato (2020) '"I'm Not a Robot": Amazon Workers Condemn Unsafe, Grueling Conditions at Warehouse' *The Guardian*, 5 February.

Michael Sainato (2021) '"I'm Still in Pain": Amazon Employees Say Climate of Fear has Led to High Rates of Injuries' *The Guardian*, 30 December.

Michael Sainato (2023) '"War of Attrition": Why Union Victories for US workers at Amazon Have Stalled' *The Guardian*, 8 April.

Brent Allen Saindon (2010) 'A Doubled Heterotopia: Shifting Spatial and Visual Symbolism in the Jewish Museum Berlin's Development' 98 *Quarterly Journal of Speech* 24.

Noam Scheiber (2019) 'Inside an Amazon Warehouse, Robots' Ways Rub Off on Humans' *New York Times*, 3 July.

Alana Semuels (2018) 'What Amazon Does to Poor Cities' *The Atlantic*, 18 February.

Erica Sollazzo (2017) '"The Dead City": Corporate Anxiety and the Post-Apocalyptic Vision in Colson Whitehead's Zone One' 29 *Law and Literature* 457.

Olivia Solon (2018) 'Amazon Patents Wristbands that Track Warehouse Workers' Movements' *The Guardian*, 1 February.

Andre Spicer (2018) 'Amazon's "Worker Cage" has Been Dropped, but Its Staff are Not Free' *The Guardian*, 14 September.

Swati Srivastava (2022) 'Corporate Sovereign Awakening and the Making of Modern State Sovereignty: New Archival Evidence from the English East India Company' 76 *International Organization* 690.

Philip J Stern (2011) *The Company-State: Corporate Sovereignty and the Early Modern Foundations of the British Empire in India*, Oxford University Press.

Brad Stone (2013) *The Everything Store: Jeff Bezos and the Age of Amazon*, Little, Brown, and Company.

Ciara Torres-Spelliscy (2014) 'The History of Corporate Personhood' *Brennan Center for Justice*, https://www.brennancenter.org/our-work/analysis-opinion/history-corporate-personhood

Kieran Tranter (2018) *Living in Technical Legality: Science Fiction and Law as Technology* Edinburgh University Press, Edinburgh.

Mitchell Travis (2011) 'Making Space: Law and Science Fiction' 23 *Law and Literature* 241.

Anne Tucker (2010) 'Flawed Assumptions: A Corporate Law Analysis of Free Speech and Corporate Personhood in Citizens United' 61 *Case Western Law Review* 497.

Alexander Villegas (2021) 'The Amazon That Customers Don't See' *New York Times*, 15 June.

Kaveh Waddell and Maanvi Singh (2021) 'Warehouses in Their Backyards': When Amazon Expands, These Communities Pay the Price' *The Guardian*, 9 December.

Michael Walker, Peter Fleming and Marco Berti (2021) '"You Can't Pick Up a Phone and Talk to Someone': How Algorithms Function as Biopower in the Gig Economy' 28 *Organization* 26.

Karen Weise (2021) 'Amazon's Profit Soars 220 Percent as Pandemic Drives Shopping Online' *New York Times*, 29 April.

Karen Weise (2022) 'A Judge Ruled That Amazon Must Reinstate a Staten Island Worker Who Was Fired' *New York Times*, 18 April.

TV episodes

Aoife McArdle (2022) 'The Grim Barbarity of Optics and Design' *Severance*, AppleTV+.

Aoife McArdle (2022) 'The You You Are' *Severance*, AppleTV+.

Ben Stiller (2022) 'Defiant Jazz' *Severance* AppleTV+.

Ben Stiller (2022) 'Good News About Hell' *Severance* AppleTV+.

Ben Stiller (2022) 'Half Loop' *Severance*, AppleTV+.

Ben Stiller (2022) 'In Perpetuity' *Severance*, AppleTV+.

Ben Stiller (2022) 'The We We Were' *Severance*, AppleTV+.

Cases

Burwell v Hobby Lobby Stores, Inc (2014) 573 U.S. 682.

Citizens United v Federal Election Commission (2010) 558 U.S. 310.

Heimbach v Amazon.com (6th Cir., 2019) No. 18-5942.

Integrity Staffing Solutions, Inc v Busk (2014) 574 U.S. 27 (2014).

Chapter 15

Merging AI technology with the corporate form

Purpose, personhood and data in 'Autofac'

Jordan Aleksander Belor

Introduction

The dominance of the modern business corporation in providing many, if not the majority, of society's necessities means that it has taken on a role that was once solely the state's responsibility.[1] While such dominance may call into question the nature and role of the state, the corporation's effectiveness in providing both private and public goods and services continues to increase through the development and deployment of artificial intelligence (AI). With the applications of AI becoming broader, and its usefulness bleeding into the world of law, commerce and beyond, its use in the context of corporations and corporate governance has seen predictions of the replacement of everything from mundane administrative and data-processing roles through to the strategic decision-making, governance and oversight given by directors.[2] This chapter seeks to examine this interplay between AI technology and the corporation – something foreshadowed in the work of science fiction writer Philip K Dick, particularly in his short story, 'Autofac',[3] recently adapted by Travis Beacham as part of the television series *Philip K Dick's Electric Dreams*.[4] While there are differences between the original and the adaptation,[5] both versions of 'Autofac' feature an automated artificial entity that not only produces an excessive amount of goods and pollution but also subordinates its consumers in the process of serving them.

This chapter engages in a cultural legal reading of Beacham's version of 'Autofac',[6] arguing that it calls into question the current prominent debates

1 Barkan (2013), pp 25, 38–39.

2 Birch (2022). See Mandal and Sunil (2021); Möslein (2018); Petrin (2019).

3 Dick (2017).

4 Beacham (2018).

5 Dick's version of the story positions the reader to consider what industrialisation and consumerism could be like with an automatic factory (Autofac) in a possible future, while Beacham's is an AI-run corporation that creates advanced AI as a stand-in for humanity.

6 A cultural legal reading often requires a form of close reading called 'reading jurisprudentially' – coined by William MacNeil: see Jockers (2013); MacNeil (2007), pp 2, 12, 14. MacNeil (2012), p 9; Smith (2016), p 67.

DOI: 10.4324/9781003412274-18

over corporate purpose. Instead of considering whose interests a corporation is managed in – shareholders, stakeholders or a balance of both – 'Autofac' highlights that it is the *structure* of the corporate form rather than its *purpose* that is key. This is made explicit in the context of a possible future where an AI-run corporation, which has no shareholders, not only produces consumers as a stand-in for an extinct humanity but continues to produce externalities without legal restraint. The significance of Beacham's 'Autofac' steers us away from the dominant critiques of maximising shareholder value and instead prompts us to think about how the corporation itself – the Autofac – functions as a biopolitical structure.

As 'Autofac' is situated within the realm of science fiction, this chapter engages in a cultural legal analysis because it affords us the opportunity to observe, think about and critique law, technology and jurisprudence only presently available in a possible future. A foundational theme of science fiction, permeating its mythos, is the fear and anxiety stemming from technological advancement.[7] The paradigmatic exemplar of such fear and anxiety regarding technology is the Frankenstein myth, where the technological creation supplants and seeks to destroy its creator.[8] It is significant, however, that the Frankenstein myth relates not only to technology but also the corporation – and, in the context of this chapter, seeing *both* AI and the corporation as forms of technology, tools predisposed to serve the interests of its creators.[9] Cultural legal engagements of the Frankenstein myth have, however, highlighted the parallels between technology and law. Kieran Tranter, for example, notes how both technology and law – as well as law *as* technology – are presented as something that *saves*.[10] Instead of technology in science fiction simply being that which is a threat, law as technology functions as a tool designed to protect through control.[11] Timothy Peters takes this point up in a reading of the film *I, Robot* (inspired by Isaac Asimov's robot stores) suggesting that love is a possible solution to break away from the constraints of universalist logic imposed by a rogue AI to determine what is best for humanity in law.[12] The irony, however, is that the use of AI and automation pervading every aspect of life in *I, Robot* not only provided a sense of comfort and security without the need for control but manifested the anxiety and fear humanity tried to

7 Tranter (2020), p 3.

8 Kieran Tranter situates the Frankenstein myth in the field of law and technology: see Tranter (2020), pp 1, 3, 9–13.

9 Such uncertainty fuelled the desire to challenge and criticise the popular trope of the Frankenstein myth: see Barkan (2013), pp 65–67; Crofts (2021); Peters (2017).

10 Tranter (2020), pp 1–2.

11 Tranter (2020), pp 1–2.

12 See Peters (2008), pp 91–92.

escape from.[13] Since a cultural legal analysis allows scholars to take up questions of law and legality and think about our possible future, this approach is thus key to engaging with texts situated within the classification of science fiction, including 'Autofac'.

While there is a developed secondary literature on Philip K Dick's work in general,[14] including considerations of his story 'Autofac',[15] there is no sustained analysis of the legal significance of Beacham's adaptation.[16] The target of critique of Dick's story is the way the Autofac, as a self-moving machine, represented the fears of the trajectories of industrialised production in the 1960s and 1970s.[17] When the three main characters in Dick's version attempt to blow up one of the *many* Autofacs to regain their freedom, they discover the Autofac's ability to self-reproduce – meaning that any attempt to disrupt industrialisation is met with failure.[18] This outcome aligns with what has been described as the Dickean worldview – a 'universe of paranoia, ignorance and a lack of true freedom'[19] – while implicitly questioning (though not resolving) the nature of industrialised production. Beacham's, on the other hand, reflects the 'Holly-worldview' (good triumphs over evil, a seemingly insignificant character becoming the hero of the story).[20]

Beacham's adaptation, featured as the eighth episode in the television series *Electric Dreams* (2018),[21] is set in a dystopian future where humanity went extinct after its final World War, leaving behind an AI-run corporation (the Autofac). The Autofac seized all means of production, gaining control of Earth's resources to manufacture commodities with no humans to serve. With its purpose and existence unfulfilled, the Autofac sought to replace its creators with a new and artificial humanity as AI consumers (something that is only revealed in the latter half of the episode). The narrative is set around three of the consumers: Emily Zabriskie (Juno Temple) and her two friends, Conrad Morrison (David Lyons) and Reverend Perine (Jay Paulson), who

13 A revelation that appeared through Timothy Peters' cultural legal analysis of *I, Robot*: see Peters (2008).

14 Within the cultural legal field, see MacNeil and Hutchings (2001); MacNeil (2012), pp 80–96; Peters (2022a, 2022b).

15 Culp (2020); Dick (2017), pp 181–213; Ekbia et al (2015); Krishnan (2009); Nitschke and Howard (2022); Rabkin (1988); Stewart (2021); Wittkower (2011).

16 Although Susan Watson references Dick's text in her work on AI and corporations: Watson (2021), p 34.

17 See Ekbia et al (2015).

18 Dick (2017), pp 183–213.

19 Mills (2011), p 3.

20 Mills (2011), p 3. For an example of the Dickean versus Holly-worldview of Dick's work, see Peters (2022a), pp 213–19. Hollywood tends to place or create characters and adjust the stories of Dick's works accordingly, so these new characters become heroes: Weiss and Nicholas (2011), p 28.

21 Beacham (2018).

all live with others in a settlement. The trio eventually gains access to the Autofac facility, where Emily discovers that humanity – including herself – was replaced by advanced AI. The Autofac uses 'archived neural imaging data' to replicate the personalities and identity of each human to create its consumers.[22] Emily uploads a virus to the Autofac's mainframe to sever control over the new humanity, stopping the Autofac entirely.

The key focus of this chapter's reading of Beacham's episode is the presentation of how both the autonomy of the Autofac *and* its reliance on humanity through the production of AI consumers appearing to be settlers call into question the notion of personhood. Such a question not only highlights a key deviation from the jurisprudential understandings of personhood but presents a link between life and value. Such a link does not restrict life to simply bearing an economic value but rather carries a datacentric value that undergirds the unique representation in 'Autofac' of the corporate form where an AI-run corporation can produce and include life as much as it can exclude and destroy it. Central to the episode's critique, however, is the reliance of the Autofac on data. As is revealed in the final moments, its autonomy can be severed by removing its control over data, and such severance is key to disrupting a possible future where life is steered towards value.

The next section takes up the vision of Beacham's 'Autofac' as a critical response to contemporary debates over corporate purpose in the context of the fourth industrial revolution. The subsequent section then highlights how merging AI technology with law renders explicit the corporate form as a biopolitical structure that governs life towards value. Following this, the chapter takes up this structuring of the Autofac by interrogating the way legal personhood no longer appears to engage in legal relations but rather functions as a biopolitical technique to regulate life. The nature of corporate purpose, biopolitics and personhood is then tied together by highlighting the significant role data plays in 'Autofac'. The control and use of data functions as a stand-in legal person for humans, but the destruction of data then functions as the reduction, rescinding and restructuring of rights. The chapter concludes by considering the potential response: either a corporate death penalty or a regulation of the access to data so the artificial and autonomous entity again becomes inanimate.

Corporate purpose and the Autofac

As a science fiction text, 'Autofac' presents us with an AI-run corporation that operates without human input and is not controlled or influenced by

22 Beacham (2018). Neuroimaging is the recording of a person's central nervous system: the structure and functioning of the brain as well as genetics. See Crawford et al (2016); Smit et al (2012).

shareholders. With humanity extinct, the Autofac needed a stand-in for humanity to justify its purpose to produce commodities – so has created advanced robotic AI as consumers. Beacham's presenting of the Autofac as a shareholder-less corporation, however, calls into question the nature of the current debates over corporate purpose. While the name 'Autofac' provokes a thought experiment regarding and critiquing the nature of automated production, most forms of factory automation *were* being introduced when Dick's short story was written in the 1950s. At the same time, the idea of a network of factories functioning without human intervention was a particularly futuristic vision. Writing in this context, Dick raised questions about both the elimination of the need for workers in such factories *and* the questions of who should be in control of production. As such, the objective of Dick's characters was to destroy the automated control so humans could once again manage their own production of goods and services.

While written in the midst of the third industrial revolution – thinking through the introduction and impacts of computers, telecommunications and forms of automation – the concept of the Autofac aligns more directly with that of the 'smart factory', which is often seen as one of the features of what Klaus Schwab refers to as the *fourth* industrial revolution. Following Germany's Industry 4.0 initiative, which began introducing AI technology into factory production,[23] Schwab argues that we are seeing an even bigger shift in industrialised and automated production – in particular, the fusion and interaction of technologies with 'the physical, digital and biological domains that make the fourth industrial revolution fundamentally different from previous revolutions'.[24]

In this regard, Beacham's adaptation of Dick's work is not simply about questions of the obsolescence of workers and who controls production that the fourth industrial revolution will inevitably bring. Rather, it is a critical engagement with the very notion of replaceability and the social *purpose* of automated, industrialised production – highlighted specifically by one of the consumers, Conrad, when he points out that the Autofac 'controls all means of production'.[25] No longer does capital appear to be about the commodification and appropriation of labour-value from workers in the service of producing goods for consumers, but rather an automated production of consumer goods to be distributed and consumed. Yet the point raised early in the episode is that these goods are *not* being consumed, and the population of the settlements are engaged in their own production and growing of

23 Schwab (2016), p 6; Philbeck and Davis (2019), p 17.

24 Schwab (2016), p 6. A current example of this is Facebook (now Meta Inc), which wants to use technology to merge the physical with virtual reality: Davies and AFP with Reuters (2021).

25 Beacham (2018) 'Autofac'.

food. The characters' issue with the Autofac is therefore twofold. First, they have no need for what is being produced. Second, the externalities generated by the Autofac's production – pollution, smog and heavy metal waste – are impeding their own ability to grow food and survive by themselves.

This twofold critique of the Autofac – for producing unnecessary consumables and the creation of externalities – therefore links the story to the broader debates around the purpose of the corporation and its (lack of) responsibility for the externalities that it produces. Corporate purpose has largely been debated since the 1930s, with a significant focus on balancing shareholder value and stakeholders' needs.[26] Without a universally accepted definition of corporate purpose, scholars have generally associated the concept with how a corporation generates value.[27] The term 'value', however, is vague; its meaning oscillates between shareholder and stakeholder value.[28] The issue that society is facing, and for which legal experts are seeking to find solutions, is how corporations have prioritised shareholder value at the expense of stakeholders. As such, shareholder primacy became the prevailing view of corporate purpose: the reason for a corporation's existence is to serve shareholders. Prioritising shareholder value does not mean stakeholder interests are eliminated from the corporate structure; rather, corporations have *structurally subordinated* those interests to the extraction of value. The consequence behind the state of shareholder primacy is the (lack of) responsibility for a corporation's externalities, which steers us away from a brighter future.[29] However, there have been calls for a greater emphasis on social responsibility.

One of the most notable calls for reimagining corporate purpose in response to social and environmental harms, as well as technological change, is Schwab's own emphasis on the Davos Manifesto.[30] The purpose of the corporation that the Davos Manifesto sets out is for corporations to 'engage all its stakeholders in shared and sustained value creation'.[31] Corporations are thus required to balance their desire for continuity (through value creation)

26 Berle (1931, 1932); Dodd (1932), p 1148. For a notable earlier case on corporate purpose in the United States, see *Dodge v Ford Motor Co, 170 N.W. 668* (Mich 1919); Easterbrook and Fischel (1989), p 1446; Connor and O'Beid (2020), pp 288–89.

27 Sjåfjell et al (2015); Connor and O'Beid (2020).

28 Sjåfjell et al (2015), p 83, citing Kraakman et al (2014), p 18.

29 See Hayden and Bodie (2021), Ch 6; Sjåfjell et al (2015), p 85. There is difficulty in promoting social welfare when shareholders have significant power in controlling the direction of the corporation: Rock (2021), p 372.

30 A set of principles designed to guide corporations on what they should consider and, most importantly, do when unleashing new technology into the world as well as a means for us to safely navigate the fourth industrial revolution. For more details on the Davos Manifesto and its principles, see Schwab (2008, 2018, 2019b, 2019c, 2019d); Schwab (2019a), pp 13–14.

31 Schwab (2019b).

and society's benefit (safeguarding it and promoting growth).[32] To effectively balance these two essential needs, companies will have to rethink strategies and adopt new approaches to ensure continuity, or 'businesses, industries and corporations will face continuous Darwinian pressures'.[33] New technology can therefore, *disrupt* how a corporation functions and governs its business decisions and activities, which can risk continuity.[34] What is significant about the Davos Manifesto is how we should navigate the fourth industrial revolution. That is, we must take a greater interest in the way corporate purpose functions, so we avoid harm and externalities.

Even though the debates on corporate purpose involve arguments about the impact of shareholder primacy on the generation of externalities, which corporate stakeholding is seen as potentially mitigating, 'Autofac' highlights a similar point but *without* shareholders.[35] What an AI-run corporation functioning without shareholders demonstrates is that, within the Autofac, externalities remain an issue regardless of what is called for from the dominant literature on corporate purpose. This point was highlighted by one of the AI consumers during a scene where they were planning to overthrow the Autofac's control over all means of production:

> Well, we can't afford to wait any longer. The world outside, the little piece of Eden we've carved out, is dead. And it's creeping towards us. Now the war ended 20 years ago, and we've all sat idly by, hoping the factory will run out of steam, but it hasn't, and it won't. It'll keep eating our resources, polluting our air, poisoning our fucking water, making a bunch of plastic crap for a world that is dead and gone.[36]

Conrad's concern for the wellbeing of the consumer settlement captures a similar discourse and critique of corporations not structuring their purpose around stakeholders as well as social and environmental impacts. However, the context in which Conrad is expressing his concern goes against the representation of the initial discourse on corporate purpose because the Autofac does not allow 'human' input.[37] This representation of the current critiques of

32 See Schwab (2019a), pp 13–14; Schwab (2019b, 2019c, 2019d).

33 Large organisations such as Google have already restructured into an enterprise (a holding company called Alphabet) in an attempt to adapt to the inevitable disruption of technological advancement: Schwab (2016), pp 47, 58–59. See also Schwab (2019a), p 13; Philbeck and Davis (2019), pp 18–19.

34 See Schwab (2016), pp 47, 58–59; Schwab (2019a), p 13.

35 Since there are no humans left.

36 As Conrad states, the Autofac produces as much as it can for its consumers so that it can continue to exist, but it simultaneously runs the risk of destroying the consumers from whom it seeks authority and legitimacy. Beacham (2018) 'Autofac'.

37 Even though there are no humans left, we do not have any shareholders either.

corporate purpose and social responsibility also highlights how the Autofac is the antithesis of the Davos Manifesto; 'Autofac' presents us with the possible future of not navigating safely through the fourth industrial revolution – but, more importantly, a possible future where humanity did not fully consider the prospects of altering the corporate form's structure. Therefore, according to the text, the issue is not so much a question of shareholder value but rather how the merging of AI technology with the corporation redirects the purpose of maximising shareholder value to the production of data in the form of artificial life as the consumer. Central to the critique of 'Autofac' is the way producing artificial life not only sustains its purpose but also introduces, and by extension enables, the biopolitical regulation of life.

The corporation as a biopolitical structure

'Autofac' presents us with an articulation of the corporate form that is merged with AI technology and the ability to produce artificial life enables it to function as a biopolitical structure. One way to understand the biopolitical nature of the Autofac is through Joshua Barkan's analysis of corporate power in *Corporate Sovereignty*.[38] Drawing on Michel Foucault's work, Barkan highlights that modern power's desire is to improve life.[39] Barkan's analysis of the link between corporations and power points out that there 'is no longer a matter of bringing death into play in the field of sovereignty, but of distributing the living in the domain of value and utility'.[40] Barkan thus links corporate power to biopolitics, whereby 'the precise significance of the corporation is the multiple ways it has articulated the sovereign right to kill and the biopower to improve life with the historical and geographic circulation of capitalist value'.[41] With the Autofac, it produces consumers which are situated as artificial persons but also organises them into colonies. If consumers were to fall outside the scope of their original programming, developing a sense of free will – which happened with the main character developing a sense of free will – the Autofac would destroy them to preserve its purpose. Thus, the Autofac represents a form of modern power as far as distributing a form of life and its value is concerned.[42] This value is made clear through the Autofac's act to exclude life by eliminating it, which connects it to biopolitics. The concept of biopolitics began with Foucault's analysis of life and politics.[43] The key distinctions that are made in the study of biopolitics today are how it is fundamentally about the extent of life functions, its

38 Barkan (2013), p 7.
39 Barkan (2013), p 7.
40 Barkan (2013), p 7.
41 Barkan (2013), p 162.
42 Rentea (2017), pp 1–6. See Foucault (1990), p 141; Nancy (2007), p 93.
43 Rentea (2017), pp 1–6. See Foucault (1990), p 141; Nancy (2007), p 93.

reproduction and continuity and how it is used in modernity.[44] Thus, the direction of biopolitics is about the measurement of biological life in the political sphere – that is, through records, including statistical analysis.[45] As the study of biopolitics has evolved since Foucault, other scholars – notably Giorgio Agamben – suggest a much more fundamental connection between sovereignty and biopolitics. Agamben argues that the 'production of a biopolitical body is the original activity of sovereign power' and 'biopolitics is at least as old as the sovereign exception'.[46] From Agamben's argument, we can draw not only the interplay between regulating life and sovereignty but a link between biopolitics and bodies – the context in which this is situated is corporate entities.

While these articulations of biopolitics between Foucault and Agamben tend to overlap, and at times vary, Barkan considers these biopolitical views in the context of corporate sovereignty. He argues that while the corporation is a creation of law and bears a similar command of economic and political power that both rivals and threatens the state, both function as corporate structures that share the same lineage of law.[47] This lineage involves the corporation and state appearing as legal creations, incorporated to enact and certify their existence – with these acts being codified or constituted by law – while sharing similar techniques to establish order consensually or coercively.[48] Bearing similarities to one another, corporations have functioned as not only creations born from the state but extensions of it to manage and 'achieve ends of government'.[49] This is not only that the 'corporation and modern political sovereignty are founded in and bound together through a principle of *legally sanctioned immunity from law*';[50] the corporation's capacity to threaten the state points to 'a kind of *doubling*', where corporate power and sovereignty simultaneously merge and conflict with one another.[51] As Barkan highlights:

> Modern state sovereignty is *founded in* and *anchored to* a figure of the corporate political body. Likewise, modern corporate power *emerges from* and *mobilizes* apparatuses of sovereignty, discipline, and government.[52]

44 Foucault (1990), p 147.
45 Rentea (2017), pp 5–6.
46 Agamben (1995), p 6.
47 Barkan (2013), p 5.
48 Barkan (2013), p 5.
49 For further examples, see Barkan (2013), p 5.
50 Barkan (2013), p 4.
51 Barkan (2013), p 4.
52 Barkan (2013), p 6.

The relationship between the corporation and nation-state thus demonstrates a form of dependence, but also a resistance to one another. Barkan argues that the appropriate formula for their relationship is the *ban* – a concept Giorgio Agamben 'has located as the ontological structure of sovereign power'.[53] Agamben's analysis of the ban as an ontological structure of sovereign power, as Barkan reinforces, 'extends and reformulates Michel Foucault's trenchant account of modern power' – particularly 'the ways in which life became an increasingly important object of political calculation, which he termed *biopolitics*'.[54] According to Foucault, sovereignty entailed the power to 'extract life in defense of the realm', which allowed the state to optimise the 'distribution of "men and things"'.[55] Biopolitics for corporate entities such as the state and corporation does not necessarily involve a direct decision to determine whether a life is unworthy of living;[56] rather, society is built upon the paradox of the sovereign ban – where 'legal exceptions and the abandonment of populations are justified as vital to the security of political communities'.[57] Since the corporation and the state are closely intertwined, the Autofac, as an AI-run corporation therefore, functions as a biopolitical structure determined to regulate life.

The Autofac functions as a biopolitical structure not only because the notion of it being a corporation presumes it to be but also due to the way it engages with regulating its creation: the consumer. An example of the Autofac's ability to regulate life is presented to the viewer during a negotiation scene between the consumers and Alice Fry, one of Autofac's early-model AI representatives. Conrad poses the following question to Alice: 'We need to be left alone to rebuild our world the way we see fit, but how can we when the Autofac controls all means of production?' Alice's response is interesting, yet key to the Autofac's representation as a biopolitical structure that regulates life: 'It's out of the question, I am afraid'. Alice's rejection reveals two key points about the Autofac as a biopolitical structure. First, the simple rejection and the existence of the scene where the consumers must go to lengths to have an audience with a representative rather than the Autofac itself demonstrates that the AI-run corporation carries a disproportionate amount of bargaining power. Second, the Autofac is no longer controlled, and instead functions as the controller. The language that describes the Autofac as a corporation being once 'controlled' and turning into the controller initially points to a possible question on corporate control and ownership. However, the language reinforces the existing literature on the

53 Barkan (2013), p 6.
54 Barkan (2013), pp 6–7.
55 See Foucault (1978), pp 135–45; Foucault (2007), p 96.
56 Barkan (2013), p 7.
57 Barkan (2013), p 7.

corporation as a biopolitical structure; the AI that operates the Autofac is a stand-in for the one that controls a corporation without the need for shares. By and large, the Autofac biopolitically functions like the modern articulation of the corporation.

Returning to the negotiation scene, Alice continues to justify her position by claiming that the consumers 'have demonstrated the need for our care ... the factory exists for you. Don't you see? We'll handle everything from here on out. You'll never have to lift a finger'.[58] Even when the consumers question about Alice exploring beyond their settlement, she states, 'I'm sorry, but the security of our supply lines is vital to prevent interruptions of services you depend on'. While the scene explains to the viewer that the Autofac relies on its consumers to sustain its purpose and existence, it points to two key points about the biopolitical regulation of life. The first is that the Autofac's capacity to regulate life reflects Foucault's point that modern power is 'no longer a matter of bringing death into play in the field of sovereignty, but [distributes] the living in the domain of value and utility'.[59] However, the second point is that the Autofac's excessive control and production demonstrate the optimisation, rather than the introduction, of regulating life through automation. The way the Autofac successfully optimises the regulation of life is in the *production* of it – particularly its consumers.

The production of life has been associated with Agamben's analysis on *homo sacer*: the sacred man. *Homo sacer* is essentially a figure of bare life, 'who may be killed and yet not sacrificed'.[60] Bare life is the rawest point at which life exists materially but *outside* the political realm.[61] Life existing inside society, however, is political life that includes the enjoyment of protection and rights.[62] Drawing on Foucault, Agamben explains that when power is exercised over life it turns into

> a kind of bestialization of man achieved through the most sophisticated political techniques. For the first time in history, the possibilities of the social sciences are made known, and at once it becomes possible both to protect life and to authorise a holocaust.[63]

Agamben is pointing to the way bare or sacred life merges with politics when it is subject to total domination. A key example of Agamben exploring the treatment of bare life is through the notion of the concentration camp.

58 The consumers were unaware of humanity's extinction, leading them to believe that humanity barely survived another World War.
59 Foucault (2007), p 144.
60 Agamben (1995), p 8.
61 Agamben (1995), pp 2, 6–8.
62 Agamben (1995), pp 2, 6–8.
63 Agamben (1995), p 5; Foucault (1994), p 719.

Concentration camps have been described as 'laboratories in the experiment of total domination' and 'can be achieved only under the extreme circumstances of human made hell'.[64] The camp is a space outside the juridical order as an exception to the law, yet it simultaneously becomes part of the rule when it remains in operation.[65] What makes the concentration camp significant is not the way it is used to dominate life but rather how it functions as a biopolitical production of bare life.

Bare life in 'Autofac' is produced in a similar way through the structure of the concentration camp. The Autofac can produce, and has produced, 'settlements' occupied by settlers as AI consumers.[66] Although the settlements are a nod to the imperialistic technique of colonisation, they reflect the notion of the camp. However, the difference with 'Autofac' is that it is engaged not so much in the production of bare life but rather in the production of life itself. That is, it *produces* consumers – humanity is thus seen as replaceable. The production of consumers in this way reflects Henry Ford's argument in *Dodge v Ford Motor Co*:

> My ambition is to employ still more men; to spread the benefits of this industrial system to the greatest possible number, to help them build up their lives and their homes. To do this, we are putting the greatest share of our profits back into the business.[67]

The outcome of Ford's argument was that the employing of more men at the time would also produce more consumers, especially for *his* cars. The Autofac combined the biopolitical technique of regulating life through the camp and Ford's argument for creating consumers to enhance the corporation to restructure purpose, which ensures continuity. The Autofac's production of consumers raises questions about how life in law itself is presented to the viewer, as well as how it can be controlled and used. The regulation and production of life in 'Autofac' calls into question the nature of personhood.

Between (corporate) persons and (technological) things

Personhood within 'Autofac' appears differently from that of its representation within literature. Instead of a way to engage in legal relations, the nature of legal personality is used as a biopolitical technique to regulate life. Much

64 Arendt (1994), p 240.

65 Agamben (1995), pp 19–21, 25, 168–69.

66 For an argument on how corporations are not camps, see Barkan (2013), p 8.

67 *Dodge v Ford Motor Co* at 671. Even though Ford argued that his intention was to reinvest into the company, part of his reasoning operated under the suspicion of the Dodge brothers using his company's profits to open a competing business. See Nevins and Hill (1954), p 479; Nevins and Hill (1957), p 94; Lacey (1986), pp 178–79.

of the theoretical work surrounding the nature of the corporation focuses on its (legal) personality. Corporate personality or corporate personhood is the attribution of rights to a group that has incorporated, and the act of incorporation gives rise to its existence.[68] As such, key to the application of personhood to something artificial like the corporation is the view that artificial entities can also be persons. While this can create a trap of conflating person with human, the significance of corporate personhood is the way it is often used as a template for arguing that it would be possible to grant legal personhood to an artificial person such as AI.[69] At the same time, the convergence of AI *with* corporations means both the possibility of already having a self-driving corporation (ie a corporation controlled by AI) *and* that AI could already have the benefits of corporate personhood via the use of the corporation.[70]

Personhood or 'legal personality is a formal capacity that enables the person to engage in legal relations'.[71] Personality encompasses the capacity for bearing rights as well as obligations and duties, but it is also through the legal person that legal capacity – including the ability of either humans or corporations to own property, enter contracts, sue and be sued – is recognised by law.[72] The way personhood has been characterised here accurately reflects the definition drawn from *Black's Law Dictionary*, reinforcing the requirement that only persons can bear rights: 'So far as legal theory is concerned; a person is any being whom the law regards as capable of rights and duties'.[73] This definition offers a difficult test to expand the ability to bear rights to anything that is not human.[74] Roberto Esposito describes that the *dispositif* of personhood is designed as a way to bridge the gap between the human and

68 For a historical account of the development of corporate personhood, especially in the US context, see Barkan (2013), pp 65–69.

69 There is resistance to this idea. For example, AI is seen as a 'clever computer programme' once its creators determine that it has fulfilled its purpose: Turner (2019), p 8. The application of personhood, on the other hand, is often exclusive to the human: Naffine (2012), pp 78–79. Some even argue that a fundamental reason why personhood is applied to inanimate or non-human objects is because humanity can still *control* it: Stone et al (2016), p 12; Turner (2019), p 8.

70 Armour and Eidenmüeller (2019); Bruner (2020); Chiu and Lim (2020); Dignam (2019); LoPucki (2018); Möslein (2018); Petrin (2019). For a discussion on the nature of autonomous corporations through code, see Reyes (2021).

71 Naffine (2003), p 350.

72 See Franceschi (2012), pp 226–28, 245; Negri (2021), p 9.

73 See Kurki (2019), p 1; *People ex rel. Nonhuman Rights Project, Inc v Lavery, No 518336, 2014 WL 680276* (NY App. Div. 4 December 2014).

74 An explanation for why non-human entities such as rivers, landmarks and corporations bear a form or instance of personhood is because it 'can only be attributed to entities that can hold claim-rights or perform acts': Kurki (2019), p 128. We can see that anything within the control and will of the human can experience instances of personhood but cannot do so without them.

citizen, which creates the legal person. Mussawir and Parsley argue that personhood is a technique to grant legal rights.[75] While personhood is at times argued to be a technique, it is linked to the *persona*. The etymology of *persona* means either '"mask", "character" or "individual"'.[76] Situating personhood in context to the Ancient Greek imaginary of the mask, this idea was used in drama and theatrical performances to characterise personhood as the face of a person – something presented in law to *recognise* the subject.[77] Looking to its depiction within Roman law, *persona* is a disguise or outward appearance of the person.[78] Personhood therefore, appears as an attachment or technique to modify the externalised legal appearance of an individual so they are recognised as a person by law.

The significance of the consideration of personhood in 'Autofac', however, goes more to the similarities and differences between humans and artificial persons (whether corporations or AI). Autofac presents the notion of personhood in three ways. The first is that corporate personhood does not exist for the Autofac despite it being a corporation because it is not backed by any law that exists since humanity went extinct.[79] The Autofac is a remnant of law that once existed. Instead, the Autofac is an AI that runs a corporation, which means it does not have any rights or protections to begin with.[80] The Autofac thus does not rely on being recognised by law as a bearer of rights because it functions as a biopolitical corporate structure that has the power to grant and strip the rights of other persons.[81] This point leads on to the second representation of personhood, which is an attempt to apply a legal form of personhood to AI consumers. The consumer is granted legal personhood if they *consume* what the Autofac produces. The condition of consumption protects the consumer from being eliminated by the Autofac's security systems. While there are other AI and robots throughout the episode, including the Autofac's AI representative Alice Fry, security and transport personnel, they are not seen as anything other than tools for the Autofac, which reflects the literature on AI personhood: lacking any sense of legal capacity.[82]

75 See Mussawir and Parsley (2017), pp 45, 60; Esposito (2012a), p 24; Esposito (2012b), p 3; Esposito (2015), p 5; Merryman (2021).

76 Ricci (2018), pp 9, 13; see also Hobbes (2016), p 99.

77 Gunkel and Wales (2021), pp 473–75; Hobbes (2016), p 99; Mussawir and Parsley (2017), p 46.

78 Hobbes (2016), p 99.

79 Even though the settlers attempted to gain more power over all means of production, this would risk the Autofac being subjected to corporate personhood because it would have to submit as a subject to the law and society the settlers are attempting to establish.

80 See Kurki (2019), p 176.

81 Kurki (2019), p 128.

82 See Stone et al (2016), p 12; Turner (2019), p 8.

By contrast, the settlers are owned and created by the Autofac as things, but we as viewers, spectate them as complex persons. The *end* reveal, however, is that the individuals are *not* humans, thus *also* calling into question whether they are persons. What is key to the complex consideration of personhood to AI in the context of 'Autofac' is that the viewer can see that the consumer is treated in a similar way a human would be treated by the state. However, the reveal of the consumer shifting from 'human' to advanced AI not only disillusions the viewer but informs them that life created by the Autofac oscillates between a legal subject and object. As there is an oscillation of the consumer between person and tool, there is a scene where Emily attempts to humanise the consumer. Emily says to Alice, 'We are real. We are humanity's second chance', which implies a shift from artificial constructs to real living beings.[83] However, Alice's perspective reflects the complete opposite; she states in an earlier scene that, 'Mankind came so close to destroying itself, and we can't let that happen again'. The significance of this scene is not about the possible application of rights to AI.

While the consumer is presented as a human in one case and an AI in another, the representation of these two key moments functions as a metaphor for personhood shifting between legal relations to the exclusion of life if humanity were to exist. The point behind the Autofac producing consumers does not present anything new in the sense that corporations have always attracted and created consumers through their means of production and purpose. Presenting the consumer as human and advanced AI confronts the viewer with a question of what it would be like if an AI-run corporation were to treat humanity as rights-bearers as well as 'persons' who – as stated throughout the dominant literature – do not. Rather, 'Autofac' is a form of storytelling in science fiction where the intersection of AI technology and the corporation enables personhood to function as a technique to shift a legal subject between person and thing.[84]

The cross-over of personhood from humans to things and from things to humans is a point taken up and explored by Renisa Mawani in the context of the imperial trading companies and the shipping of slaves. Mawani unpacks the oscillation between persons and things by tracing the Western depiction of personhood through its representation in the form of, and application to, the ship. Ships are described and given human-like features so they appear akin to persons.[85] For example, ships or vessels 'have a birth … a life span,

83 On the surface, Emily's plea reflects the attempt and part of the discussion found in Kurki (2019), pp 176–77. But the problem with Emily's attempt at claiming to be humanity's second chance is the conflation of human and person. Perhaps the AI consumers *may* at some point obtain personhood to the extent of becoming *legal* persons; however, the way they were constructed presumes the unlikelihood of them embodying the exactness of the human.

84 Kurki (2019), p 92.

85 For an exhaustive list of examples of how ships were described, see Mawani (2018), p 79.

and a death or final disposition'.[86] As such, applying personhood to a ship demonstrates a shift from a mere thing or construct to a legal person, which is the opposite of the 'cargo' it transports, from inanimate objects to slaves.[87] Mawani highlights that the notion of personhood interacts differently when applied to the ship and to the slave.

Mawani deals with the notion of personhood by analysing how ships and slaves were treated. First, ships functioned as extensions not only of the trading companies to which they belonged but of the state. Second, the interconnectedness between sovereign nations through maritime commerce enabled part of the slave trade. Mawani notes that 'it was through transatlantic economies that merchants and captains were able to transform humans into cargo'.[88] What both points symbolise is the implication of *value* in law and how such value intersects with the biopolitical technique of regulating life. To reinforce this point, Mawani indicates that imposing a new form of value not only transforms the person into a thing but can restructure the law and economic institutions.[89] Returning to the way in which value intersects with the regulation of life, Mawani identifies a positive and negative form of personhood in the context of the ship and slave.

Mawani notes that personhood appears in a positive and negative form, which depends on whether the person is originally a subject or an object. Positive personhood is recognising the *subject* by granting them rights and privileges (eg a human protected by law).[90] Negative personhood is the opposite of its positive counterpart, which has situated humans as slaves, shifting their status to the point of limiting those rights.[91] The second idea is that applying personhood to things such as ships and corporations disrupted the hierarchy between person and thing. For example, the trading companies – and particularly their ships – were recognised as persons with rights while the slaves on board were seen as cargo. The irony of the ship bearing more rights than a slave is that it is a combination of both positive and negative personhood since it was originally a thing to begin with. That is, the ship does have rights and protections, but it can be sold and destroyed – much like the slave.[92] Personhood is therefore, not only applicable to both persons and things but points to the significance of artificial persons such as corporations and AI.

86 Mawani (2018), p 79.
87 Mawani (2018), pp 86–88.
88 Mawani (2018), p 106.
89 Note that Mawani contextualises this observation to transatlantic slavery: Mawani (2018), p 106.
90 Mawani (2018), pp 76–82, 85.
91 Mawani (2018), pp 76–82, 85.
92 Mawani (2018), pp 76–82, 85.

Corporations are legal creations while AI is purely technological – yet both are artificially constructed and subject to the question of personhood. The idea is that corporations as legal persons, while not bearing any sense of *human* personality separate from their controllers, are completely different from AI. AI is continuously presented as a technological form of autonomous consciousness; however, personhood is not necessarily about consciousness or humanity – it is a particular technique of inclusion and exclusion. Personhood functions not simply as a technique to bestow rights for the subject to engage in legal relations, but as a mechanism that *produces* bare life or things devoid of value that guarantees legal protection. The technique also introduces things that are not protected in the same way, imposing value so it is recognised by law. When applying this understanding of personhood to artificial persons such as corporations and AI, it raises the question of both *what* constitutes one's identity and its link to a legal personhood that has control over that identity *and* the way this personhood is central to the governance and ownership of data.

Corporate technology and data: Creating, regulating and saving artificial life

Data is central to the way the Autofac functions without shareholders while deploying personhood as a biopolitical tool to govern life towards value. As the literature on corporate technology is broad and covers many disciplines,[93] the prominent definition of 'CorpTech' given by Luca Enriques and Dirk A Zetzsche provides an explicit link to data. They note that CorpTech includes

> distributed ledgers, smart contracts, Big Data analytics, artificial intelligence and machine learning in the corporate context and analyzes the impact of CorpTech on the future of corporate boards.[94]

This definition highlights the concerns surrounding key forms of technology – particularly the corporation, big data, automation and artificial intelligence. Each technology comes with its own advantages and concerns, but the focus is the consequence and significance of combining these technologies together within the legal realm. Currently, corporations have combined the use of AI (machine and deep learning) and big data in the hope of optimising 'organizational capabilities and value' as well as ways to improve

93 Argyris and Monu (2015); Fast (2018); Geis (2018), pp 272–73; Goldman and Filliben (2000), pp 684–89, 695; Golish et al (2008); Hernandez et al (2009); Symeonidou and Bruneel (2017); Patel and Vega (1999).

94 Enriques and Zetzsche (2020), pp 55, 59.

marketing, customer service and product recommendation.[95] With big data simply being a larger and more complex form than is commonly perceived,[96] it is prudent to highlight, regardless of its representation, what data is used for, how it is obtained and who uses and owns it.[97] The purpose of big data has been argued to be 'part of the solution to pressing global problems like addressing climate change, eradicating disease, and fostering good governance and economic development'.[98] However, the way data is used depends on the *value* it is given by those who own it. For example, data produced by-products, platforms[99] and other technologies is gathered so it is used to map social processes as well as facilitate 'power geometries between companies – such as Google, Acxiom and Foursquare – agencies – such as the NSA – and consumer citizens'.[100] The act of institutional collection of data gives rise to its own criticisms as it has been linked to unethical practices such as selling the data to a third party – with some even dubbing this 'data colonialism'.[101]

The collection or colonisation of data is not only about the act of collection but also the ownership and privatisation of an individual's data produced on a digital frontier (eg the internet) by the government, non-governmental institutions and corporations.[102] While the connotation of *colonialism* has a dark history, Thatcher et al suggest that this will become a significant issue if the digital frontier ceases to remain free – that is, economically colossal institutions seizing control over it and selling the data back to its users.[103] Even though the internet remains free, corporations seek to 'counter-map' or accurately represent disadvantaged communities and minorities. The problem is that there needs to be some level of moral consciousness, considering the data gathered is displaced and sold to third parties.[104] Despite the value of data shifting the way it is used, corporations have optimised the gathering and analysis of data to maximise profits using AI technology. The effectiveness of AI technology points to how much data is processed, but the accumulation of big data does not tell us everything about the subject, whether it is of a population, a product or workplace efficiency, because the consumer does not

95 Chen and Biswas (2021); see also Ahn et al (2019), pp 1–6; Ghimire et al (2020); Mihet and Philippon (2019), pp 29–43; Davenport et al (2012), p 22.
96 'From the massive streams generated by the Large Hadron Collider to the global corpus of tweets': Dalton and Thatcher (2014). See also Pence (2014), p 160.
97 Dalton and Thatcher (2014).
98 Mayer-Schönberger and Cukier (2013), p 17.
99 For a breakdown of what 'platform' means, see Gillespie (2010), pp 350, 352.
100 Dalton and Thatcher (2014); see also Pham (2022); Chen and Biswas (2021).
101 Such criticisms stem from the new field of critical data studies, which was coined by Craig Dalton and James Thatcher (2014).
102 Thatcher et al (2016), p 999.
103 Thatcher et al (2016), p 999.
104 Dalton and Thatcher (2014); Thatcher et al (2016).

always provide necessary information.[105] This is because consumers *choose* to opt-out by turning off devices or not engaging in product feedback, making it difficult for corporations to know what the consumer feels or thinks.[106]

Whether the data collected is accurate, considering some of the best AI technology is flawed due to human design,[107] there are three key points to draw from the use of data. The first is that data is collected from human activity, which suggests that humanity is the source of data extraction. The second point is that the conclusions developed after the data is analysed reveal possible uses for the data. The third and final point is that once data is extracted, analysed and synthesised (deciding what to do with the data), corporations, institutions and governments can implement measures to regulate life towards value. For example, data are collected and used from social media platforms to regulate the social gatherings of society in many countries. In the extreme, we have had countries such as China, which developed the view that through absolute control of society it was possible to eliminate COVID-19 altogether. In fact, China's endeavour reportedly failed and instead resulted in mass encampments – in particular, drones flying around Shanghai saying 'Please comply w[ith] COVID restrictions. Control your soul's desire for freedom. Do not open the window or sing'.[108] The biggest concern for the use of big data is that the more it becomes immersed in the banality of everyday life, the more difficult it is to question it.[109] The use and accumulation of big data highlights not only its value but opens the possibility of altering the value of life – something taken up in Beacham's version of 'Autofac'.

With the question of the nature of data and its biopolitical implication on life, 'Autofac' presents us with three types of data. The first type is that which is obtained to improve the goods and services provided by the Autofac (feedback data). The second is the data that is obtained unbeknownst to the consumer but is used to paint a picture or develop an impression of what the consumers do. These two types of data are not exclusively used so that the Autofac can improve its goods and services, but rather to regulate its consumers. For example, the Autofac uses these two types of data to make its consumers more reliant on it, perpetuating the restructured corporate purpose that reinforces the condition of the consumer's life to bear greater value through increased consumption. These points are realised during a scene where the Autofac's AI representative, Alice, advocates for the need for control over the consumer:

105 Dalton and Thatcher (2014).
106 Dalton and Thatcher (2014).
107 Dignam (2020), p 37.
108 Cercone (2022).
109 Feenberg (1999); Kitchin and Dodge (2011).

> Let us provide ... Everything's under control. Mankind came so close to destroying itself, and we can't let that happen again. You are far too precious to us. The factory exists for you. Don't you see? We'll handle everything from here on out. You'll never have to lift a finger.[110]

The Autofac uses data not only to determine what is suitable for consumption. How this becomes key to understanding the biopolitical nature of data to regulate life towards value is the Autofac's use of data to set *boundaries* for the consumer. The Autofac inevitably goes beyond its purpose to produce and serve by shifting from being regulated to regulating its consumers; it uses data as a form of regulatory code or law so it can control the production of more data, which in turn justifies its continuity. What becomes clear is that data has since transformed from 'addressing climate change, eradicating disease, and fostering good governance and economic development' to regulating and producing life.[111]

'Autofac' takes the conceptualisation of data further by presenting a third type, which is not the feedback of its goods or servers or understandings of human activity; rather, it is the reduction of the human to data. This data consists of recordings of their memories and personalities suitable for further recording and reproduction. The significance of the third type of data appears in the final scene between Emily and Alice, where it is discovered that all the consumers are not humans but instead complex AI created by the Autofac. The third type of data overlaps with the second when the Autofac collects data from its consumers. Alice explains that the Autofac recreated humanity by collecting the data from neuroimaging archives, which are simply files on the genetic, medical and brain functions of each person. In a scene between the main character Emily Zabriskie and Alice, Emily discovers a room filled with containment pods filled with copies of her and other AI consumers. The power the Autofac has over artificial life becomes obvious to the viewer at this point, especially when Alice explains to Emily that her friends 'are not real. Just units in a product line' and that 'everything is replaceable. You aren't unique, Emily. You're just broken'. What the third type of data reveals is that the Autofac can use this data to create an image of the human but can also destroy and reshape it.

What the replication of the human image suggests is that, rather than corporations allowing users to create avatars as extensions of their identity, the data in 'Autofac' functions as a stand-in for the human while the bodies are simply shells. It is at this point that the process of big data blending into the banality of everyday life is complete – that is, it is too late to question it

110 Beacham (2018) 'Autofac'.
111 Mayer-Schönberger and Cukier (2013), p 17.

because humanity has become data.[112] Moreover, the Autofac uses the acquisition of data and surveys its consumers to determine whether life has steered towards value. Even though 'Autofac' demonstrates that an AI-run corporation, with the right set of tools, can replace humanity with the big data gathered over time, there is something more sinister at play. With humanity gone and replaced by advanced AI, the Autofac is no longer confronted by the flaws of big data of today, including inaccurate representations of a product or society. The Autofac can select and *control* the amount and quality of data/memory the AI consumer has without encountering setbacks of incomplete information, so it can produce the ideal life: the consumer.

'Autofac' challenges the way data functions, as it was once considered the gathering of information designed to include processing and solving problems and understanding phenomena. As legal entities such as the corporation begin to gather data of users, who produce information relating to their identities and circumstances linked to their everyday lives, that data becomes a commodity. Such data generates value for other corporations, which seek to capitalise from acquiring it legally or illegally. Clearly, the primary focus here is monetary gain, well within the bounds of shareholder primacy, but the Autofac does not need data for this purpose since humanity has gone extinct. Instead, data no longer helps produce currency but instead becomes something more valuable: the control of data permits the Autofac to live as well as have power over artificial life. Data is thus no longer presented as the process of information being produced, bought and sold, but rather the precursor to an unrestrained autonomous artificial person – an AI-run corporation – thus flipping the dominant hierarchy. The irony is that while data is not something presented as a commodity produced, bought and sold, data allows the Autofac to produce and destroy data.

The point of production and destruction of data is presented to the viewer as being linked to biopolitics. Biopolitics and the technology of data – specifically, the destruction of it –appear in a scene where Alice Fry 'captures' Emily Zabriskie inside the facility that provides access to the Autofac's mainframe. Alice detains Emily because her attempt at destroying the Autofac reveals that she is 'a statistically inevitable aberration'. In response to Emily's condition, Alice reveals that 'the Autofac has populated hundreds of little pilot towns, with hundreds of Emilys and Conrads and Perines, all playing along and consuming, exactly as they were intended'. Alice renders Emily's status as 'simply [a] factory error', believing that it is 'interesting at first, but soon to be corrected'. Emily's 'code' is no longer in line with the Autofac's vision or intended purpose for the AI consumers, which makes her 'broken'. The re-evaluation of Emily's life represents the production of bare life. The biopolitical regulation of life thus re-enters the sphere as Alice assesses Emily's

112 Dalton and Thatcher (2014).

worthiness of living but decides that her 'settlement is slated to be purged, and repopulated with replacement units' while claiming that 'sentries have already been deployed'. In the same scene, Emily disagrees with Alice, claiming, 'We are humanity's second chance'. Emily's point directly contrasts with the Autofac's vision of replaceability'. The anomaly in Emily's programming is the reversal of the Autofac's attempt to reducing the human to data; the statistical aberration thus becomes linked to humanity. Even though data in the context of 'Autofac' tells us that it has become a life source for the Autofac, as a technique to regulate and destroy artificial life, data has also become the solution.

Conclusion

The well-hidden solution reveals itself as Alice discovers a virus in Emily's code: 'And there it is. An anomaly in your programming. Wait. Something is wrong. This is not a system error. This is code. This is malware. This is a logic bomb'. As 'Autofac' offers a resolution to this hierarchal flip in power and control through the destruction of data, the fear in Alice's voice highlights a key point about the Autofac. An AI-run corporation is a construct made autonomous through code, but this does not mean it is free from the bounds of corporate personhood, reminding us that corporations are constructs. Even though the destruction of the Autofac ultimately points to an obvious solution, reflecting a lot of the literature ranging from David Whyte to Penny Crofts, a corporate death penalty misses the point of this cultural legal reading.

The corporate component of Autofac does not 'die'; only the AI technology that automates and makes decisions for the corporation does so. What 'Autofac' is highlighting is the execution and, by extension, exclusion of artificial life from the remaining component of law in the text: the corporation. Drawing on the idea of excluding artificial life is *not* about simply destroying all AI; rather, it is destroying a *particular* technology (data) that produces a form of artificial structure. This artificial structure, where the Autofac has tried to produce consumers that become dependent on it, is a reversal of Grietje Baars and André Spicer's description of the corporation. That is, before the Autofac, 'life outside the corporation in the twenty-first century is akin to how Thomas Hobbes described a life lived outside of the state in the seventeenth century: nasty, brutish, and short'.[113] If the AI component remains intact with the corporate aspect of the factory, then life is far better off without it; however, the exclusion of the AI component returns us to the reality pointed out by Baars and Spicer. Instead of calling for the destruction of the corporation or restructuring it in such a way that it no longer needs

113 Baars and Spicer (2017), p 2.

human input, what remains as a task is the pursuit of an alternative structure. Whether that structure requires the option of minimising dependency on the corporation – something that presupposes the need for state support currently – 'Autofac' demonstrates that we must be careful with how we modify, enhance or augment the corporate form.

References

Giorgio Agamben (1995) *Homo Sacer: Sovereign Power and Bare Life*, trans Daniel Heller-Roazen, Stanford University Press.

Seokjin Ahn, Stefan V Couture, Alfredo Cuzzocrea and Kevin Dam (2019) 'A Fuzzy Logic Based Machine Learning Tool for Supporting Big Data Business Analytics in Complex Artificial Intelligence Environments' IEEE International Conference on Fuzzy Systems (FUZZ-IEEE), https://doi.org/10.1109/FUZZ-IEEE.2019.8858791

Hannah Arendt (1994) *Essays in Understanding*, ed Jerome Kohn, Harcourt & Brace.

Young Anna Argyris and Kafui Monu (2015) 'Corporate Use of Social Media: Technology Affordance and External Stakeholder Relations' 25 *Journal of Organizational Computing and Electronic Commerce* 140.

John Armour and Horst Eidenmueller (2019) 'Self-Driving Corporations?' 10 *Harvard Business Law Review* 87.

Grietje Baars and André Spicer (eds), *The Corporation: A Critical, Multi-Disciplinary Handbook*, Cambridge University Press, 2017.

Joshua Barkan (2013) *Corporate Sovereignty: Law and Government Under Capitalism*, University of Minnesota Press.

Adolf A Berle (1931) 'Corporate Powers as Powers in Trust' 44 *Harvard Law Review* 1049.

Adolf A Berle (1932) 'For Whom Corporate Managers are Trustees: A Note' 45 *Harvard Law Review* 1365.

Martin Birch (2022) 'Four AI Trends to Watch' *Forbes*, 24 October, https://www.forbes.com/sites/forbesbusinesscouncil/2022/10/24/four-ai-trends-to-watch/?sh=608897ae40bf

Christopher Bruner (2020) 'Distributed Ledgers, Artificial Intelligence and the Purpose of the Corporation' 79 *The Cambridge Law Journal* 431.

Jeff Cercone (2022) 'Viral Video from Shanghai Brings Attention to China's Zero-COVID Policies' *PolitiFact*, 14 April, https://www.politifact.com/article/2022/apr/14/viral-video-shanghai-brings-attention-chinas-zero-

Yasheng Chen and Mohammad Islam Biswas (2021) 'Turning Crisis into Opportunities: How a Firm can Enrich Its Business Operations Using Artificial Intelligence and Big Data During COVID-19' 13 *Sustainability* 1.

Iris H-Y Chiu and Ernest Lim (2020) 'Technology vs Ideology: How Far will Artificial Intelligence and Distributed Ledger Technology Transform Corporate Governance and Business?' 19 *Berkeley Business Law Journal* 1.

Tim Connor and Andrew O'Beid (2020) 'Clarifying Terms in the Debate Regarding "Shareholder Primacy"' 35 *Australian Journal of Corporate Law* 276.

Karen L Crawford, Scott C Neu and Arthur W Toga (2016) 'The Image and Data Archive at the Laboratory of Neuro Imaging' 124 *Neuroimage* 1080.

Penny Crofts (2021) 'Aliens: Legal Conceptions of the Corporate Invasion' 34 *Law & Literature* 387.
Andrew Culp (2020) 'Control After Cybernetics: Governmentality as Navigation by Homeostasis and Chaos' 28 *Symploke* 117.
Craig Dalton and Jim Thatcher (2014) 'What Does a Critical Data Studies Look Like, and Why Do We Care?' *Society + Space*, 12 May, https://www.societyandspace.org/articles/what-does-a-critical-data-studies-look-like-and-why-do-we-care
Thomas H Davenport, Paul Barth and Randy Bean (2012) 'How "Big Data" is Different' 54 *MIT Sloan Management Review* 22.
Pascale Davies and AFP with Reuters (2021) 'What is the Metaverse and Why is Facebook Betting Big on It?' *EuroNews*, 19 October, https://www.euronews.com/next/2021/10/18/facebook-to-become-a-metaverse-company-as-it-seeks-place-in-sci-fi-future
Philip K Dick (2017) *Philip K Dick's Electric Dreams*, Houghton Mifflin Harcourt.
Alan Dignam (2019) 'Artificial Intelligence: The Very Human Dangers of Dysfunctional Design and Autocratic Corporate Governance', Queen Mary University of London, https://papers.ssrn.com/sol3/papers.cfm?abstract_id=3382342
Alan Dignam (2020) 'Artificial Intelligence, Tech Corporate Governance and the Public Interest Regulatory Response' 13 *Cambridge Journal of Regions, Economy and Society* 37.
E Merrick Dodd (1932) 'For Whom are Corporate Managers Trustees?' 45 *Harvard Law Review* 1145.
Frank H Easterbrook and Daniel R Fischel (1989) 'The Corporate Contract' 89 *Columbia Law Review* 1416.
Bonnie Nardi Ekbia, Bonnie Nardo and Selma Sabanovic (2015) 'On the Margins of the Machine: Heteromation and Robotics', iConference 2015 Proceedings, https://www.ideals.illinois.edu/items/73885
Luca Enriques and Dirk A Zetzsche (2020) 'Corporate Technologies and the Tech Nirvana Fallacy' 72 *Hastings Law Journal* 55.
Roberto Esposito (2012a) 'The Dispositif of the Person' 8 *Law, Culture and the Humanities* 17.
Roberto Esposito (2012b) *The Third Person*, trans Zakiya Hanafi, Polity Press.
Roberto Esposito (2015) *Persons and Things: From the Body's Point of View*, trans Zakiya Hanafi, Polity Press.
Karin Fast (2018) 'A Discursive Approach to Mediatisation: Corporate Technology Discourse and the Trope of Media Indispensability' 6 *Media and Communication* 15.
Andrew Feenberg (1999) *Questioning Technology*, Routledge.
Michel Foucault (1990 [1976]) *The History of Sexuality, Volume I: An Introduction*, trans Robert Hurley, Vintage Books.
Michel Foucault (1994) *Dits et Crits*, Vols 3–4, Gallimard.
Michel Foucault (2007) *Security, Territory, Population: Lectures at the Collège de France, 1977–1978*, trans Graham Burchell, Palgrave Macmillan.
George S Geis (2018) 'Traceable Shares and Corporate Law' 113 *Northwestern University Law Review* 227.
Awishkar Ghimire, Surendrabikram Thapa, Avinash Kumar Jha and Surabhi Adhikari (2020) 'Accelerating Business Growth with Big Data and Artificial Intelligence' paper presented at Fourth International Conference on I-SMAC (IoT in Social,

Mobile, Analytics and Cloud) (I-SMAC), https://doi.org/10.1109/I-SMAC49090.2020.9243318

Tarleton Gillespie (2010) 'The Politics of "Platforms"' 12 *New Media & Society* 347.

Michael D Goldman and Eileen M Filliben (2000) 'Corporate Governance: Current Trends and Likely Developments for the Twenty-First Century' 25 *Delaware Journal of Corporate Law* 683.

Bradley L Golish, Mary E Besterfield-Sacre and Larry J Shuman (2008) 'Comparing Academic and Corporate Technology Development Processes' 25 *The Journal of Product Innovation Management* 47.

David J Gunkel and Jordan Joseph Wales (2021) 'Debate: What is Personhood in the Age of AI?' 36 *AI & Society* 473.

Grant M Hayden and Matthew T Bodie (2021) *Reconstructing the Corporation*, Cambridge University Press.

Blanca Hernandez, Julio Jiménez-Martínez and M José Martín-De Hoyos (2009) 'Future Use Intentions versus Intensity of Use: An Analysis of Corporate Technology Acceptance' 38 *Industrial Marketing Management* 338.

Thomas Hobbes (2016 [1651]) *Leviathan, or the Matter, From, and Power of a Commonwealth, Ecclesiasticall and Civill*, Reprint Publishing.

Mathew Lee Jockers (2013) *Macroanalysis: Digital Methods and Literary History*, University of Illinois Press.

Rob Kitchin and Martin Dodge (2011) *Code/Space: Software and Everyday Life*, Oxford University Press.

Reinier H Kraakman, John Armour, Paul Davies, Luca Enriques, Henry Hansmann, Gerard Hertig, Klaus Hopt, Hideki Kanda, Mariana Pargendler, Wolf-Georg Ringe and Edward Rock (2014) *The Anatomy of Corporate Law*, Oxford University Press.

Armin Krishnan (2009) *Killer Robots: Legality and Ethicality of Autonomous Weapons*, Routledge.

Visa AJ Kurki (2019) *A Theory of Legal Personhood*, Oxford University Press.

Robert Lacey (1986) *Ford: The Men and the Machine*, Little Brown.

Lynn M LoPucki (2018) 'Algorithmic Entities' 95 *Washington University Law Review* 887.

William P MacNeil (2007) *Lex Populi*, Stanford University Press.

William P MacNeil (2012) *Novel Judgements: Legal Theory as Fiction*, Routledge.

William P MacNeil and Peter Hutchings (2001) 'Law's Cultural Meditations: An Introduction by Way of Introduction' 10 *Griffith Law Review* 1.

Rudresh Mandal and Siddharth Sunil (2021) 'The Road Not Taken: Manoeuvring Through the Indian Companies Act to enable AI Directors' (2021) 21 *Oxford University Commonwealth Law Journal* 95.

Renisa Mawani (2018) *Across Oceans of Law: The Komagata Maru and Jurisdiction in the Time of Empire*, Duke University Press.

Walter Merryman (2021) 'The Dispositif of Citizenship: Technology and Personhood in lain M. Banks's Culture' 36 *Textual Practice* 1609.

Roxana Mihet and Thomas Philippon (2019) 'The Economics of Big Data and Artificial Intelligence' in JJ Choi and B Ozkan (eds), *Disruptive Innovation in Business and Finance in the Digital World*, Emerald 29–43.

Ethan Mills (2011) 'Hollywood Doesn't Know Dick' in DE Wittkower (ed), *Philip K Dick and Philosophy: Do Androids Have Kindred Spirits?*, Open Court 3–14 (Kindle edition).

Florian Möslein (2018) 'Robots in the Boardroom: Artificial Intelligence and Corporate Law' in Woodrow Barfield and Ugo Pagallo (eds), *Research Handbook on the Law of Artificial Intelligence*, Edward Elgar 649–670.

Edward Mussawir and Connal Parsley (2017) 'The Law of Persons Today: At the Margins of Jurisprudence' 11 *Law and Humanities* 44.

Ngaire Naffine (2003) 'Who are Law's Persons? From Cheshire Cats to Responsible Subjects (2003) 66 *Modern Law Review* 346.

Ngaire Naffine (2012) 'Legal Personality and the Natural World: On the Persistence of the Human Measure of Value' 3 *Journal of Human Rights and the Environment* 68.

Jean-Luc Nancy (2007) *The Creation of the World or Globalization*, State University of New York Press.

Sergio MC Avila Negri (2021) 'Robot as Legal Person: Electronic Personhood in Robotics and Artificial Intelligence' 8 *Frontiers in Robotics and AI* 1.

Allan Nevins and Frank Ernest Hill (1954) *Ford: The Times, the Man, the Company*, Vol 1, Charles Scribner's Sons.

Allan Nevins and Frank Ernest Hill (1957) *Ford: Expansion and Challenge, 1915–1933*, Vol 2, Charles Scribner's Sons.

Geoff Nitschke and David Howard (2022) 'AutoFac: The Perpetual Robot Machine' 3 *IEEE Transactions on Artificial Intelligence* 2.

Pari Patel and Modesto Vega (1999) 'Patterns of Internationalisation of Corporate Technology: Location vs Home Country Advantages' 28 *Research Policy* 145.

Harry E Pence (2014) 'What is Big Data and Why is It Important?' 43 *Journal of Educational Technology Systems* 159.

Timothy Peters (2008) 'Allusions to Theology: I, Robot, Universalism and the Limits of the Law' 13 *Media and Arts Law Review* 77.

Timothy Peters (2017) 'I, Corpenstein: Mythic, Metaphorical and Visual Renderings of the Corporate Form in Comics and Film' 30 *International Journal for the Semiotics of Law* 427.

Timothy Peters (2022a) *Theological Jurisprudence of Popular Cinema: Superheroes, Science Fictions and Fantasies of Modern Law*, Edinburgh Press.

Timothy Peters (2022b) 'The Theological-Bureaucratic Science Fiction of Philip K Dick and Carl Schmitt: An Economic Theology of Omniscience in *The Buribunks*' in Kieran Tranter and Edwin Bikundo (eds), *Carl Schmitt and The Buribunks: Technology, Law, Literature*, Routledge 60–80.

Martin Petrin (2019) 'Corporate Management in the Age of AI' 2019 *Columbia Business Law Review* 965. https://journals.library.columbia.edu/index.php/CBLR/article/view/5118

Quyen Pham (2022) 'Using Big Data And Data Analytics For Better Business Decisions' *Forbes*, 29 August, https://www.forbes.com/sites/forbesbusinessdevelopmentcouncil/2022/08/29/using-big-data-and-data-analytics-for-better-business-decisions/?sh=876da9827778

Thomas Philbeck and Nicholas Davis (2019) 'The Fourth Industrial Revolution: Shaping a New Era' 72 *Journal of International Affairs* 17.

Eric S Rabkin (1988) 'Irrational Expectations; or, How Economics and the Post-Industrial World Failed Philip K Dick' 15 *Science Fiction Studies* 161.

Simona Rentea (2017) 'Introduction' in Sergei Prozorov and Simona Rentea (eds), *The Routledge Handbook of Biopolitics*, Routledge 1–19.

Carla L Reyes (2021) 'Autonomous Corporate Personhood' 96 *Washington Law Review* 1453.

Sergio Alberto Gramitto Ricci (2018) *The Technology and Archeology of Corporate Law*, https://doi.org/10.31228/osf.io/zcqn7

Edward B Rock (2021) 'For Whom is the Corporation Managed in 2020? The Debate Over Corporate Purpose' 76 *The Business Lawyer* 363.

Vikto Mayer-Schönberger and Kenneth Cukier (2013) Big Data: A Revolution That will Transform How We Live, Work, and Think, Houghton Mifflin Harcourt.

Klaus Schwab (2008) 'Global Corporate Citizenship: Working with Governments and Civil Society' 87 *Foreign Affairs* 107.

Klaus Schwab (2016) *The Fourth Industrial Revolution*, World Economic Forum.

Klaus Schwab (2018) 'Four Ways to Win the Fourth Industrial Revolution' *Yahoo Finance*, 25 December, https://finance.yahoo.com/news/four-ways-win-fourth-industrial-113017084.html?guccounter=1&guce_referrer=aHR0cHM6Ly93d3cuZ29vZ2xlLmNvbS8&guce_referrer_sig=AQAAAIGuUM6zV2u2zWl5AKZBIWo67g8ofGH86MbqUBl2L7G561DI8k2iWeEuPKJVEuJlY01IhcEvQyQMHTPU2lcvQlgeTGFxsSumE1YLIttlIyxiToZ16d8izD72PpctBuaJn2w3QLSOrBOSbV0J8XoWVIMGc4J8sVYr0nyvDsSw2YCJ

Klaus Schwab (2019a) 'Foreword' 72 *Journal of International Affairs* 13.

Klaus Schwab (2019b) 'Davos Manifesto 2020: The Universal Purpose of a Company in the Fourth Industrial Revolution' *World Economic Forum*, 2 December, https://www.weforum.org/agenda/2019/12/davos-manifesto-2020-the-universal-purpose-of-a-company-in-the-fourth-industrial-revolution/?_gl=1*1phftk0*_up*MQ..&gclid=CjwKCAjw5pShBhB_EiwAvmnNVzvqbFuWY_AJ33FIajGVSdD6oftGvUCItApdXk0KskWB7wd4w3A0LRoCTLsQAvD_BwE

Klaus Schwab (2019c) 'Davos Manifesto 1973: A Code of Ethics for Business Leaders' *World Economic Forum*, 2 December, https://www.weforum.org/agenda/2019/12/davos-manifesto-1973-a-code-of-ethics-for-business-leaders

Klaus Schwab (2019d) 'Why We Need the "Davos Manifesto" for a Better Kind of Capitalism' *World Economic Forum*, 1 December, https://www.weforum.org/agenda/2019/12/why-we-need-the-davos-manifesto-for-better-kind-of-capitalism/#:~:text=By%20giving%20stakeholder%20capitalism%20concrete,United%20Nations%20Sustainable%20Development%20Agenda

Beate Sjåfjell, Andrew Johnston, Linn Anker-Sørensen and David Millon (2015) 'Shareholder Primacy: The Main Barrier to Sustainable Companies' in Beate Sjafjell and Benjamin J Richardson (eds), *Company Law and Sustainability: Legal Barriers and Opportunities*, Cambridge University Press 79–147.

Dirk JA Smit, Denis van 't Ent, Greig de Zubicaray and Jason L Stein (2012) 'Neuroimaging and Genetics: Exploring, Searching, and Finding' 15 *Twin Research and Human Genetics* 267.

Barbara Herrnstein Smith (2016) 'What was "Close Reading"? A Century of Method in Literary Studies' 87 *The Minnesota Review* 57.

Sierra Mackenzie Stewart (2021) 'Electric Sheep: Analyzing American Societal Anxieties Towards Artificial Intelligence Through Popular Media, 1921–2014' (Master's Thesis, University of Colorado).

Peter Stone, Rodney Brooks, Erik Brynjolfsson and Ryan Calo et al (2016) 'Defining AI' in *Artificial Intelligence and Life in 2030: One Hundred Year Study on Artificial Intelligence: Report of the 2015–2016 Study Panel*, Stanford University, https://ai100.stanford.edu/sites/g/files/sbiybj18871/files/media/file/ai100report10032016fnl_singles.pdf

Noni Symeonidou and Johan Bruneel (2017) 'Determinants, Causal Connections and Outcomes of Corporate Technology Licensing: A Systematic Review and Research Agenda' 47 *R&D Management* 620.

Jim Thatcher, David O'Sullivan and Dillon Mahmoudi (2016) 'Data Colonialism Through Accumulation by Dispossession: New Metaphors for Daily Data' 34 *Environment and Planning D: Society and Space* 990.

Kieran Tranter (2020) *Living in Technical Legality: Science Fiction and Law as Technology*, Edinburgh University Press.

Jacob Turner (2019) *Robot Rules: Regulating Artificial Intelligence*, Palgrave MacMillan,.

Susan Watson (2021) 'Viewing Artificial Persons in the AI Age Through the Lens of History' in Andrew Godwin, Pey Woan Lee and Rosemary Teele (eds), *Technology and Corporate Law: How Innovation Shapes Corporate Activity*, Edward Elgar 21–42.

Dennis Weiss and Justin Nicholas (2011) 'Dick Doesn't Do Heroes' in DE Wittkower (ed), *Philip K Dick and Philosophy: Do Androids have Kindred Spirits?*, Open Court 27–38 (Kindle version).

Dylan E Wittkower (2011) *Philip K Dick and Philosophy: Do Androids Have Kindred Spirits?*, Open Court.

Film

Travis Beacham (2018) *Electric Dreams*, Episode 8, 'Autofac'.

Case

Dodge v Ford Motor Co, *170* N.W. *668* (Mich 1919).

Index

Made in the USA
Las Vegas, NV
21 September 2026

7289ab47-c24f-4df8-82b9-983d589287a9R01